Manias, Panics, and Crashes

Robert Z. Aliber · Charles P. Kindleberger ·
Robert N. McCauley

Manias, Panics, and Crashes

A History of Financial Crises

Eighth Edition

Robert Z. Aliber
Booth School of Business
University of Chicago
Chicago, IL, USA

Charles P. Kindleberger
Massachusetts Institute of Technology
Cambridge, MA, USA

Robert N. McCauley
Global Development Policy Center
Boston University
Boston, MA, USA

Faculty of History
University of Oxford
Oxford, UK

ISBN 978-3-031-16007-3 ISBN 978-3-031-16008-0 (eBook)
https://doi.org/10.1007/978-3-031-16008-0

This Palgrave Macmillan imprint is published by the registered company Springer Nature Switzerland AG
The registered company address is: Gewerbestrasse 11, 6330 Cham, Switzerland

Prologue by Henry Kaufman

The word 'classic' can seem a bit stodgy. Now in this eighth edition, *Manias, Panics, and Crashes* became a classic many years ago, although it is difficult to say exactly when. Indeed, the first edition, written by MIT's esteemed economic historian Charles Kindleberger, immediately attracted notice and praise. But it is because this book has continued to evolve along with its topic rather than solidifying in its original form that *MPC* still deserves our attention and praise.

In retrospect, the Wall Street of 1978—the year the first edition was published—now seems foreign, almost quaint. In the United States, the decade had opened with the spectacular collapse of the Pennsylvania Central Railroad, thanks to its overdependence on commercial paper. Hard to imagine now, the Dow Jones Industrial Average didn't top the 1,000-point milestone for the first time until 1972. Two years later, Franklin National Bank—a heavy borrower in Eurodollar interbank markets—also went belly up. As the decade wrapped up, another financial crisis roiled markets, this one caused by the Hunt brothers' efforts to corner the silver market, their positions funded heavily by Wall Street. How many of these events are familiar to today's investors?

More than any other free market institution, Wall Street underscores Joseph Schumpeter's observation that 'creative destruction' dooms those who stand still in a capitalist economy. Financial markets have become the epicenters of that reality. The same can be said of those—including the authors

of this new edition—who aspire to chronicle the history of extreme financial gyrations. *Manias, Panics, and Crashes* remains a classic, not because it is frozen in time but because—through its various editions and through the contributions of the two co-authors who joined Kindleberger's original enterprise—it has remained a living document.

Some consider me somewhat of a Wall Street 'classic.' Longevity certainly has played a role: I've been a Wall Streeter for seven decades, starting with stints at a commercial bank and at the New York Federal Reserve, then for twenty-six years at Salomon Brothers. The Salomon research departments I oversaw pioneered powerful new methods in financial and business analysis and forecasting—especially regarding interest rates. It was a heady era, one filled with an ample share of booms, bubbles, and busts, as documented in the pages that follow. Along with the US crises noted above, we lived through the collapse of Drysdale Government Securities, Inc. and Penn Square Bank; witnessed the massive bailouts of Mexico and Continental Illinois Bank; and endured the Savings and Loan Crisis. I wasn't just a passive observer; sometimes my macroeconomic or interest rate predictions moved markets. When after many years of bearish forecasts (some called me 'Dr. Doom') I released a memo August 17, 1982 predicting the secular reversal of long-term interest rates, markets reacted with the largest one-day bull market since World War II.

Living through and somewhat shaping those many years on Wall Street not surprisingly instilled some lessons in me about financial crises. As this book amply demonstrates, excessive use of credit is a common denominator in most crises. Indeed, prior to each crisis, investors typically come to depend heavily on leverage. Excessive credit expansion furthermore is commonly driven by a sense of market enthusiasm, at times even euphoria, or the widespread belief that the old rules no longer apply. Sometimes 'glamour industries' that drive up stock and bond markets prove to be real; but too often (as with the so-called dot.com bubble) they do not. And not infrequently—as during the classic tale of Wall Street in the 1920s—justified enthusiasm morphs into reckless speculation. One of the great strengths of this book is its melding of history and theory, as in its discussion of the work of economist Hyman Minsky, whose penetrating insights into the dynamics of bubbles and crashes were not fully appreciated during his lifetime.

Less well recognized has been the grim fact that the aggressive expansion or over-expansion of credit typically is accompanied by a discernable decline in credit quality. Consider the sharp decline in the number of Fortune 500 companies with AAA credit ratings during the last several decades. Meanwhile, heavy consolidation within the financial sector, including the rise of

'too-big-to-fail' financial conglomerates, also has worked to undermine the competitiveness and stability of financial markets.

As this book generously chronicles and as I learned and often wrote about, US and non-US governments alike have at best posted a mixed record of anticipating, preventing, or correcting financial crises. Even in the modern period, when crises sometimes inspired regulatory reforms, the overall trend has been toward market liberalization and greater risk-taking. It is the great challenge of our financial markets to balance their entrepreneurial drive for profit with their fiduciary role as custodians of our financial assets. Because that challenge is so great—and too often ends in calamity—the story told in thes pages is far from over. In the meantime, we can be thankful this edition of *MPC* brings both history and theory up-to-date in what remains the best single volume on the topic between covers.

Preface to the Eighth Edition

Charles P. Kindleberger, the second author, has died before the publication of this book.

I first met Charles Kindleberger ('call me Charlie') in his fall 1976 European economic history course at MIT. The course eventually became his 1984 book, *A Financial History of Western Europe*. In its acknowledgments, he thanked me among many 'in my MIT classes, some students attending from Harvard.' In those days, in economics, Harvard was running a trade deficit with MIT, to which I contributed three times, twice with Charlie and once with Rudi Dornbusch.

In 1976, Charlie gave me draft chapters from *Manias, Panics and Crashes*. I learned that the 1970s enthusiasm for lending to developing countries had many precedents. Charlie ascribed the 1970s lending boom not to the common explanation of the first oil shock, which flooded banks in London with so-called petro-dollars, but to easy US monetary policy early in the decade and the resultant failure of international monetary coordination:

> Our problem started with the attempt of the United States in 1971–72 to achieve low interest rates, when Germany was striving to restrict inflation through tight money policies. Money poured out of the United States into the Euro-currency market, and out of the Euro-currency market into Germany and other countries. The Euro-currency market swelled up like a frog in the mating season, and started lending to developing countries in ways reminiscent of the 1820s, 1860s, 1880s, 1910-1913, and the 1920s.[1]

Sadly, the frog metaphor did not make it into *Manias, Panics and Crashes.*

Later, I took Charlie's undergraduate international economics class, using the 5th edition (1973) of his textbook by the same title. This textbook was unusually rich in history and institutions compared to the narrower competing texts. My work over the years probably drew more on this class than any other. At the end of his undergraduate class, he recalled that I had taken his graduate history class and quipped that he expected to see me next semester in his kindergarten class.

Paul Krugman reports that Charlie's international macro class was 'full of wisdom' but left him uninspired—'who feels wise in his 20s?'.[2] The history class inspired me to follow in Charlie's pre-MIT footsteps by working first at the New York Fed and then at the Bank for International Settlements (BIS). His erudition, and the way his writing could carry it lightly, were not so easy to follow.

What was Charlie's contribution to *Manias, Panics and Crashes*? One answer is that he applied Hyman Minsky's model to history, which led him to the prescient forecast that the mania of lending to developing countries would once again see panic and crash. Another answer is Charlie's argument for the international lender of last resort.

Charlie did not just apply Minsky to experience; he memorably formulated a key social psychological insight: 'There is nothing so disturbing to one's well-being and judgment as to see a friend get rich.'

On the relationship with Minsky, Brad de Long and Barry Eichengreen wrote in their forward to the fortieth-anniversary edition of Charlie's *The World in Depression*[3]:

> Kindleberger amply acknowledged his intellectual debt to Minsky. But we are not alone if we suggest that Kindleberger's admirably clear presentation of the framework, and the success with which he documented its power by applying it to historical experience, rendered it more impactful in the academy and generally.

My experience bears out this judgment. I first saw Minsky at a Federal Reserve Bank of New York colloquium in the early 1990s. He presented his framework with gusto but without applying it to the recent mania for corporate leveraged buyouts or for commercial real estate that drove big US banks to the brink of failure. Colleagues Judy Ruud and Frank Iacono joined me in applying Minsky's model to the corporate leveraging mania of the 1980s in *Dodging Bullets: Changing Corporate Capital Structures in the 1980s.*

In retrospect, what is striking is how little recent material Charlie had to work with. But what he had to work with, he got right. The first rip-roaring

financial crisis of global significance after the Second World War came with the developing country debt crisis that hit in August 1982 as Mexico ran out of dollars to service its debt. Charlie had warned over five years before about the accumulation of debt by countries borrowing eurodollars.[4]

This ran against conventional wisdom. The tendency at the Federal Reserve and US Treasury was to see the 'recycling' of payments surpluses of oil countries as supporting global demand. In a celebrated 1981 *Brookings Paper*, Jeff Sachs focused on flows and argued that 'If my analysis is correct, much of the growth in LDC [less developed country] debt reflects increased investment and should not pose a problem of repayment… This is particularly true for Brazil and Mexico…'[5] In the official sector, few other than Alexandre Lamfalussy at the BIS and Henry Wallich at the Board of Governors of the Federal Reserve shared Charlie's apprehensions.

On the policy front, Charlie's contribution was to argue for an international lender of last resort. His stint at the BIS in 1939-40 and his following of central bank cooperation there in the 1960s equipped him to recognize central bank swaps as the closest approximation to the international lender of last resort. At the time, and for most of the rest of the twentieth century, economists and officials looked to the International Monetary Fund as the closest approximation. Charlie saw from the first days of the swap lines their potential to be extended in an unlimited fashion, anticipating practice in October 2008.

With the fifth through seventh editions, *Manias, Panics and Crashes* has another author, Bob Aliber. I first met him in 1991 when he invited me and my co-author Steve Zimmer to present our work comparing the cost of capital across countries to his class in international finance at the Graduate Business School at the University of Chicago. He was kind enough to introduce us as having written an article that he wished he had written. Steve and I had described differences in the cost of capital that Bob had already used to explain why some countries are on balance homes for multinationals (eg. Switzerland) and why others are hosts.[6] At the time, the competitive challenge of Japanese banks had hinged on their very low cost of equity during the bubble years.

Bob nominated me to teach two courses, International Financial Policy and The Multinational Firm, for two terms at the Chicago Business School in 1992. Commuting weekly from New York proved a real treat for me if not the students. Using Bob's notes to teach these courses amounted to a challenging way of taking his classes. Our dialog since has spanned more than three decades.

In the fifth through seventh editions of *Manias, Panics and Crashes*, Bob has in his turn made two major contributions. First, he has posed the question of how capital flows lead to manias and crashes, bringing in elements from the debate over German reparations after WWI. Second, he has posed the question of the link between successive waves of manias, including exchange rates and capital flows.

The WWI version of the capital flow problem posed the question of how the payment of an indemnity by Germany to France could lead to more net exports from the payer and lower net exports from the receiver. Keynes' polemical answer in the *Economic Consequences of the Peace* centered on how much Germany's prices would have to fall relative to those of its trading partners—by way of suggesting the impossibility or at least the harshness of the reparations. Ohlin ironically answered in a more Keynesian fashion using income changes. In particular, higher German taxes or lower German government expenditure, and the reverse in France, would affect incomes. Germans would reduce spending not only on exports and imports but also on home goods and services like haircuts and thereby release resources to produce more goods for export. The French would increase spending with the opposite effects.

Aliber re-cast this so-called transfer problem into the question of how an economy responds not to official flows but to a big inflow of private capital. His answer is that it can set in motion a mania. It raises the prices of stocks and bonds, adding to private wealth. It can stimulate and fund bank lending and other credit creation, giving a particular lift to real estate prices. With a floating exchange rate, the capital inflow appreciates the exchange rate. If firms have borrowed in foreign currency, currency appreciation flatters their balance sheets, reducing debt relative to equity and increasing the supply of bank loans. All of these lead to greater domestic spending relative to domestic production and thereby a deterioration in external trade. The current account deteriorates to match the capital inflow. The transfer is made to happen not, as with Ohlin's story, through changes in the government budget, but rather through the effect on private spending of easier credit, lower financing costs, higher wealth, and exchange rate appreciation. In this story, the exchange rate movements contribute to the unsustainable accumulation of debt rather than adjusting to maintain equilibrium, as foreseen by the proponents of floating exchange rates. When the capital inflow reverses, boom turns to bust.

This view does not take it as a coincidence if several countries experience manias simultaneously. Rather, attention should be paid to similar inflows of capital.

Tiny Iceland's outsized equity bubble and deterioration of its trade accounts in the years before 2008 played an important role in clarifying these dynamics to Bob. Michael Lewis' *Boomerang* recounts Bob's 2006 prescient call that Iceland had passed the point of no return and would encounter a traumatic crash.[7] A friend quipped that just as Darwin had to go to the Galapagos Islands to grasp evolution, so Aliber had to go to Iceland to recognize the manic power of capital inflows with a floating exchange rate.

The 7th edition's epilogue on the Chinese real estate market proved timely and insightful when big Chinese real estate companies became distressed in the middle of 2021. It remains an epilogue in this edition, though the story is updated.

Bob's second major contribution is the question of how successive major manias in different countries since the 1970s are linked. His answer is that the outcome of the previous mania and crash unleash exchange rate changes and capital flows that set the stage for the next wave of crises.

Charlie and Bob are tough acts to follow.

My main contribution to this 8th edition is the new chapter on the lender of last resort in this century; the conclusion focuses on the same issue. Another new chapter concerns the mania for cryptocurrencies, on the grounds that it is the most speculative asset ever invented by the human mind. My first stab at the topic within weeks of the November 2021 peak of crypto prices generated heavy web traffic, an appearance on CNBC, and not a little vitriol from crypto 'bros' on Twitter.[8] By May 2022, my return to the same venue to describe crypto runs and collapses faced much more competition.[9]

Porto, Portugal Robert N. McCauley

Notes

1. Charles P. Kindleberger, 'Discussion of C McMahon's "Central banks as regulators and lenders of last resort in an international context: a view from the United Kingdom",' in *Key Issues in International Banking*, Federal Reserve Bank of Boston *Conference Series no 18, Proceedings of a Conference Held at Melvin Village, New Hampshire, October, 1977*, p. 112.
2. Paul Krugman, 'Remembering Rudi Dornbusch,' unpublished manuscript, www.pkarchive.org, July 28, 2002, accessed July 4, 2022.
3. Bradford DeLong and Barry Eichengreen, 'New Preface to Charles Kindleberger, *The World in Depression 1929–1939*,' *VoxEU*, June 12, 2012.

4. Charles P. Kindleberger, 'Debt Situation of the Developing Countries in Historical Perspective,' in S. Goodman, ed., *Financing and Risk in Developing Countries, Proceedings of a Symposium on Developing Countries' Debt Sponsored by the Export-Import Bank of the United States in April 1977* (New York: Praeger, 1978), pp. 3–11.

5. Jeffrey Sachs, 'The Current Account and Macroeconomic Adjustment in the 1970s,' *Brookings Papers in Economic Activity*, 1981:1, p. 243.

6. Robert Aliber, R. (1984): 'International Banking: a Survey,' *Journal of Money, Credit and Banking*, vol. 16, no. 4, part 2, November 1984, pp. 661–678, and *The Multinational Paradigm* (Cambridge: MIT Press, 1993).

7. Michael Lewis, *Boomerang* (New York: Norton, 2011), p. 21.

8. Robert McCauley, 'Why Bitcoin Is Worse Than a Madoff-style Ponzi,' *Financial Times Alphaville*, December 22, 2021; 'Here's Why Bitcoin Looks Worse than a Madoff-style Ponzi Scheme, Says Robert McCauley,' *CNBC*, December 27, 2021, https://www.cnbc.com/video/2021/12/27/heres-why-bitcoin-looks-worse-than-a-madoff-style-ponzi-scheme-says-robert-mccauley.html, accessed July 13, 2022; https://twitter.com/ftalphaville/status/1473612539791560707?lang=en, accessed July 15, 2022.

9. Robert McCauley, 'How Stablecoins Are Destabilising Crypto,' *Financial Times Alphaville*, May 12, 2022.

Contents

List of Figures

List of Tables

1

Financial Crises: A Hardy Perennial

[handwritten annotation: long time or occurring continually]

When this work first appeared, it looked back a long way to the financial crisis of the 1930s and revived interest in an old theme. Few books on the subject appeared during the several decades after World War II, following the spate of the 1930s, because the industry that produces them is anticyclical in character,[1] and recessions from 1945 to 1973 were few, far between, and exceptionally mild.

This work also looked forward, four years it turned out, to the developing country debt crisis of 1982. In the decades since, 1982 proved just the first of four waves of financial crises. Debtors in three, four, or more countries defaulted at about the same time and the prices of real estate and securities in these countries fell sharply. Each country that experienced a financial crisis also had a recession as household wealth declined in response to the sharp fall in the prices of securities and real estate, and as the banks became much more reluctant suppliers of credit as their own capital was depleted. The Great Recession that began in 2008 was the most severe and the most global since the Great Depression of the 1930s.

The first wave of financial crises broke in the early 1980s when Mexico, Brazil, Argentina, and other developing countries defaulted on hundreds of billions of US-dollar-denominated debt to international banks. The second wave occurred in the early 1990s and engulfed Japan and two of the Nordic countries—Finland and Sweden; Norway had had a similar crisis a few years earlier. The Asian Financial Crisis that began in mid-1997 was the third wave; initially, it hit Thailand, Malaysia, and Indonesia and subsequently South

© The Author(s), under exclusive license to Springer Nature
Switzerland AG 2023
R. Z. Aliber et al., *Manias, Panics, and Crashes*,
https://doi.org/10.1007/978-3-031-16008-0_1

Korea, Russia, Brazil, and Argentina. The financial crisis that hit Mexico during its presidential transition at the end of 1994 served in some ways a dress rehearsal for the crisis in Southeast Asia thirty months later. The fourth wave began in September 2008 with the failure of Fannie Mae and Freddie Mac, the two large US-government-sponsored mortgage lenders and the collapse of Lehman Brothers a few days later; the debacle of these lenders followed a sharp decline in the price of US real estate that had started in 2006. Britain, Spain, Ireland, and Iceland also were involved in the fourth wave.

Financial crises strike at the peaks of business cycles. We are not interested in the business cycle as such, the rhythm of economic expansion and contraction, but only in the financial crisis that is the culmination of a period of expansion and leads to downturn. Raymond Goldsmith's pithy definition comes close: a financial crisis is 'a sharp, brief, ultracyclical deterioration in all or most of a group of financial indicators – [private?] short-term interest rates, asset (stock, real estate, land) prices, commercial insolvencies and failures of financial institutions.'[2] Business cycles without financial crises lie outside our interest. Isolated financial crises that prove so manageable as to have no effects on the economic system are also neglected to an extent. The financial crises we shall consider here are major both in size and in effect and, as a rule, international in scope.

By no means does every upswing in business excess lead inevitably to mania and panic. But the pattern occurs sufficiently frequently and with sufficient uniformity to merit renewed study. What happens, basically, is that some event changes the economic outlook. New opportunities for profits are seized, and overdone, in ways so closely resembling irrationality as to constitute a mania. Investors and firms leverage their positions with borrowed money and credit expands rapidly. Once the excessive character of the upswing is realized, the financial system experiences a sort of 'distress,' in the course of which the rush to reverse the expansion process may become so precipitous as to resemble panic. In the manic phase, people of wealth or credit switch out of money or borrow to buy real or illiquid financial assets. In a panic, the reverse movement takes place, from real or financial assets to money, or repayment of debt, with a crash in the prices of commodities, houses, buildings, land, stocks, bonds—in short, in whatever has been the subject of the mania.

The issues to be probed are several. Are markets so rational that manias—irrational by definition—cannot occur? If, on the other hand, such manias do occur, should they be allowed to run their course without governmental or other authoritative interference—at the risk of financial crisis and even panic that may spread through propagation by one means or another to other

financial markets at home and possibly abroad? Or is there a salutary role to be played by a 'lender of last resort,' who comes to the rescue and provides the public good of stability that the private market is unable to produce for itself? And if the services of a lender of last resort are provided nationally, by the government or by such official institutions as a central bank, what agency or agencies can furnish stability to the international system, for which no government exists?

Charles Kindleberger's *The World in Depression, 1929–1939* concluded that the 1930s depression was wide, deep, and prolonged because there was no international lender of last resort.[3] Britain was unable to act in that capacity because it was exhausted by World War I, obsessed with pegging the British pound to gold at its pre-1914 parity, and groggy from the aborted economic recovery of the early 1920s. The United States was unwilling to act as an international lender of last resort; few Americans had thought through what the United States might have done if it had chosen to take on that role. The present work started as an attempt to extend the analysis more widely in time and space.

Speculative excess, referred to concisely as a mania, and revulsion from such excess in the form of a crisis, crash, or panic looks to be, if not inevitable, at least historically common. The four waves of crises of the last 40 years offer all too much evidence.

During a crisis, many firms that recently appeared robust can suddenly become bankrupt because the failure of a few lenders leads to a withdrawal of credit, fire sales of securities, and a slowdown in the economy. When the prices of securities decline sharply, government intervention may be desirable to prevent the price changes from becoming self-justifying and thereby to provide the public good of stability. At such times a lender of last resort can provide financial stability or attenuate financial instability. The policy dilemma is that if investors know in advance that governmental support will be forthcoming at such times, they will be less cautious in their purchases of securities and crises might occur more frequently.

The role of the lender of last resort in coping with a crash or panic is fraught with ambiguity and dilemma. Thomas Joplin commented on the behavior of the Bank of England in the crisis of 1825: 'There are times when rules and precedents cannot be broken; others, when they cannot be adhered to with safety.'[4] Breaking the rule establishes a precedent and a new rule that can be adhered to or broken as the occasion demands. In these circumstances, intervention is an art rather than a science. The general rules that the state should always intervene or that the state should never intervene are both wrong.

This same question about the wisdom of intervention reappeared in the last century. Should the US government have rescued Chrysler in 1979? Should the State of New York have rescued New York City in 1975? Should the federal banking authorities have rescued Continental Illinois Bank in 1984? (Continental Illinois was nationalized, although the depositors, both insured and uninsured, in the bank were made whole.). Similarly, should the Bank of England have rescued Baring Brothers in 1995 after the rogue trader Nick Leeson in its Singapore branch office had depleted the firm's capital through hidden transactions in option contracts? Should the International Monetary Fund have lent to Mexico, Brazil, and Argentina in the 1980s, and Mexico, Thailand, Indonesia, South Korea, Brazil, and Russia in the 1990s?

And the question reappeared in the present century. Should the Fed not have rescued Bear Stearns and AIG? Should the Fed have lent to Lehman Brothers? Should the Bank of England have intervened earlier in the run on Northern Rock? Should many governments have injected equity into many, many banks in 2008? The list of questions emphasizes that the problem of financial crisis is still very much with us.

The monetary aspects of manias and panics are important and are examined at length in several chapters. The monetarist view—or at least one monetarist view—is that a mania would not occur if the rate of growth of the money supply were low and stable. (The twenty-first century version might be that the mania would not occur if the central bank sets policy interest rates according to an inflation-targeting Taylor rule linking policy to inflation and unemployment.) To be sure, banking crises in which monetary growth accelerates early or late in the process should be distinguished from those in which the growth in the money supply did not increase significantly. But in principle, this view overlooks the capacity of bank credit to grow rapidly on the basis of non-money liabilities, including domestic near money and cross-border wholesale funding. In particular, many surges in credit within economies draw on surges in cross-border inflows of funds.[5] And it overlooks the propensity of nonbank financial institutions to gain share in extending credit in a boom. And it overlooks the possibility of direct credit, whether vendor financing or peer-to-peer lending. In practice, the conventional monetary measure of M2 plus CDs did not flash a strong red signal during the bubble years of the late 1980s in Japan. The rate of increase in US stock prices in the second half of the 1920s was exceptionally high relative to the rate of growth of the money supply, and similarly, the rate of increase in the prices of NASDAQ stocks in the second half of the 1990s was exceedingly high relative to the growth of the US money supply.

The earliest manias discussed in the first edition of this book were the South Sea and Mississippi bubbles of 1719–1720. The earliest manias analyzed in this edition are the *Kipper- und Wipperzeit*, a monetary crisis (1619–1622) that occurred at the outbreak of the Thirty Years War, and the much-discussed 'tulipmania' of 1636–1637.

The early historical treatment focuses on European experiences. The most recent full-scale crises covered in this edition center on the real estate markets in the United States, Britain, Ireland, Spain, and Iceland that began in 2008. More recent events treated include the international lender of last resort in March 2020, and boom and distress if not bust in crypto assets and Chinese housing. The concentration on the financial crises in Britain in the nineteenth century reflects both the central importance of London in international financial arrangements and the abundant writings by contemporary analysts. In contrast, Amsterdam was the dominant financial power for much of the eighteenth century, but events there are slighted because of the difficulties in accessing the Dutch literature.

The waves of surges in the supply of credit and the subsequent financial crises since the mid-1970s suggest that these market events have become more global than in the past. Most of the countries that have experienced surges in the supplies of credit that led to sharp increases in the prices of real estate and securities also experienced increases in cross-border investment inflows. These inflows led to increases in the prices of currencies unless they were anchored to parities and to increases in the prices of securities. Each country experienced an economic boom—'the times could not be better.' Perhaps because of the increases in the prices of currencies, the upward pressures on prices of goods have been smaller than they would have been had the currencies been pegged. Nevertheless, the central banks in many countries raised interest rates to dampen inflationary pressures due to the boom—which attracted more money from abroad.

Technological innovations in communications and computing mean that the costs of cross-border investment inflows have declined; investors shift funds to a foreign center for a small anticipated incremental return. Moreover, there is a larger pool of liquid funds denominated in the US dollar in the offshore market that investors can tap when they want to buy securities and assets in countries whose financial and economic prospects suddenly look much brighter.

The Story Chapter by Chapter

Chapter 2 presents a stylized model of speculation, credit expansion, financial distress, and then crisis that ends in a panic and crash. The model follows the early classical ideas of 'over-trading' followed by 'revulsion' and 'discredit'—musty terms used by earlier generations of economists including Adam Smith, John Stuart Mill, Knut Wicksell, and Irving Fisher. These concepts were developed further by Hyman Minsky, who argued that the US financial system is unstable, fragile, and prone to crisis. The Minsky model has great explanatory power for earlier crises in the United States and in Western Europe, for the surges in the prices of real estate and equities in Japan in the second half of the 1980s, and for the sharp increases in real estate prices in the United States, Britain, Ireland, Spain, and Iceland between 2002 and 2007. Each of these crises followed a surge in real estate prices that followed an increase in the supply of credit.

The analysis itself, with copious historical illustrations, begins in Chapter 3 with its focus on speculation, the mania phase. The central issue is whether speculation can be destabilizing as well as stabilizing—whether, in other words, markets are always rational. Do investors in real estate and in stocks anticipate prices on the basis of recent increases in the prices of these assets—the bubble case—or do they anticipate prices on the basis of their estimates of their earning power? The nature of the outside, exogenous shock that triggers the mania is examined in different historical settings including the onset and the end of a war, a series of good harvests and a series of bad harvests, the opening of new markets and of new sources of supply and the development of different innovations—the railroad, electricity, the automobile, and the internet. A particular displacement that has shocked the system has been financial liberalization or deregulation in Japan, the Nordic countries, some Asian countries, Mexico, Russia, and Iceland. Deregulation has led to both domestic credit expansion and to increases in borrowing in foreign centers to finance domestic loans and speculative investment. Ronald McKinnon and Edward Shaw condemned government restraints on banking as financial repression in the 1970s and many since have taken increases in the ratio of private credit to GDP as signs of increased welfare.[6]

Investors have speculated in commodities, agricultural land, urban building sites, railroads, new banks, discount houses, stocks, bonds (both foreign and domestic), glamor stocks, conglomerates, condominiums, shopping centers, and office buildings. Moderate excesses burn themselves out without significant damage to the economy although individual investors encounter large losses. One question is whether the euphoria of the economic

upswing endangers financial stability only if it involves at least two or more objects of speculation, a bad harvest, say, along with a railroad mania or an orgy of land speculation, or a bubble in real estate and in stocks at the same time.

Chapter 4 analyzes the monetary dimensions of both manias and panics. On occasion a boom or a panic results from a monetary event—a recoinage, a discovery of precious metals, a change in the ratio of the price of gold to the price of silver under bimetallism, an unexpected success of some flotation of a stock or bond, a sharp reduction in interest rates as a result of a massive debt conversion, or a rapid expansion of the monetary base. Innovations in finance, as in productive processes, can shock the system and lead to over-investment in some types of financial services, especially if competition and lack of experience lead innovations to be underpriced.[7] The financial sector expanded rapidly in the United States during its real estate boom because of the rapid increase in the demand for mortgages following the introduction of private-label mortgage-backed securities (MBSs) that sliced up claims to the interest income and the principal of a large number of mortgages that were held in a trust.

The problems associated with managing the monetary mechanism to avoid manias and bubbles deserve stress. Many monetarists insist that many, perhaps most, of the cyclical difficulties of the past have resulted from mismanagement of the monetary mechanism. Such mistakes were frequent and serious. The argument advanced in Chapter 4, however, is that even when the supply of money was adjusted to the economy's demands, the financial system may proceed to produce many close substitutes for money, just as lawyers find new loopholes in tax laws as fast as legislation closes up the old ones. The evolution of money from coins to bank notes, bills of exchange, bank deposits, and finance paper illustrates the point. The Currency School may have been right about the need for a fixed supply of money, but it was wrong to believe that it could be achieved. Moreover, banks or nonbank lenders can access wholesale funding, especially from abroad, to fund credit extension. Then, credit to households and developers can grow faster than money and enable surges in the prices of real estate.

Chapter 5 describes the crisis stage, with an emphasis on domestic aspects. One question is whether manias can be halted by official warnings—moral suasion or jawboning. By and large, the evidence suggests that they cannot, or at least that many crises followed warnings that were intended to head them off. One widely noted remark was that of Alan Greenspan, chairman of the Federal Reserve Board, who stated on December 6, 1996, that he thought the New York stock market was 'irrationally exuberant,' This was at a time

when the Dow Jones industrial average was 6400. It subsequently rose to over 11,000. The NASDAQ was 1300 at the time of the Greenspan remark and peaked at more than 5000 four years later. A similar warning had been issued in February 1929 by Paul M. Warburg, a private banker who was one of the fathers of the Federal Reserve system, without slowing the stock market's upward climb. The nature of the event that ultimately produces a turning point is discussed: some bankruptcy, defalcation, or troubled area revealed or rumored, a sharp rise in the central bank discount rate to halt the hemorrhage of cash into domestic circulation or abroad. And then there is the interaction of falling prices—the crash—and its impact on the liquidity of the economy.

Chapter 6 considers swindles and defalcations. Sometimes, the revelation of some misfeasance, malfeasance, or malversation (the corruption of officials) engendered during the mania precipitates a crash and panic. Other times the crash and panic reveal frauds and swindles that had proliferated in the froth of the mania. It seems clear from the historical record that swindles are a response to the greedy appetite for wealth stimulated by the boom: demand creates its own supply. Demand is strong: short-seller Jim Chanos claims that 'we are in the golden age of fraud.'[8] It is remarkable that recent corporate frauds, including Theranos, a Silicon Valley startup whose young female founder promised a blood test based on drops of blood, and Wirecard, a German company booking bogus profits from electronic payments, came to light in mid-boom. By contrast, the rogue's gallery of corrupt business firms of the 1990s, Enron, MCIWorldCom, Tyco, Dynergy, and Adelphia were revealed after the crash of tech stocks in 2000. The regularity remains that the revelation of swindles occurs as a mania passes from euphoria to distress to crash. And as the monetary system gets stretched, institutions lose liquidity, and unsuccessful swindles are about to be revealed, the temptation to take the money and run becomes virtually irresistible.

Chapter 7 deals with domestic propagation or contagion. It was mentioned just now that a financial crisis may be more serious if two or more, rather than just one, good or asset is the subject of speculation. History seems to show that a boom in one market spills over into others. When and if a crash comes, moreover, it may seize up the banking system and, quite apart from any change in the quantity of money, lead banks to ration credit all around. The connections between the stock and commodities markets were especially strong in New York in 1921 and 1929, and those linking shares and real estate again in 1929, and in 1987, and notably in Japan and the Nordic countries in 1988–1990.

Chapter 8 traces the international contagion of manias and crises from the seventeenth to the first half of the twentieth century; two, three, four, or

more countries experienced similar manias at the same time. There are two competing narratives. One invokes the metaphor of the sun and the moon, with the mania initiated in one country, often a large one, and then 'beamed' to its smaller neighbors or trading partners. An alternative posits that these countries are subject to the same displacement or innovation. Connections run through many linkages among countries, including trade, arbitrage of securities, capital flows, changes in central bank reserves of gold or foreign exchange, and direct contagion of speculators in euphoria or gloom. Some surges in the supply of credit are national, others global in that two, three, or more countries are involved. Some crises are national, others international. What constitutes the difference? Did, for example, the 1907 panic in New York precipitate the collapse of the Società Bancaria Italiana via pressure on Paris communicated to Turin by withdrawals of bank deposits? There is a fundamental ambiguity here. Tight money in one financial center can serve either to attract funds or to repel them, depending on the expectations that a rise in interest rates generates. With inelastic expectations—no fear of crisis or that the price of the currency might decline—an increase in the discount rate attracts funds from abroad and helps provide the cash needed to ensure liquidity; with elastic expectations of changes—of falling prices, bankruptcies, or the decline in the price of the currency—raising the discount rate may suggest to foreigners the need to take more funds out rather than bring new funds in. The trouble is familiar in economic life generally. A rise in the price of a commodity may lead consumers to postpone purchases in anticipation of a decline or to speed up purchases before prices rise further. And even where expectations are inelastic, and the increase in the discount rate at the central bank sets in motion the right reactions, lags in responses may be so long that the crisis begins before the Marines arrive.

One complex but not unusual trigger that leads to a financial crisis is a sudden halt to foreign lending, perhaps because of a domestic boom. Thus the boom in Germany and Austria in 1873 led to a decline in money outflows and contributed to the difficulties of Jay Cooke in the United States. Similar developments occurred with the Baring crisis in 1890, when troubles in Argentina led the British to halt lending to South Africa, Australia, the United States, and the rest of Latin America. The stock market boom in New York in the spring of 1928 led Americans to cut off buying bonds of Germany and various Latin American countries, which in turn caused these countries to slide into depression. A halt to foreign trading is likely to precipitate depression abroad, which may in turn feed back to the country that launched the process.[9]

The discussion in Chapter 9 takes up international contagion since the mid-twentieth century and highlights the four waves of banking crises since the early 1980s and the relationships among the successive waves. The likelihood that these four waves are independent and unrelated seems low. The first of these waves was preceded by the surge in bank loans to governments and government-owned firms in Mexico and other developing countries in the 1970s, and the second surge was in Tokyo in the second half of the 1980s; was there a connection between the developing country debt crisis and the surge in property prices in Japan? The third wave was in Thailand, Malaysia, Indonesia, Russia, and other developing countries in the mid-1990s, while the fourth wave occurred in the real estate markets in the United States, Britain, Ireland, Iceland, and Spain ten years later. Surges in the prices of real estate cannot occur without the rapid growth of credit, either in the aggregate or to particular groups of borrowers. The theme of this chapter is that there was a systematic relationship among these waves, or at least between the first and the second, and the second and the third. The surge in the supply of credit to Mexico and other developing countries in the 1970s had responded to the growth of the offshore dollar market that took off when the United States and Germany set different interest rates in 1971. When these credit flows slowed sharply the prices of the currencies of these countries declined and the dollar rose. When the dollar fell after 1985, the Bank of Japan resisted the pressure toward the increase in the price of the yen in the second half of the 1980s amid deflation by lowering its interest rates and keeping them low. When property prices and stock prices in Japan began to decline at the beginning of the 1990s, the price of the yen increased and Japanese firms rapidly increased their investments in production facilities in Southeast Asia. The prices of the currencies of these countries increased unless they were prevented from doing so, and the prices of real estate increased. When stock prices and real estate prices in Bangkok and the other Asian capitals began to decline in 1997, the prices of the Asian currencies declined sharply, and there was a surge in the flow of money to New York as Asian borrowers repaid their foreign loans.

Domestic crisis management is reviewed in Chapters 10 and 11. The first of these two chapters considers the range of domestic responses to a crisis; at one extreme the government may take a hands-off approach, and at the other there is a range of miscellaneous measures. Those who believe that the market is rational and can take care of itself prefer the hands-off approach; according to one formulation, it is healthy for the economy to go through the purgative fires of deflation and bankruptcy to get rid of the mistakes and excesses of the boom. Among the miscellaneous devices are legal holidays, bank holidays, the

issue of scrip, guarantees of liabilities, issuance of government debt, deposit insurance, and the formation of special institutions like the Reconstruction Finance Corporation in the United States in 1932 and the Istituto per la Ricostruzione Industriale (IRI) in Italy in 1933. The Italian literature calls the process the 'salvage' of banks and companies; the British in 1974–1975 referred to saving the fringe banks as a 'lifeboat' operation.

Chapter 11 addresses the policy choices related to a domestic lender of last resort—whether there should be such a lender, who this lender should be and how it should operate. A key topic is 'moral hazard'—if market participants are confident that they will be 'bailed out' by a lender of last resort, their self-reliance is weakened. But on the other hand, policymakers may choose to halt the panic today rather than worry about the adverse effects on incentives tomorrow. If there is a lender of last resort, however, whom should it save? Insiders? Outsiders and insiders? Only the solvent, if illiquid? The distinction between solvent and insolvent firms depends on the scope and duration of the panic. These are political questions, and they are raised in particular when it becomes necessary to legislate to increase the capital of the deposit insurer when it runs out of funds to support banks in trouble in a time of acute stress. The issue was particularly acute in the 1990s in Japan, where the collapse of the Nikkei stock bubble in 1990 uncovered all sorts of bad real estate loans by banks, credit unions, and other financial houses, confronting the government with the headache of deciding how much of a burden to put on the taxpayer. If the taxpayers didn't take the hit, then the owners of bonds and stocks would incur very large losses because the prices of these securities would decline further. Particularly troubling in this context was the catatonic state of government in Japan in the 1990s—slow to decide how to meet the crisis and even slower to act.

One of the key issues that a domestic lender of last resort must deal with is whether to extend credit to banks that may be insolvent. The Bagehot doctrine was that the lender of last resort should supply unlimited credit to illiquid but solvent institutions but not supply credit to an insolvent institution. Whether a bank is solvent depends on the prices of the securities and loans in its portfolio. During a crisis, cash is king, and the potential buyers of securities are hiding in the woodwork; a large decline in the prices of securities is necessary to induce them to part with cash. Even though the sale occurred at fire-sale prices, the banks that own these securities must use the sales price in valuing their own portfolios, even though these prices seem exceptionally low relative to the interest income on these securities.

Chapter 12 discusses the role of the international lender of last resort in providing global monetary stability up until the end of the twentieth century.

There was no responsible government or agency of government with the de jure responsibility for providing this public good of global monetary stability. The key question is where the international lending of last resort comes from. Before World War II, the central bank of the leading financial center of the world, often assisted by other countries, might play this role. But it might not, with adverse consequences.

After World War II, a hybrid international lender of last resort emerged. The International Monetary Fund (IMF) was established as a treaty-based global organization to reduce the likelihood that countries would manage the prices of their currencies to secure a competitive advantage in the production of exports. It could lend to finance temporary deficits in international trade in goods and services, but its lending was by design slow, limited and conditional. It evolved from lending to countries trying to stabilize their currencies exchange rates through the 1970s to lending to developing countries trying to manage their external debts in the 1980s and 1990s. But leading central banks also continued to play a role. In the Latin American debt crisis of the 1980s, creditor country central banks helped to organize the rescheduling of private bank claims, and they returned to this role with South Korea in the Asian Financial Crisis. Starting in the early 1960s, major central banks agreed to provide each other with short-term credits known as swaps. These were extended for the short term, mostly to manage exchange rates, with the understanding that the borrower would refinance over the medium term with the IMF if necessary. In the 1980s and to a lesser extent in the 1990s, swaps were extended to some emerging market countries as 'bridges' to IMF borrowings.

The international lender of last resort changed so much in the twenty-first century that it merits a separate Chapter 13 in this edition. Non-US banks suffered from a major loss of dollar funding in 2008 and again in 2020, and the Fed advanced dollars to a range of central banks that in turn provided them to banks in their home markets. What had only been a possibility since the inception of the swap lines in the early 1960s became a reality: the Fed offered swaps with no ex ante limits to its partner central banks. The object of the episode mixed strong, if often overlooked, self-interest—lowering key market rates that set debt-servicing costs for US firms and households—with service to the global good of financial stability—countering a run on non-US banks' global dollar borrowing. Taking into account regional swaps extended in modest amounts by the ECB and the Swiss National Bank, central banks, predominantly the Fed, had become the global lenders of last resort.

This chapter also tells the story of the Fed as stabilizer of global dollar bond markets in early 2020. As the COVID pandemic broke out, panic selling of

US Treasury and corporate bonds hit what is usually the world's broadest, deepest, and most liquid bond market. Runs on bond mutual funds threatened a spiral of lower prices and fire-sale bond selling. The Fed's response in buying US Treasury and even US corporate bonds did not just stabilize these markets, but also the $6 trillion market for dollar bonds issued by borrowers outside the US. However domestic its focus, the Fed brought stability not only to the global banking market but also to the global bond market.

Chapter 14 profiles the mania in cryptocoins, coded anonymous money produced and traded privately over the internet. At a peak aggregate valuation of $3 trillion in November 2021, its sheer scale does not necessarily merit a chapter. But these assets soared in value while offering no cash flow, no ultimate redemption, little use value, and, for the largest, environmental damage. But crypto engages so intriguingly with so many of the themes of this book that it deserves consideration. More than anything, the judgment to buy them arose from the sight of friends (and more remote objects of comparison) getting rich overnight. The account here emphasizes the illusion of decentralization in crypto and asks what risks arise from its central institutions, including both trading platforms and its pseudo-money, so-called stablecoins. While its anonymity and vulnerability attracted criminals and hackers, in the main crypto is not strictly a fraud. But its cash flows are often likened to those of a financial swindle, but the question is which kind of swindle bears the best likeness?

Chapter 15 concludes. The lender of last resort should exist but its presence should be doubted. For example, uncertainty about whether New York City would be helped, and by whom, may have been the appropriate policy in the long run, so long as help was finally provided, and so long as there was doubt right to the end as to whether it would be forthcoming. This is a neat trick: eventually always come to the rescue, in order to prevent needless deflation, but always leave it uncertain whether rescue will arrive in time or at all, so as to instill caution in other speculators, banks, cities, or countries. In Voltaire's *Candide*, the head of a general was cut off 'to encourage the others.' A sleight of hand may be necessary to 'encourage' the others (without, of course, cutting off actual heads) not to anticipate the lender of last resort because the alternative of not providing it has such unhappy consequences for the economic system.

An epilogue updated from the 7th edition focuses on the implosion of property prices and the decline in real estate construction that threatens the Chinese economy. The economic achievements of China since the early 1980s have been brilliant; three hundred to four hundred million have moved into the middle class, with clean water in and dirty water out. Property prices have soared and are extraordinarily high, and at the same time, there are thirty

or fifty million empty apartments. The combination of high prices and empty apartments suggests the relevance of the quip of the great Yogi Berra: 'It's so expensive no one can afford to live there.'

Ponzi Finance, Chain Letters, Pyramid Schemes, Manias, and Bubbles

Ponzi finance, chain letters, bubbles, pyramid schemes, and manias are somewhat overlapping terms for non-sustainable patterns of financial behavior, in that the prices of securities today are not consistent with the anticipated prices at distant future dates. Ponzi schemes generally involve promises to pay an interest rate of 30 or 40 or 50 percent a month; the entrepreneurs that develop these schemes always claim they have discovered a new secret formula so they can earn these high rates of return. They make the promised interest payments for the first few months with the money received from their new customers attracted by the promised high rates of return. But by the fourth or fifth month, the money received from these new customers is less than the monies promised to the first sets of customers and the entrepreneurs go to Brazil or jail or both. Bernie Madoff ran one of the largest Ponzi schemes ever, and his posted returns were in the range of ten to twelve percent—but steady. And he remained in business for more than fifteen years—probably long enough to merit the top position on the hit parade of longest-running Ponzi scheme.

A chain letter is a particular form of pyramid arrangement; the procedure is that individuals receive a letter asking them to send $1 (or $10 or $100) to the name at the top of the pyramid and to send the same letter to five friends or acquaintances within five days; the promise is that within thirty days they will receive $64 for each $1 'investment.'

Pyramid arrangements often involve sharing of commission incomes from the sale of securities or cosmetics or food supplements by those who actually make the sales to those who have recruited them to become sales personnel.

A bubble involves the purchase of an asset, usually real estate or a security, in anticipation that the asset or security can be sold to someone else at an even higher price; the term 'the greater fool' has been used to suggest the last buyer was always counting on finding someone else to whom the stock or the condo apartment or the baseball cards could be sold. The term 'bubble' suggests that when the prices stop increasing, they are likely—indeed almost certain—to decline.

The term 'mania' describes the frenzied pattern of purchases, often an increase in prices accompanied by an increase in trading volumes; individuals are eager to buy before the prices increase further.

Chain letters and pyramid schemes rarely have macroeconomic conse-quences, but rather involve isolated segments of the economy and involve the redistribution of income from the latecomers to those who were initially involved.

Notes

1. See the list of books and films about the 2008 Great Financial Crisis in Chapter 1 of the 7th edition of this work.
2. Raymond W. Goldsmith, 'Comment on Hyman Minsky's *The Financial Insta-bility Hypothesis; Capital Processes and the Behavior of the Economy*', in C. P. Kindleberger and J.-P. Laffargue, eds., *Financial Crises: Theory, History and Policy* (Cambridge: Cambridge University Press, 1982), p. 42.
3. C. P. Kindleberger, *The World in Depression, 1929–1939*, 2nd edn (Berkeley: University of California Press, 1986).
4. Thomas Joplin, *Case for Parliamentary Inquiry into the Circumstances of the Panic in a Letter to Thomas Gisburne, Esq.* (London: F. Ridgeway & Sons, n.d. [after 1832]), p. 28.
5. Stefan Avdjiev, Robert McCauley and Patrick McGuire, 'Rapid Credit Growth and International Credit: Challenges for Asia', *BIS Working Papers* No. 377, April 2012; Claudio Borio, Robert McCauley and Patrick McGuire, 'Global Liquidity and Credit Booms', in B. Winkler, A.v. Riet, and P. Bull, eds., *A Flow-of-Funds Perspective on the Financial Crisis* (London: Palgrave Macmillan, 2014).
6. Edward Shaw, *Financial Deepening in Economic Development* (New York: Oxford University Press, 1973); Roland I. McKinnon, *Money and Capitalism in Economic Development* (Washington, DC: Brookings Institution, 1973). A detailed study of regulation in developing countries is 'A Survey of Financial Liberalization' by John Williamson and Molly Mohar, *Essays in International Finance*, no. 221 (Princeton: International Finance Section, November 1998).
7. *Recent Innovations in International Banking* (Basel: Bank for International Settlements, 1986).
8. Harriet Agnew, 'We Are in the Golden Age of Fraud', *Financial Times*, July 24, 2020.
9. See C. P. Kindleberger, 'Panic of 1873', in *Historical Economics* (New York: Harvester Wheatsheaf, 1990), pp. 310–25; idem, 'International Propagation of Financial Crises: the Experience of 1888–93', in idem, *Keynesianism vs. Mone-tarism and Other Essays in Financial History* (London: Allen & Unwin, 1985), pp. 226–39; Henrietta M. Larson, *Jay Cooke, Private Banker* (Cambridge, MA: Harvard University Press, 1936); Matthew Simon, *Cyclical Fluctuations in the International Capital Movements of the United States, 1865–1897* (New York: Arno, 1979).

2

The Anatomy of a Typical Crisis

History vs. Economics

Historians view each event as unique. In contrast, economists search for patterns in the flow of events, and for systematic relationships between an event and its antecedents. History is particular; economics is general.

An economic model of a general financial crisis is presented in this chapter, while the phases of the speculative manias that eventually lead to crisis and collapse are set out in the following chapters. This model of a crisis covers only the boom and the subsequent bust and centers on the episodic nature of the mania and the subsequent events.

Thus the model does not deal with the full turn of the business cycle. The business cycle is a standard feature of market economies; increases in investment spending lead to increases in household incomes and in GDP growth. Macroeconomics focuses on the explanations for the cyclical variations in the rates of growth of GDP around the long-run trend rates of growth and why these trend rates vary over time and place.

The mania model also differs from models that focus on the periodicity of economic expansions and contractions, including the Kitchin inventory cycle of thirty-nine months, the Juglar cycle of investment in plant and equipment that has a periodicity of seven or eight years, and the Kuznets cycle of twenty years that highlights the rise and fall in housing construction.[1] The mania model is silent on the once regular, then ragged spacing of crises. In the first two-thirds of the nineteenth century, crises occurred regularly at ten-year intervals (1816, 1826, 1837, 1847, 1857, 1866), thereafter, less regularly

© The Author(s), under exclusive license to Springer Nature
Switzerland AG 2023
R. Z. Aliber et al., *Manias, Panics, and Crashes*,
https://doi.org/10.1007/978-3-031-16008-0_2

(1873, 1907, 1921, 1929). Evidently, some time must elapse after one speculative mania that ends in crisis before investors have recovered sufficiently from their losses and disillusionment to be willing to take a flyer again.

The Model

We start with the model of the late Hyman Minsky, a man with a reputation among monetary theorists for being particularly pessimistic, even lugubrious, in his emphasis on the fragility of the monetary system and its propensity to disaster.[2]

Minsky highlighted that the changes in the supply of credit are procyclical; the supply of credit increases when the economy is booming and decreases as the growth rate slows. Investors become more optimistic as an economy expands and they revise upward their estimates of the profitability of a wide range of investments, and they become more eager to borrow. At the same time, both the lenders' assessments of the risks of individual investments and their risk averseness decline and they become more willing to make loans, including some for investments that they previously had deemed too risky. Eventually, debts weigh, the economy slows, and investors become less optimistic. The lenders also became more cautious as their loan losses increase, especially if these losses lead to declines in their capital.

Although Minsky was a monetary theorist rather than an economic historian, his model lends itself effectively to the interpretation of economic and financial history. Indeed, in its emphasis on the instability of the credit system, it is a lineal descendant of a model, set out with personal variations, by a host of classical economists including John Stuart Mill, Alfred Marshall, Knut Wicksell, and Irving Fisher. Like Fisher, Minsky attached great importance to the role of debt structures in causing financial difficulties, and especially debt contracted to leverage the acquisition of speculative assets for subsequent resale. Financial economists are working to render aspects of Minsky's model into formal, mathematical models.[3]

> **Minsky's Three-Part Taxonomy of Finance**
> Minsky distinguished among hedge finance, speculative finance, and Ponzi finance—on the basis of the relation between the operating income of individual firms and their debt service payments. A firm is in the hedge finance group if its anticipated operating income is more than sufficient to pay both the interest and the scheduled reduction in its indebtedness. A firm is in the

speculative finance group if its anticipated operating income is sufficient to pay the interest on its indebtedness; however, the firm must use cash from new loans to pay part or all of the amounts due on maturing loans. A firm is in the Ponzi group if its anticipated operating income is smaller than the amount needed to pay all of the interest on its indebtedness on the scheduled due dates, so the firm must either increase its indebtedness or sell some assets to get the cash for these interest payments.

Minsky hypothesizes that the longer an economic upturn continues the more firms that had been in the hedge finance group move to the speculative finance group and the more firms that had been in this latter group move to the Ponzi finance group. Good economic times reward firms that adopt fragile financial structures; their growth leads to aggregate financial instability.

Minsky's use of the term 'Ponzi finance' memorializes Carlo Ponzi, who operated a small 'near bank' or deposit-taking firm, in a Boston suburb in the early 1920s. Ponzi promised to pay interest on the firm's IOUs at the rate of 30 percent a month and his financial transactions went smoothly for three months. In the fourth month, however, the inflow of cash from new depositors was smaller than the interest payments promised to the older depositors and soon Ponzi was on his way to prison.

Ponzi finance is now a generic term for a non-sustainable pattern of finance. The borrowers can only meet their commitments to pay the high interest rates on their outstanding loans if they can obtain cash from new loans. Initially many of the depositors are so pleased with their high rates of return that they allow their interest income to compound; the cliché is that they are 'earning interest on the interest.' Since in many Ponzi schemes, the interest rates are very high, often 30–40 percent a year, the continuation of the arrangement requires a continuous inflow of new money and often at an accelerating rate. The arrangement can operate only as long as the cash withdrawals are smaller than the inflow of new money.

According to Minsky, events leading up to a crisis start with a *displacement*, some exogenous, outside shock to the macroeconomic system. The nature of this displacement varies from one speculative boom to another. It may be the outbreak or end of a war, a bumper harvest or crop failure, the widespread adoption of an invention with pervasive effects—canals, railroads, the automobile, information technology, and the internet—some political event or surprising financial success, or a debt conversion that precipitously lowers interest rates. Financial liberalization has in various places opened up the credit taps and set off a speculative boom. An unanticipated change of monetary policy might constitute such a displacement.

But whatever the source of the displacement, if it is sufficiently large and pervasive, it will alter the economic outlook by changing profit opportunities in at least one important sector of the economy. Displacement brings opportunities for profit in some new or existing lines and closes out others. As a result, business firms and individuals with savings or credit seek to take advantage of the former and retreat from the latter. If the new opportunities dominate those that lose, investment, and production pick up. A boom is under way.

In Minsky's model, the boom is fed by an expansion of bank credit that enlarges the total money supply. Banks typically can expand money, whether by the issue of bank notes under earlier institutional arrangements or by lending through an addition to the borrower's deposit account. Bank credit is, or at least has been, notoriously unstable, with banks easing conditions in the upswing and tightening in the downswing, and the Minsky model rests squarely on that fact. This feature of the Minsky model is incorporated in what follows, but we go further. Before banks had evolved, and afterward, additional means of payment to fuel a speculative mania were available in the virtually infinitely expansible nature of personal credit and vendor finance. For a given banking system at a given time, monetary means of payment may be expanded not only within the existing system of banks but also by the formation of new banks, the development of new credit instruments, and the expansion of personal credit outside of banks. Crucial questions of policy turn on how to control all these avenues of monetary expansion. But even if the instability of old and potential new banks were corrected, instability of personal credit would remain to provide means of payment to finance the boom, given a sufficiently strong stimulus.

Let us assume, then, that the urge to speculate is present and is transmuted into effective demand for goods or financial assets. After a time, increased demand presses against the capacity to produce goods or the supply of existing financial assets. Prices increase, giving rise to new profit opportunities and attracting still further firms and investors. Positive feedback develops, as new investment leads to increases in income that stimulate further investment and further income increases. At this stage, we may get what Minsky called *euphoria*. Speculation for price increases is added to investment for production and sale. If this process builds up, the result is often, though not inevitably, what Adam Smith and his contemporaries called 'overtrading.'

Now, overtrading is by no means a clear concept. It may involve pure speculation for a price rise, an overestimate of prospective returns, or excessive 'gearing' (or leverage, or borrowing against assets).[4] Pure speculation, of course, involves buying for resale rather than use in the case of commodities

or for resale rather than income in the case of financial assets. Overestimation of profits comes from euphoria, affects firms engaged in productive and distributive processes, and requires no explanation. Excessive gearing arises from cash requirements that are low relative both to the prevailing price of a good or asset and to possible changes in its price. It means buying on margin, or by installments, under circumstances in which one can sell the asset and transfer with it the obligation to make future payments. As firms or households see others making profits from speculative purchases and resales, they tend to follow: 'There is nothing so disturbing to one's well-being and judgment as to see a friend get rich.'[5] Similarly, banks may increase their loans because they are reluctant to lose market share to other lenders and to show lower profit growth.

When the number of firms and households indulging in these practices grows large, bringing in segments of the population that are normally aloof from such ventures, speculation for profit leads away from normal, rational behavior to what has been described as a *mania* or *bubble*. The word mania emphasizes the irrationality; bubble foreshadows the bursting. In the technical language of some economists, a bubble is any deviation from 'fundamentals,' whether up or down, leading to the possibility and even the reality of negative bubbles, which rather gets away from the thrust of the metaphor. More often small price variations about fundamental values (as prices) are called 'noise.' In this book, a bubble is an upward price movement over an extended range that then implodes. Investors' forecasts of the price of an asset, whether stocks, property, or cryptocurrency, on Friday, are based on the increase in its price from Monday to Thursday. An extended negative bubble is a crash.

As we shall see in the next chapter, the object of speculation may vary widely from one mania or bubble to the next. It may involve primary products, especially those imported from afar (where the exact conditions of supply and demand are not known in detail), or goods manufactured for export to distant markets, domestic and foreign securities of various kinds, contracts to buy or sell goods or securities, land in the country or city, houses, office buildings, shopping centers, condominiums, and foreign exchange. At a late stage, speculation tends to detach itself from really valuable objects and turn to delusive ones. A larger and larger group of people seeks to become rich without a real understanding of the processes involved. Not surprisingly, swindlers and catchpenny schemes flourish.

Although Minsky's model focuses on the pro-cyclical changes in the supply of credit in a single country, overtrading has historically tended to spread from one country to another. The conduits are many. Internationally traded

commodities and assets that go up in price in one market will rise in others through arbitrage. The foreign-trade multiplier communicates surging income in a given country to others through increased imports. For instance, the bubble in Japan in the 1980s had significant impacts on South Korea and Taiwan, because the firms in these economies were links in the Japanese supply chain and exported to firms in Japan; when Japan experienced a high rate of growth, South Korea and Taiwan also had high growth rates. Capital flows constitute a third link. Money flows of gold, silver (under the gold standard or bimetallism), or foreign exchange are a fourth. And there are purely psychological connections, as when investor euphoria or pessimism in one country infects investors in others. The declines in prices on October 24 and 29, 1929, and October 19, 1987, were practically instantaneous in all financial markets (except Japan), far faster than can be accounted for by arbitrage, income changes, capital flows, or money movements.

Credit expansion in a booming country may be echoed abroad, even though in an ideal gold standard world, a gain of specie for one country would be matched by a corresponding loss for another, so that the resulting expansion in money and credit in the first case would be offset by the contraction in the second. In the real world, however, while the boom in the first country may gain speed from the increase in the supply of reserves, or 'high-powered money,' credit may also rise in the second despite the loss in monetary reserves, as investors respond to rising prices and profits abroad by joining in the speculative chase. In other words, the potential contraction from the shrinkage on the monetary side may be overwhelmed by the increase in speculative interest and the rise in demand. For the two countries together, in any event, the credit system is stretched tighter.

As the speculative boom continues, interest rates, the velocity of circulation, and prices all continue to mount. At some stage, a few insiders decide to take their profits and sell out. At the top of the market, there is hesitation, as new recruits to speculation are balanced by insiders who withdraw. Prices begin to level off. There may then ensue an uneasy period of *financial distress*. The term comes from corporate finance, where a firm is said to be in financial distress when it must contemplate the possibility, perhaps only a remote one, that it will not be able to meet its liabilities.

For an economy as a whole, the equivalent is the awareness on the part of a considerable segment of the speculating community that a rush for liquidity—to get out of other assets and into money—may develop, with disastrous consequences for the prices of goods and securities, and leaving some speculative borrowers unable to pay off their loans. As distress persists, speculators realize, gradually or suddenly, that the market cannot go higher.

It is time to withdraw. The race out of real or long-term financial assets and into money may turn into a stampede.

The specific signal that precipitates the crisis may be the failure of a bank or firm stretched too tight, the revelation of a swindle or defalcation by someone who sought to escape distress by dishonest means, or a fall in the price of the primary object of speculation as it, at first alone, is seen to be overpriced. In any case, the rush is on. Prices decline. Bankruptcies increase. Liquidation sometimes is orderly but may degenerate into panic as the realization spreads that there is only so much money, not enough to enable everyone to sell out at the top. The word for this state—again, not from Minsky—is revulsion. Revulsion against commodities or securities leads banks to cease lending on the collateral of such assets. In the early nineteenth century, this condition was known as discredit. Overtrading, revulsion, and discredit—all these terms have a musty, old-fashioned flavor. They are imprecise, but they do convey a vivid story.

Revulsion and discredit may go so far as to lead to panic (or as the Germans put it, Torschlusspanik, 'door-shut-panic'), with people crowding to get through the door before it slams shut. The panic feeds on itself, as did the speculation, until one or more of three things happen: (1) prices fall so low that people are again tempted to move back into less liquid assets; (2) trade is cut off by setting limits on price declines, shutting down exchanges, or otherwise closing trading; or (3) a lender of last resort succeeds in convincing the market that money will be made available in sufficient volume to meet the demand for cash. Confidence may be restored even if a large volume of money is not issued against other assets; the mere knowledge that one can get money is frequently sufficient to moderate or even to eliminate the demand.

Whether there should be a lender of last resort is a matter of some debate. Those who oppose the function argue that it encourages speculation in the first place. Supporters worry more about the current crisis than about forestalling some future one. There is also a question of the place for an international lender of last resort. In domestic crises, government or the central bank (when there is one) has responsibility. At the international level, there is neither a world government nor any world bank adequately equipped to serve as a lender of last resort. Central banks providing short-term credits to each other have shown themselves capable of discharging the role, but can they keep doing so?

Dilemmas, debates, doubts, and questions abound. We shall have more to say about these questions later on.

The Psychology of Ponzi Schemes and Market Manias
By Clark McCauley*

It is easy to suppose that greed is the explanation for manias and Ponzi schemes, with panics and crashes the sad but inevitable result. Greed, according to Merriam-Webster, is an intense and selfish desire for something. Surely it must be greed that pushes people into the latest fad investment. Greed is not only selfish but solitary: Silas Marner, communing with his gold coins by candlelight, or Scrooge McDuck, dancing alone in his vault under a shower of cash.

Kindleberger had a different idea: 'There is nothing so disturbing to one's well-being and judgment as to see a friend get rich.' This well-polished line reliably elicited a nervous laugh from his audiences. The insight here is that manias are not the result of greed but of fear—the fear of falling behind. The psychology at the bottom of this fear is social comparison theory—the idea that humans are driven to evaluate themselves by comparison with others. FOMO (fear of missing out) is more accurately seen as FOFB (fear of falling behind).

Most of us do not aspire to be the world's richest; we just don't want to fall behind friends, relatives, neighbors, and co-workers. We want to keep up with the Joneses. Investing in a Ponzi scheme or market mania is not an individual failure reflecting an individual character flaw like greed. Rather it reflects the fact that humans are social creatures: we care about others and care how we compare with others.

Kindleberger refers to the effect of watching a friend get rich—a motivating comparison to the extent that we are falling behind. But comparison extends beyond friends. Comparison can occur across generations: it is disturbing if we do not do as well as our parents. Comparison also occurs over time, within one person's experience: it is disturbing to see yourself poorer today than you were five years ago.

Motivating comparison is only half the story of Ponzi frauds. The other element is trust.

Trust is a reciprocal expectation: you trust them to look out for you, and they trust you to look out for them. The importance of trust comes through in the prevalence of *affinity frauds* in Ponzi schemes.

In a landmark study, the *Marquet Report on Ponzi Schemes* reviewed 329 Ponzi cases revealed between 2002 and 2011.** Nearly one in four Ponzi schemes was an affinity fraud—a group with ingroup trust scammed by a member or supposed member of the ingroup. Eighty-five percent of affinity group frauds targeted an ethnic, religious, or elderly/retired group. Ingroup identity brings ingroup trust to the scammer.

For the three quarters of the *Marquet Report* Ponzi schemes that were not affinity frauds, trust had to come from something other than ethnicity, religion, or age. Most likely it was trust in family or friends. Family and friends constitute a personal rather than demographic identity group, a personalized affinity group. Trust in family and friends in this network is likely greater than trust in a demographic identity, and the Ponzi power of family and friends is thus greater than the power of an affinity group.

A market mania or bubble can be understood as a naturally occurring Ponzi—a boom and bust with no Charles Ponzi at the center of it. The motive is the same kind of social comparison that powers a Ponzi—fear of falling behind. But comparisons in a mania are less about personal contact and more about mass media, which in recent years means not only journalistic news sources but also web sites such as Facebook, Twitter and Reddit.

In the US today, there is a sociological form of motivating comparison—between the rich and the rest. Wealth inequality in the United States has been increasing since 1990. In March 2022, the top ten percent of US households had about 70 percent of the wealth; the bottom fifty percent had 3 percent.*** The result of increasing inequality has been to focus more attention on wealth, strengthen stereotypes of the rich and the rest, and enhance 'us' versus 'them' comparisons of the rich and the rest.**** When Bill Gates (Microsoft), Mark Zuckerberg (Facebook), and Jeff Bezos (Amazon) are summoned to testify in Washington, they become targets of motivational comparison; they have grown richer as most Americans became (relatively) poorer.

They also become advertisements for risky investment. What price/earnings ratio would have been too high to get in on the ground floor with these corporate heroes? For many Americans, a risky investment looks like a lottery ticket—the only chance to avoid falling behind.

The stock market can look to non-experts like a lottery. Suppose I am looking at a rising market. The market may be the whole S&P 500, or a sector like the NASDAQ, or a particular stock like Tesla. Should I invest? Should I buy a ticket?

The first argument for investing is that many others have, enough others to produce the rising market. If they trusted this investment, I can. And they have made big money with this investment. I am falling behind those who have already invested.

Of course, the market could go down. So there are four possibilities. I invest, the market continues up, and I am no longer falling behind. Or I invest, the market goes down. I am still not falling behind, my rank in the order of wealth stays the same. Or I don't invest, the market continues up, and I fall further behind. (*Have fun staying poor!* is the crypto jibe.) Or I don't invest, the market goes down, and I move ahead in the order of wealth.

This gain is undermined, however, by the fact that my dollar wealth has not increased.

Looking at the four outcomes, I am much better off investing if the market continues up. I am better off not investing if the market goes down, but I only feel slightly better because my money value is unchanged. Balancing these possibilities, I am likely to follow the crowd into the rising market.

A further consideration is that there is no reason to think the market will go down. When the market is up, pundits, politicians, and economists compete for the news hole in which to explain WHY it is going up. There is much less space for those who might explain why the market is likely to go down next month. The result is that when the market is rising, most stories will explain why it is rising. Most of these explanations will have time signatures that predict further rise on top of the current rise being explained.

So why do Ponzi frauds and no-fraud manias keep happening? Because we humans care about others (trust), and care how we are doing in relation to others (social comparison). All that is required to shut down manias and Ponzi schemes is to shut down trust and social comparison, and look out for number one.

* Emeritus Professor of Social Psychology, Bryn Mawr College

** Marquet International, *The Marquet Report on Ponzi Schemes: A White Collar Fraud Study of Major Ponzi-Type Investment Fraud Cases Revealed from 2002 to 2011*, June 2, 2011, http://media.cleveland.com/business_impact/other/marquet_report_on_ponzi_schemes.pdf, accessed June 18, 2022.

*** https://www.federalreserve.gov/releases/z1/dataviz/dfa/distribute/chart/#quarter:130;series:Net%20worth;demographic:networth;population:1,3,5,7;units:shares;range:1989.3,2022.1, accessed June 23, 2022.

**** Jolanda Jetten, Kim Peters, Belén Álvarez, Bruno Gabriel Salvador Casara, Michael Dare, Kelly Kirkland, Ángel Sánchez-Rodríguez, Hema Preya Selvanathan, Stefanie Sprong, Porntida Tanjitpiyanond, Zhechen Wang, and Frank Mols, 'Consequences of Economic Inequality for the Social and Political Vitality of Society: A Social Identity Analysis', *Political Psychology*, vol. 42, issue 1, December 2021, pp. 241–266.

The Validity of the Model

Three criticisms have been directed at the Minsky model. One is that each crisis is unique, so a general model is misplaced. A second is that changes in the economic environment mean that this type of model is no longer relevant. A third is that asset price bubbles are highly improbable because 'all

the information is in the price' and this price reflects the fundamentals—the mantra of the efficient-market view of finance.

The first criticism is that each crisis is the product of a unique set of circumstances, or that there are such wide differences among financial crises that they should be arranged into various species, each with its own particular features. Banking crises were frequent in the first two-thirds of the nineteenth century and in the last third of the twentieth century. In this view, each crisis is unique and a product of a specific series of historical accidents—which was said about 1848 and about 1929,[6] and may be inferred from the historical accounts of separate crises noted throughout this book. Each crisis also has its unique individual features—the nature of the shock, the object of speculation, the form of credit expansion, the ingenuity of the swindlers and the nature of the incident that touches off revulsion. But if one may borrow a French phrase, the more something changes, the more it remains the same. Details proliferate; structure abides. Virtually every banking crisis has followed two, three, or more years when the rates of growth of the borrowers' indebtedness exceeded 10 or even 20 percent a year—rates of growth that were too high to be sustained for an extended period.

More compelling is the suggestion that the genus 'crises' should be divided into commercial, industrial, monetary, banking, fiscal, and financial (in the sense of financial markets) sub-species or into local, regional, national, and international groups. A large number of taxonomies can follow from this suggestion. A taxonomic approach is not accepted in this book because the primary concern is with international financial crises that involve a number of critical elements—speculation, increase in the supply of credit and borrowers' indebtedness, rise in asset prices followed by a sharp fall, and rush into money. The test is whether the Minsky model provides insights about the broad features of crises.

The second criticism is that the Minsky model of the instability of the supply of credit is no longer relevant because of structural changes in the institutional features of the economy, including the rise of large corporations and of big labor unions and big governments, modern banking, and speedier communications. Alvin Hansen claimed that something akin to the Minsky model applied satisfactorily to the world economy prior to the middle of the nineteenth century but then ceased to apply because the institutional structure underwent a sea change.

> Theories based on uncertainty of the market, on speculation in commodities, on 'overtrading', on the excesses of bank credit, on the psychology of traders and merchants, did indeed reasonably fit the early 'mercantile' or commercial

phase of modern capitalism. But as the nineteenth century wore on, captains of industry... became the main outlets for funds seeking a profitable return through savings and investments.[7]

Hansen—who was a foremost expositor of the Keynesian model of the business cycle and especially of the recently re-invoked risk of persistently high levels of unemployment amounting to 'secular stagnation'—wanted to downplay the significance of any explanations for declines in economic activity other than increases in household or business saving. However, Hansen's emphasis on the importance of the relationship between savings and investment does not require the rejection of the view that changes in the supply of credit and the extent of leveraged speculation can have important impacts on the prices of securities and the level of economic activity.

The financial debacles in Mexico, Brazil, Argentina, and more than ten other developing countries in the early 1980s are consistent with the Minsky model and his notion of Ponzi finance (see Box above); the external indebtedness of these countries increased much more rapidly than their interest payments on their loans in a pattern that could not be sustained. The surges in real estate prices and stock prices in Japan in the second half of the 1980s and the subsequent sharp declines in these prices are also consistent with the Minsky model. The booms and the subsequent busts in the second half of the 1990s in Thailand, Indonesia and Korea and then in Russia feature the same pattern of cash flows; initially the borrowers' indebtedness increased much more rapidly than their interest payments on the indebtedness.

The third criticism is that bubbles are impossible because market prices always reflect the economic fundamentals, and that sharp declines in the prices of securities usually reflect 'policy switching' by governments or central banks. Those who take this position dismiss the possibility that the surges in the prices of securities are the result of herd behavior, positive feedback, or bandwagon effects—credulous suckers following smart insiders. These critics suggest instead that the model is 'mis-specified,' that is, that something was going on and not taken into account by the theory, and that more research is needed.[8] Some of the research that these critics want is offered in this book.

The Relevance of the Minsky Model in the Twenty-First Century

The Minsky model readily applies to the US real estate mania in the first decade of the twenty-first century that culminated in the Great Financial Crisis, which involved Iceland (see Box below), Spain, Ireland and others. The US displacement around the turn of the century was the private securitization of home mortgages. Securities that bundled mortgages guaranteed by the government or its agencies had been around for decades, and techniques for slicing cash flows to create 'tranches' with different exposures to the risk that homeowners would repay the mortgage early were also well developed. What was new was that bankers bundled together mortgages without a government guarantee and used the slicing technique to concentrate the resulting credit risk of homeowners defaulting in some tranches, leaving others able to make full payments in all but the most dire Great Depression-type scenarios. Thus, a given bundle of mortgages could give rise to 'collateralised mortgage obligations' or 'collateralised debt obligations' carrying a mix of mostly top investment grade ratings underpinned by securities carrying bottom junk bond ratings.

This innovation increased the amount of money available for mortgages and propelled US house prices upward. Private mortgages could offer less money down than the government agencies had demanded to extend their guarantees, and loan to value ratios on the privately securitized mortgages rose toward 100 percent. Often mortgages that had qualified for government guarantees were refinanced with high leverage, allowing households to extract equity in a rising market. Or, households traded up to bigger houses, stretching to afford them with the help of low down payments and adjustable-rate mortgages. These could carry low 'teaser' rates for the first two years, by which time continued house price appreciation promised to make a new refinancing possible. The very predictability of the Fed's interest rate hikes allowed mortgage bankers to count the cost of the teaser rates and undermined the rate hikes' power to restrain.

The boom of the early 2000s turned to euphoria in 2005–2006. The share of mortgages extended without government guarantees and with easy down payments reached a high level of 55 percent. Adjustable-rate mortgages—most priced off of the London interbank rate, Libor—amounted to 62 percent of private label mortgage-backed securities.[9]

Lower down payments and rising house prices piled debt onto household balance sheets. The Case-Shiller index of house prices rose 93 percent from the beginning of 2000 to the peak in the first quarter of 2006 at a time of low overall inflation. Prices more than doubled in the hot markets responsible for disproportionate growth of mortgage debt. The ratio of household debt to GDP rose from 71 percent in 2000 to 99 percent in 2007.[10]

Leverage rose not only in the mortgage *instrument* and in the household *sector*, but also in *financial institutions*, both large banks and securities dealers. US banks were constrained by a simple leverage ratio, so they used the wheeze of special-purpose investment vehicles to fund and to hold mortgage securities off their balance sheets. US securities firms faced no such constraints and piled 40 or 50 or so dollars of debt on each dollar of equity. So did major banks headquartered outside of North America, likewise unconstrained by any limit on overall leverage.

As home prices rose, so did investment in housing. Sales of new single-family homes rose from a peak annual rate of less than a million in the previous cycle to a peak near 1.4 million in July of 2005.[11] Even with the boom in house prices with the Covid pandemic, sales have not sustained a rate of a million a year since then.

The boom drew strength from international propagation, discussed further in Chapter 9, which took place on balance sheets in the United States and spanning the Atlantic. Non-US banks were key players in the process from producing private mortgage-backed securities to the holding of them. Foreign banks' US securities affiliates ranked high among underwriters and when top-rated insurer AIG stopped guaranteeing the top-rated securities, foreign banks 'ate their own cooking' and held them on their US balance sheets. European banks' credit also took a round trip across the Atlantic: they borrowed from US money market funds, shipped the dollars to Europe, and funded holdings there of private mortgage-backed securities. And European banks borrowed dollars offshore to fund the securities. Adding it all up, foreign nationals ended up holding an estimated 40 percent of the private mortgage-backed securities with European banks doing the heavy lifting.

After house prices peaked in 2006, distress arrived in the summer of 2007. Two Bear Stearns mortgage-backed securities funds blew up in June. In August BNP Paribas suspended redemptions of its euro-denominated funds invested in US mortgage securities because it could not obtain prices for them. October 2007 saw the peak of stock prices. Distress persisted for over a year. 'Rather like a brontosaurus that has been bitten on the tail and most of the body hasn't noticed yet, the signal is working its way up the vertebrae,' observed investor Jeremy Grantham in July 2007.[12]

The Minsky moment, or panic, arrived with the failure of Lehman Brothers in mid-September 2008. Officials responded with lending of last resort at the domestic and international levels. Chapter 13 highlights the breakthrough in the international lender of last resort in 2008. Often overlooked, the Fed entered the market for short-term private securities as buyer of last resort in 2008. In doing so, it set a precedent for last resort buying of corporate bonds in March 2020 that in the event gave support to dollar bonds issued by borrowers from all over the world. In 2008, governments injected equity into many banks and guaranteed bank borrowing. Crash was averted at the expense of unprecedented government intervention in a broad swathe of economies.

So the Minsky model has proven its worth once in this century by drawing attention to the phased links among leverage, asset prices and real activity in the Great Financial Crisis. By 2022, was another proof on its way?

In early 2022, the Fed belatedly began to reverse the monetary expansion that fueled what some consider the fifth great modern bubble following the United States in 1929, Japan in 1989, the dot.coms in 2000 and the Great Financial Crisis in 2008. Equity, housing and bond prices—and cryptocurrencies in the fringes—all reached high levels in late 2021. The argument that high bond prices (low bond yields) justified high equity prices recalled the University of Tokyo professors' argument that high Japanese property prices in 1989 justified high equity prices.

Yet from the Minsky perspective, indicators of private indebtedness sent mixed signals. During the pandemic, US households used government transfers to pay down credit card debt and to stash an untidy sum in banks. The ratio of US corporate debt to GDP remained on its long-term trend, and corporate rating upgrades well exceeded downgrades into 2022. Bank solvency seemed strong. Nevertheless, the supply of credit was abundant, with private equity operators able to leverage up companies with a free hand to which the corporate raiders of the late 1980s only aspired. Likewise the composition of junk bonds had never been so skewed to the junkiest.

One risk that is not captured in debt indicators is that investors and nonbank financial institutions jointly behave as if they were leveraged. If investors in bond funds sell their shares when bond prices decline, then the bond funds must dump bonds into a declining market. Securities markets rather than banks can suffer runs that seize up the credit mechanism. It would be a mistake to assume that the Great Financial Crisis is the twenty-first century's last demonstration of the relevance of the Minsky model.

The Saga of Iceland's 'Perfect' Bubble

Iceland is the smallest advanced economy—370,000 people—with its own currency. Between 2002 and 2007, prices of residential real estate doubled, which was not exceptional, while the prices of stocks increased by a factor of nine, which was exceptional. In 2002, the value of the assets owned by the three Icelandic banks was 150 percent of the country's GDP, while in 2007 the value of these assets was eight times Iceland's GDP. Moreover, Iceland's GDP in 2007 was 20 percent larger than in 2002. Iceland's banks were the most rapidly growing banks in the world. And then in September 2008 stock prices declined by 90 percent; the prices of real estate tumbled; the market for the Icelandic krona outside of central bank transactions disappeared; and the economy went into a recession—severe by Iceland's standards but modest by those of other countries.

Because Iceland is so small, the financial processes associated with a bubble are more readily visible than in larger countries. The saga began in 1998 when a market-oriented government began to privatize the three main banks, a process that was completed in 2003. The buyers of the shares and the new owners of the banks were politically connected businessmen; in one case the purchase of one of the privatized banks was financed by another bank.

In 2002, the price of the Icelandic krona began to increase in response to three inflows of money. First, Icelandic banks marketed foreign currency loans to businesses in Iceland, which could seemingly profit from lower interest rates abroad. Eventually 80 percent of business loans were foreign currency denominated; as the kroner appreciated, firms' balance sheets strengthened, their profits rose and banks increased the supply of credit. In addition, 20 percent of household debt came to be denominated in foreign currency, mostly auto loans but also some mortgages. With the supply of bank credit increasing, business and household debt rose rapidly. Second, some foreign investors bought Icelandic securities, looking for both an interest rate pickup ('carry') and exchange rate gains. The flow of money to Iceland was part of an increase in investment inflows to the United States, Britain, Ireland, Spain, South Africa, and Australia. Third, the Icelandic banks in various ways lent in foreign currency for the purchase of Icelandic stocks, including their own shares. One wheeze was the banks' lending to their own offshore affiliates to buy bank shares; another was loans to insiders to buy bank shares.

All three of these inflows of money pushed up the exchange value of the krona and share prices. Since banks owned large amounts of the stocks of Icelandic firms, their profits and capital rose. And, as described, the banks were making sure that their own share prices were rising. Stock prices were increasing by 65–70 percent a year, and bank capital was increasing at the same rate.

With household wealth rising and the krona strengthening, consumption and imports increased despite the interest rate hikes of the central bank. These hikes, of course, only increased the incentives for residents to borrow foreign currency and for global investors to hold krona. Iceland's trade balance morphed from a small surplus to a deficit of nearly 20 percent of its GDP. The external indebtedness of Iceland exploded. The flow of money to Iceland was a multiple of the interest payments of the Icelandic residents to their foreign creditors.

The newly privatized Icelandic banks sold their own IOUs to banks in London and Frankfurt and other foreign banking centers in order to fund their foreign currency loans to Icelandic firms and households. They traded on the country's high rating and faced an elastic supply of interbank funding, especially from German banks. As Icelandic banks' equity grew rapidly, the world was their oyster. They borrowed even more from banks to fund the purchase of high street stores in London and Copenhagen. The banks increased their loans at a pace that was almost as rapid as the increase in their capital. In 2005, the government commissioned a report on how to make Reykjavik an international financial center, like Luxembourg, Zurich, or Hong Kong.

Events in 2006 and 2007 challenged the Icelandic banks' business model of heavy dependence on interbank funding in foreign currency. The krona and the stock market fell by a quarter in March 2006 when rating agency Fitch revised its sovereign outlook from stable to negative.* In response, the Iceland Chamber of Commerce commissioned a report with a prominent American economist as co-author that drew soothing conclusions about financial stability in Iceland.** The stock market resumed its climb. In March 2007, Fitch Ratings downgraded the Icelandic sovereign from AA+, citing a current account deficit of 27 percent of GDP in 2006, with interest payments accounting for half that sum.*** (Fitch's reference to 'high standards of governance' and 'strong transparent institutions' would not age well.) As noted above, distress was felt in international financial markets with the halting of redemptions at the BNP Paribas funds in August 2007. In the fall, the Iceland Chamber of Commerce commissioned a critical but again ultimately reassuring report on Icelandic banks with a prominent American economist as co-author.**** One of the Icelandic banks relied increasingly on retail funding in Britain and the Netherlands through an internet brand known as Icesave, whose depositors came to rival in number the whole population of Iceland. At this stage, some foreign observers began to wonder whether the Icelandic banks had not grown too large for even a top-rated government to backstop.

When Lehman Brothers failed in mid-September 2008, the Icelandic banks lost their remaining capacity to roll over their wholesale debt and could not pay the interest to foreign banks. Stock prices tanked, and first one and

then within days the other two large banks defaulted. The loan losses of the Icelandic banks soared. The banks were put into receivership by the Icelandic authorities, who had no foreign exchange to pay to Icesave's retail depositors in the UK and Netherlands. The UK authorities paid out to the UK retail depositors, and an ugly dispute ensued between Iceland and the UK and the Netherlands. In the end, the foreign assets of the Icelandic bank ended up covering the deposits, and the German banks and others holding the Icelandic bank's bonds were left holding the bag.

Iceland is famous for having prosecuted and jailed dozens of bankers, including CEOs, for a collective century of jail time. But as investigator Jared Bibler in his 2022 book *Iceland's Secret: The Untold Story of the World's Biggest Con* makes clear, the story is more ominous than this fact suggests. Bibler was lead investigator at Icelandic regulator the Financial Supervisory Authority whose probes into the banks' manipulation of their own share prices culminated in bankers' serving time in jail. But Bibler reports that the probes were only allowed to go so far before funding was cut off.

Thanks are due to Gylfi Zoega for comments on this box, but he is not responsible for any of its limitations.

* Fitch Ratings, 'Iceland—Macro Imbalances Trigger Negative Outlook', in Robert Aliber and Gylfi Zoega, eds., *Preludes to the Icelandic Financial Crisis* (Basingstoke, Hampshire: Palgrave Macmillan, 2011), Chapter 7, pp. 77–88.

** Frederic S. Mishkin and Tryggvi T. Herbertsson, 'Financial Stability in Iceland', in Aliber and Zoega, eds., *Preludes to the Icelandic Financial Crisis*, Chapter 9, pp. 107–159.

***Fitch Ratings, 'Fitch Downgrades Iceland to "A+"/"AA+"; Outlook Stable', March 15, 2007, https://www.fitchratings.com/research/sovereigns/fitch-downgrades-iceland-to-a-aa-outlook-stable-15-03-2007, accessed June 25, 2022.

**** Richard Portes, Friðrik Már Baldursson and Frosti Ólafsson, 'The Internationalization of Iceland's Financial Sector', in Aliber and Zoega, eds., *Preludes to the Icelandic Financial Crisis*, Chapter 10, pp. 160–240.

Notes

1. Joseph A. Schumpeter, *Business Cycles: a Theoretical, Historical and Statistical Analysis of the Capitalist Process* (New York: McGraw-Hill, 1939), vol. 1, chap. 4, esp. pp. 161ff.
2. Hyman P. Minsky, *John Maynard Keynes* (New York: Columbia University Press, 1975); idem, 'The Financial Instability Hypothesis: Capitalistic

Processes and the Behavior of the Economy', in C. P. Kindleberger and J.-P. Laffargue, eds, *Financial Crises: Theory, History and Policy* (Cambridge: Cambridge University Press, 1982), pp. 13–29. For a view of the work of Hyman Minsky in historical context, see Perry Mehrling, 'The Vision of Hyman P. Minsky', *Journal of Economic Behavior and Organization*, vol. 39 (1999), pp. 125–58.

3. See Markus K. Brunnermeier and Martin Oehmke, 'Bubbles, Financial Crises, and Systemic Risk', in George Constantinides, M. Harris and René Stulz, eds. *Handbook of the Economics of Finance, Volume 2B, Financial Markets and Asset Pricing* (Oxford: North Holland, 2013), pp. 1221–88.

4. See R. C. O. Matthews, 'Public Policy, and Monetary Expenditure', in Thomas Wilson and Andrew S. Skinner, eds, *The Market and the State: Essays in Honour of Adam Smith* (Oxford: Oxford University Press, Clarendon Press, 1976), p. 336.

5. See James B. Stewart, *Den of Thieves* (New York: Touchstone Books [Simon & Schuster], 1991, 1992), p. 97: 'What really fueled the takeover boom [in the 1980s] was the sight of other people making money, big money, by buying and selling companies.'

6. See C. P. Kindleberger, *The World in Depression, 1929–1939*, 2nd edn (Berkeley: University of California Press, 1986), pp. 1–3.

7. Alvin Hansen, *Business Cycles and National Income* (New York: W. W. Norton, 1957), p. 226.

8. Robert D. Flood and Peter W. Garber, *Speculative Bubbles, Speculative Attacks and Policy Switching* (Cambridge, MA: MIT Press, 1964), pp. 73–4, 85, 96, 98, etc.

9. Robert McCauley, 'The 2008 Crisis: Transpacific or Transatlantic?', *BIS Quarterly Review*, December 2018, p. 45.

10. BIS, Residential property prices: detailed series (nominal). https://www.bis.org/statistics/pp/pp_detailed.xlsx and Credit to the non-financial sector. BIS Statistics: time-series details A:US:H:A:M:770:A, accessed 2 April 2022.

11. Federal Reserve Bank of St. Louis, FRED Data. https://fred.stlouisfed.org/series/HSN1F, accessed 2 April 2022.

12. Quoted by Justin Fox, 'The End of Easy Money', *Time*, July 19, 2007. www.content.time.com, accessed 6 May 2022.

3

Speculative Manias

Rationality of Markets

The word 'mania' suggests a loss of a connection with rationality, perhaps mass hysteria. The loss of connection with rationality reflects that the investors, lenders, borrowers, and the bank and financial regulators fail to recognize that a crash always is the end game for the mania. Economic history is replete with manias that involved the construction of canals, railroads, and homes and commercial properties as well as manias that involved stock prices. Economic theory assumes that men and women are rational—and hence manias would not develop. The rationality assumption is disconnected from the observation that manias occur episodically. This chapter focuses on the increases in the investor demand for a particular type of security or asset and the next chapter is centered on increases in the supply of credit.

The 'rational expectations' assumption is that investors react to changes in economic variables as if they are always fully aware of the long-term implications of each of these changes, either because they are clairvoyant or because they have Superman-like vision. Thus, the cliché that 'all the information is in the price' reflects the view that prices in each market change immediately and fully in response to every news item so that no 'money is left on the table'—so that none of the market participants earns an excess return and presumably, none incurs exceptionally large losses.

Contrast the rational expectations assumption with the adaptive expectations assumption that the prices of certain securities or assets at various future dates are extensions of their recent prices—the assumption that is implicit

© The Author(s), under exclusive license to Springer Nature Switzerland AG 2023
R. Z. Aliber et al., *Manias, Panics, and Crashes*,
https://doi.org/10.1007/978-3-031-16008-0_3

in the view that there are 'trends' in the changes in the prices of securities. The cliché that 'the trend is your friend' reflects that prices will continue to increase if they have been increasing. In contrast the thrust of the rational expectations view is that the prices that are anticipated next week and next month determine the prices that prevail today, in effect a backward-looking view from the anticipations about the future to the present. Thus the price of gold in the spot market today is based on the anticipated prices of gold as revealed in a futures market on contracts that mature two or three or more years from now; these anticipated spot prices are discounted to the present by an appropriate interest rate, usually the one on risk-free US Treasury securities. The Canadian dollar price of the US dollar today is the anticipated price of the US dollar for a distant future date discounted to the present by the difference between US and Canadian interest rates.

If a government reduces tax rates to stimulate consumption spending or investment spending, the rational expectations view implies that investors immediately realize that the increase in the fiscal deficit today implies higher tax rates tomorrow and so they will increase the amounts they save in anticipation of the projected increase in their tax bills.

What does it mean to say that investors are rational?[1] One assumption is that most investors behave rationally most of the time. A second is that all investors behave rationally most of the time. A third is that each and every participant in the markets has the same intelligence, the same information, the same objectives and uses the same economic model. A fourth is that each investor behaves rationally all the time.

Each of these assumptions has different implications for the way that investors behave and respond to changes in the prices of securities and of commodities, including gold. Obtaining agreement on the assumption that most investors behave rationally most of the time is easier than obtaining agreement on the assumption that each investor behaves rationally all of the time. Frequently the argument is between two polar positions, one that holds that no investor is ever rational while the other asserts that all investors are always rational. Harry G. Johnson offered this description of the difference between an older group of economists and a younger group interested in international monetary reform in the 1960s:

> The difference can be encapsulated in the proposition that whereas the older generation of economists is inclined to say 'the floating rate system does not work the way I expected, therefore the theory is wrong, the world is irrational and we can only regain rationality by returning to some fixed rate system to be achieved by cooperation among national governments' while the younger group is inclined to say 'the floating rate system is a system that should be

expected to operate rationally, like most markets; if it does not seem to work rationally by my standards, my understanding of how it ought to work is probably defective; and I must work harder at the theory of rational maximizing behavior and its empirical consequences if I am to achieve understanding'. This latter approach is the one that is being disseminated, and intellectually enforced, through the [younger] network.[2]

Rationality is an a priori assumption about the way the world should work rather than a description of the way the world has actually worked. The assumption that investors are rational in the long run is a useful hypothesis because it illuminates an understanding of changes in prices in different markets; in the terminology of Karl Popper, it is a 'pregnant' hypothesis. Hence it is useful to assume that investors are rational in the long run and to analyze economic issues on the basis of this assumption. One interpretation of the rationality assumption is that prices in a particular market today must be consistent with the prices one and two months from now and with prices one and two years from now adjusted for the 'costs of storage'; otherwise, there would be a profitable and relatively riskless arbitrage opportunity.

Ragnar Nurkse summarized his survey of changes in the prices of the French franc and of the German mark in the 1920s with the statement that speculation in the currency market had been destabilizing. Milton Friedman asserted that destabilizing speculation cannot occur—or at least is unlikely to persist—because investors that bought as prices were increasing and sold as prices were declining 'would be buying high and selling low'; because of their losses, they would either go out of business or change their strategy. The Friedman view is that since the destabilizing speculators would fail to survive, destabilizing speculation cannot occur.[3] One response is that from time to time some investors follow strategies that lead to such large losses that they go out of business.

There have been many historic episodes of destabilizing speculation, although at times the language has been imprecise and at other times hyperbolic. Consider some of the phrases in the literature: *manias ... insane land speculation ... blind passion ... financial orgies ... frenzies ... feverish speculation ... epidemic desire to become rich quick ... wishful thinking ... intoxicated investors ... turning a blind eye ... people without ears to hear or eyes to see ... investors living in a fool's paradise ... easy credibility ... overconfidence ... overspeculation ... overtrading ... a raging appetite ... a craze ... a mad rush to expand.*

Fernand Braudel used the terms 'craze' and 'passion' when he discussed everyday life in Europe from the fifteenth to the eighteenth centuries, largely

in connection with consumption but also extended to spices, styles of dress, craving for knowledge, and purchases of land.[4]

The principals in the London banking firm of Overend, Gurney, which crashed on Black Friday in May 1866, were said to be 'sapient nincompoops.'[5] 'These losses,' said Bagehot, 'were made in a manner so reckless and so foolish that one would think a child who had lent money in the City of London would have lent it better.'[6]

Clapham's description of the Baring firm in 1890 is understated in a characteristic British fashion: 'They had not considered these enterprises or the expected investors in them coolly or wisely enough [but had] gone far beyond the limits of prudence.'[7]

Consider Adam Smith's comment on the South Sea Bubble: 'They had an immense capital dividend among an immense number of proprietors. It was naturally to be expected, therefore, that folly, negligence, and profusion should prevail in the whole management of their affairs. The knavery and extravagance of their stock-jobbing operations are sufficiently known [as are] the negligence, profusion, and malversation of the servants of the company.'[8]

And finally a description by the usually restrained Alfred Marshall:

> The evils of reckless trading are always apt to spread beyond the persons immediately concerned ... when rumors attach to a bank's credit, they make a wild stampede to exchange any of its notes which they may hold; their trust has been ignorant, their distrust was ignorance and fierce. Such a rush often caused a bank to fail which might have paid them gradually. The failure of one caused distrust to rage around others and to bring down banks that were really solid; as a fire spreads from one wooden house to another until even fireproof buildings succumb to the blaze of a great conflagration.[9]

Rationality of the Individual, Irrationality of the Market

Manias are associated on occasion with 'irrationality' or mob psychology. The relationship between rational individuals and an irrational group of individuals can be complex. A number of distinctions can be made. One assumption is that of mob psychology, a 'group think' when virtually each of the participants in the market changes his or her views at about the same time and moves as a member of a 'herd.' Alternatively, various individuals change their views about prospective developments in markets at different times as part of a continuing process; most start rationally and then more of them lose contact with reality, gradually at first and then more quickly. A third possible

case is that rationality differs among different groups of traders, investors, and speculators, and that an increasing number of individuals in these groups succumb to the hysteria as the prices of securities or currencies or commodities increase. A fourth case is that all the market participants fail to recognize the 'fallacy of composition,' the view that from time to time the behavior of the group of individuals differs from the sum of the behaviors of each of the individuals in the group. The fifth is that there is a failure of a market with rational expectations as to the *quality* of a reaction to a given stimulus to estimate the appropriate *quantity*, especially when there are lags between the stimulus and the reactions. Finally, irrationality may exist because investors and individuals use the wrong model, fail to consider a particular and crucial bit of information, or suppress information that does not conform to the model that they have implicitly adopted. The irrationality of the gullible and greedy in accepting the sales chatter of swindlers is described in Chapter 6.[10]

Mob psychology or hysteria is well established as an occasional deviation from rational behavior. Some economic models highlight the demonstration effect, which leads the Smiths to spend more than their incomes—at least for a while—as they seek to keep up with the Joneses. Another is the Duesenberry effect: both the Smiths and the Joneses increase their consumption expenditures when their incomes increase and both are reluctant to reduce their spending when their incomes decline. Politics has its 'bandwagon effects' when individuals back the most probable winners (or 'rats desert the sinking ship' when they turn from losers—though if the ship is sinking the most rational rats are the first to leave). The French historian Gustave LeBon discussed this subject in *The Crowd*.[11] Charles MacKay in his review of the South Sea Bubble[12] mentioned a banker who purchased £500 worth of South Sea stock in the third subscription list of August 1720, saying, 'When the rest of the world are mad, we must imitate them in some measure.'[13] In 2008 Chuck Prince, then the Chair of Citigroup, said 'You have to keep dancing as long as the music is playing.'

Minsky highlighted a mild form of this type of irrationality in his discussion of 'euphoria' in markets. In an earlier day, such waves of excessive optimism perhaps followed by extreme pessimism might have been explained by 'sunspots'[14] or the paths of Venus or of Mars through the heavens. In Minsky's formulation, these waves of optimism start with a 'displacement' or shock that leads to an increase in the optimism of investors and business firms and of bank lenders. More confident expectations of a steady stream of prosperity and of an increase in profits induce investors to buy riskier stocks. Banks make riskier loans to more leveraged and less liquid firms in

this more optimistic environment. The optimism increases and may become self-fulfilling until it evolves into a mania.

An earlier alternative explanation for this un-sober upswing was provided by Irving Fisher and by Knut Wicksell who emphasized that from time to time the real rate of interest was too low.[15] Consumer prices increase in economic expansions and, while interest rates increase, they increase less rapidly so the real rate of interest declines. Lenders have 'money illusion' and ignore the decline in the real rate of interest. In contrast, borrowers do not have money illusion; they recognize that the real rate of interest has declined. (The puzzle is to explain why one group of market participants has money illusion and another does not—and while the intuition is that the lenders are more likely to be rational than the borrowers, the lenders lose their money and often their livelihoods when banks and other financial institutions fail.) Rational investors buy more stocks or real estate in this environment of increases in anticipated profits and lower real interest rates. (The Fisher and Wicksell explanations were effective descriptions of the changes in the relationship between nominal interest rates and real interest rates in the 1970s; the decline in real interest rates as the price level increased reflected that investors lagged in estimating the increases in the goods price level.)

This model unpersuasively relies on the ad hoc assumption that two groups of market participants systematically differ in their sensitivity to money illusion.

Too low an interest rate is a special case of what is perhaps a wider phenomenon—the pricing of financial innovations. Initially, these innovations may be underpriced as 'loss leaders' so they will be more readily accepted, but the low price may lead to excess demand. Alternatively, undue risks may be taken by recent entrants in an industry as they reduce their selling prices to increase their market share. One notable example is that of Jay Cooke, the last prominent banker of the early 1870s to back a railroad, the Northern Pacific.[16] Other examples include Roger Caldwell in the municipal bond market of the late 1920s,[17] Bernard K. Marcus of the Bank of the United States in mortgages in the same era,[18] and Michele Sindona of Franklin National Bank in the early 1970s.[19]

Angelo Mozilo, the New York butcher who founded Countrywide Financial, wanted his firm to become the largest US mortgage lender, which would involve a significant increase in its market share. That meant Countrywide had to charge interest rates lower than most of its traditional competitors, and extend credit to some borrowers whose applications for loans had been rejected by other lenders.

Speculation often develops in two stages. In the first, sober stage house-holds, firms, and investors respond to a shock in a limited and rational way; in the second, the anticipations of revaluation profits from increases in the prices of securities and assets play an increasingly dominant role. 'The first taste is for high interest but that taste soon becomes secondary. There is a second appetite for large gains to be made by selling the principal.'[20] In the 1830s US investors initially bought land to cultivate more high-priced cotton; thereafter they purchased land for the anticipated profits from the increase in the price of land. In the 1850s farmers and planters both culti-vated and speculated in land. In ordinary times they bought more land than they cultivated as a hedge against the decline in the price of the acres that they planted; in booms this more or less sound basis was discarded, and farms were heavily mortgaged to buy *more* land, which in turn was mort-gaged so they could buy still more land to profit from anticipated further increases in land prices.[21] The 1830s railway boom in Britain also had two stages: the first prior to 1835 when the projects were not bubbles, and a second after 1835 when they were. In the first phase, shares were sold by promoters to local chambers of commerce, Quaker capitalists, and hard-headed Lancashire businessmen, both merchants and industrialists—that is, to men of substance who anticipated that new business enterprises would flourish from the construction of the railroads. These groups were able to meet both the initial 5–10 percent payment and the subsequent calls for payment as the construction progressed. In the second phase, professional company promoters—many of them rogues interested only in quick profits—tempted a different class of investors, including ladies and clergymen.[22] The same stages were evident in building sites in Vienna in the early 1870s; initially, these sites were bought for construction but then later were snapped up like speculative poker chips for profitable resale.[23] Ilse Mintz noted a two-stage process in the sale of foreign bonds in New York in the 1920s; these bonds were sound prior to 1924 and the Dawes loan (which touched off the boom) and inferior thereafter.[24] The loans to Mexico and Brazil in the early 1970s were based on the realistic assessments of the credit standing of the borrowers; thereafter the banks wanted to increase their loans and they had less concern with the quality of the projects that were being financed. Loans to subprime borrowers in the United States after 2004 surged because the supply of credit was larger than the demand for credit from prime borrowers; the lenders had to look under stones and in the woodwork for additional borrowers.

The markets in recently completed and in unfinished houses in southern California, sold from one person to another at ever-higher prices with the

help of an active market in second mortgages, peaked in 1981 and then collapsed, with price declines of 40 percent.[25] There was a condominium 'craze' in Boston in 1985 and 1986; 60 percent of the buyers intended to sell the units. The condo market turned soft in 1988,[26] in a pattern similar to the 'flat craze' in Chicago in 1881.[27] A similar boom and dip occurred in the apartment market in Chicago in 2003. Speculators traded titles to condominium apartments in buildings that were still under construction in the real estate boom in Florida between 2003 and 2006. One wag developed a 'Condo-Flip' website.

Essentially there was a reversal between the objective and the process, and eventually, the objective became the process. The lenders became so enthusiastic about the process that they failed to appreciate the end game and provide an answer to the standard question about the source of the money that the borrowers would rely on to pay the interest when the money was no longer available from new loans. Initially, the junk bond market may have been rational, but then the supply of junk bonds surged and the creditworthiness of the borrowers declined more or less continuously. A lot of attention in the US housing debacle that began in 2007 has been given to the defaults on 'subprime mortgages,' whose share of the market for new mortgages had increased from 8 percent in 2004 to 20 percent in 2005 and 2006, because the supply of prime mortgage loans was too small to satisfy the lenders that wanted to buy more mortgage loans.

The analysis in terms of two stages suggests two groups of investors, the insiders and the outsiders. The insiders destabilize by driving the price up and then at or near the top sell to the outsiders, whose losses are necessarily equal to the gains of the insiders. Johnson pointed out that for every destabilizing speculator there must be a stabilizing one.[28] But the professional insiders initially destabilize by exaggerating the upswings; these insiders follow the mantra that the 'trend is my friend.' At a much earlier stage, these investors were known as 'tape watchers'; more recently they have been called 'momentum investors.' The outsider amateurs who buy high and sell low are the victims of euphoria that affects them late in the day; the 'Belgian dentists' or Italian doctors bought the bonds of the Argentinean government in 1999 and 2000 to increase their interest income. After they lose, they go back to their normal occupations to save for another splurge in five or ten years.

The evidence from the gold panic of 1869 is consistent with the hypothesis that Gould and Fisk first drove up the gold price and then sold at the top in a manner that is consistent with destabilizing speculation, although Larry Wimmer does not agree that speculation had been destabilizing.[29] The information available to the two groups of speculators differed. In the early stage,

Gould tried to persuade the US government of the desirability of forcibly reducing the price of the US dollar by driving up the 'agio' or premium on gold to increase grain prices, while the outsider speculators operated on the expectation derived from past performance that the US government would seek to drive the agio down so that greenbacks would again be convertible into gold at the pre-Civil War parity. On 16 September the outsiders abandoned this expectation and adopted Gould's; they bought gold and the price went up. On 22 September Gould learned from his associate, President Grant's brother-in-law, that the outsiders originally had been right and that his plan was not going to be adopted; Gould then sold. Belatedly the outsiders saw they were wrong. The result was the collapse of stock prices on Black Friday of 23 September 1869.

Another case that involves two sets of speculators, insiders and outsiders, is the 'bucket shop.' This term has nearly disappeared from the language since the Securities and Exchange Commission declared the practice illegal, but the men and women who run the boiler shops are the children of those who ran bucket shops. Bucket shops are described in novels; a classic picture is given in Christina Stead's excellent *House of All Nations*.[30] The insiders in a bucket shop take orders from the public to buy and sell securities but do not execute these orders because they assume that the outsider's bet will prove to be wrong. And the bucket shop has the advantage of a hedge. If the outsiders should turn out to be right by 'buying low and selling high,' the bucket-shop operators decamp and leave for Brazil. In *House of All Nations*, Jules Bertillon in 1934 fled to Latvia.

Bucket shops evolved into boiler shops that hustled untutored investors with promises of quick sure-fire gains. The owners of the boiler shops had brought forth their own firms; initially, they owned nearly all or all of the shares in these firms. Robert Brennan of First Jersey Securities owned and operated or was associated with a series of boiler shops; the names kept changing but the scam was always the same. Their buddies hustled increases in the prices of stocks of very small, little-known firms; once the stock prices were increasing, they used tele-marketing to sell the stocks in small towns all over America after touting how rapidly prices had been increasing.

The great Master of the Mint, Issac Newton, a world-class scientist, provides another example of an outside destabilizing speculator who bought high and sold low. In the spring of 1720, he stated: 'I can calculate the motions of the heavenly bodies, but not the madness of people.' On 20 April, accordingly, he sold his shares in the South Sea Company for £7000, a 100 percent profit. Later an infection from the mania gripping the world that spring and summer caused him to buy a larger number of shares near the

market top and he lost £20,000. In the irrational habit of so many who experience financial disaster, he put it out of his mind and for the rest of his life he could never bear to hear the name South Sea.[31]

Yet euphoric speculation with insiders and outsiders may also lead to manias and panics when the behavior of every participant seems rational. Consider the fallacy of composition when the whole differs from the sum of its parts. The action of each individual is rational—or would be if many other individuals did not behave in the same way. If an investor is quick enough to get in and out ahead of the others, he may do well, as insiders generally do. Carswell quotes a rational participant on the South Sea Bubble:

> The additional rise above the true capital will only be imaginary; one added to one, by any stretch of vulgar arithmetic will never make three and a half, consequently all fictitious value must be a loss to some person or other first or last. The only way to prevent it to oneself must be to sell out betimes, and so let the Devil take the hindmost.[32]

'Devil take the hindmost,' '*sauve qui peut*,' '*die Letzen beissen die Runde*' ('dogs bite the laggards'), are variants on the 'greater fool theory' and are recipes for a panic. The analogy is someone yelling 'fire' in a crowded theater. The chain letter is another analogy; because the chain cannot expand infinitely, only a few investors can sell before the prices start declining. It is rational for an individual to participate in the early stages of the chain and to believe that all others will think they are rational too.

Closely akin to the fallacy of composition is the standard 'cobweb' demonstration in elementary economics in which demand and supply are linked with a lag rather than simultaneously as in an auction that clears the market at each moment. 'Displacement' consists of events that change the economic or financial environment, extend the horizon and alter expectations. In such cases, otherwise rational expectations of some investors fail to recognize the strength of similar responses by others. When there appears to be a shortage of physicists or mathematicians or schoolteachers many young people enter graduate school to prepare for one of these professions; by the time they have finished their studies, there may be an 'excess supply' of individuals trained for careers in this field. After the belated surge in supply, job opportunities suddenly become scarce. But the excess supply becomes known only after the long gestation period. Responses to shortages of coffee, sugar, cotton, or some other commodity may be similarly excessive. The price increases sharply in response to the initial surge in demand and then declines even more rapidly as the new supply eventually becomes available.

The history of manias and panics is full of examples of destabilizing 'cobweb' responses to exogenous shocks. When Brazil opened as a market for British goods in 1808, more goods from Manchester were sent to the market in a few weeks than had been consumed there in the previous twenty years, including ice skates and warming pans that, as Clapham noted, proved to be the accepted illustration of commercial madness among nineteenth-century economists.[33] In the 1820s, the independence of the Spanish colonies triggered a boom in loans to the new Latin American governments, investments in mining shares and in exports to these countries; the surge in investment proved excessive. 'The demand is sudden, and as suddenly stops. But too many have acted as if it were likely to continue.'[34]

In the 1830s the cobweb fluctuation had a two-year periodicity. 'Each merchant would be ignorant of the amounts that other merchants would be bringing forward by the time his own merchandise was on the market.'[35] The same was true in the United States in the 1850s following the discovery of gold in California:

> The extraordinary and undue expectations entertained not only in the United States but in this country [Britain] as to the capability of California – after the 1849 gold discovery – unquestionably aided in multiplying and extending the disaster consequent on the American crisis. [It] was again and again stated, both in London and in Boston, in regard to all shipments to San Francisco, that six, or at most eight, moderately-sized or assorted cargos per month were all that were required or could be consumed; instead of that eastern shippers dispatch twelve to fifteen first-class ships a month, fully laden.[36]

A rather far-fetched line of reasoning led from the phylloxera that ruined many vineyards and set back wine production in France to the 1880s boom in brewery shares in Britain, as one after another private brewery sold shares to investors for the first time in the public company mania. Among them, Arthur Guinness and Co. was bought for £1.7 million and sold for £3.2 million.[37] 'The success of the issue was like the firing of a starting pistol; by November 1890, 86 other brewery companies had appealed to the public for funds [issued new shares to the public for the first time].'[38]

There was a boom in Britain at the end of World War I when businessmen thought victory would ensure the elimination of German competition in coal, steel, shipping, and cotton textiles. Prices of industrial assets, ships, stocks, and even houses increased. Companies were merged; many of the mergers were financed with large amounts of credit. Then the sober realization set in from the summer of 1920 to the coal strike of the second quarter of 1921.[39]

Three more cases are on the borderline of rationality. The first—the Duesenberry effect noted earlier—deals with individuals who get used to a certain level of income and find it difficult to reduce their spending when their incomes decline. The counterpart in labor supply is the 'backward-bending supply curve,' which suggests that higher wages or salaries produce not more work but less and that the way to increase effort is to lower the wage per unit of time. In economic history books, this principle is known as 'John Bull can stand many things but he cannot stand 2 percent.' John Stuart Mill put it thus:

> Such vicissitudes, beginning with irrational speculation and ending with a commercial crisis, have not hitherto become less frequent or less violent with the growth of capital and the extension of industry ... Rather they may be said to have become more so: in consequence, it is often said, of increased competition; but, as I prefer to say, of a low rate of profit and interest, which makes the capitalists dissatisfied with the ordinary course of safe mercantile gains.[40]

In France at the end of the Restoration and the beginning of the July Monarchy—that is, between 1826 and 1832—speculation was rife despite the 'distrust that the French always feel toward ill-gotten money.' Landowners earned 2.25–3.75 percent on their assets; industrialists tried to earn 7–9 percent on their fixed investments, 2–4 percentage points more than the long-term interest rate. Merchants and speculators in raw materials sought returns in the range of 20–25 percent.[41] Charles Wilson noted that earlier the Dutch were converted from merchants into bankers (accused of idleness and greed); they developed habits of speculation because of the decline in the rate of interest in Amsterdam to 2.5 percent.[42] Large-scale conversions of public debt in 1822 and 1824, and again in 1888 led to a decline in the rate of interest and induced British investors to buy more foreign securities.[43] Andréadès observed that 'When interest goes down, the English commercial world, unable to reduce its mode of life, deserts its usual business in favor of the more profitable, but on that very account more risky undertakings ... speculation leads to disaster and ultimately must be borne by the central bank.'[44]

The boom in bank-syndicated loans to Mexico and other developing countries in the 1970s followed a sharp decline in interest rates in the spring of 1970 as the Federal Reserve flooded the New York market with money to combat the 1970 stock market crash. The funds flowed to the Eurodollar market, where they drove interest rates far down. Banks, chock-a-block with liquidity, looked around for attractive borrowers which they found in governments and government-owned firms in Mexico, Brazil, Argentina, and ten

other developing countries. The 1960s had been a decade of accelerating internationalization for the major US banks and they had rapidly increased the number of their foreign branches. Because commodity prices were increasing rapidly, nominal and real incomes in Mexico, Brazil, and most other developing countries were growing at above-trend rates. Commodity prices declined sharply in the early 1980s in response to the surge in interest rates on US dollar securities, and then nominal and real incomes declined in these indebted countries. Should the banks have foreseen that the decline in commodity prices was inevitable?

The second borderline case involves hanging on to an investment that has gone sour in the hope of some improvement or failing to take a specific type of action when circumstances change. Note the failures of the New York Warehouse and Security Company, of Kenyon, Cox & Co., and of Jay Cooke and Co. on 8, 13, and 18 September 1873, because of loans made to railroads (respectively, the Missouri, Kansas, and Texas, the Canada Southern, and the Northern Pacific) with which they were associated. These railroads were unable to sell bonds to obtain the funds they needed to complete construction because investors in Berlin and in Vienna had stopped buying US dollar securities.[45] Similarly, American investors became much more interested in buying stocks in 1928 in the very frothy market and stopped buying German bonds, although New York banks and investment houses continued to make short-term loans to German borrowers. When riding a tiger or holding a bear by the tail, it seems rational to hang on—at least for a while.

For an error of omission, note the plight of Hamburg banks that had made large loans to Swedish banks that were financing smuggled goods into Russia during the Crimean War; the Hamburg banks failed to cancel these loans when peace came. The Swedish banks used the money to speculate in shipbuilding, factories, and mining, which helped embroil Hamburg in the world crisis of 1857.[46]

The third borderline case is to have a rational model in mind, but the wrong one. The most famous example in another field is the French 'Maginot Line psychology,' though this may be thought of less as a case of irrational expectations than one of an undistributed lag. '"When a man's vision is fixed on one thing," thought Ponzi, "he might as well be blind".'[47] Or Bagehot on Malthus: 'Scarcely any man who has evolved a striking and original conception ever gets rid of it.'[48] In the 1760s, Hamburg merchants were not hurt by the fall in commodity prices until the end of the Seven Years' War. Thus in 1799 while the Napoleonic Wars were continuing they were unprepared for the decline in prices that came with the penetration of the blockade of Napoleon's 1798 Continental system.[49] Or consider the French bankers and

industrialists who formed the copper ring in 1888, patterned after the cartel movement in iron and steel, steel rails, coal, and sugar in the early part of the decade, attracted by the successes of the diamond syndicate in South Africa and of the Rothschilds' mercury monopoly in Spain. By 1890 the French syndicate owned 160,000 tons of high-priced copper plus contracts to buy more; the older mines were being reworked, firms were beginning to process scrap and the copper price was sinking like a stone. The collapse of the copper price from £80 to £38 a ton in 1889 almost buried the Comptoir d'Escompte, which was saved by an advance of 140 million francs from the Bank of France, reluctantly guaranteed by the Paris banks.[50] Perhaps extrapolating from the success of the Organization of Petroleum Exporting Countries in increasing the price of petroleum in the 1970s, Bunker Hunt failed in his attempt to corner the world silver market in 1980. Parallels to the French copper corner included the reworking of mining tailings, huge drives to collect scrap, and short sales by the opposition, but not a suicide by a banker.

Earlier paragraphs have touched upon sudden declines in interest rates from debt conversion that led investors to embrace riskier investments in order to maintain their incomes, and the mistake in monetary policy that flooded the Eurocurrency market in 1970–1971, before the OPEC price hike, and stimulated multinational banks to embark on lending programs to the Third World that became excessive. Financial innovations may also be underpriced and constitute a species of displacement.

One more such displacement deserves attention: deregulation or liberalization. Ronald McKinnon led an intellectual attack on 'financial repression' in the early 1970s, that is, the segmentation of financial markets in developing countries from those in the global economy, which led to preferential treatment for the large firms and the government borrowers in these countries that were involved in foreign trade.[51] The message appealed particularly to Latin American countries already influenced by the Chicago doctrine of liberalism. Some countries deregulated their financial systems, which was followed by the rapid growth of new banks and surges in the supply of credit and then inflation; subsequently, some of the new banks collapsed.[52] McKinnon concluded that the several steps in the process of deregulation should be staged carefully.[53]

The same question appeared again in Poland and in the former Soviet Union in the early 1990s in fierce debates over whether the shift from a command economy to a market economy should be carried through rapidly or slowly. The success of a transition from a command economy seems to depend on the extent to which individuals in the socialist economy remember

the institutional arrangements of capitalism. The memory of the market economy was far greater in Poland than in Russia; long years of socialism and corruption had eradicated the memory of market institutions in Russia. Such memory is more important to transitional success than the speed of decontrol and the privatization of state monopolies.

One purely irrational case involves a society that pins its hopes on some outstanding event of limited relevance to its current economic circumstances and another is when a society ignores evidence that it would prefer not to think about. Many Austrian enterprises had invested extensively in anticipation of the increase in business activity that would follow from the opening of the World Exhibition in Vienna on 1 May 1873; already at the outset of the year, firms' liquid liabilities greatly exceeded their liquid assets and they had acute financial distress. The objective of each of these world fairs was to increase business activity, so there was a significant investment in facilities to accommodate those who would visit. The credit at banks was stretched to the limit; a move from commodities, land, shares, and debt back into money was under way and the chain of accommodation bills was extended as far as it would go. Nonetheless, the firms and the banks that had lent to them hung on, waiting for the exhibition to open, because they thought or at least hoped that the surge in revenues from the visitors would be large enough so the investments would somehow prove to be profitable. When the exhibition opened and the increase in sales was disappointing, the market collapsed in early May.[54]

As an illustration of repression of contradictory evidence—the cognitive dissonance case—consider J. W. Beyen's analysis of the German failure to restrict short-term borrowing from abroad at the end of the 1920s. He suggested that the dangers were not faced, even by Schacht, the German finance minister, and added: 'It would not have been the first nor the last time that consciousness was being "repressed".'[55] These examples suggest that despite the general usefulness of the assumption of rationality, markets have on occasions—infrequent occasions—acted in ways that were irrational even when each participant in the market believed he or she was acting rationally.

Displacements

A displacement is an outside event or shock that changes horizons, expectations, anticipated profit opportunities, behavior—'some sudden advice many times unexpected.'[56] The shock must be sufficiently large to have an

impact on the economic outlook. Each day's events produce some changes in outlook, but few are significant enough to qualify as a shock.

War is a major shock. Some crises occur immediately at the beginning or end of a war, or soon enough after the end to permit a few expectations to be falsified. For beginnings, the most notable is the crisis of August 1914. The displacements at the end of wars include the crises of 1713, 1763, 1783, 1816, 1857, 1864, 1873, and 1920. Moreover, there has been an impressive series of crises seven to ten years after the end of a war, long enough for expectations formed at the end of the original crisis to be falsified; these included 1720, 1772, 1792, 1825, 1873 in the United States, and 1929.

Far-reaching political developments may also jar the system and displace expectations. The Glorious Revolution of 1688 gave rise to a boom in company promotion. By 1695 there were 140 joint-stock companies with a total capital of £4.5 million; more than 80 percent had been formed in the previous seven years. By 1717 total capitalization had reached £21 million.[57] The Bubble Act of July 1720 forbade the formation of new joint-stock companies without the explicit approval of parliament, a limitation that lasted until 1856. Although this legislation has normally been interpreted as a reaction against speculation in the shares of the South Sea Company, Carswell asserts that it was undertaken to support the South Sea Company, as the king and parliament sought to repress the development of rival companies that might attract cash that was intensely needed by the South Sea promoters.[58]

The events of the French Revolution, Terror, Directorate, Consulate, and Empire, along with incidents of the Napoleonic Wars themselves, similarly served as displacements, setting in motion large-scale specie movements in 1792–1793 and 1797 and opening and closing markets in Europe and elsewhere for British and colonial goods. Further political events of the kind in France were the Restoration (1815), the July Monarchy (1830), the February 1848 revolution, and the Second Empire (1852). The Sepoy Mutiny in India in May 1857, followed by a Hindustan military revolution, contributed to the distress in the London financial markets.[59] These events were a precedent for the Invergordon disorder of September 1931, when a contingent of British sailors came close to striking over reductions in their pay decreed by the new national government. Continental Europeans interpreted this response as a mutiny by the navy, a great British institution, which contributed to the British decision to stop pegging the pound to gold.[60]

War, revolution, restoration, change of regime, and mutiny come largely from outside the system; they are beyond the usual set of risky events that can be modeled as a probability distribution—hence they qualify as a 'black swan.' Monetary and financial displacements are more difficult to describe as

exogenous. But maladroit recoinage, tampering with gold-silver ratios under bimetallism, conversions undertaken to economize on government revenue that unexpectedly divert investor attention to other avenues, new lending that proves successful beyond all anticipation—these also are displacements.

The *Kipper- und Wipperzeit* of 1619–1623 noted earlier received its name from the actions of money changers who took the debased coins that were coming from the increase in the number of princely mints and rigged their scales as they sought to exchange bad money for good with naive peasants, shopkeepers, and craftsmen. Rapidly rising debasement spread from state to state until the coins used in daily transactions became worthless.[61]

Two later German recoinages provide a study in contrast. In 1763, Frederick II of Prussia bought silver in Amsterdam on credit to provide for a new coinage to replace that which had been debased during the Seven Years' War. He withdrew the old, debased money from circulation before the new money was issued, which precipitated a deflationary crisis and the collapse of a chain of discounted bills.[62] More than 100 years later, after the Franco-Prussian indemnity, the German authorities issued new money but this time before the old money was withdrawn to save on their interest payments. In three years the circulation of coins rose threefold from 254 million thalers (762 million marks). The result was goods price inflation.[63]

The crisis of 1893 in the United States arose from the threat to gold convertibility from the Sherman Silver Act of 1890 and has already been noted. So have the British debt conversions of 1822, 1824, 1888, and 1932, although the last was associated with a boom in housing that did not lead to a crisis. In France, conversion of the 5 percent *rente* was discussed after 1823 as the money supply expanded and the rate of interest would have fallen had investors not been reluctant to buy *rentes* at a premium. Each of three bankers had a different idea of the purpose of the conversion: Rothschild wanted to sell more *rentes*; Greffuhle (and Ouvrard) hoped to attract investors into canals while Laffitte wanted to ensure the development of industry. Political obstacles prevented passage of the necessary legislation, and the market finally gave up its objection to maintaining the *rente* at a premium. This sharp decline in interest rates touched off speculation.[64] Canals were built by the government with private money[65] and the faint glow of a railroad boom could be seen in France along the Loire, the Rhone, and the Seine. But the main object of speculation was building in and around the major cities— Toulouse, Lyons, Marseilles, Le Havre.[66] Honoré de Balzac's novel *César Birotteau*, written in 1830, was inspired by this experience; he recounted the doleful story of a perfumer who was enticed into buying building lots in the

vicinity of the Madeleine on borrowed money for 'one quarter of the value they were sure to have in three years.'[67]

The success of loans in recycling reparations or indemnities after the Napoleonic and Franco-Prussian wars and World War I was a displacement. Any surprising success of a security issue with a large multiple over-subscription and a quick premium for subscribers attracts borrowers, lenders, and especially investment bankers. The Baring loan of 1819—'the first important foreign loan contracted by a British bank'[68]—led quickly to a series of issues for France, Prussia, Austria, and, later, the newly independent countries in Latin America that had been Spanish colonies. The Thiers *rente* made French banking houses salivate in the hope of foreign loans, a hunger that received a further fillip from the 1888 conversion loan for czarist Russia that bailed out German investors and sent French investors down a trail that was to end, after the revolution in 1917, with a whimper rather than with a bang. The Dawes loan in 1924 opened the eyes of American investors to the romance of buying foreign securities. The Thiers *rente* was oversubscribed fourteen times, and the Dawes loan eleven times; far more important than the size of the multiple, however, was that investors became more enthusiastic about buying these securities. Rosenberg described the three French loans of 1854 and 1855 as sensational since they were oversubscribed almost two to one (468 million francs on an offering of 250 million), four to one (2175 million francs for an issue of 500 million), and five to one (3653 million against 750 million). In Austria and Germany, however, when the speculative boom of the 1850s was under way, the Credit Anstalt opening stock sale was oversubscribed 43 times, largely by people who had stood in line all night; and when the Brunswick Bank sought 2 million thalers in May 1853, it was offered 112 times that amount in three hours.[69]

Among major recent displacements have been the deregulation of banks and financial institutions, derivatives (which existed earlier on a much more modest scale), mutual funds, and hedge funds, Real Estate Investment Trusts (REITS), bank flotation of loans and mortgages as marketable securities, and the initial public offerings (IPOs) of private companies.

The deregulation of financial markets and financial institutions was a major contributory factor to the asset price bubble in Japan in the 1980s and especially during the second half of that decade. Each Japanese bank was keenly interested in its position on the hit parade of banks in terms of the size of its assets and deposits; each wanted to move to a higher position on this hit parade ladder—which meant that each had to 'grow its loans' more rapidly than one or two of the banks that had a higher position on this ladder.

The technological revolution in the 1920s—the sharp increase in automobile production, the electrification of much of America, the rapid expansion of the telephone system, the increase in the number of movie theaters—was a major shock. Investment surged. Similarly, in the 1990s, especially in the second half of the decade, there was a major technological information revolution. The venture capital firms, especially those in the San Francisco Bay area, were eager suppliers of finance to many of the engineers who had ideas. Then, at a later stage, these firms received 'mezzanine financing.' The next stage was that the firms had an initial public offering (IPO) arranged by one of the major investment banks including Merrill Lynch, Morgan Stanley, and Credit Suisse First Boston. The investment banks would arrange 'road shows' for these firms as they were about to sell their shares to the public; entrepreneurs would visit the mutual funds and the pension funds and the managers of other pools of money. Based on the demand, the investment banks would price the shares at $19 or $23 or $31, and perhaps 10–20 percent of the firms' outstanding shares would be sold. Often the price of the shares at the end of the first day's trading was three or four times the IPO price.

The 'pop' in the share price on the first day's trading was an advertisement that stock prices only increase, and often very rapidly. During the late 1990s, an extremely high proportion of new stock issues experienced these large price surges on the first day of trading, which encouraged strong investor demand and many more new stock offerings.

Displacement to Crisis: It Takes Two Objects of Speculation?

How likely is it that a displacement will lead to a crisis? Assume that destabilizing speculation can occur in a world of normally rational individuals. Then assume a displacement, giving rise to prospects that these individuals misjudge. At some stage, investment for use gives way to investment for profit, especially for short-term gains. How likely is the speculation to lead to trouble?

One question is whether two or more objects of speculation such as real estate and stocks must or are likely to be involved before 'overtrading' reaches sufficient dimensions to lead to a crisis. Consider several occasions when two or more objects have been involved in speculation.

The South Sea and Mississippi bubbles in 1720 were related, as Chapter 8 explains, and powerfully stoked by monetary expansion in Britain and France

that supported a high head of speculative steam. Speculation that started in the securities of the South Sea Company and the Sword Blade Bank in England, and in those of the Mississippi Company and John Law's *banques* in France spread rapidly to other ventures and to commodities and to land; many of these other ventures were swindles. The South Sea Company failed because of its attempt to suppress rival speculations by bringing proceedings under the Bubble Act of June 1720 against York Buildings, Lustrings and Welsh Copper boomeranged.[70] The spread of speculation from one object to another, to generalize the rise of prices, occurred because the speculators that had the foresight to sell South Sea stock when prices were approaching their peak purchased banks and insurance stocks, and country houses.[71] Then the price of land began to move with the price of South Sea stock.[72] In France land prices rose in the fall of 1719 as successful speculators started to take their profits from the Mississippi Bubble.[73]

The 1763 boom was based exclusively on government war expenditure and its finance through chains of discount bills. The DeNeufville Brothers, whose failure set off the panic, sold 'commodities, ships, and securities like so many Dutch firms,'[74] with hundreds of thousands of florins in acceptance liabilities while they rarely kept more than a few thousand guilders in cash reserves. Some contribution to the downturn may have come from an unparalleled drought in England in 1762 that led to shortages of hay and scarcities of meat, butter, and cheese.[75] In any case, speculation leading up to the crisis seems to have had multiple objects.

The crisis of 1772 was precipitated by speculation in Amsterdam and London in the stock of the East India Company and by the collapse of the Ayr Bank (Douglas, Heron & Co.). Numerous complex details were involved, including the political reverses of the East India Company and restriction on its credit by the Bank of England; the practice of the thrusting new Ayr Bank (which was left bad loans by the established banks) to borrow in London when its acceptances came due; and the flight in July 1772 of Alexander Fordyce, who had lost his firm's money selling East India Company stock prematurely. When the price of the stock fell in the autumn, Clifford & Co., the Dutch bank that had headed a syndicate trying to push the price up, failed. These phenomena seem superficial, however. Extensive investment in Britain in houses, turnpikes, canals, and other public works had put a strain on resources.[76] One source relates the fall in coffee prices beginning in 1770 to the financial crisis of 1772–1773,[77] but this is not mentioned by Wilson, the standard source, or by Ashton, Clapham or Buist.[78]

In 1793 a flow of money to London was stimulated by several causes—the expansion of country banks, the construction of more canals, the Reign of

Terror—as well as bad harvests. In 1799 the tightening and loosening of the blockade led to further flows of money to London. Contrariwise, the crisis of 1809–1810 had 'two separate causes: a reaction from the speculation in South America; and a loosening and then tightening of the continental blockade.'[79]

In 1815–1816, the surge in exports to Europe and the United States was larger than the amount that could be sold; the economy slowed as a result of the combination of the excess supply and the fall in the price of wheat. Canals and South American government bonds and mines combined in 1825; British exports, cotton, land sales in the United States, and the beginning of the railroad mania contributed to the crisis in the mid-1830s. The crisis of 1847 was caused by the railway mania, the potato blight, a wheat crop failure one year, and a bumper crop the next, followed by revolution in Continental Europe.

Thus at least two objects of speculation and two markets (as argued in Chapter 8) were involved in most of the significant crises. Just as the national markets were connected, so the speculation was connected by the underlying credit conditions. But when a crisis like that of 1847 arose from developments as disparate as railroads and wheat, there is some basis for suggesting that the crisis is accidental in origin unless the monetary conditions that fed it were systematic.

National Difference in Speculative Temperament

One suggestion is that investors in some countries are more likely to speculate than those in others. Despite Ruth Benedict's distinction between cultures with Apollonian (balancing) and those with Dionysian (orgiastic) temperaments,[80] the proposition is dubious. And despite this implausibility, the opinion among historians is that the Brabanters had a strong gambling temperament in the sixteenth century and that those tens of thousands who migrated to the United Provinces after the sack of Antwerp in November 1576 and its devastating siege in 1585 took this temperament with them.[81] In the Dutch Republic, the gambling instinct of bankers, investors, and even common folk existed in great tension with Calvinist and Lutheran frugality and abstemiousness.[82] There may be substance to the view that banking institutions facilitate more speculation in some countries than in others; Canada did not experience the surges in property prices that preceded the US banking crisis in 2008. Juglar claims the French crises in the eighteenth century were less abrupt and less violent than those of Britain because (after the John Law affair) credit in France was less used and less abused.[83] A different view ascribes French experience to a more severe bankruptcy law:

A high standard of business honesty prevails in France, perhaps because of education, the force of law, tradition, and roles of established institutions. The act of sons in toiling for years to pay the debts of their fathers, and of notaries in paying for the defalcations of one of their number, for the sake of the profession, although without personal association with him, indicates a standard of compliance with business obligations which strongly influences the material prosperity of the country. It may be surprising that the nation whose soldiers are so noted for dash in war should furnish financiers and business men who are the embodiment of conservatism in their methods, but such is clearly the case.

This author continues, 'England is the country in which a spirit of adventure and speculation has done most to promote crises and depressions.'[84]

One historian has suggested that mining and sheep grazing contributed to a love of gambling, and that Australians, starting with the gold discoveries of 1851–1852, developed a particular love of gambling, expressed both through horse racing and speculation in land.[85]

A common view is that the United States is 'the classic home of commercial and financial panics,' presumably because of wildcat banking.[86] This was observed in the 1830s by Michel Chevalier who contrasted French moderation with American speculation (but who believed, however, that the latter was a stimulus to the construction of canals, railroads, roads, factories, and villages).[87] Letter 25 of his letters from America to France is devoted to a discussion of speculation: 'All the world speculates and it speculates on everything. From Maine to the Red River (in Arkansas) the United States has become an immense Rue Quincampoix [the Wall Street of the Mississippi Bubble].'[88] Partly the origins lie in permissive institutions. But it is easy to find abundant and contradictory views on the demand side for other countries: 'The French nation is prudent and economical, the English nation is enterprising and speculative.'[89] 'France has not shown proofs of prudence equal to those of Scotland; its nerves are extremely susceptible, impressionable in matters of credit.'[90] 'The character of this nation [Britain] is in carrying everything to excess ... virtue, vice.'[91] After 1866, a new arrogance was said to have taken hold of the Germans, but they surpassed the French only in 'stock-market swindling and speculation horrors.'[92] Morgenstern found ten waves of panic in France, two more than in the United States, which is 'not surprising, given the unstable character of French politics.'[93] (His remarks address displacements rather than the love of speculation.) Contrast, however, the opinion of a French financier who claims that 'the French love money not for the possibilities of action which it opens, but for the income it assures.'[94]

Or consider two views, at the level of a Harvard–Yale debate, from a fictional Frenchman and an Englishman in 1931:

WILLIAM BERTILLION: England's such a Christmas tree for share-pushers. Noble lords will sit on the board of any company for a couple of quid a sitting. And the public. Loco or idiotic. God, I've never heard of such people, except perhaps some peasants in Bessarabia, or the niggers in the from Cameroons, who believe in what they believe in. Magic. Put up any sort of business that sounds impossible and they gulp it down.[95]

STEWART: England's the world's banker. Never failed yet, never failed yet. She keeps her word, that's why ... None of this – none of this speculation you get in the American stock market. Every Tom, Dick and Harry trying to make a pile – like in France.[96]

It's a stand-off. The speculative temperament may differ among countries. The amount of speculation in a country may change as the national mood swings between elation and depression.

Notes

1. John F. Muth, 'Rational Expectations and the Theory of Price Movements', *Econometrica*, vol. 29 (July 1961), pp. 313–35.
2. Harry G. Johnson, 'Destabilizing Speculation: a General Equilibrium Approach', *Journal of Political Economy*, vol. 84 (February 1976), p. 101.
3. Milton Friedman, 'The Case for Flexible Exchange Rates', in *Essays in Positive Economics* (Chicago: University of Chicago Press, 1953). On one occasion, Friedman moved to a different position: 'Destabilization speculation is a theoretical possibility, but I know of no empirical evidence that it has occurred even as a special case, let alone as a general rule.' Milton Friedman, 'Discussion' of C. P. Kindleberger, 'The Case for Fixed Exchange Rates, 1969', in Federal Reserve Bank of Boston, *The International Adjustment Mechanism* (Boston: Federal Bank of Boston, 1979), pp. 114–5.
4. See Fernand Braudel, *The Structures of Everyday Life*, vol. 1 of *Civilization and Capitalism: the Limits of the Possible*, trans. Siân Reynolds (New York: Harper and Row, 1981), pp. 220, 221, 281, 315, 318, 335, etc.
5. H. M. Hyndman, *Commercial Crises of the Nineteenth Century* (1892; 2nd edn [1932], reprinted, New York: Augustus M. Kelley, 1967), p. 96.
6. Walter Bagehot, *Lombard Street: a Description of the Money Market* (1873; reprint edn, London: John Murray, 1917), p. 18.
7. Sir John Clapham, *The Bank of England: a History* (Cambridge: Cambridge University Press, 1945), vol. 2, p. 326.

8. Adam Smith, *An Inquiry into the Nature and Causes of the Wealth of Nations* (1776; reprint edn, New York: Modern Library, 1937), pp. 703–4.

9. Alfred Marshall, *Money, Credit and Commerce* (1923; reprint edn, New York: Augustus M. Kelley, 1965), p. 305.

10. More and more economic theorists are moving away from unswerving reliance on the assumption that market participants are uniformly intelligent, informed, and independent in thought, introducing such concepts as asymmetric information (different knowledge available to different participants), cognitive dissonance (unconscious suppression of information that fails to fit a priori views), herd behavior, procrastination that results in failure to act in timely fashion, and so on. Those interested should consult the work especially of George Akerlof and Richard Thaler. For relevant studies, see Frederic S. Miskin, 'Asymmetric Information and Financial Crises: a Historical Perspective', in R. Glenn Hubbard, ed., *Financial Markets and Financial Crises* (Chicago: University of Chicago Press, 1991), pp. 69–108; and Thomas Lux, 'Herd Behavior, Bubbles and Crashes', *Economic Journal*, vol. 105 (July 1995), pp. 881–96.

11. Gustav LeBon, *The Crowd: a Study of the Popular Mind* (London: T. Fisher Unwin, 1922).

12. Charles Mackay, *Memoirs of Extraordinary Delusions and the Madness of Crowds* (1852; reprint edn, Boston: L. C. Page Co., 1932).

13. John Carswell, *The South Sea Bubble* (London: Cresset Press, 1960), p. 161.

14. David Cass and Karl Shell, 'Do Sunspots Matter?' *Journal of Political Economy*, vol. 91, no. 2 (April 1983), pp. 193–227. This concept of a completely extraneous event was included in the first edition more or less randomly. Since 1983, however, 'sunspots' has become a word of art to cover general uncertainty as opposed to the 'fundamentals' that feature in rational expectations.

15. Irving Fisher, *The Purchasing Power of Money: Its Determination and Relation to Credit, Interest and Crises*, 2nd edn (New York: Macmillan, 1911), esp. chap. 1, dealing with crises; Knut Wicksell, *Interest and Prices* (London: Macmillan, 1936) (first published 1898).

16. Henrietta M. Larson, *Jay Cooke, Private Banker* (Cambridge, MA: Harvard University Press, 1934).

17. John Berry McFerrin, *Caldwell and Company: a Southern Financial Empire* (Chapel Hill: University of North Carolina Press, 1939; reprint, Nashville: Vanderbilt Press, 1969).

18. Peter Temin, *Did Monetary Forces Cause the Great Depression?* (New York: W. W. Norton, 1976), pp. 90–3.

19. Joan Edelman Spero, *The Failure of the Franklin National Bank: Challenge to the International Banking System* (New York: Columbia University Press, 1980).

20. Bagehot, *Lombard Street*, pp. 131–2.

21. George W. Van Vleck, *The Panic of 1857: an Analytical Study* (New York: Columbia University Press, 1953), p. 31.
22. R. C. O. Matthews, *A Study in Trade-Cycle History: Economic Fluctuations in Great Britain, 1832– 1842* (Cambridge: Cambridge University Press, 1954), pp. 49, 110–1; M. C. Reed, *Investment in Railways in Britain: a Study in the Development of the Capital Market* (London: Oxford University Press, 1976).

The ladies and clergymen—in American parlance, 'widows and orphans'—may more properly belong to a third stage when the securities have become seasoned in the market. The French call such investments suitable for 'the father of a family'. Charles Wilson, in *Anglo-Dutch Commerce and Finance in the Eighteenth Century* (Cambridge: Cambridge University Press, 1941), produces a number of variations on investor groups: in the Netherlands 'spinsters, widows, retired naval and army officers, magistrates, retired merchants, parsons and orphanages' (p. 118); 'hundreds of other merchants ... as well as thousands of civil servants, magistrates, widows and orphans and charitable institutions' (p. 135); 'widows, parsons, orphanages, magistrates and civil servants' (p. 162); 'country gentry, wealthy burghers and officials of Amsterdam, widows and wealthy spinsters' (p. 181); 'spinsters, theologians, admirals, civil servants, merchants, professional speculators, and the inevitable widows and orphans' (p. 202).

In the quotation from Bagehot that constitutes one of the epigraphs of this book, owners of the blind capital who lacked the wisdom to invest it properly were characterized in the excised portion as 'quiet ladies, rural clergymen and country misers' and again as 'rectors, authors, grandmothers'. See Bagehot, 'Essays on Edward Gibbon', quoted in Theodore E. Burton, *Financial Crises and Periods of Industrial and Commercial Depression* (New York: Appleton, 1902), pp. 321–2.

In his essay on Lord Brougham (1857), Bagehot quotes his subject on the crisis of 1814:

> The frenzy, I can call it nothing less ... descended to persons in the humblest circumstances, and the farthest removed by their pursuits, from commercial cares ... Not only clerks and labourers, but menial servants, engaged the little sums which they had been laying up for a provision against old age and sickness ...
>
> The great speculators broke; the middling ones lingered out a precarious existence, deprived of all means of continuing their dealings either at home or abroad; the poor dupes of the delusion had lost their little hoards and went on the parish. (Norman St. John-Stevas, ed., *Bagehot's Historical Essays* [New York: New York University Press, 1966], pp. 118–9)

Another British expression for the naive and innocent who were drawn into the last phases of a bubble is 'greengrocers and servant girls'. The American

1929 categories were 'bootblacks and waiters', whereas a more modern characterization is 'house painters and office girls' (John Brooks, *The Go-Go Years* [New York: Weybright and Talley, 1973, p. 305]). Classes of current well-to-do amateurish and sometimes badly advised investors in the United States include successful doctors and dentists and professional athletes.

23. Max Wirth, *Geschichte der Handelskrisen*, 4th edn (1890; reprint edn, New York: Burt Franklin, 1968), p. 480.
24. Ilse Mintz, *Deterioration in the Quality of Bonds Issued in the United States, 1920–1930* (New York: National Bureau of Economic Research, 1951).
25. Benjamin Stein, 'The Day Los Angeles's Bubble Burst', *New York Times*, 8 December 1984.
26. 'For Investors, Condo Craze Ends: Once Hot Market Makes Do Without Speculators', *Boston Globe*, 14 February 1988.
27. Homer Hoyt, *One Hundred Years of Land Values in Chicago* (Chicago: University of Chicago Press, 1933), p. 136.
28. Johnson, 'Destabilizing Speculation', p. 101.
29. Larry T. Wimmer, 'The Gold Crisis of 1869: Stabilizing or Destabilizing Speculation under Floating Exchange Rates', *Explorations in Economic History*, vol. 12 (1975), pp. 105–22.
30. Christina Stead, *House of All Nations* (New York: Knopf, 1938).
31. Carswell, *South Sea Bubble*, pp. 131, 199.
32. Ibid., p. 120.
33. Clapham, *Bank of England*, vol. 2, p. 20. Hyndman, a socialist, sarcastically ascribes this example to the 1820s: 'The most ridiculous blunders were made by the class which was supposed to be carrying on business for the general benefit. Warming-pans were shipped to cities within the tropics, and Sheffield carefully provided skaters with the means of enjoying their favorite pastime where ice had never been seen. The best glass and porcelain were thoughtfully provided for naked savages, who had hitherto found horns and cocoa-nut shells quite hollow enough to hold all the drink they wanted.' (See H. M. Hyndman, *Commercial Crises of the Nineteenth Century* [1892; 2nd edn, 1932, reprinted, New York: Augustus M. Kelley, 1967], p. 39.) Clapham is right and Hyndman wrong. The source for both is J. R. McCullough, *Principles of Political Economy*, 2nd edn (Edinburgh, 1830), which refers to 1810 not 1825.

The announcement of the formation of the South Sea Company in May 1711 produced expectations of a strong demand for British goods in Latin America that would provide 'a triumphant solution to the [British] financial problem and need for expansion for the support of our way of life'. Booming markets were anticipated in 'Colchester bays [a type of cloth], silk handkerchiefs, worsted hose, sealing wax, spices, clocks and watches, Cheshire cheese, pickles, scales and weights for gold and silver' (see Carswell, *South Sea Bubble*, p. 55).

34. William Smart, *Economic Annals of the Nineteenth Century* (1911; reprint edn, New York: Augustus M. Kelley, 1964), vol. 2, p. 292.
35. Matthews, *Trade-Cycle History*, p. 25.
36. D. Morier Evans, *The History of the Commercial Crisis, 1857–1858, and the Stock Exchange Panic of 1859* (1859; reprint edn, New York: Augustus M. Kelley, 1969), p. 102.
37. Max Wirth, 'The Crisis of 1890', *Journal of Political Economy*, vol. 1 (March 1893), p. 230.
38. P. L. Cottrell, *Industrial Finance, 1830–1914: the Finance and Organization of English Manufacturing Industry* (London: Methuen, 1980), p. 169. Cottrell notes that the Guinness flotation was for £6 million, was handled by Baring, and was oversubscribed many times.
39. A. C. Pigou, *Aspects of British Economic History, 1918–25* (London: Macmillan, 1948).
40. J. S. Mill, *Principles of Political Economy, with Some of Their Applications to Social Philosophy* (1848; 7th edn, reprint edn, London: Longmans, Green, 1929), p. 709.
41. Maurice Lévy-Leboyer, *Les banques européennes et l'industrialisation internationale dans la première moitié du XIXe siècle* (Paris: Presses universitaires de France, 1964), p. 715.
42. Charles Wilson, *Anglo-Dutch Commerce and Finance in the Eighteenth Century* (Cambridge: Cambridge University Press, 1941), p. 25. For a series from the early seventeenth century, see J. G. van Dillen, 'The Bank of Amsterdam', in *History of the Principal Public Banks* (The Hague: Martinus Nijhoff, 1934), p. 95.
43. For 1822 and 1824, see Smart, Economic Annals, vol. 2, pp. 82, 215. For 1888, see W. Jett Lauck, *The Causes of the Panic of 1893* (Boston: Houghton Mifflin, 1907), p. 39.
44. A. Andréadès, *History of the Bank of England* (London: P. S. King, 1909), pp. 404–5, see also p. 249.
45. O. M. W. Sprague, *History of Crises under the National Banking System* (1910; reprint edn, New York: Augustus M. Kelley, 1968), pp. 35–6.
46. Great Britain, Parliamentary Papers (Monetary Policy, Commercial Distress), 'Report of the Select Committee on the Operation of the Bank Acts and the Causes of the Recent Commercial Distress, 1857–59' (Shannon: Irish University Press, 1969), vol. 4; Consular report from Hamburg, no. 7, 27 January 1858, p. 438.
47. This statement appears in italics in Donald H. Dunn's fictionalized book, *Ponzi, the Boston Swindler* (New York: McGraw-Hill, 1975), p. 98.
48. *The Collected Works of Walter Bagehot*, ed. Norman St. John Stevas (London: The Economist, 1978), vol. 11, p. 339.
49. Wirth, *Handelskrisen*, p. 109.
50. Wirth, 'Crisis of 1890', pp. 222–4; Alfred Pose, *La monnaie er ses institutions* (Paris; Presses universitaires de France, 1942), vol. 1, p. 215. Lauck puts the

cost of the rescue operation at 25 million francs from the leading banks and 100 million francs from the Bank of France; see Causes of the Panic of 1893, p. 57.

51. Ronald I. McKinnon, *Money and Capital in Economic Development* (Washington, DC: Brookings Institution, 1973).

52. Carlos F. Diaz-Alejandro, 'Goodbye Financial Repression, Hello Financial Crash', *Journal of Development Studies*, vol. 18, no. 1 (September–October 1985), pp. 1–24.

53. Ronald I. McKinnon and Donald J. Mathieson, 'How to Manage a Repressed Economy', in *Essays in International Finance*, no. 145 (Princeton: International Finance Section, Princeton University, 1981).

54. Wirth, *Handelskrisen*, p. 519. An apparent parallel can be found in a major exhibition in Melbourne, Australia, to celebrate the hundredth anniversary of European settlement, which boosted the city's economy briefly. See Geoffrey Serle, *The Rush To Be Rich: a History of the Colony of Victoria* (Melbourne: Melbourne University Press, 1971), pp. 285–7.

55. J. W. Beyen, *Money in a Maelstrom* (New York: Macmillan, 1959), p. 45.

56. The expression is that of Gerald Malynes in 1686, quoted in Violet Barbour, *Capitalism in Amsterdam in the 17th Century* (Ann Arbor: University of Michigan Press, 1963), p. 74.

57. William R. Scott, *The Constitution and Finance of English, Scottish and Irish Joint-Stock Companies to 1720*, 3 vols. (London, 1922), as summarized by J. A. Schumpeter, *Business Cycles* (New York: McGraw-Hill, 1939), vol. 1, p. 250.

58. Carswell, *South Sea Bubble*, p. 139.

59. Hans Rosenberg, *Die Weltwirtschaftskrise von 1857–59* (Stuttgart-Berlin: W. Kohlhammer, 1934), p. 114.

60. David Divine, *Indictment of Incompetence: Mutiny at Invergordon* (London: Macdonald, 1970).

61. C. P. Kindleberger, 'The Economic Crisis of 1619 to 1623', *Journal of Economic History*, vol. 51, no. 1 (March 1991), pp. 149–75.

62. Wirth, *Handelskrisen*, p. 92.

63. Ibid., p. 458.

64. Bertrand Gille, *La Banque et le crédit en France de 1815 à 1848* (Paris: Presses universitaires de France, 1959), p. 175.

65. Lévy-Leboyer, *Banques européennes*, p. 673.

66. Gille, Banque et crédit, p. 304.

67. Honoré de Balzac, *César Birotteau* (Paris: Livre de Poche, 1972), esp. pp. 13–4.

68. Leland H. Jenks, *The Migration of British Capital to 1875* (New York: Knopf, 1927), p. 34.

69. Rosenberg, *Weltwirtschaftskrise*, pp. 50, 100–1. See also Stewart L. Weisman, *Need and Greed: the Story of the Largest Ponzi Scheme in American History* (Syracuse: University of Syracuse Press, 1999).

70. Carswell, *South Sea Bubble*, p. 171.
71. Ibid., pp. 140, 155.
72. Ibid., p. 159.
73. Guy Chaussinand-Nogaret, *Les financiers de Languedoc au XVIIIe siècle* (Paris: S.E.V.P.E.N., 1970), p. 146. This author observed that the financiers were much more realistic than John Law, stimulating the speculation (agiotage) but keeping themselves aloof from the fever and ruining the system by converting their notes when they judged the moment to be the most favorable. Ibid., p. 129.
74. Clapham, *Bank of England*, vol. 2, p. 239.
75. T. S. Ashton, *Economic Fluctuations in England, 1700–1800* (Oxford: Oxford University Press, Clarendon Press, 1959), p. 151.
76. Ibid., p. 127.
77. See the review of Johannes van der Voort, *De Westindische Plantage van 1720 tot 1795* (Eindhoven: De Witte, 1973), in *Journal of Economic History*, vol. 36 (June 1976), p. 519.
78. Wilson, *Anglo-Dutch Commerce*, pp. 169–87; Ashton, *Economic Fluctuations*, pp. 127–9; Clapham, *Bank of England*, vol. 1, 242–9; Martin G. Buist, *At Spes non Fracta, Hope & Co., 1770–1815: Merchant Bankers and Diplomats at Work* (The Hague: Martinus Nijhoff, 1974), pp. 21ff.
79. Arthur D. Gayer, W. W. Rostow and Anna J. Schwartz, *The Growth and Fluctuation of the British Economy, 1790–1850* (Oxford: Oxford University Press, Clarendon Press, 1953), vol. 1, p. 92.
80. Ruth Benedict, *Patterns of Culture* (Boston: Houghton Mifflin, 1934).
81. See Herman van der Wee, *The Growth of the Amsterdam Market and the European Economy* (The Hague: Martinus Nijhoff, 1963), vol. 2, p. 202; J. A. van Houtte, 'Anvers', in *Amitore Fanfani*, ed., Città Mercanti Dottrine nell' Economia Europea (Milan: A. Guiffre, 1964), p. 311; Simon Schama, *The Embarrassment of Riches: an Interpretation of Dutch Culture of the Golden Age* (Berkeley: University of California Press, 1988), pp. 347–50; Ernest Baasch, *Holländische Wirtschaftsgeschichte* (Jena: Gustav Fischer, 1927), p. 240, quoting Büsch.
82. Schama, *The Embarrassment of Riches*, pp. 503, 505.
83. Clement Juglar, *Des crises commerciales et leur retour périodiques en France, en Angleterre et aux Etats-Unis*, 2nd edn (1889; reprint edn, New York: Augustus M. Kelley, 1967).
84. Theodore E. Burton, *Financial Crises and Periods of Industrial and Commercial Depression* (New York: D. Appleton, 1902), pp. 39–41.
85. The real prices of Australian land rose from 100 in 1870 to 450 in 1895, fell to about 360 before 1900, and then took off again to 600 by 1905. See Kevin H. O'Rourke and Jeffrey G. Williamson, *Globalization and History* (Cambridge, MA: MIT Press, 1999), Fig. 3.1.
86. Francis W. Hirst, *The Six Panics and Other Essays* (London: Methuen, 1913), p. 2.

87. Michel Chevalier, *Lettres sur l'Amérique du Nord*, 3rd edn (Brussels: Société belge du librairie, 1838), vol. 1, pp. 261–2.
88. Ibid., vol. 2, pp. 151ff.
89. Andréadès, *Bank of England*, p. 404.
90. Louis Wolowski, testimony before Ministère des Finances et al., *Enquête sur les principes et les faits généraux qui régissent la circulation monétaire et fiduciaire* (Paris: Imprimerie imperiale, 1867), vol. 2, p. 398.
91. Wilson, *Anglo-Dutch Commerce*, p. 77, quoting Isaac de Pinto, Jeu d'Actions (eighteenth century).
92. Fritz Stern, *Gold and Iron: Bismarck, Bleichröder, and the Building of the German Empire* (London: Allen & Unwin, 1977), p. 500, quoting Constantin Franz in 1872.
93. Oskar Morgenstern, *International Financial Transactions and Business Cycles* (Princeton: Princeton University Press, 1959), p. 550.
94. Robert Bigo, *Les banques françaises au cours du XIXe siècle* (Paris: Sirey, 1947), p. 262.
95. Stead, *House of All Nations*, p. 233.
96. Ibid., p. 244.

4

Fueling the Flames: The Expansion of Credit

Axiom number one: You can't have inflation without the rapid growth in the money supply.

Axiom number two: You can't have a real estate bubble without the rapid growth of the supply of credit.

Speculative manias gather speed through the expansion of credit. Most increases in the supply of credit do not lead to a mania—but nearly every mania has been associated with rapid growth in the supply of credit to a particular group of borrowers. In the last hundred years, the increases in supplies of credit have been provided in part by the banks, in part by the development of new financial instruments and in part by cross-border investment inflows. The mania in tulip bulbs in the seventeenth century occurred because the sellers of the bulbs provided credit to the buyers.[1] John Law had his Banque Générale, later the Banque Royale, as his source of credit while the South Sea Company relied on the Sword Blade Bank. In 1763 credit expansion in Holland was financed by the *Wisselruiti*, or chains of accommodation bills (think post-dated checks) from one merchant to another. The British canal mania of 1793 was fed by spending facilitated by loans from many newly established country banks to the entrepreneurs who were developing the canals.

In many cases, the expansion of credit resulted from the development of substitutes for more traditional monies. In the United States in the first part of the nineteenth century, the innovation was that bills of exchange (again

© The Author(s), under exclusive license to Springer Nature
Switzerland AG 2023
R. Z. Aliber et al., *Manias, Panics, and Crashes*,
https://doi.org/10.1007/978-3-031-16008-0_4

think post-dated checks) replaced silver in the triangular trade among the United States, China, and Britain. The United States had a bilateral trade deficit with China and China had a bilateral trade deficit with Britain. Previously the United States bought silver from Mexico which was then shipped to China to finance the bilateral trade deficit with China; the silver then was shipped to London to finance China's trade deficit with Britain. The institutional innovation was that American merchants sent bills of exchange that specified payment in the British pound for US imports from China; these bills then were shipped to London to finance China's bilateral trade deficit with Britain. The transaction costs involved in making cross-border payments using bills of exchange were much smaller than those that involved the shipment of silver. The result of this innovation was that the silver stayed in the United States and the US money supply did not decline, which meant that economic activity no longer slowed when payments were made to China.[2]

The global boom of the 1850s followed from the combination of new gold discoveries, the formation of new banks in Britain, France, Germany, and the United States, the establishment of clearinghouses by the banks in New York and in Philadelphia and the expansion of the London clearing house. The growth in bank clearinghouses led to the increased use of credit in the transactions among the participating banks; payments imbalances among them were settled by transfer of clearinghouse certificates—a new form of 'money.' (The use of certificates, a specialized IOU, in payments among banks, meant that each bank held a much smaller number of notes and coins for payments to other banks.) The expansion of credit in Britain in 1866 resulted from the increase in loans by the newly formed joint-stock discount houses. The boom in Central Europe in the 1870s was based on the gold reparations payments from France to Prussia and on the creation of *Maklerbanken* (brokers' banks) in Germany, which spread into Austria, and *Baubanken* (construction banks) in Austria, which expanded into Germany.

One of the many different institutional avenues for the expansion of credit that occurred in France in 1882 was based on a system of fortnightly clearing of stock exchange transactions that provided credit to buyers of stocks through a system of delayed payments called *reportage*. The buyers of stocks had up to fourteen days before they had to pay for their purchases; in effect, they got interest-free loans until the date of payment (although the value of the loans to the buyers of the stocks probably meant they paid higher prices for the stocks).[3] Similarly the expansion of the supply of credit in the call-money market in New York helped finance the stock market boom in the late 1920s. The catalyst for the expansion of credit in the United States in 1893 was the addition of silver coins to the US money supply; in 1907,

the increase in the supply of credit resulted from increases in loans by trust companies. In the years before and after World War I, the development of the gold-exchange standard led to an expansion of the international credit base so that a larger volume of international trade could be financed with the existing holdings of monetary gold. The rapid increase in installment credit in the United States in the 1920s contributed to the surge in automobile ownership (the dramatic increases in the number of automobiles and other consumer durables led to rapid growth in demand for staggered payment arrangements for the purchase of durable assets).

After World War II, the development of negotiable certificates of deposit (CDs) contributed to the expansion of credit. In the 1870s the Austrian banks had developed a new financial instrument (the *Cassenscheine*) that paid interest; the increase in the demand for these instruments led to an increase in the supply of credit and then to an increase in spending. In the 1950s and the 1960s, large US banks began to practice liability management, which meant that they funded their loans by borrowing in the interbank market rather than by the sale of their deposits or IOUs to business firms and households. Liability management enabled the banks to be much more aggressive in increasing their loans.

One unique form of the expansion of 'bank credit' occurred in Kuwait between 1977 and 1982 when shares and real estate were bought and sold on the Kuwaiti Souk al-Manakh (stock exchange) with post-dated checks. Eventually, the value of these checks in circulation increased to the dinar equivalent of near US$100 billion—much more than the country's GDP. The values of post-dated checks written by the buyers of the shares and real estate were much, much larger than their bank deposits. The sellers of the shares and real estate increased their spending as their wealth increased; they hoped—and prayed—that there would be money in the bank accounts of the payors when they deposited the checks that they had received for the sale of shares and real estate. In July 1982 some of these checks bounced when they were deposited.[4]

These examples suggest that the expansion of credit is a systematic development that has occurred in spurts for several hundred years as the participants in financial markets seek to reduce the costs of transactions and the costs of holding money balances. The form each event takes may seem accidental—the substitution of bills of exchange for silver in payments to China, or the development of deposits in the Eurocurrency market because price ceilings prevented US banks from increasing the interest rates that they could pay on demand deposits in New York and other US cities. The development of new credit instruments occurs episodically in response to changes in

institutional arrangements, which sometimes follows from changes in technology and sometimes from changes in regulations. Monetary expansion is systematic and endogenous rather than random and exogenous.

During economic booms, the money supply defined as means of payment has increased and the existing stock of money has been used more efficiently to finance both increases in economic activity and the purchases of real estate and securities. The efforts of central bankers to limit and control the growth of money have been offset in part by the development of new and close substitutes for money. Such efforts have a long history, including the resumption of specie payments and the return to convertibility of national currencies into gold after the end of wars. The demonetization of the lesser metallic monies—initially copper was displaced by silver and subsequently silver's monetary role was eclipsed by gold—was an effort by the monetary authorities to obtain greater control over increases in the money supply. Central banks wanted a monopoly on the issue of currency notes; initially, the government restricted and then eliminated the right of private, country, and joint-stock (corporate) banks to issue currency notes. Legislation and custom limited the amount of deposit money that could be issued against primary bank reserves, starting shortly after the Bank Act of 1844 and continuing through the application by the Federal Reserve System of reserve requirements on both demand and time deposits (as embodied in the Federal Reserve Act of 1913) and then on certificates of deposit and subsequently on the borrowing by US banks from their branches in London and other offshore financial centers. The process is Sisyphean, a *perpetuum mobile*; the history of money is a story of continuing innovations so that the existing supply of money can be used more efficiently and the development of close substitutes for money that circumvent the regulatory requirements applied to the increases in the money supply in the form of bank deposits.

The Eurocurrency deposit market surged in the 1960s as an end-run around the regulations imposed on US banks by the Federal Reserve and the Federal Deposit Insurance Corporation; the US dollar deposits produced by the branches of US banks in London and other offshore centers were not subject to interest rate ceilings, reserve requirements, and deposit insurance premiums. The costs incurred by the offshore branches of US banks when they produced deposits were below those that the head offices of these banks would incur if they produced the same amount of deposits, and hence the offshore branches could afford to pay higher interest rates on deposits than their head offices. A marvelous example of regulatory arbitrage. In the 1970s the US stock brokerage firms developed money market funds that produced quasi-deposits or IOUs that paid market rates and were a close substitute

for bank deposits, although these IOUs were not insured or guaranteed by any agency of the US government. (During the financial crisis of 2008, the owners of these deposits received a 'free lunch'—their quasi-deposits were guaranteed by the US government to reduce the likelihood that anyone would seek to shift funds from a money market fund to a bank that offered government-guaranteed deposits.)

Selling Money by S. C. Gwynne
Sam Gwynne was hired by the Cleveland Trust Company (subsequently the AmeriTrust Company) in 1977 when he was 24 to be a traveling loan officer. After less than two years at the bank, he had traveled to twenty-five countries and was one of four officers at the bank that managed a portfolio of $150 million of international loans.

Cleveland was a vibrant American industrial city with a large number of major manufacturing firms that sold machine tools and other capital goods to foreign buyers. The senior management of the Cleveland Trust wanted to protect its long-standing relationships with the firms in Ohio and the Midwest from incursions by the major US banks headquartered in New York, Chicago, and San Francisco. Citibank, Chase, and Bank of America wanted to parlay their ability to provide financing for the foreign customers of US firms to obtain more of the US domestic banking business from these American firms.

One reason Cleveland Trust wanted to increase its foreign loans was to grow its assets more rapidly than was possible if its loans were limited to the Cleveland metropolitan area—although some of its loan officers traveled to visit potential borrowers on the East and West Coasts and in Pittsburgh, Detroit, and St. Louis. And it wanted to protect its relationships with the Ohio-based industrial firms from the competitive threats of larger banks based in other US cities.

Sam Gwynne's task was to find attractive borrowers in the cities that he visited. It's a safe bet that each of these borrowers previously had been visited by loan officers from thirty or forty other American banks and from loan officers from Canadian, Japanese, British, and other foreign banks. Many of those who wanted to borrow some of the money that Cleveland Trust might bring to them had previously had their requests for loans denied by one of these other US and foreign lenders.

When Cleveland Trust found an attractive borrower, it would source the money for the loan by selling its own IOU in the interbank market, or in the offshore deposit market.

During the expansion phase of the credit cycle, the lenders chase the borrowers; some lenders seek to increase their market share while the more established lenders seek to defend their market share.

Currency School Vs. Banking School

One feature of the history of monetary theory is a continuing debate between two different views—the Currency School and the Banking School—about how to manage the growth of the money supply. The proponents of the Currency School advocated a firm limit on the expansion of money to avoid increases in the price level. The adherents of the Banking School believed that as long as the increases in the supply of money corresponded with the increase in business transactions, the inflation rate would not increase. The same distinction in ideology and economic analysis separated the hard money school from the populists in the 1890s—the former was concerned with inflation while the latter believed prices would not increase as long as the increases in the money supply were no more rapid than the increase in economic activity. The debate between these two views of managing the growth in the money supply has continued for three hundred years.

The Currency School wanted a simple rule that would fix the growth of the money supply at 2 or 4 or 5 percent a year, much like today's monetarists.[5] Viner's discussion of the nineteenth-century controversy is succinct:

> The currency school tended also to minimize or to deny the importance of bank credit in other forms than notes as a factor affecting prices, or as in the case of Torrens, to claim that the fluctuations in the deposits were governed closely by the fluctuations in the note issues. They had a hankering also for a simple automatic rule, and could find none suitable for governing the general credit operations of the Bank. They also had laissez faire objections to extending legislative control of the banking system any further than seemed absolutely necessary.[6]

Neither the Currency School nor the Banking School paid much attention to the expansion of nonbank credit. The Bank of Amsterdam, founded in 1609, issued warehouse receipts or notes against deposits of precious metals; initially, the amounts of these notes were tied one-for-one to the amounts of the deposits of the metals. Hence at first the Bank of Amsterdam did not expand credit; subsequently, in the eighteenth century, the bank increased its loans in an effort to rescue the Dutch East India Company during the fourth Anglo-Dutch War. The Bank of Amsterdam was also a *Wisselbank* where bills of exchange (*Wissel* in Dutch, *Wechsel* in German) were paid. Merchants kept deposits at the Bank of Amsterdam to meet bills presented for collection. Deposits of precious metals enabled the Bank of Amsterdam to earn seignorage—the profit or spread between the purchasing power of a coin or deposit and the costs of producing each type of money—when it

produced coins. Moreover, the Bank paid a low-interest rate on deposits. In 1614 the Municipality of Amsterdam established a Bank of Lending (*Huys van Leening*) that enabled merchants to establish their own credit efficiently but it was not an active lender.[7] This credit created by the merchants led to an excessive expansion of the *Wisselruiti*; when the chain of bills of exchange broke in 1763 because one of the merchants did not have the money to pay on a maturing bill, the DeNeufville bank failed.

The Swedish Riksbank, established in 1668, had two departments, a Bank of Exchange patterned after the Bank of Amsterdam (*Wisselbank*) and a Bank of Lending (*Liinebank*).[8] These two departments foreshadowed the Bank Act of 1844 in Britain, which was a compromise between the two schools; an Issue Department would produce bank notes against deposits of coin or bullion above a specified fiduciary issue that represented the Bank of England's holdings of British government debt, and a Banking Department that would make loans and discounts up to a multiple of its reserves of bank notes that had been produced by the Issue Department. The establishment of the Issue Department was a victory for the Currency School, which had criticized the loans made by Bank of England after the suspension of the gold standard in 1797. (The Bank of England's defense was that these loans did not lead to an increase in the inflation rate because they financed an increase in trade.) The establishment of the Banking Department was a victory for those who believed that an expansion of credit would help finance the initial upswing in the early stages of an economic recovery.

The view of the Currency School that the expansion of credit would eventually lead to inflation was correct. The Banking School's view that an increase in the supply of credit was needed at the start of an economic expansion was also correct. The Currency School's view that the amount of its discounts be limited to acceptances that were related to actual commercial transactions became known as the 'real bills doctrine.' The larger the volume of business transactions, the greater the scope for discounting, and the larger the increase in the money supply and eventually the higher the inflation rate. The central policy questions, once an expansion of credit has started, are whether it is practicable to decree a stopping place and whether this limit could be determined by an automatic rule.

The core issue is that it is easier to define money than it is to measure the effective money supply. Walter Bagehot wrote 'Men of business in England do not … like the currency question. They are perplexed to define accurately what money is: *how* to count they know, but *what* to count they do not know.'[9]

The stylized fact is that every time the monetary authorities stabilize or control some quantity of money, M, either in absolute volume or at a predetermined rate of growth, more of the money and the near-money substitutes will be produced in periods of euphoria. If the definition of money is fixed in terms of designated liquid securities the euphoria may lead to the 'monetization' of credit in ways that are beyond the scope of the definition; the velocity of money (velocity is defined either as total spending or national income divided by the money supply) will increase even if the amount of money defined in the traditional way remains unchanged. The debate was over whether money should be defined as M_1, currency plus demand deposits; M_2, equal to M_1 plus time deposits; M_3, consisting of M_2 plus highly liquid government securities; or some other designation.

The process seemed endless; fix any M_1 and in economic booms, the market will create new forms of money and near-money substitutes to get around the limit if it proves profitable to develop these substitutes. The Radcliffe Commission in Britain in 1959 claimed that in a developed economy there is 'an indefinitely wide range of financial institutions' and 'many highly liquid assets which are close substitutes for money, as good to hold, and only inferior when the actual moment for a payment arrives.' The Radcliffe Commission did not use the concept of velocity of money because it 'could not find any reason for supposing, or any experience in monetary history indicating, that there is any limit to the velocity of circulation.'[10] The commission recommended that a complex of controls of a wide range of financial institutions be developed as a substitute for the traditional control of the money supply: 'Such a prospect would be unwelcome except as a last resort, not mainly because of its administrative burdens, but because the further growth of new financial institutions would allow the situation continually to slip out from under the grip of the authorities.'[11]

Economists have debated for more than two hundred years which assets should be included in 'money.' One view is that the most appropriate definition is the group of assets that provides the strongest correlation with changes in economic activity. Measuring economic activity is relatively unambiguous. The identification of the group of assets that have the highest correlation with economic activity might change over time and differ across countries. 'In common parlance, *bank currency means circulating bank notes*—"paper money." Yet some writers include checks and *promissory notes*, if not also loans and deposits' (italics in original) in their measure of money.[12]

The debate was neatly summarized by John Stuart Mill:

The purchasing power of an individual at any moment is not measured by the money actually in his pocket, whether we mean by money the metals, or

include bank notes. It consists, first, of the money in his possession; secondly, of the money at his banker's, and all the other money due him and payable on demand; thirdly of whatever credit he happens to possess.[13]

One approach is to include all securities in the measurement of the money supply. But in theory, the question is the one raised by Mill—how much credit can households, firms, and governments command at a given time? The amounts are certain to vary because access to credit depends on satisfying certain conditions, which is likely to be easier in euphoric periods than at other times.[14] But in theory the analyst wants to know, with Mill, the amount of credit that a household, firm, or government would be able to command at a given time, and the amount varies over a wide range because access to credit depends on satisfying certain conditions and both households and firms are better able to satisfy these conditions in euphoric periods. Banks and other lenders have often extended credit lines to firms and household borrowers, but the amount of credit available under a line at any moment may require that the borrowers satisfy specific requirements.

Consider the rapid growth of US dollar deposits in London and other offshore banking centers in the 1960s, the 1970s, and the 1980s, which was a response to the increases in interest rates on these deposits relative to interest rates on bank deposits in New York and other American cities that were subject to regulatory ceilings. The banks that sold these offshore deposits used the funds to make US dollar loans to American and non-American firms as well as to various governments that they might otherwise have made from one of their US offices. The firms that borrowed US dollar funds from the offshore banks in London were as likely to spend these funds in the United States as if they had borrowed the US dollar funds in New York or some other US city. Should the US dollar deposits produced in London and other offshore banking centers be included in the US money supply? (Yes).

The home equity credit line is a recent financial innovation; banks and other lenders offer to lend homeowners an amount that may be equal to eighty or ninety percent of the value of their equity in their homes or in some cases a modestly larger amount. (At an earlier period the loans that used the equity in the home as collateral were known as second mortgages; a home equity credit line represents potential borrowing until the homeowner draws on the line, while the second mortgage was an actual loan.) The availability of home equity credit lines means that homeowners economize on their holdings of money and near-monies; households engage in liability management of the type that business borrowers developed thirty and forty years earlier, and the increase in these lines leads to higher levels of spending with the same money supply.

The purchasing power of the household cannot readily be extrapolated to that of a country, since an increase in the amount of credit extended to one individual may or may not subtract from the amounts of credit available to others, depending on both banking institutions and on the scope of euphoria. As one novelist wrote about credit:

> Beautiful credit! The foundation of modern society. Who shall say this is not the age of mutual trust, of unlimited reliance on human promises? That is a peculiar condition of modern society which enables a whole country to instantly recognize point and meaning to the familiar newspaper anecdote, which puts into the speculator in lands and mines this remark: 'I wasn't worth a cent two years ago, and now I owe two million dollars.'[15]

The basis for this generalization is the historical development of close substitutes for money that led to increases in the amount of credit and total spending. Consider only bills of exchange, call money, and the gold-exchange standard from a list that also includes bank notes, bank deposits, clearing-house certificates, the liabilities of specialized banks (for example, *banques d'affaires, Maklerbanken*, or *Baubanken*), the liabilities of trust companies, negotiable CDs, Eurocurrency deposits, installment credit, credit cards, and NOW accounts.

Quality of Debt[16]

Credit rating agencies were established to rank the quality of the debt of individual borrowers—firms, governments, and even households. Minsky developed a taxonomy to rank the quality of corporate debt; his three-part distinction was based on the relationship between the cash flows to the borrowers from their operating activities and their projected debt-servicing payments. 'Hedge finance' occurs when the cash from the firm's operating activities is larger than the cash needed for its scheduled debt-servicing payments. 'Speculative finance' occurs when the cash from the firm's operating activities is large enough to enable the firm to pay the interest on its debt on a timely basis; however, the firm would need to borrow to get the cash to pay some or all of the principal due on maturing loans. 'Ponzi finance' occurs when the cash from the firm's operating activities is not large enough for all of the scheduled interest payments on a timely basis. The firms involved in Ponzi finance either will need to borrow or they will need to sell assets to get the cash to pay the interest.[17] (This distinction between Ponzi finance and speculative finance is comparable to that used in the public finance literature

between a 'primary fiscal balance' which involves the relationship between the government's tax and other receipts and its total payments exclusive of its interest payments. A government with a primary fiscal deficit must increase its indebtedness to obtain all of the funds that it needs for its current scheduled interest payments.)

Minsky emphasized the 'quality' of debt to gauge the fragility of the credit structure; the terms 'speculative' and 'Ponzi' highlight fragility. The implication of the term 'Ponzi finance' is that the firm may not be able to make a scheduled debt service payment in the absence of a 'miracle.'[18] An edifice of debt contracted to finance risky ventures is inherently unstable. Buyers of homes in California and Nevada and Arizona who used subprime mortgages bet that the increase in property prices would be sufficiently rapid so they could borrow against the increase in the equity of their homes to get the money to pay the interest on the indebtedness that they had incurred to buy the property. The lenders made the same bet. Many of these homeowners and their lenders lost these bets.

The model in the previous chapter emphasizes that in periods of economic euphoria the quantity of debt increases because the lenders and investors become less risk-averse and more willing—or less unwilling—to make loans that had previously seemed too risky. During economic slowdowns, many firms experience less rapid increases in their revenues than they had anticipated with the result that some that had been in the hedge finance group are shunted into the speculative finance group while some firms that had been in the speculative finance group move into the Ponzi finance group.

Drexel Burnham Lambert, Michael Milken, and 'junk bonds'

One of the great financial innovations in the 1980s was the development of 'junk bonds'—the bonds of highly leveraged firms that had been ranked in a 'speculative grade' by one of the major credit rating agencies. The interest rates on these bonds were generally three to four percentage points higher than the interest rates on the bonds that had been ranked in an 'investment grade' by the credit rating agencies. Many of the junk bonds were 'fallen angels'—issued by firms when their economic circumstances had been more favorable and they then had received a credit rating. A series of mishaps led to a reduction in the credit rating and eventually to the lowest investment grade; one more mishap and the credit rating agencies would move the firm to the non-investment grade or speculative ranking.

Many financial institutions are prohibited by the regulatory authorities or their investment mandates from holding bonds that are below investment

grade, and once this threshold was crossed, such institutions were required to sell these bonds; the interest rates on these bonds then increased sharply.

The sales pitch by the sellers of junk bonds was that the buyers of junk bonds—say of a diversified portfolio of junk bonds—had a 'free lunch' because the additional interest income would be more than enough to cover the losses when one or several of these bonds tanked because the borrowers went bankrupt.

The innovation in the 1970s and 1980s was that Drexel Burnham Lambert, then a third-tier investment bank, began to issue junk bonds, known in more polite circles as high-yield bonds; the mastermind of this innovation was Michael Milken. The firms that issued these bonds had to pay high interest rates to attract buyers. Many firms issued junk bonds to get the cash to finance leveraged buyouts; often the senior executives of a firm would seek to buy all of its publicly traded shares. Fear of a takeover motivated the management of Revco, a drugstore chain, to do a leveraged buyout that ended in bankruptcy 19 months later, an astonishingly brief period during an ongoing economic expansion.[19] Or Firm A might issue high-yield bonds to get the cash to acquire Firm B before Firm B issued junk bonds to get the cash to buy Firm A.

So much for the facts, which are not in dispute. What is in dispute is whether some of the underwriting transactions by Milken were illegal or unethical. The polite critics note that many of the firms that were buyers of junk bonds were savings and loan associations, and other thrift institutions and insurance companies; the managers and the owners of some of these firms had used Drexel as the underwriter to raise the money so they might buy ownership and control of various firms. The captive thrift institutions relied on the deposit guarantee of the US government; they offered high interest rates and used the money from the sale of deposits to buy the junk bonds that Drexel had underwritten.

Many of the firms that had issued the junk bonds through Drexel Burnham Lambert went bankrupt and as a consequence, the thrift institutions incurred large losses; many of the institutions that had provided the ready market for the high-yield bonds went bankrupt with losses to the American taxpayers of many tens of billions. But it was legal.

In a Cassandra-like book, Henry Kaufman decried the increase of all kinds of debt—consumer, government, mortgage, and corporate, including junk bonds; Kaufman argued that the quality of debt declined as the quantity of debt increased.[20] Felix Rohatyn, a distinguished investment banker and the head of the US office of Lazard Frères, called the United States 'a junk-bond casino.'

Still, the owners of junk bonds earned much higher interest rates than the owners of traditional bonds—at least for a while.

Even before the economic slowdown of the late 1980s and early 1990s, many of the firms that had issued junk bonds went bankrupt. A new set of studies showed that the owners of defaulted junk bonds on average lost one-third of their money and that the additional three to four percentage points of interest income per year of these bonds were insufficient to compensate for the losses on the defaulted bonds.

The large number of failures among the issuers of junk bonds was consistent with Minsky's taxonomy: most of these bonds would have been in his speculative group and some were in his Ponzi group when they were initially issued. ('Payment-in-kind' bonds allowed the issuer to hand out more of the bonds in lieu of paying interest in cash: ex ante Ponzi finance.) When the US economy moved into a recession, the cash receipts of these firms declined, and many bonds would have been shifted to the Ponzi group. An economic miracle would have been necessary to avoid a default.

A very expensive free lunch. Milken went to jail and paid a large fine. His fortune when he was released from jail and after he had paid the fine was many hundreds of millions of dollars.

Bills of exchange were claims for future payment and a form of vendor financing that the sellers of goods provided as incentives to the buyers.[21] The sellers provided a 90 or 120-day credit to the buyers. The sellers of the goods then often sold the bills of exchange to the banks at a discounted price below their face values and in return the banks provided the sellers with cash in the form of bank notes or coin or, in the nineteenth century, bank deposits. The bills of exchange often were used directly in payment. Once the seller of the goods had received a bill of exchange from the buyer, the seller transferred the bill to someone else in payment. Each recipient of a bill would add his name to the bill, much like endorsing a check. The endorsement was a form of guarantee; there were five or ten endorsers on some bills. Anyone who endorsed the bill was legally responsible to pay the owner of the bill in case the firm that initially had issued the bill defaulted on the payment. 'The bill was now money.' Ashton said that even if some of the parties in the chain of endorsers were of doubtful credit, the bill would still circulate as if it were a bank note.[22] In the first half of the nineteenth century, some bills for as little as £10 circulated with fifty or sixty names.

Payment practices differed among regions. Bank notes were disliked in Lancashire, and at the beginning of the nineteenth century, coins and bills of exchange were the primary items used for payments.[23] Because of the increase in the use of bills of exchange in payments, Bank of England note circulation declined by £9 million during the economic expansion from 1852 to 1857,

even though the demand for money increased. The deposits of five banks in London increased from £18 million to £40 million. The average volume of bills of exchange in circulation, however, expanded from £66 million to £200 million, according to the contemporary estimates of Newmarch.[24]

Initially, the bills of exchange were issued in connection with specific transactions and the amount of each bill matched the exact value of the sale. Subsequently, the link between the sale of goods and the issue of a bill of exchange was relaxed. In 1763 in Sweden, Carlos and Claes Grill bills on Lindegren in London could not be identified with particular shipments, which often were made in rapid succession, but were drawn when the firm needed to pay sellers.[25] Thus the credit of a firm or individual was gradually separated from particular transactions and the bill had become 'accommodation paper' or a promissory note—an IOU.

Some economists were firmly opposed to 'accommodation paper' because they were believed to be of lower quality than self-liquidating, commercial bills since there was less assurance that the firms that issued the bills would have the cash to pay the holders when the bills matured.[26] In a period of falling prices, however, the merits of the higher quality commercial bills were exaggerated, since the buyers of the goods might not have the cash to settle their obligations because they might not be able to sell the goods at a profit.[27] The ratio of the amount of the debt to the borrower's income or wealth is a more meaningful measure of the quality of credit.

The bill of credit, as Franklin said,

> is found very convenient in Business; because a great Sum is more easily counted in them, lighter in Carriage, concealed in less Room, and therefore safer in Travelling or Laying Up, and on many other Accounts they are very much valued. The Banks are the General Cashiers of all Gentlemen, Merchants and Great Traders ... This gives Bills a Credit; so that in England they are never less valuable than Money, and in Venice and Amsterdam they are generally more so.[28]

The statement that in Britain bills were 'never less valuable than Money' is optimistic, but the efficiency of bills when they were as good as money is clear. During the first half of the nineteenth century, there was a continuous debate as to whether bills of exchange were 'money,' 'means of payment' or 'purchasing power.' The members of the Currency School agreed that only the supply of bank notes needed to be controlled and that there was no need to control or limit the amounts of bills of exchange and of bank deposits.[29]

Problems were likely to arise when the ratio of the debt represented by the outstanding value of bills of exchange issued by a borrower became large

relative to the borrower's wealth or income, which often happened in periods of euphoria. Drawing bills of exchange in chains was infectious. Described by Adam Smith as a normal business practice, it could easily be overdone.[30] A draws on B, B on C, C on D, and so on, which increases the supply of credit. The vice of the accommodation bill, according to Hawtrey, was its 'use for construction of fixed capital when the necessary supply of bona-fide long-run savings cannot be obtained from the investment market.' Hawtrey claimed the system was particularly abused before the London crisis of 1866 and before the New York crisis of 1907.[31] The spectacular failure of the DeNeufvilles in Amsterdam in 1763 has been noted, which produced panics in Hamburg and in Berlin, and to a lesser extent in London and Amsterdam because long chains of bills were unraveled. If one bank in the chain of banks that had endorsed the bill failed, the chain collapsed and might bring down firms with relatively low ratios of outstanding IOUs to capital because each was responsible for payment. Accommodation bills enabled traders with limited capital to borrow large amounts of money, and these short-term loans often stretched into longer-term loans because they were rolled over when they matured. During the suspension of the gold standard at the beginning of the Napoleonic Wars in the early nineteenth century, there was no need to be concerned about the impacts of the expansion of credit on the price of the pound. Sir Francis Baring knew of clerks worth less than £100 who were allowed discounts of £5000 to £10,000. The 'phrenzy of speculation' during this period strongly influenced the Currency School.[32] In 1857 John Ball, a London accountant, reported knowing firms with capital under £10,000 and obligations of £900,000 and claimed it was a fair illustration.[33] In Hamburg during the same boom, Schäffle reported a man with capital of £100 and £400,000 worth of acceptances outstanding.[34]

Long-Term Capital Management borrowed more than $125 billion when its capital was $5 billion. Its leverage ratio of 25 to 1 was much higher than the ratios of most other hedge funds, which generally were less than 10 to 1. In the eighteenth century, however, many firms, according to Wirth, speculated for ten to twenty times their capital during the boom of 1763.[35] Lehman Brothers' leverage was more than 30 to 1 in the several years prior to its collapse—and toward the end of each quarter, Lehman transferred some of its securities to affiliates to reduce the leverage ratios in its quarterly reports.

Finance or accommodation bills could lead to excessive credit expansion. From time to time fictitious names were introduced into the chain so the chain would appear more creditworthy. Moreover, such bills were written for odd amounts to suggest an underlying commercial transaction. Claims

were sometimes made (for example, by German banks drawing on Dutch and American banks after the halt in American lending) that the banks knew it was finance paper disguised as commercial bills.[36]

Securitization

Securitization contributed to the surge in US real estate prices between 2002 and 2006; the investment banks created new Mortgage-Backed Securities (MBSs) that were claims on the interest and principal of a bundle of mortgages with similar attributes in terms of maturity and credit risk; each of these mortgages had been placed in a trust. Moreover, the investment banks created new Asset-Backed Securities (ABSs) that were claims on various tranches of MBSs.

MBSs were much more liquid than the individual mortgages that were in the trust. Moreover, the MBSs provided a way for firms to diversify the credit risks attached to individual mortgages. Because of these advantages, the supply of credit for mortgages increased and the interest rates on mortgages declined.

Credit card debt and student loan debt also were securitized. The advantages were identical to those associated with MBSs—the borrowers were able to diversify the credit risks, and the securities were more liquid.

Call Money

The expansion in the use of call money to finance the purchase of stocks was important prior to the crash of 1882 in France, which was a classic mania financed by call money, or money lent to stockbrokers by banks 'on call,' that is, for one day (in French, *reports*).[37] The stockbrokers used the money to finance their holdings of an inventory of stocks and they anticipated that they would be able to renew the one-day loans day after day.

The Union Générale was a bank in Paris started by Eugène Bontoux in 1878, an engineer who had worked with Rothschild and then left to initiate rival operations in Austria, Serbia, and southeastern Europe. An earlier Union Générale, founded in 1875, was not a success. France was entering a boom based on the expansion of the railroads and the construction of the Suez Canal. The boom peaked in December 1881 and the crash followed in the next month. Bouvier's interest was whether Bontoux, a Catholic, failed because of his mistakes as a lender or whether he was 'done in' by a conspiracy

of establishment Jewish and Protestant bankers that resented an intruder. Bouvier concluded with a Scottish verdict of 'not proven.'

Bontoux's Union Générale initially was capitalized at 25 million francs, which was increased in the spring of 1879 to 50 million francs and increased again in January 1881 to 100 million francs; a third increase, planned for January 1882, would have raised the capital to 150 million francs. Only one-fourth of the capital was paid in.[38] With each increase in capital, the investors had to pay a premium above the par value of 500 francs into the reserves of the bank in response to the increase in the market price of the stock. These premiums were 20, 175, and 250 francs, respectively. Shares were registered in the names of buyers even though they still owed three-quarters of the par value for the purchases of shares; nevertheless, roughly half of the 200,000 original shares floated in the trading market.

Trading in securities was conducted through fortnightly settlements in both Paris and Lyon. A purchaser would pay 10 percent down, and borrow 90 percent from an *agent de change* or broker who in turn borrowed the money in the call-money market. Money was invested in *reports* by banks, by special *caisses* (funds created especially by banks and other investors for this outlet) and by individuals. A bank and *caisse*, moreover, could favor brokers who specialized in trading in a particular stock. Thus banks such as the Union Générale and the Banque de Lyon et de la Loire—not to mention three or four less successful if less spectacular banks created during the boom—could support their own stock indirectly. When changes in stock prices were modest, speculators realized small gains and small losses, and the brokers would typically pay out or receive relatively little money. If stock prices increased, some speculators would withdraw money from the market and then more capital would need to be invested. Assume a speculator bought a share for 100 francs, paid 10 francs down and borrowed 90 francs. If the speculator sold the share at 110 francs and withdrew his 20 francs, 11 francs of the 20 francs withdrawn from the market would come from the new speculator, and 9 francs had to be a new *report* and borrowed from the call money market. As stock prices increased the interest rates on call money (*taux des reports*) increased to attract new money; the interest rate on call money increased from 4 to 5 percent at the end of 1880 to 8–10 percent in the spring of 1881, and reached a peak of 12 percent in the autumn of 1881.[39]

When the share prices declined the speculators needed more money to comply with margin requirements. If the speculator bought a share at 100 francs, again with 10 francs down and the share price fell to 90 francs, the speculator had to produce 9 more francs to comply with the 10 percent margin requirement. If the speculator had been fully leveraged earlier and did

not meet the margin call, the broker sold the speculator's stocks. If the price dropped below 90 francs, the broker, bank, or individual that had made the loan lost money. The stock of the Union Générale went from 1250 francs in March 1881 to a peak of 3040 on 14 December as the mania gathered speed. Thereafter a period of distress followed with price quotations at 2950 francs on 10 January 1882, and 2800 francs on 16 January. On 19 January the price was 1300 francs. Brokers were short 18 million francs on that day, as speculators could not produce the cash needed to meet margin requirements, and short 33 million francs when it came to the month-end liquidation on 31 January.[40]

The collapse of Banque de Lyon et de la Loire was more spectacular as the share price went from a peak of 1765 francs on 17 December 1881 to 1550 francs on 28 December, when it was supporting its own stock, to 1040 francs on 4 January 1882, 650 francs on 10 January, and finally to 400 francs on 19 January, the day after it closed its doors.[41] The signal for the collapse was the approval given to Bontoux to establish a Banque de Crédit Maritime at Trieste, which was announced on 4 January 1882. The coup boomeranged.[42] Investors with losses on their holdings of shares in Banque de Lyon et de la Loire sold their Union Générale shares. The combination of highly leveraged speculation and a credit mechanism that rested on bank and personal credit cycled through the call money market and the result was the collapse among banks, caisses, brokers, individuals, and businesses in a few days. Economic activity was adversely affected in advance of the collapse of the stock market, not because of a change in the money supply but because at the peak of the fever the business world of Lyons turned to speculation in Union Générale: 'silk merchants, cloth manufacturers, industrialists, tradesmen, dry-goods merchants, grocers, butchers, people with fixed incomes, janitors, shoemakers'; 'A lot of capital was diverted from regular business to the stock market both in securities and in call money.'[43]

Some of the features of the US stock market crash of 1929 were similar to those in the collapse of the French banks nearly fifty years earlier: a preoccupation with speculation and a decline in economic activity as stock prices peaked. More money was used to support the higher level of stock prices and less money was available for economic activity. Another similarity is that as stock prices peaked, call loans of 'all others' as opposed to New York banks and banks outside New York increased from just under $2 billion at the end of 1926 to nearly $4 billion two years later and to more than $6.6 billion on 4 October 1929. Margin credit was extensive. Brokerage firms might require that the buyers of stocks pay 10 percent down; the buyers borrowed the remaining 90 percent. Meanwhile, brokers' loans of New York banks declined

from $1.6 billion at their height at the end of 1928 to $1.1 billion on 4 October 1929.[44]

With the crash, 'all others' and banks outside New York took call funds from the market. They were fearful that the Stock Exchange might be closed as it had been in 1873, which would have frozen their liquid day-to-day loans.[45] At this stage, New York banks slightly increased their brokers' loans. Similarly, in 1882, one consortium of Paris banks headed by the Banque de Paris et des Pays-Bas (Paribas) advanced 18 million francs in five loans to the Union Générale directly, while another group headed by the Rothschild bank loaned 80 million francs to the company of brokers to get them through the end of January settlement and allow them time to work out their payment arrangements. In both crises many brokers, clients and (in 1882) banks and their caisses went bankrupt. The money market banks eased the adjustment, but in Paris, in 1882 they did not save the Union Générale.

Buying stocks on margin in the United States was curbed in the 1930s by a Federal Reserve regulation that fixed margin requirements at no more than 50 percent. Financial institutions were able to make end runs about this regulation. The regulation applied to organized exchanges for shares, including the New York Stock Exchange, but not to the Chicago Mercantile Exchange, which dealt in Standard and Poor's (S&P) 500 stock index futures and where the margin requirement was 10 percent of the value of the investor's positions in futures contracts. Arbitrageurs linked prices in two markets so in effect they were one market. An investor who bought an S&P 500 futures contract in Chicago with a 10 percent margin was in effect buying stocks in New York with a 10 percent margin; as the price of futures contracts increased in Chicago, the arbitrageurs would sell the futures contracts and at the same time buy a representative basket of stocks of the companies that dominated the index.

In the aftermath of the 19 October 1987 collapse, there was some support for the idea of regulating the Chicago and New York markets by a single agency—the Federal Reserve Board or the Securities and Exchange Commission—and some for tightening margin regulations in the futures market, and some for banning futures trading in stocks altogether.

The Gold-Exchange Standard

A third example of the expansion of credit on a fixed money base is represented by the gold-exchange standard, which involved central banks' holdings of liquid securities denominated in the British pound and in the US dollar.

This practice began before World War I, although it is sometimes thought to have been based on the recommendations of the Genoa Conference of 1922 and the Gold Delegation of the League of Nations. This innovation had been strongly supported by Governor Montagu Norman of the Bank of England who sought to increase foreign holdings of British pound securities to provide relief for Britain's balance of payments problem and especially its modest holdings of gold relative to foreign holdings of short-term securities denominated in the British pound.[46] The boom in world lending of 1913–1914 was financed by increases in central bank holdings of securities denominated in the British pound, the French franc, and the German mark.

Just as it is less costly to use currency notes and bills of exchange rather than coins in payments, ownership of securities denominated in the currency of a country with a large capital market was more attractive than ownership of monetary gold as long as financial conditions were stable. These securities are easier to use in transactions, free of the need for transport, safeguarding, and assay. A country can increase its holdings of international reserve assets by selling bonds in London or in New York and then use the money receipts to buy short-term securities denominated in the British pound or the US dollar. Since the British or US monetary authorities are not likely to regard the increase in the foreign holdings of liquid securities denominated in their currency as a reason to contract their own credit superstructure, these transactions lead to an expansion of credit.

International lending on the gold standard may have the same unstable character as on the gold-exchange standard. Before countries borrowed foreign money that they would use as reserves for domestic monetary expansion, they borrowed gold. During the nineteenth century, American firms and state governments borrowed in London during economic upswings both to finance imports and to increase the gold base of the US banking system. Transactions in gold helped with the transfer of goods and services; gold loans enabled the borrowers to expand the supply of credit without inducing credit contractions in the lending countries.[47]

Instability of Credit and the Great Depression

The notion that manias and crashes result from the instability of the supply of credit is an old one. Alvin Hansen, writing on business cycles, discussed this view in a general survey of 'early concepts' and in a chapter on mid-nineteenth-century economists—John Stuart Mill and Alfred Marshall—entitled 'Confidence and Credit.'[48] Hansen believed that these views had

become obsolete because they neglected the investment and savings decisions of large firms. Theories that attach importance to the instability of credit persisted into the twentieth century. Hawtrey was a classic economist in this vein, and so was A. C. Pigou, whose book *Industrial Fluctuations* (1927) has a chapter dealing with panics.[49] The paradox is that the role of the instability of credit began to be neglected about the time of the Great Depression of the 1930s.

The monetarist view of the Great Depression is set out in a monumental study by Milton Friedman and Anna Schwartz. They maintained that the sharp decline in economic activity in the first half of the 1930s was the result of policy mistakes by the Federal Reserve; they focused on the decline in the money supply from August 1929 to March 1933. Whenever the question turns to the start of the depression, they note that the money supply did not increase in 1928 and 1929, and that it declined 2.6 percent from August 1929 to October 1930 when it should have been increased to offset the weakness in the economy. Friedman and Schwartz contend that the stock market crash of October 1929 had little or nothing to do with the intensity of the decline in industrial output and that the depression was the consequence of US domestic policies and had only a tangential connection with international cross-border investment inflows, changes in the prices of currencies, and deflation in Europe and in other countries.[50] Their view of the depression has held sway in the United States for an extended period.[51]

Peter Temin challenged this monetarist view from a Keynesian point of view. He asked whether the decline in spending resulted from a decline in the money supply or whether instead the decline in the money supply followed from the decline in spending; he used sophisticated econometrics to choose between these two views. Much of Temin's argument centered on how much actual consumption deviated from forecasts of the levels based on the relationships among consumption, income, wealth, and similar variables that should be specified in forecasting a 'normal' trend in consumption. In addition, he examined the relationship between the timing of changes in the US money supply and the changes in interest rates on US dollar securities; thus if the increases in spending preceded the increase in the money supply then interest rates should have increased whereas if the increase in the money supply preceded the increase in spending interest rates should have declined. Since interest rates declined sharply after the 1929 crash (except for interest rates on high-risk bonds which increased because of the greater concern with default risk) he concluded that the decline in spending preceded the decline in the money supply. Temin also examined the changes in real money balances (the nominal money supply adjusted for changes in the consumer price level)

and concluded that real balances increased between 1929 and 1931 by 1–18 percent, depending on the choice between M_1 and M_2 and on whether a wholesale price deflator or a consumer price deflator was used to adjust changes in nominal GDP to changes in real GDP. Annual averages further dampened the movement; on the basis of monthly figures, and averaging M_1 and M_2 expressed as percentages or relatives of a base year and the two price indexes, the money supply increased 5 percent between August 1929 and August 1931 if seasonal influences are minimized. Temin concluded that there is no evidence that changes in the money supply between the stock market crash and the British departure from the gold standard in September 1931 caused the depression.[52]

Temin's analysis did not provide an explanation of the depression even though it was a strong challenge to the monetarist view. One analyst claimed that the stock market crash led banks to ration credit to borrowers and thus started the depression without reducing the money supply.[53] Another suggested that the sharp decline in share prices reduced nominal wealth and household spending; the implicit assumption was that the decline in consumption followed from the decline in the real value of wealth.[54]

These arguments ignore the speed of the decline in industrial production in 1929 that began four or five months before the stock market crash. Industrial production fell from 127 in June to 122 in September to 117 in October, 106 in November, and 99 in December; automobile production declined from 660,000 units in March 1929 to 440,000 in August, 319,000 in October, and 92,500 in December. These declines were much too large to be explained by changes in the US money supply.

Instead, these declines are best explained by the instability in the supply of credit, and the reduction in the supply of credit available for purchases of automobiles and other durables as more credit was diverted to the stock market. As stock prices increased in the first ten months of 1929, funds were channeled to the call-money market; the volume of call money rose from $6.4 billion at the end of December 1928 to $8.5 billion in early October 1929. Moreover, first, the New York banks and then banks headquartered in other US cities became more cautious lenders to stock market participants and to other borrowers. When the stock market crashed, the credit system suddenly froze. Loans to finance imports declined sharply, in part because of the sharp decline in the prices of imports.

The debate between the monetarists and the Keynesians ignores the instability of the supply of credit and the fragility of the banking system and the negative impacts on production and prices when the credit system became paralyzed because declines in the prices of many commodities and goods

caused many borrowers to default on their loans—which explains the events in the early stages of the 1929 depression. This view was largely ignored except by Minsky and Henry Simons, the Chicago economist who thought the Great Depression was caused by declines in business confidence that led through an unstable credit system to declines in liquidity and in the willingness of banks to increase their loans.[55]

Simons's views were set forth in *Economic Policy for a Free Society*,[56] written after World War II under the strong influence of the 1930s depression. He recommended a 100 percent currency reserve against bank deposits to prevent changes in deposits arising from changes in the willingness of the public to hold currency and a vigorous effort to stamp out the variability in the supply of credit elsewhere in the system. He proposed restrictions on open-book credit and installment loans as well as limitation of government debt to non-interest-bearing money at one end of the spectrum and very long-term debt (ideally, perpetual obligations) at the other. Simons advocated a system in which all financial wealth would be held in equity form with no fixed money contracts so that only banks could create effective money substitutes. He was concerned about the speculative temper of the community and the ease with which short-term nonbank borrowing and lending made society vulnerable to changes in business confidence.

Simon's recommendations to limit the character of money and financial securities were very different from Friedman's liberal propensity to let market forces determine the demand and supply for different types of financial securites.[57] Friedman was confident that control of the growth of the money supply would prevent major business cycles and that there was no need to fear that the credit mechanism would not be stable. Even if Simons's positive proposals were desirable (and there is grave doubt on this score) they are utopian and hence not practical. Nevertheless, Simons's diagnosis of the tendency of the system toward unstable short-term borrowing and repayment is similar to the Minsky view.

In the last several decades still another viewpoint on the relations of money and banking to economic stability has come into prominence from the neo-Austrian school that wants to decontrol money and banking entirely. This group, led by Friedrich Hayek in Britain, Roland Vaubel in Germany, and Richard Timberlake, Leland Yeager, Lawrence White, and George Selgin in the United States, seeks to abolish an active monetary policy. Any bank, company or person would be allowed to issue 'money'; they believe that market forces will determine which firms issue good money. Each firm will compete to ensure that its money is accepted, and so good money will drive out bad. White defends the position on the basis of the experience of the

Scottish banks that were unregulated between the failure of the Ayr Bank in 1772 and the Bank Act of 1845 which applied the Bank Act of 1844 to Scotland.[58]

During this period the leading commercial banks accumulated the notes of the lesser ones and were ready to convert them to specie if they thought the supply of currency notes issued by any bank was increasing too rapidly. The large banks served as informal controllers of the money supply. But several historical experiences—the country banks in England from 1745 to 1835, wildcat banking in Michigan in the 1830s, and the latest experience with bank deregulation in Latin America and especially in East Asia—do not support the view that 'good money drives out bad.'

The global inflation of the 1970s resulted from a combination of expansive US monetary policy and expansive monetary policies in Europe and Japan as their large balance of payments surpluses led to rapid growth in their holdings of international reserve assets and in their money supplies. Central bank holdings of international reserve assets increased rapidly in the mid and late 1990s.[59] Three years later a French economist, Pascal Blanqué, wrote of a US credit bubble.[60] In a similar view, Graciela Kaminsky and Carmen Reinhart blame foreign countries for printing money and the United States for running a persistent balance of payments deficit.[61]

The central question is whether a central bank can restrain the instability in the supply of credit and slow speculation to avoid its dangerous extension. If the monetary authorities fix some proxy for the money supply or liquidity, or if they focus directly on the rate of interest, can the upswing and subsequent decline that leads to a crisis be moderated or eliminated? There is no a priori way to determine whether a central bank policy of holding the money supply constant, limiting the liquidity of the money market or raising the discount rate at the first sign of euphoric speculation would prevent the manias that subsequently morph into crises. Economists cannot conduct carefully controlled experiments. Nevertheless, the weight of historical evidence favors the view that while a somewhat different monetary policy might have moderated booms and busts it would not have eliminated them.

The Bank of England was severely attacked for its blindness to an approaching crisis in 1839 and its failure to raise interest rates sooner. The general view that it had been dilatory is said to have been the proximate cause of the Bank Act of 1844.[62] In the early 1850s the glut of gold led to declines in interest rates in 1852 and 1853. Thereafter interest rates increased although not by enough to forestall the severe crisis of 1857.[63] The number of bills of exchange in circulation continued to increase as the discount rate rose, and declined as it fell, rather than responding to policy changes in the opposite

direction; speculation based on bill creation seems to have been uninhibited by the increases in discount rates.[64] One mid-1850s proposal was that the Bank of England should vary its discount rate as its reserves changed so the public would have a clear idea of what to expect—a suggestion Elmer Wood claims shows no grasp of Bank of England transactions.[65] In 1863 and 1864 the Bank of England twice raised the interest rate to 9 percent, which perhaps delayed but did not prevent the 1866 crash. Liquidation was completed in France in 1864; there were two shakeouts in Britain that year, but the main deflation was delayed.[66] In July 1869 the National Bank of Austria-Hungary raised interest rates but the increases came too late to forestall a crash in the fall of 1869 which was a pale forerunner of the Great Crash of 1873 in Vienna.[67] The Bank raised its discount rate again in 1872, although Wirth said the rate still was too low.[68] In a similar fashion, with the same timing and the same absence of result (unless it precipitated the crisis), the Federal Reserve Bank of New York raised its discount rate from 5 to 6 percent on 9 August 1929.

In 1873 the Bank of England changed its discount rate twenty-four times and avoided the financial crises that seized Austria and Germany in May and the United States in September. In November the rate was raised to 9 percent to prevent the Germans from withdrawing money that had been in London since the French-German reparation payments.[69] Whether this represented successful fine-tuning against the possibility of a crisis or merely increasing sensitivity to short-term capital movements cannot be determined from secondary sources.

In the panic of 1907, the preparatory expansion had involved lending of unknown amounts by out-of-town banks in New York, together with large borrowing in London by New York banks—a combination of two of the methods of expansion discussed earlier, if one equates out-of-town banks lending in New York to the gold-exchange standard. Since the United States did not have a central bank, it was not possible to take discretionary actions to increase interest rates. American borrowing led to gold exports from London and to increases in interest rates, and the Bank of England advised the market that further acceptance of American finance bills was unwelcome because it was a menace to stability.[70] This statement slowed the boom but failed to prevent the 'rich man's panic' of March 1907 and the full-scale panic of October.

If central bankers were omniscient and omnipotent, they might be able to manage interest rates and reserve requirements to stabilize the supply of credit; they could then correct the instability in the supply implicit in the

infinite expansibility of credit. But 'there are no positive limitations to the expansion of individual credit.'[71]

Central banking arose to impose control on the growth and instability of the supply of credit. The evolution of central banking from profit-oriented private banking is a remarkable achievement. By 1825 there was implicit agreement on the division of labor between the private banks and the central bank; private bankers in London and the provinces would finance the boom while the Bank of England would 'finance the crisis' so it would not become self-justifying. In the United States, which was without a central bank after 1837, the major banks in New York were caught between the profit-making role that led them to contribute to the instability in the supply of credit and their role as holders of deposits of out-of-town banks that might contribute to instability if they were withdrawn. There was a conflict between the short-run concern with profitability and the long-run concern with financial stability, the private good with the public good. No one decreed that the New York banks should act responsibly in the public interest; it may or may not have been to their advantage to do so. The problem is a general one in politics and business and centers on who should look out for the public interest.

Notes

1. At least as far as I can tell from limited sources. Typically at the height of the bubble, sellers had no bulbs, and some (many?) buyers made down-payments, if at all, in kind, that is, in personal possessions or commodities, presumably because they lacked cash. The difference between the value of the down payment and the negotiated price was personal credit. See N. W. Posthumus, 'The Tulip Mania in Holland in the Years 1636 and 1637', *Journal of Economic and Business History*, vol. 1 (1928–29), reprinted in W. C. Scoville and J. C. LaForce, eds, *The Economic Development of Western Europe*, vol. 2, *The Sixteenth and Seventeenth Centuries* (Lexington: D. C. Heath, 1969), p. 142; Simon Schama, *The Embarrassment of Riches: an Interpretation of Dutch Culture in the Golden Age* (Berkeley: University of California Press, 1987), p. 358; Robert P. Flood and Peter M. Garber, *Speculative Bubbles, Speculative Attacks and Policy Switching* (Cambridge, MA: MIT Press, 1994), p. 60.

2. Peter Temin, *The Jacksonian Economy* (New York: W. W. Norton, 1969), pp. 79–82.

3. Jean Bouvier, *Le Krach de l'Union Générale, 1878–1885* (Paris: Presses universitaires de France, 1960), pp. 129–34.

4. 'Kuwait's Great $70 Bn Paper Chase', *Financial Times*, 25 September 1982; 'Kuwait Aide Says Speculators Own "Price of Follies"', *International Herald*

Tribune, 29 October 1982; 'Kuwaitis Try a New Exchange', *New York Times*, 16 December 1984, sec. D.

5. Milton Friedman, *The Optimum Quantity of Money and Other Essays* (Chicago: Aldine, 1969), pp. 1–50.

6. Jacob Viner, *Studies in the Theory of International Trade* (New York: Harper, 1937), pp. 232–3.

7. J. G. van Dillen, 'The Bank of Amsterdam', in *History of the Principal Public Banks* (The Hague: Martinus Nijhoff, 1934), pp. 79–123.

8. Eli F. Heckscher and J. G. van Dillen, eds, 'The Bank of Sweden in Its Connection with the Bank of Amsterdam', in ibid., p. 169.

9. Walter Bagehot, 'The General Aspect of the Banking Question', no. 1, a letter to the editor of *The Economist*, 7 February 1857, in *The Collected Works of Walter Bagehot*, ed. Norman St. John Stevas (London: *The Economist*, 1978), vol. 9, p. 319.

10. Great Britain, Committee on the Working of the Monetary System, *Report* (Radcliffe Report), Cmnd 827 (London: HM Stationery Office, August 1959), pp. 133–4, 391–2.

11. Ibid., pp. 134, 394.

12. James S. Gibbons, *The Banks of New York, Their Dealers, the Clearing House and the Panic of 1857* (New York: D. Appleton, 1859), pp. 376–7.

13. J. S. Mill, in *Westminster Review*, vol. 41 (1844), pp. 590–1, quoted in Jacob Viner, *Studies in International Trade*, p. 246.

14. See Benjamin M. Friedman, 'Portfolio Choice and the Debt-to-Income Relationship', *American Economic Review*, vol. 75, no. 2 (May 1985), pp. 338–43; and idem, 'The Roles of Money and Credit in Macro-economic Analysis', in James Tobin, ed., *Macroeconomics, Prices, and Quantities: Essays in Memory of Arthur Okun* (Washington, DC: Brookings Institution, 1983), pp. 161–89.

15. Samuel L. Clements (Mark Twain) and Charles Dudley Warner, *The Gilded Age: a Tale of Today* (New York: Harper & Brothers, 1873; reprint edn, author's national edn, 10 vols, 1915), vol. 1, p. 263.

16. For an extended discussion see C. P. Kindleberger, 'The Quality of Debt', in D. B. Papadimitriou, ed., *Profits, Deficits and Instability* (Basingstoke: Macmillan, 1992), reprinted in idem, *The World Economy and National Finance in Historical Perspective* (Ann Arbor: University of Michigan Press, 1995), pp. 117–30.

17. See Hyman P. Minsky, 'The Financial-instability Hypothesis: Capitalist Processes and the Behavior of the Economy', in C. P. Kindleberger and J. P. Laffargue, eds, *Financial Crisis: Theory, History and Policy* (Cambridge: Cambridge University Press, 1982), pp. 13–39.

18. See the comments on the Minsky paper by J. S. Flemming, Raymond W. Goldsmith and Jacques Melitz, in ibid., pp. 39–47.

19. 'Revco Drugstore Chain in Bankruptcy Filing', *New York Times*, 29 July 1988, sec. D.

20. Henry Kaufman, *Interest Rates, the Markets and the New Financial World* (New York: Times Books, 1986).
21. Alfred Marshall noted that paper money was used in China 2000 years before his writing, and that the apt term *flying money* was given there to bills of exchange 1000 years ago. See Appendix E, 'Notes on the Development of Banking, with Special Reference to English Experience', in *Money, Credit and Commerce* (1923; reprint, New York: Augustus M. Kelley, 1965), p. 305n.

 In Europe the bill of exchange was developed by Italian merchants to balance accounts at fairs. Net debtors at the end of trading paid in bills drawn on a fair in a different location or on the next fair at the same place. This 'private money' was needed because there was not enough coin (money of the prince) to square accounts. See Marie-Thérèse Boyer-Xambeu, Ghislain Deleplace, and Lucien Gillard, *Private Money and Public Currencies: The 16th-Century Challenge*, translated from the French (Armonk: M. W. Sharpe, 1984).
22. T. S. Ashton, 'The Bill of Exchange and Private Banks in Lancashire, 1790–1830', in T. S. Ashton and R. S. Sayers, eds, *Papers in English Monetary History* (Oxford: Oxford University Press, Clarendon Press, 1953), pp. 37–8.
23. Francis C. Knowles, *The Monetary Crisis Considered* (1827), referring to the House of Lords Committee on Scottish and Irish Currency of 1826; quoted in J. R. T. Hughes, *Fluctuations in Trade, Industry and Finance: a Study of British Economic Development, 1850–1860* (Oxford: Oxford University Press, Clarendon Press, 1960), p. 267.
24. Ibid., p. 258.
25. Kurt Samuelsson, 'International Payments and Credit Movements by Swedish Merchant Houses, 1730–1815', *Scandinavian Economic History Review*, vol. 3 (1955), p. 188.
26. For an early example of such attitudes, see the hypothetical discussion of the board of directors at a New York bank in the 1850s by James S. Gibbons, The Banks of New York, Their Dealers, the Clearing House, and the Panic of 1857, p. 50. A director is pleading the loan application of a Mr. Black, 'rich beyond a contingency,' who wants to build a new house on Fifth Avenue for $60,000 and to spend $40,000 to furnish it, and proposes expanding his firm's discount line at the bank by the whole amount. Another director objects:

 > Mr. President, my notion is, that we have no right to discount any thing at the Board but a *bona fide* commercial note that will be paid when due. And on top of that the indorser must be able to take it up himself, if the drawer should fail or die. Don't you see that we are discounting this paper to pay for Mr. Black's house and furniture, just for his single enjoyment? This isn't commercial paper, sir! It's accommodation paper in the true sense.

Gibbon's book, with chapters on the various tasks in a bank, is a mid-nineteenth-century precursor to Martin Mayer's *The Bankers* (New York: Ballantine Books, 1974).

27. R. G. Hawtrey, *The Art of Central Banking* (London: Longmans, Green, 1932), pp. 128–9.
28. See Herman E. Krooss, ed., *Documentary History of Banking and Currency in the United States* (New York: Chelsea House, 1969), vol. 1, p. 31.
29. Viner, *Studies in International Trade*, pp. 245ff., esp. pp. 249–50.
30. Adam Smith, *An Inquiry into the Nature and Causes of the Wealth of Nations* (1776; reprint edn, New York: Modern Library, 1937), pp. 293–7.
31. R. G. Hawtrey, *Currency and Credit*, 3rd edn (New York: Longmans, Green 1930), p. 224.
32. Arthur D. Gayer, W. W. Rostow and Anna Jacobson Schwartz, *The Growth and Fluctuation of the British Economy, 1790–1850* (Oxford: Oxford University Press, Clarendon Press, 1953), vol. 1, p. 105.
33. Great Britain, *Parliamentary Papers* (*Monetary Policy, Commercial Distress*), 'Report of the Select Committee on the Operation of the Bank Acts and the Causes of the Recent Commercial Distress, 1857–59' (Shannon: Irish University Press, 1969), vol. 4, p. 113, question 1661, and p. 115, question 1679.
34. Albert E. Fr. Schäffle, 'Die Handleskrise von 1857 in Hamburg, mit besonderer Rucksicht auf das Bankwesen', in Schäffle, Gesammelte Aufsätze (Tübingen: H. Haupp'schen, 1885), vol. 2, p. 31.
35. Wirth, *Handelskrisen*, p. 91.
36. See C. P. Kindleberger, *The World in Depression, 1929–1939*, 2nd edn (Berkeley: University of California Press, 1986), p. 133 and note.
37. Bouvier, Le Krach, pp. 130–1.
38. After the bank's dissolution, the French prosecutor of Bontoux wrote that there had been grave irregularities in the issuance of the shares and in the increases in capital. Subscriptions to the capital had been made by the bank both in its own name and in the names of fictitious client subscribers. A rival bank, the Banque de Lyon et de la Loire, formed in April 1881 with a capital of 25 million francs (raised to 50 million in November) and with one-quarter of its capital theoretically paid in, was similarly a bubble. Of 50,000 shares originally issued, more than half had not paid amounts due, and the bank had less than half of the 6.5 million francs of capital claimed at the outset.
 The Union Générale also bought its own securities in the open market and, as we shall see, loaned money to others to buy them (Bouvier, *Le krach*, pp. 123, 164–5, 167).
39. Ibid., p. 131.
40. Ibid. For prices, see tables 7 and 8, pp. 136 and 144; for the shortfall, see p. 144.
41. Ibid., tables 7 and 8, pp. 136, 144, 145.
42. John Carswell, *The South Sea Bubble* (London: Cresset Press, 1960), p. 171.

43. Bouvier, *Le krach*, pp. 112, 113.

44. Federal Reserve System, *Banking and Monetary Statistics* (Washington, DC: Board of Governors of the Federal Reserve System, 1943), p. 494.

45. Alexander Dana Noyes, *The Market Place: Reminiscences of a Financial Editor* (Boston: Little, Brown, 1937), p. 353.

46. Peter H. Lindert, *Key Currencies and Gold, 1900–1913*, Princeton Studies in International Finance, no. 24 (August 1969).

47. Jeffrey G. Williamson, *American Growth and the Balance of Payments, 1830–1913: a Study of the Long Swing* (Chapel Hill: University of North Carolina Press, 1964).

48. Alvin H. Hansen, *Business Cycles and National Income* (New York: W. W. Norton, 1957), chaps 13, 15.

49. A. C. Pigou, *Industrial Fluctuations* (London: Macmillan, 1927), pt. 1, chap. 7, and p. 274.

50. Milton Friedman and Anna J. Schwartz, *A Monetary History of the United States, 1867–1960* (Princeton: Princeton University Press, 1963). Chapter 10 of the book is published separately as *The Great Contraction, 1929–1933* (Princeton: Princeton University Press, 1965).

51. This assertion was made by Thomas A. Mayer in a seminar on money and the Great Depression, University of California, Berkeley, 11 May 1977.

52. Peter Temin, *Did Monetary Forces Cause the Great Depression?* (New York: W. W. Norton, 1976), passim.

53. Ben S. Bernanke, 'Nonmonetary Effects of the Financial Crisis in the Propagation of the Great Depression', *American Economic Review*, vol. 73, no. 3 (June 1983), pp. 237–76.

54. Frederic S. Miskin, 'Illiquidity, Consumer Durable Expenditure, and Monetary Policy', *American Economic Review*, vol. 66 (September 1976), pp. 642–54.

55. See Minsky's review of Temin, in Challenge, vol. 19, no. 1 (September/October 1976), pp. 44–6; and see Milton Friedman, 'The Monetary Theory and Policy of Henry Simons', in *Friedman, Optimum Quantity of Money*, pp. 81–93.

56. Henry Simons, *Economic Policy for a Free Society* (Chicago: University of Chicago Press, 1948).

57. Friedman, 'Henry Simons', p. 83.

58. See Friedrich A. Hayek, 'Choice in Currency: A Way to Stop Inflation', Occasional Paper no. 48 (London: Institute of Economic Affairs, 1982); Roland Vaubel, 'Free Currency Competition', *Weltwirtschaftliches Archiv*, vol. 113 (1977), pp. 435–59; Richard H. Timberlake, 'Legislative Construction of the Monetary Control Act of 1980', *American Economic Review*, vol. 75, no. 2 (May 1985), pp. 97–102; Leland B. Yeager, 'Deregulation and Monetary Reform', *American Economic Review*, vol. 75, no. 2 (May 1985), pp. 103–7: Lawrence H. White, *Free Banking in Britain: Theory, Experience and Debate* (New York: Cambridge University Press, 1984); George Selgin, *The Theory of*

Free Banking (Totowa: Rowan and Littlefield, 1989). For a defense of central banking, see Charles Goodhart, *The Evolution of Central Banks* (Cambridge: Cambridge University Press, 1989).

59. 'The Post-1990 Surge in World Currency Reserves', *Conjuncture*, 26th year, no. 9 (October 1996), pp. 2–12.
60. Pascal Blanqué, 'US Credit Bubble.com', Conjuncture, 29th year, no. 4 (April 1999), pp. 12–21.
61. Graciela L. Kaminsky and Carmen W. Reinhart, 'The Twin Crises: the Causes of Banking and Balance-of-Payments Problems', *American Economic Review* (June 1999), pp. 433–500.
62. Gayer, Rostow, and Schwartz, *Growth and Fluctuation*, vol. 1, p. 300.
63. Hughes, *Fluctuations*, p. 12.
64. Ibid., p. 261.
65. Elmer Wood, *English Theories of Central Banking Control, 1819–1858, with Some Account of Contemporary Procedures* (Cambridge, MA: Harvard University Press, 1939), p. 147.
66. A. Andréadès, *History of the Bank of England* (London: P. S. King, 1909), pp. 356–7.
67. Wirth, *Handelskrisen*, p. 463.
68. Ibid., pp. 515–16.
69. E. Victor Morgan, *The Theory and Practice of Central Banking, 1797–1913* (Cambridge: Cambridge University Press, 1943), pp. 184–5.
70. O. M. W. Sprague, *History of Crises under the National Banking System* (1910; reprint edn, New York: Augustus M. Kelley, 1968), p. 241.
71. Gibbons, *Banks of New York*, p. 375.

5

The Critical Stage: When the Bubble Is About to Pop

Changing Expectations

The standard model of the sequence of events that leads to a financial crisis is that a shock triggers an economic expansion that morphs into an economic boom and then euphoria develops: the prices of securities and real estate increase rapidly, much more rapidly than GDP. Then there is a pause in the pace of these increases in the price of securities. A few savvy or lucky investors sell some of their securities to park their speculative gains in a secure store of value. The slowing of the increases in the prices of securities and real estate may induce a more cautious approach by others. Distress is likely to follow as the prices of securities begin to decline. The pattern is biological in its regularity. A panic is likely and then a crash may follow. Lord Overstone, the leading British banker of the middle of the nineteenth century, saw a similar pattern and was quoted with approval by Walter Bagehot: 'quiescence, improvement, confidence, prosperity, excitement, overtrading, CONVULSION [sic], pressure, stagnation, ending in aquiesence.'[1] Overstone identified five stages of euphoria before the financial crisis, or, in his words, the convulsion.

The theory of rational expectations assumes that investors' expectations change more or less instantaneously in response to each shock and that investors immediately see through to the impacts of each shock on the long-run equilibrium prices for real estate and stocks and commodities. In contrast, the insight from financial history is that expectations change slowly at some times and rapidly at others as various groups realize—sometimes at

© The Author(s), under exclusive license to Springer Nature Switzerland AG 2023
R. Z. Aliber et al., *Manias, Panics, and Crashes*,
https://doi.org/10.1007/978-3-031-16008-0_5

different moments and at other times more or less simultaneously—that the current forecasts of prices in the distant future differ from earlier projections of these same prices.

The change in the mindsets of investors from confidence to pessimism compounds the instability in the credit markets as some lenders eventually realize that the borrowers' indebtedness is too large relative to their incomes. The lenders slow their willingness to buy more of the IOUs from the borrowers. The borrowers adjust to their new perceptions about the future by reducing their spending so they will have the cash to pay the interest and to reduce debt. Some firms may sell divisions and operating units to get the cash to repay loans. The lenders recognize that they have too many risky loans and they seek repayment of outstanding loans from the riskier borrowers and they become reluctant to renew these loans as they mature and they raise the credit standards for new loans.

The period of financial distress may last weeks, months, or even several years, or it may be concentrated in a few days. US property prices began to decline at the end of 2006 and economic growth was positive although less rapid throughout 2007 and in the first half of 2008; the third quarter of 2008 was the first one when the level of GDP declined—until then the rate of growth had slowed more or less quarter by quarter. Then the collapse of Lehman Brothers in September 2008 triggered panic and a crash.

Government policies play a central role in the formation of expectations. Can the government head off a financial crisis by dampening the expectations that develop in the euphoria?

Warnings

One proposal is that a government should make its knowledge or publish its own forecast if it believes that the prices of securities and assets are too high—if it thinks it knows more than the speculators.[2] Thus the government might calm the concerns or fears of investors by making that knowledge publicly available.[3] Many individuals within the government have views about the economic and financial outlook but their views often are at variance with those of others in the government so that developing a 'government view' could occur only if someone—the prime minister, the head of the central bank, the minister of finance—developed a consensus.

Chairman Greenspan of the Federal Reserve warned about 'irrational exuberance' when he commented on stock prices in December 1996. That remark clearly was a warning. But investors ignored the warning.

The historical record provides little support for the view that statements from government officials have had much of an impact in dampening euphoria. In some cases 'a word to the wise' may be sufficient but in others, the warnings are not likely to be adequate to forestall further increases in the prices of securities. The likelihood that investors and speculators would heed the warnings of a government official when the prices of securities and assets have been increasing at annual rates of 20–30 percent a year is not especially high.

The first such warnings on the record were made in 1825. Although many writers have viewed the Bubble Act of June 1720 as a warning by Robert Walpole and King George II against speculation, the primary objective of that legislation was to repress competitors of the South Sea Company because the other bubbles were draining cash that the South Sea Company wanted and needed.[4] The Bubble Act, which had been strengthened in 1749, made both swindles and starting a legitimate business more difficult and was not repealed until the nineteenth century.

The banking authorities began to warn about speculative booms in the nineteenth century. In the spring of 1825, Prime Minister Canning, the Chancellor of the Exchequer, Lord Liverpool, Sir Francis Baring, and W. R. McCulloch in *The Scotsman* warned against the excesses of speculation. The warning contributed to the crisis—but the crisis was probably inevitable. In the panic and crash of December 1825, Lord Liverpool did not rescue the speculators because nine months earlier he had said he would not.[5] In 1837 the President of the Board of Trade, J. Poulett Thomson, excoriated the prevalent spirit of speculation, which differed from that of 1825 in that individuals were investing in Britain rather than abroad.[6]

In the autumn of 1837, the gambling spirit crossed the Channel, and the Belgian and French authorities attempted to repress speculation by forbidding the quotation of the prices of notes and the prices of shares of corporations. Their efforts were futile; speculation had gone beyond the narrow framework of the Bourse and non-professionals such as *rentiers* and even 'women and foreigners' were becoming involved. Chambers of Commerce in Liège, Vervier, and Antwerp condemned stock market speculation. The Belgian king refused to charter a proposed bank, the Mutualité Industrielle. Investment slowed as a result of a decline in economic activity rather than in response to the statements from the administration and business establishment.[7] In July 1839, Lamartine in the French Chamber of Deputies spoke against speculation and especially warned about the guarantee of railroad securities.[8]

The only suggestion that official condemnation of speculation may have been effective was from a French observer who commented on the 1857

crisis. In March 1856 the minister of the interior brought legal action against certain swindlers. Emperor Napoleon III congratulated O. de Vallée, the author of *Les Manieurs d'Argent*, which dealt sternly with dubious financial practices. The Senate passed laws; the Bank of France raised the discount rate to 10 percent and Napoleon III published a letter in *Le Moniteur* on 11 December that indicated that the government would provide support only for those catastrophes that were beyond human anticipation. According to d'Ormesson, speculative exuberance declined and the memory of the 1857 crisis reflected a certain glory on French commerce.[9] But Rosenberg concluded that the warnings had been too late.[10]

Restrictions by the Austrian National Bank in 1869 produced a 'great crash' that proved to be modest compared with the one that followed in 1873.[11] The warnings and revelations of Eduard Lasker, a member of the Diet who in February 1873 had exposed the scandalous connections between the Prussian government and its commerce ministry and the railroad concessionaires had no significant impact in dampening speculative sentiment.[12]

More timely were warnings issued by *The Economist* in 1888 against commitments to buy *cedulas*, the Argentinean land bonds. In April *The Economist* said that 'the bonds … might … become a very inadequate security. Just at present all real estate at the River Plate commands inflated prices, but the occurrence of financial difficulties might easily render them unsaleable.'[13] Then in May 'A collapse of the "boom" in real estate, which is easily conceivable, would be sure to severely depress the value of the cedulas.'[14] The warnings proved ineffective.

More memorable is the Cassandra-like utterance of Paul Warburg, a partner of Kuhn, Loeb & Co. and one of the founders of the Federal Reserve System, who in February 1929 warned the American public that US stock prices were too high and showed symptoms reminiscent of the 1907 panic; his statement followed a similar statement from the Chairman of the Federal Reserve Board. Investors paused briefly and then stock prices again increased. The ineffectiveness of Federal Reserve Chairman Greenspan's December 1996 statement about 'irrational exuberance' in the high level of US stock prices was noted earlier. In August 1999 Greenspan stated that the Fed would consider the level of stock prices when it set interest rates after the Fed had increased the discount rate by 0.25 percent. Again the stock market barely noticed.

If prices of real estate and stocks continue to increase despite these warnings, then it appears that the warnings lack credibility. Economic forecasters may know—or at least think they know—the long-run equilibrium prices for

real estate and for stocks, but the ability to foretell when market prices will decline toward their long-run average values rather than away from them is modest. Roger Babson sold his clients' stocks in 1928 and he then appeared foolish as stock prices continued to increase for more than a year.

The question of the appropriate time for the authorities to issue a warning is complex. If the government authorities want their warnings to be effective, they need to provide their cautionary statements early enough to forestall some of the excesses of the euphoric period and late enough so their statements are credible. Neither task is easy.

Attempting to convince speculators of the errors of their ways is generally futile.

Financial Distress

Distress is widely discussed in connection with financial crises. The term is imprecise: one meaning is a state of suffering and another is of a hazardous situation. Commercial distress reflects the first definition, and financial distress the second. Commercial distress implies that prices and economic activity and profitability have declined and that many mercantile and industrial firms have gone bankrupt—or are on their path to bankruptcy. Financial distress for an individual firm means that it is incurring significant losses and that there is a non-trivial probability that it will not have enough cash to pay the interest on its debt according to the agreed-upon schedule.[15] The credit panic in the last several months of 2008 led to a sharp decline in automobile sales, and both General Motors and Chrysler became bankrupt. Financial distress for an economy also has a prospective significance and implies the need for economic adjustments; firms may be on the verge of bankruptcy and the exceptionally large loan losses of the banks are likely to mean that some may need additional capital. The US government developed a $700 billion-plus Troubled Assets Relief Program (TARP) that made money available to strengthen the capital positions of banks and other financial firms; in effect, the US government purchased newly issued preferred shares in each of these banks. The US government was reluctant to indicate which banks had the most desperate need for additional capital and hence it required that a large number of banks sell newly issued preferred shares to the US Treasury.

Many investment projects become stalled because the developers could not obtain the money that they needed to complete construction. The eyeball test is that there may be a lot of construction cranes at the various building sites,

but many may not be moving because the developers are unable to borrow the additional money that would move the projects toward completion.

Other words used to describe the interval between the end of euphoria and the onset of what classic writers called revulsion and discredit (or crash and panic) are *uneasiness, apprehension, tension, stringency, pressure, uncertainty, ominous conditions, fragility*. More colorful expressions include *an ugly drop in the market*[16] or *a thundery atmosphere*.[17] Meteorological metaphors have been used frequently: 'One feels again the oppressive atmosphere that precedes a storm.'[18] And geological metaphors have been used: two years before the panic of 1847 Lord Overstone wrote to his friend G. W. Norman (the grandfather of Montagu Norman, the Governor of the Bank of England in the 1920s): 'We have no crash at present, only a slight premonitory movement of the ground under our feet.'[19] The seismographic metaphor was also used by Michel Chevalier who wrote from America about President Jackson's war against the Second Bank of the United States: 'A general collapse of credit, however short the time it lasts, is more fearful than the most terrible earthquake.'[20] Another French writer noted the 'presentiment of disaster.'[21] A German metaphor spoke of the 'bow being so bent in the fall of 1782 that it threatened to snap.'[22]

Distress is not an easily measured condition for an economy. Investors may have become apprehensive when the prices and values of certain variables diverged significantly from their long-run averages; some of these variables include the gold reserve ratios of central banks, the ratio of debt to capital of a large number of firms or individuals, the losses of banks in relation to their capital, the ratios of a country's external debt service payments to its export earnings, and the price-earnings ratios for stocks and the rental rate of return on real estate. Investors may be increasingly aware of the approach to a limit, such as the ceiling on the note issues by the Bank of England stipulated in the Bank Act of 1844, the $100 million gold minimum requirement of the US Treasury in 1893, the ceiling on advances from the Bank of France to the French Treasury in 1924, the gold reserve ratio of the Reichsbank under the Dawes Plan in June 1931, or the free gold available to the Federal Reserve System prior to the passage of the Glass-Steagall Act in February 1932. A ratio of external debt to GDP of 60 percent for a country has been viewed as a premonitory indicator by investors; the 'ice is thin' for a country when this ratio is much higher. Similarly, a ratio of government debt to GDP of significantly more than 60 percent often has been viewed as too high. Limits excite, as one Chancellor of the Exchequer noted in 1857:

Now when you impose a limit, there is no question that the existence of that limit, provided it makes itself felt at a time of crisis, must increase the alarm. People feel at the moment that a peril presses on them, they begin to calculate how much remains of that fund to which they look for assistance in times of commercial difficulty, and in whatever way you fix the limit, whether by Act of Parliament, or, as Mr. Thomas Tooke [a leader of the Banking School] proposed, by a sort of usage, or, as in France, by the discretion of the Government acting on the Bank of France, there is no doubt that in moments of crisis the limit must aggravate the alarm.[23]

A French official expressed the same idea two decades later when he defended the tradition that the Bank of France should maintain a specie reserve of about one-third of its demand liabilities but without a hard and fast legal requirement: 'A fixed ratio is not required. That would be unwise … the terror of a limit fixed and absolute.'[24] Overshooting of the limit may have psychological significance. In March 1924, although sophisticated bankers knew that a small increase in the French money supply would not be dangerous, the public had come to regard the ceiling on the advances from the Bank of France to the French Treasury as an index of economic health. As one minister put it, the French were close to the upper limit of elasticity of confidence in their own currency.[25]

Causes of distress and the symptoms of distress are observed at the same time and include sharply rising interest rates in some or all segments of the capital market, an increase in the interest rates paid by subprime borrowers relative to the interest rates paid by prime borrowers, a sharp decline in the price of the currency, an increase in bankruptcies, and an end of price increases in commodities, securities, and real estate. These developments are often related and show that the lenders have become over-extended and are trying to reduce their exposure to risks and especially to large risks.

Financial distress in the nineteenth century was compounded by the arrangements for purchases of newly issued stock that provided for a series of payments by the buyers in response to 'calls' from the issuers of stocks as construction work proceeded. In 1825 and again in 1847 in Britain and in 1882 in France some of the buyers of the stocks did not have the cash to meet the calls; they may have counted on selling the stocks at a profit before the next call. Thomas Tooke describes this embarrassment in 1825 as acute because the call for cash payment was immediate and pressing while prospects for earnings on the stock were remote and uncertain.[26] Distress developed in January 1847 when railroad calls amounted to £6.5 million in one month.[27]

The chain letter aspect of security issues became evident in the finances of the South Sea Company in June, July, and August 1720 with repeated

attempts to raise cash through new issues of stock. In 1881 more than 125 new issues with a market value of 5 billion francs were sold in Paris when France's annual savings were estimated at 2 billion francs.[28] Nor was this an era when private companies were going public in large numbers, as in the late 1880s in Britain and the late 1920s in the United States; in both cases, there was no need for an increase in savings because the newly issued publicly owned shares were exchanged for privately owned shares.

The end of a period of rising prices for securities and assets leads to distress whenever a significant number of investors have based their purchases of these securities on the anticipation that their prices will continue to increase at a rapid rate—or even at a slow rate. Some of these investors then may have a 'negative carry' because the interest rates on the funds borrowed to buy the securities and assets exceed the cash income on these securities; these investors anticipated that they would be able to use the increase in the prices of securities and of assets as collateral for new loans that would provide them with the cash that they would need for interest payments. When the prices of securities stop increasing, these investors are shunted into distress mode since they have no ready way to get the cash that they need to pay the interest.

The Date of No Return

One of the best-selling American novels in the late 1940s was J. P. Marquand's *Point of No Return*. The concept implicit in the title can be readily modified into the 'Date of No Return.' The banking crisis in Iceland occurred in September 2008, about the time that Lehman Brothers failed. The Icelandic banks failed because they could no longer borrow enough money from the major international banks to pay the interest that they owed to these lenders. If these foreign banks had stopped lending to the Icelandic banks on the fourth of July 2008, the Icelandic banks almost certainly would have failed the next day. Similarly, if the foreign banks had stopped lending to the Icelandic banks on the fourth of July 2007, the Icelandic banks almost certainly would have closed within a day or two. The cutoff in the supply of new loans would have meant that the price of the Icelandic krona would have declined sharply, which would have led to the surge in the indebtedness of those Icelandic borrowers with IOUs denominated in the euro or the Swiss franc. Some of these borrowers would have defaulted on their foreign loans as well as on their domestic loans.

The earlier the date when the foreign banks would have blown the whistle on additional lending to the Icelandic banks, the smaller the likelihood that the Icelandic banks would have defaulted. Still, the likelihood seems high that if this whistle had been blown at any time after the spring of 2005, it

would have followed because the price of the Icelandic krona was high and the external indebtedness was high.

One question raised by this observation is why the lenders continued to increase their loans to Iceland after the borrowers had long since passed the date of no return. And, similarly, why did the International Monetary Fund and the Organization for Economic Cooperation and Development fail to recognize that a crisis in Iceland was inevitable or highly likely or even fifty percent probable?

The date of no return question can be applied to the analysis of the US financial crisis of September 2008. That crisis was not an Act of God, a bolt from the blue, that suddenly hit the US financial markets. Instead the crisis was the crescendo of a set of prior events that led to surges in indebtedness to levels that were too high to be sustained.

Distress enveloped the market for subprime mortgages toward the end of 2006 and 2007 when US real estate prices began to fall. The hallmark of these mortgages is that the down payment by the homebuyers often was less than ten percent of the purchase price and in some cases, the homebuyers had negative equity from the first day because the amounts of their mortgage loans were increased to cover closing costs; when prices began to fall, these borrowers immediately had 'upside-down mortgages.' One response to the distress was 'jingle mail'—to ship the keys to the properties to the lenders.

Distress may arise from an increase in the flow of funds out of the country—a bad harvest may require an increase in imports and an increase in interest rates in a major international financial center may attract funds from the domestic financial market. Credit in the domestic credit market might become less readily available—tighter—because of a reduction in the reserves of the banking system.

The potential investment outflow from a country has been a source of distress; there was distress in the London money market in 1872 when the French payment of reparations to Prussia meant that the Reichsbank acquired substantial money market securities denominated in the British pound that could be readily converted into gold. Similarly, there was an investment inflow to London prior to April 1925 in anticipation that the price of the British pound would increase to its pre-war gold parity; once the pound was again pegged to gold, the owners of these deposits had modest incentives to keep them in London. The Bank of England's interest rate policy was constrained by the concern that some of these funds might leave London. The Bank of France acquired large British pound balances in an effort to

limit the increase in the price of the French franc after the successful mone-
tary stabilization at the end of 1926; the likelihood that the French might use
part or all of these balances to buy gold was a bargaining chip that increased
nervousness at the Bank of England.

The essence of financial distress is loss of confidence. What comes next—
greater confidence in the future as imbalances in the economy are corrected,
or instead runs on banks, panics, and the collapse of prices?

The issue is concisely posed by James S. Gibbons:

> Bank officers are not always insensible to alarm when respectable merchants,
> failing in their best endeavors, are driven into a corner and assume an air
> of desperation. They know the danger that hangs over the market. Credit is
> prodigiously extended; the public excitement is wrought up to a high pitch
> of apprehension, and there need be but a single failure of a 'great house' to
> explode the 'mighty bubble.' Who knows that it is a bubble? Who knows that
> the highest point of pressure is not reached today, and that tomorrow the
> waters will not begin to subside? And then gradually things fall into their old
> channels, confidence revives and it is proved that there was no bubble to burst
> after all.[29]

How Long Does Distress Last?

Financial distress may subside as in France in 1866 and in Britain in 1873
and 1907 and panic may not follow the distress. In the United States, there
was great concern over the failed attempt by Bunker Hunt to corner the
silver market in 1979, the failure of the Continental Illinois Bank in 1984,
and the debacle of Long-Term Capital Management in 1998. There were
extended periods of distress after August 1982 over bank loans to Mexico,
Brazil, and other developing countries and over loans by the thrift institu-
tions in Louisiana, Oklahoma, and Texas to borrowers who had based their
exploration activities on the prospect that the oil price would increase to $70
or $80 a barrel. After the collapse of hundreds of US banks and thrift insti-
tutions at the end of the 1980s, the US Resolution Trust Corporation (RTC)
acquired tens of billions of dollars of real estate that had been the collateral
for mortgage loans that were in default. Eventually these properties were sold
to the public but the uncertainty about the amounts that the buyers would
pay for these properties depressed their prices.

The sharp decline in stock prices on Monday 19 October 1987 proved
to be a correction rather than a panic because it did not spread to other
US markets, although there were nearly simultaneous sharp declines in stock

prices in nearly every other country except Japan. Distress lasted for several weeks while investors waited to see whether the decline in stock prices would have significant impacts on other markets.

The crash or panic that follows financial distress may do so immediately, in a matter of weeks, or with a delay of several years. John Law's system peaked in December 1719 and collapsed in May 1720—five or six months from glory to disaster. In the South Sea Bubble of 1720, the lunatic note sounded clearly at the end of April, the ugly drop in the market occurred in August, and the collapse came in the first days of September. In 1763 distress developed in March while the actual crisis precipitated by the failure of DeNeufville in Amsterdam occurred in July. The Bank of England raised its discount rate early in 1772; the Ayr Bank curtailed its operations in May, but it was too late. Fordyce absconded on 10 June and the news precipitated panic in Britain on 22 June; the consequent distress in Amsterdam lasted until the failure of Clifford & Co. in December.

The timing of crises from 1789 to 1815 was dominated by individual apocalyptic events, including the guillotining of Louis XVI in January 1793 (losing one's head almost always is apocalyptic), the landing of the French army at Fishguard on the southwestern tip of Wales in February 1797, and the penetration of the continental blockade in 1799. The periods of distress on these occasions were short because the panic was almost immediate. In 1809–10 the setback arose from a tightening of the continental blockade and overtrading in exports to Brazil. Pressure mounted slowly from the middle of 1809, then more rapidly from mid-1810 to the climax of bankruptcies in January 1811.

Calls for further payments on subscriptions to the shares in railroads in January 1847 set the background of tension against which speculation in grain peaked in May, collapsed in August, and led to a panic in November. The crisis of 1866 was the delayed result of the 1864 collapse of cotton prices that had brought panic to France in that year. Britain had two 'critical moments' in 1864, one in January—the real crisis that was related to the collapse in cotton prices—and another in the fourth quarter.[30] British treatment of the period tends to look more to speculative expansion that affected the discount houses and that started in the previous year, and to a series of firms that resembled the Credit Mobilier and were using the funds received from selling new share issues to buy their own shares to pump up the wealth of their investors. W. T. C. King wrote that one Albert Gottheimer used the name Albert Grant to float the imposing Credit Foncier and Mobilier of England, which ultimately achieved a paid-up or rather called-up capital of £1 million.[31] The conversion of the discount house of Overend, Gurney &

Co. to a public company in July 1865 at the peak of the boom and 'dividend race' led to a 100 percent premium on the stock in October. The Bank of England responded by raising its discount rate from 3 to 7 percent; the crash did not occur until May 1866. The distress in Britain lasted seven months, from October 1865 to May 1866, while the distress in France lasted nearly thirty months.

Periods of financial stringency and crisis and panic (in the United States) occurred in the autumn when Western banks in the grain-producing areas borrowed large sums of money from the banks in the East to finance the payment for the purchases of cereals from the farmers by the grain dealers.[32] Sprague noted that the crisis of 1873 came in September because of the early harvest, that the outbreak of a crisis invariably came as a surprise to the business community and that the crisis of 1873 was not an exception.[33] The seasonal tightness of money was well known and nevertheless the puzzle is that it was a surprise. The 'excessive tightness' of money from September 1872 to May 1873 caused the railroads to borrow short-term funds rather than issue bonds, which could have been seen as a sign of distress, and then the seasonal tightness precipitated the crash.[34]

Distress may be continuous or it may oscillate in its own rhythm. The crash of the Union Générale in January 1882 was preceded by three separate tense periods, in July, October, and December 1881.[35] The panic of October 1907 was anticipated (although Sprague indicated its exact timing was not foreseeable) and preceded by a 'rich man's panic' in March when Union Pacific stock, the security most widely used as collateral for finance bill operations, dropped 50 points.[36] Markets recovered from this blow and from the failure of an offering of New York City 4 percent bonds in June (only $2 million was tendered for an offering of $29 million of these bonds) and from the collapse of the copper market in July, and from the $29 million fine levied against the Standard Oil Company for antitrust law violations in August—only to succumb to the failure of the Knickerbocker Trust Company in October.[37] In 1929 distress lasted from June to the last week in October.

Distress in Tokyo extended in the 1990s until the runs and nationalizations in 1997–1998. On any 'mark to market' test most of the large Japanese banks were bankrupt for most of the decade and they kept 'zombie' firms alive with new lending. Yet they did not experience any runs by domestic depositors who understood that they would be made whole by the government if any of the banks closed. Nevertheless, the uncertainty about the Japanese government's policies toward these failed institutions caused distress: would the government close these failed banks or would the government provide new capital to them on favorable terms?

Argentina experienced an extended period of distress at the end of the 1990s and in 2000 before its currency collapsed in January 2001. At the end of the 1980s, Argentina had suffered through two years of hyperinflation. The incoming government of President Carlos Menem pegged the new Argentinean peso to the US dollar at the rate of one Argentinean peso to one US dollar; at the same time, Argentina adopted a currency board arrangement that meant that its central bank would increase the supply of peso liabilities only if its holdings of US dollars increased—more or less a very strict application of the Currency School doctrine. During the 1990s, the tax revenues of the Argentinean government were smaller than its expenditures and the fiscal deficit was financed partly with the receipts from privatization of government-owned firms and partly by government borrowing. The hyperinflation of the 1980s had sharply reduced the real value of the Argentinean government debt and so investors purchased the Argentinean government bonds denominated in the US dollar because the government looked like a good credit risk; initially the ratio of government debt to the country's GDP was low. As the ratio of Argentinean government debt to the country's GDP increased, the interest rates that the government had to pay to sell new bonds increased. There was a recession in Argentina toward the end of the decade because as the price of the US dollar increased during its stock market boom, the price of the peso increased at the same time, Argentinean imports increased relative to its exports, economic activity slowed and the Argentinean fiscal deficit increased as its tax receipts declined relative to its expenditures. The recession was intensified by the decline in the price of the Brazilian real in January 1998 because Brazil was Argentina's major trading partner. The policy question was whether Argentina would be able to reduce its fiscal deficit while maintaining the established parity of one Argentinean peso for each US dollar. (The Argentineans do not have an established tradition of paying taxes, so tax rates tend to be high and tax collections low, while government salaries tend to be high and the performance of government officials low.) The efforts to raise taxes and cut government expenditures led to a series of political problems; Argentinean citizens were extremely reluctant to pay more taxes when the economy was doing poorly. The country was moving in slow motion toward a disaster. In the end, the price of the Argentinean currency declined sharply and the government defaulted on its external debt.

Suppose the monetary authorities, instead of standing there with moral suasion, actually do something and tighten credit to raise the cost of speculation. When the prices in the commodity and the security markets move together, up or down, the direction that monetary policy should take is clear.

But when share prices or real estate or both soar while commodity prices are stable or falling the authorities face a dilemma. The Federal Reserve encountered this dilemma in the 1920s; President Benjamin Strong of the New York Fed agonized over the appropriate policy in 1925 and again in 1927. Policymakers cannot kill two birds with one stone, or more precisely they cannot achieve two policy targets with one policy instrument, or in what is perhaps a better metaphor, it is difficult to pick off a target if it is standing next to another target that one wants to leave untouched and the weapon is a shotgun rather than a rifle. In 1929 and 1990, monetary policy was at last and reluctantly pressed into service, to set off, if it did not 'cause,' the New York 1929 and the Tokyo 1990 crashes.[38]

Fed Chairman Greenspan was concerned that US stock prices were too high or increasing too rapidly when he remarked about 'irrational exuberance' in December 1996. The Fed proved reluctant to raise interest rates to dampen the increase in stock prices because of the negative impacts on economic growth and employment. In 1999 the Fed became concerned (obsessed?) with the Y2K problem, the likelihood that US computer systems would collapse because so many software programs were not designed to recognize the transition to the year 2000. In the last several months of the year, the Fed provided the monetary system with abundant liquidity to forestall any problems associated with the end-of-the-millennium transition and in the meantime the money—which had to go somewhere—led to further increases in stock prices.

Bear Stearns, Fannie Mae and Freddie Mac, and Lehman Brothers

Over a year of distress preceded the Lehman panic. One of the first signs of adjustment in the United States to the extraordinary increase in home prices and the large excess supply of homes that began in 2002 was a surge in the bankruptcies of mortgage brokers that started in the last few months of 2006; these firms were 'middlemen' and wholesalers who acquired mortgages from home buyers. These brokers set the terms of the mortgages that they would acquire and then sold the mortgages to the investment banks, who placed mortgages with similar terms in a trust that they would use as collateral for issuing mortgage-backed securities (MBSs). The investment banks retained the right to 'put' any mortgage loan back to a broker if the borrower stopped making the required monthly payments within the first 12 or 18 months after the mortgage was originated. As borrowers failed to make their scheduled

loan payments, the investment banks returned these mortgage loans to the brokers and asked for the return of their money. The brokers that were unable to repay went bankrupt, and the investment banks then were stuck with tens of billions of dollars of failed mortgages.

The combination of the default by those who had recently borrowed to buy homes and the failure of the mortgage brokers led to a sharp decline in the supply of credit available for mortgages. The pace of home purchases slackened. The property developers that had built homes in anticipation of future sales experienced a surge in their inventories of unsold properties.

House prices in some of the regional markets peaked toward the end of 2005, and at the national level at the end of 2006. The decline of housing prices of nearly 15 percent in 2007 led to a dramatic fall in new housing starts.

The first major casualty was associated with Bear Stearns; two of the leveraged hedge funds that it managed tanked in June 2007, and the investors in these funds lost most of their money. Then in early August BNP Paribas froze investments in funds invested in mortgage securities. Then there was a run on Countrywide Financial, the largest US mortgage lender, in mid-August 2007. At the same time, there was a run on Northern Rock, which was the largest mortgage lender in Britain. Both firms had been aggressive in their efforts to increase their share of the market for mortgages, both had relied on short-term wholesale funding for much of the money that they used to buy mortgage loans. In effect both Countrywide and Northern Rock had obtained some of the cash that they used to buy more mortgages from selling their short-term IOUs; the buyers of these IOUs were the firms that had extra cash.

Countrywide Financial was rescued by Bank of America, which initially made a capital investment through the purchases of preferred shares and subsequently acquired Countrywide. Northern Rock was rescued by the Bank of England, which initially provided liquidity; subsequently, the British government acquired shares in Northern Rock and became its owner.

The next striking development was the two runs on Bear Stearns in March 2009, one by the owners of its shares and the other by those who owned fixed-price claims on Bear and were reluctant or unwilling to acquire new claims on Bear as the ones they owned matured. The Federal Reserve facilitated JPMorgan Chase's acquisition of Bear by agreeing to accept up to $29 billion of losses on 'toxic' securities of dubious quality that Bear owned.

Fannie Mae and Freddie Mac, the two very large government-sponsored enterprises that carried more than 50 percent of the credit risk attached to US home mortgages, were placed in conservatorship (in effect, 'nationalized')

by the US Treasury in the second week of September 2008. The owners of their shares were wiped out, including banks that held their preferred shares. Thus the bankruptcy of Freddie and Fannie led to a decline in the capital of banks that owned the preferred shares in Freddie and Fannie.

Lehman Brothers went bankrupt, three days after Freddie and Fannie were taken over by the US Treasury, because the US government had decided that it didn't want to 'save Lehman.' Officials at the US Treasury and the Federal Reserve said that they didn't have the authority to save Lehman. Perhaps they could have found the authority if they had tried harder. Or they could have provided some temporary financial assistance to enable Lehman to avoid bankruptcy while they acquired the legal authority to save Lehman.

The decision not to 'save Lehman' triggered the most massive US credit crisis in the last one hundred years; credit spreads soared. Lehman had issued commercial paper; when Lehman closed, this market was disrupted in a massive way, and the firms that had relied on the sale of their IOUs in this market for short-term financing were placed in a serious bind.

The households and business firms that owned shares in money market funds—established primarily by brokerage firms as an alternative to government-guaranteed bank deposits—became more cautious and withdrew money from these funds.

The standard narrative is that the decision not to 'save Lehman' reflected that government officials were concerned by the public outrage about 'bailing out' the rich bankers. They—like officials and analysts in the previous two hundred years—believed that saving a large firm would encourage risky financial behavior ten and twenty and thirty years in the future. But there are several backstories. One is that there was intense personal enmity between Richard Fuld of Lehman and Hank Paulson, then the Secretary of the US Treasury; previously Paulson had been the number one at Goldman Sachs. Fuld is said to have had a lot of Goldman envy.

Then on Tuesday 14 September—the day after Lehman failed—the Federal Reserve lent $85 billion to AIG; the loan gave the Fed the option to buy 79.9 percent of AIG's stock. AIG was primarily an insurance company, although it owned a bank. One subsidiary of the insurance company had written billions of dollars of credit default swaps (CDSs), which provided their buyers with the guarantee that if some of the bonds they owned went into default, the subsidiary would ensure that the owner of the swap would be made whole. Investors who owned private mortgage-backed bonds had bought the CDSs from the AIG subsidiary to minimize the loss if such bonds defaulted. The AIG subsidiary's motivation for selling the CDSs was the premiums that it would receive from the buyers of the CDSs. The fear

was that AIG would not have enough cash to pay the owners of the CDSs if the insured bonds tanked. The 'too-big-to-fail' doctrine had been revived. The concern was that if AIG closed, runs on many other financial institutions would occur, and the dramatic rush for cash would lead to the collapse of many other firms.

The interplay between the decline in real estate prices and bank loan losses was inevitable and predictable, although not all of the names of the firms that would be pummeled and fail during the crisis could have been predicted. However, those firms that recently had rapidly increased their market share—Countrywide, Northern Rock, Washington Mutual—had done so on the basis of short-term funds borrowed in the wholesale market and hence were much more vulnerable to runs on their liabilities than the lenders that relied almost exclusively on deposits for the money to buy mortgages. And to cope with a run, these firms would have to sell securities at a time when potential buyers would be scarce because lenders would be in a 'save cash' mode.

The major question is whether the decline in US real estate prices was predictable, and then how many of these subsequent developments were predictable in response to the decline in real estate prices. The market value of US real estate had nearly doubled in four years after 2002. The excess supply of unsold homes was increasing; many had been purchased by investors who anticipated selling these properties at even higher prices.

At some stage, it was inevitable that property prices would stop increasing, and that they would then begin to decline. The net worth of millions of households would decline as property prices fell. Several millions of these households then would have 'upside-down mortgages'—the amounts that they would owe on their mortgage loans would be greater than the market value of their homes. Millions would walk away from these properties, and leave the lenders with losses.

Onset of a Crisis

Students of logic have discussed the damp squib thrown by A that lands at B's feet which is then thrown from B to C and from C to D, and so on only to explode after Y throws it in Z's face. Who is to blame? A, *causa remota*? Or Y, *causa proxima*? *Causa remota* of any crisis is the expansion of credit and speculation while *causa proxima* is some incident that saps the confidence of the system and induces investors to sell commodities, stocks, real estate, bills of exchange or promissory notes, and increase their money holdings. The *causa proxima* may be trivial: a bankruptcy, a suicide, a flight, a revelation

of fraud, a refusal of credit to some borrowers, or some change of view that leads a market participant with a large position to sell. Prices fall. Expectations are reversed. The pace of the decline in prices accelerates. To the extent that investors have used borrowed money to finance their purchases of stocks and real estate, the decline in prices is likely to lead to calls for more margin or cash and to further sales of stocks or real estate. As prices fall further, bank loan losses increase and one or more trading firms, banks, discount houses or brokerages fail. The credit system appears shaky, and there is a race for money and liquidity.

Identifying the original sellers is difficult. Conspiracy theories abound. One can single out bear speculators like Joseph P. Kennedy, Sr, or Bernard Baruch in 1929; the Protestant-Jewish cartel that allegedly did in Eugène Bontoux in 1882; or Thomas Guy, who liquidated £54,000 of South Sea stock over six weeks between April and June 1720, never selling more than shares worth £1000 at a time. (He used his fortune to endow Guy's Hospital in London, 'the best memorial of the Bubble.')[39]

Someone sells. Occasionally it is a foreigner. In 1847, for example, the French (according to one S. Saunders, quoted by Evans) bought up surplus wheat and sent it to Britain in June and July where it was sold at prices much below the then-prevailing market prices, which fell from 96 to 56 shillings per quarter (a quarter is equal to eight bushels) and brought about the bankrupt-cies of a large number of firms connected with the corn trade.[40] The story is not persuasive. The price of wheat had risen from 46 shillings in August 1846 to 93 shillings in May 1847 because of the violent storms that had ruined the crop and because of the potato blight in Ireland and on the Continent. The price dropped in July 1847 with favorable weather and the prospect of a good crop. Imports of wheat and flour rose from 2.3 million quarters in 1846 to 4.4 million in 1847, aided by the repeal of the Corn Laws[41]; the 70,000 quarters are a trivial proportion of this sum. In 1846 France had its smallest crop of wheat in 100 years (a problem exacerbated by the potato crop failure); in 1847 the crop was the largest in 100 years. But the condition was general, and British wheat speculation had been excessive.

One view is that the Baring crisis of 1890 was triggered by the sale of Argentinean bonds by German investors, who had stopped buying these bonds two years earlier either because of general uneasiness,[42] or because they were concerned about the instability of the Argentinean currency,[43] or because the domestic boom led them to sell foreign bonds including Russian bonds.[44] German sales of the Argentinean bonds contributed to distress rather than to a crisis since British investors then acquired more of the Argen-tinean bonds. In November 1888 a £3.5 million offering of the Buenos Aires

Drainage and Waterworks Company failed, and Baring felt obliged to lend to Argentina through acceptance credits. Declining primary product prices in 1890 meant that the Argentine government did not have the money to repay these loans as they came due. The Baring crisis of November 1890, after two years of distress, resulted from a warning from the Bank of England to Baring Brothers to limit the level of its acceptances (which stood at £30 million in the summer of 1890), from the crisis in New York in October, and from the maturing of £4 million of acceptances in November.

New information may precipitate a crash, as when it was revealed that the Paris-Lyons-Marseilles railroad would cost 300 million francs instead of the projected 200 million.[45] *Causa remota*, and much more important, were the large balance of payments deficits from extensive imports of railroad materials and, especially, the crop failure of 1846 followed by the glut of 1847. The Granger movement helped precipitate the collapse of cereal prices in the United States in 1873. The Grangers, who in some ways resembled today's environmentalists, started in the late 1860s and early 1870s as activists for legislation that would control interstate transportation by prohibiting discriminatory freight rates, establish regulatory commissions, and set maximum freight rates.[46] A very large volume of railroad securities had been sold on credit—including a number of 'superfluous and ridiculous' enterprises like the Rockford, Rock Island and St. Louis line which had been sold at par and then declined to 6 cents on the dollar as the prospect of local control of freight rates put an end to optimism and triggered sales and then liquidation of these bonds.

One 'accidental' detonator of a crisis has been the sinking of a ship. In 1799, when interest rates ranged between 12 and 14 percent and the price of sugar was 35 percent below the peak before the convoy had broken through the continental blockade, British merchants shipped £1 million on the frigate *Lutine* destined for Texel in an attempt to assist in the Amsterdam crisis. The ship sank in a storm off the Dutch coast and the hope of alleviating the crisis was dashed.[47] During the 1857 crisis in New York the news that the steamer *Central America*, bound from Panama to New York with a cargo including $2 million in gold, was overdue came at the time of extreme distress in Philadelphia, Cincinnati, and Chicago. Two days later it was learned that the ship had gone down, uninsured.[48]

An accident may precipitate a crisis, but so may action designed to prevent it—or action by the authorities adopted to achieve other objectives. The matter was well put by H. S. Foxwell apropos the crisis of 1808–1809:

> To refuse accommodation altogether is always held to be dangerous. To make personal reference is invidious, especially for a National Bank. It is just possible

that the Bank might have resorted to the expedient used in 1795–96, I mean the granting of pro rata discounts ... [In seeking to contract the circulation] it must have put severe pressure on the market and risked the creation of a panic ... The Bank was responsible for the solvency of this crowd of small, ill-managed institutions [country banks], but dared not call them to account, on peril of provoking a general collapse of credit.[49]

Foxwell posed the dilemma neatly. Not applying discipline will let the credit market expand to dangerous levels; applying discipline may prick the bubble and induce collapse.

Policies adopted to deal with a crisis often encounter lags. Raising the discount rate in the face of an external drain of cash may induce a return flow. In the folklore of the City of London, an increase in the discount rate of the Bank of England to 10 percent can 'draw gold from the moon,' but how long would it take to produce that result? The issue was debated between the Banking and the Currency schools in the context of the Bank Act of 1844 and the need either to suspend the Act or for the Bank to act as a lender of last resort. In 1825 and again in 1836, speculation in an economic boom led to an outflow of gold and financial stringency. On one interpretation, the boom broke before the Bank of England belatedly raised its discount rate in an effort to reduce its liabilities by encouraging demand for securities. Thus a combination of tight money and declining commodity prices produced the crisis and induced the Bank to reverse course and to reduce interest rates.[50] The Banking School believed that the increase in the discount rate produced an immediate inflow of money. One of the two wings of the Currency School, on the other hand, also believed there would be an immediate inflow, and the other, represented by Lord Overstone, thought that the increase in the discount rate would have an impact only after a lag and that a lender of last resort would be required to fill the gap.[51]

Even after the Bank of England had learned how to adjust its Bank rate better than in the 1820s and 1830s, there were still crises and in some cases crashes and panics. Hawtrey pointed to a lag at the level of commercial banks and internal drains, based on order backlogs:

Bankers may take proper steps, but panic because they work slowly: They may have really checked the fundamental danger of the position ... stopped the stress of new orders ... and yet the demand for fresh credits and the drain of cash may go undiminished. The consequence may be a state of panic among the bankers, who, unaware of the cause of the apparent ineffectiveness of the measures they have taken [the working off of the backlog of old orders], despair of saving themselves from failure, call in existing loans regardless of

the embarrassment of debtors, and precipitate a series of bankruptcies among their customers and themselves.

The fact is that there is no golden rule for keeping the extension of credits within bounds.[52]

Apart from lags and mistakes in discount policy, the authorities may precipitate a panic by brusque action in the early stages of distress. In the summer of 1836, with credit extended in acceptances drawn by American houses on British joint-stock banks, the Bank of England refused to discount any bills that carried the name of a joint-stock bank and specifically instructed its Liverpool agent not to rediscount any paper of the three so-called 'W banks' (Wiggins, Wildes, and Wilson) among the seven American banks in Britain, an action that 'seemed vindictive'[53] and led immediately to panic.[54] The Bank of England then reversed its policies and had long conferences with the 'W banks' in October; it had extended credit to them in the first quarter of 1837 but was unable to prevent their failure in June of that year. The Bank acted to dampen the extension of too large an amount of credit. But credit is delicate; expectations can quickly be altered.

Panic in the form of a run on a bank or a group of banks has usually been started by small depositors as happened in the 1980s in Ohio and Maryland and Rhode Island, where some of the state-chartered banks relied on state-chartered insurance arrangements because they charged lower premiums than the FDIC. (All federally chartered banks and thrifts were required to participate in the federal government's deposit insurance programs.) In contrast, panics in the stock markets often resulted from selling by big-money insider investors or institutional investors such as mutual funds, pension funds, and insurance companies, because several follow similar program-trading algorithms. The run on Franklin National Bank was initiated by other banks, especially the large money-center banks in New York that refused to take the counterpart of Franklin's forward foreign exchange contracts or to lend it federal funds or to lend to Franklin through repurchase agreements, except at rates of interest that reflected deep distrust.[55] Similarly the run on the Continental Illinois Bank in 1984 was triggered by the reluctance of other large banks to renew loans to the bank in the federal funds market and in the offshore deposit market. Smaller depositors were protected by FDIC deposit insurance. In the stock market meltdown in the autumn of 1987, the Fidelity group of mutual funds of Boston was a large seller in the London market before the New York Stock Exchange opened on 19 October. These orders were communicated to New York; by the time the New York market opened for trading a mountain of sell orders had been accumulated. Fidelity's sales were a response to the redemptions by the holders of its mutual funds

rather than for its own position, although it may have wanted to raise cash in anticipation of future redemptions—and before stock prices fell further.

The clumsiness of the International Monetary Fund triggered a run on many of the banks in Indonesia during the early days of the Asian crisis in July 1997. The IMF induced the Indonesian government to take over and support fifteen of the large private banks, in effect guaranteeing their deposits. But the remaining fifty or so other private banks then were placed in a nether-world position and were subject to runs as the depositors scrambled to withdraw funds before the banks collapsed.

Crashes and Panics

A crash is a collapse of the prices of assets, or perhaps the failure of an important bank or firm. A panic, 'a sudden fright without cause' (from the god Pan, known for causing terror), may occur in the markets for securities and involve a rush from less liquid securities to money or government securities— in the belief that governments do not go bankrupt because they can always print more money. A financial crisis may involve one or both and in either order. The collapse of the stock of the South Sea Company and the Sword Blade Bank almost brought down the Bank of England. The 1929 crash and panic in the New York Stock Market had adverse consequences in both the commodity and the real estate markets, and the seizure in the credit markets led to sharp declines in income and employment and output. But there was no panic in the money market; interest rates did not increase because the Federal Reserve provided liquidity to the market.[56] In 1893 the lack of confidence in the ability of the US government to adhere to its commitment to sell gold at the stipulated parity under pressure from the silver interests led to increases in short-term interest rates, bank failures, and declines in the prices of securities.[57]

The financial system has positive feedback. The debt-deflation cycles involve a decline in prices of securities and commodities which leads to a reduction in the market prices of collateral for bank loans and induces the lenders to call loans or refuse new ones; firms sell commodities and inventories because their prices are falling, and the decline in prices causes more and more firms to fail. Households sell securities and firms postpone borrowing and investing and prices fall still further. Further declines in the market prices of the securities offered as loan collateral lead to further liquidation. The failure of firms means that the banks incur loan losses and fail. As banks fail,

depositors withdraw their money, especially before deposit insurance became readily available.

Deposit withdrawals require more loans to be called, more securities to be sold. Trading firms, industrial firms, investors, banks in need of ready cash—their riskiest securities cannot be sold at any price, they are forced to sell their least risky securities to minimize their losses, and the prices of these securities decline. The banks may carry the firms, corporations, and households that are known to be in trouble for a time in the expectation or hope that prices will increase again and refloat the frail bark of credit. Bank examiners may *in extremis* look the other way as banks continue to value loans and securities at cost rather than at market value, extend loans due or add to loans of delinquent borrowers so they can pay some of the interest. But when bankruptcy occurs, the nettle of bad loans must be grasped. Prices, solvency, liquidity, and the demand for cash—in German *Bargeld*, in French *numéraire*—are related. Not only banking institutions: as Sprague stated, households, firms, and banks are 'very similar to a row of bricks, the fall of one endangering the stability of the rest.'[58] The metaphor is a cliché, but nonetheless appropriate.

At the height of the panic, money is said to be unavailable. Descriptions are frequently exaggerated, not least about 1825:

> Bankers in Lombard Street called on the Governor [of the Bank of England] on Sunday [after the panic of country banks had reached Pole, Thornton & Co. on 12 December] to warn that if such a house, drawn on by 47 country banks, were allowed to stop, a run would take place on every bank in London.
>
> It was allowed to stop. A panic seized upon the public, such as had never been witnessed before: everybody begging for money – money – but money was hardly on any condition to be had. 'It was not the character of the security,' observes the **Times**, 'that was considered: but the impossibility of producing money at all.'[59]

This was the occasion when the failure of seventy-three banks brought Britain, according to Huskisson, within twenty-four hours of barter.[60] 'It was, as the Duke said of Waterloo, "a damned nice thing – the nearest run thing you ever saw in your life".'[61] Barter was avoided by exchanging silver for gold with the Bank of France, and by luck of the Bank of England in finding, just as it ran out of £5 and £10 notes (which were then all it issued), a block of £1 notes left in the vault from 1797. With government approval, these were issued on 17 December and 'worked wonders.'[62]

In 1857 the price of the shares of the New York Central Railroad went from 93 to 61, Reading from 96 to 36.[63] The price of pork fell from $24 a barrel to $13; flour from $10 to $5.[64] In September interest rates rose from

15 to 24 percent as 150 banks in Pennsylvania, Maryland, Rhode Island, and Virginia failed in the last four days of the month. The panic reached a peak in October when 1415 banks in the United States failed and interest rates rose from 60 to 100 percent per annum—for monies borrowed for a few days.[65] Very high rates of interest, such as 4 percent a day, have sometimes been quoted for a particular kind of loan, as for call money in 1884, when commercial discounts continued at 4.5–5 percent a day for first-class endorsed paper[66]; or 5 percent a day at the peak as a premium for cash at the onset of the panic of 1907.[67] Perhaps the apogee of the liquidity squeeze was recorded in 1907 when one bank paid $48 per $1000 for the cash gate receipts of the Harvard–Yale football game.[68]

Will the storm subside, the flood crest and fall? We come to this question ultimately. Before that, we turn to swindles that may be revealed during distress and may even precipitate panic. And then come chapters on how boom and crash spread from one market and country to another and the steps taken locally and internationally to halt panic and reverse the damage it does.

Notes

1. *The Collected Works of Walter Bagehot*, ed. Norman St. John Stevas (London: The Economist, 1978), vol. 9, p. 273.
2. Milton Friedman, 'In Defense of Destabilizing Speculation', in *The Optimum Quantity of Money and Other Essays* (Chicago: Aldine, 1969), p. 288.
3. Harry G. Johnson, 'The Case for Flexible Exchange Rates, 1969', in Federal Reserve Bank of St. Louis, *Review*, vol. 51 (June 1969), p. 17.
4. John Carswell, *The South Sea Bubble* (London: Cresset Press, 1960), p. 139.
5. W. R. Brock, *Lord Liverpool and Liberal Toryism, 1820–1827* (Cambridge: Cambridge University Press, 1941), p. 209.
6. R. C. O. Matthews, *A Study of Trade-cycle History: Economic Fluctuations in Great Britain, 1832–1842* (Cambridge: Cambridge University Press, 1954), p. 162.
7. Maurice Lévy-Leboyer, *Les banques européennes et l'industrialisation internationale dans la première moitié du XIX^e siècle* (Paris: Presses universitaires de France, 1964), pp. 618–20.
8. Ibid., p. 713.
9. Wladimir d'Ormesson, *La grande crise mondiale de 1857: L'histoire recommence, les causes, les remèdes* (Paris-Suresnes: Maurice d'Hartoy, 1933), pp. 110ff.
10. Hans Rosenberg, *Die Weltwirtschaftskrise von 1857–59* (Stuttgart: Verlag von W. Kohlhammer, 1934), p. 210.

11. Max Wirth, *Geschichte der Handelskrisen*, 4th edn (1890; reprint edn, New York: Burt Franklin, 1968), p. 463.
12. Fritz Stern, *Gold and Iron: Bismarck, Bleichröder, and the Building of the German Empire* (London: Allen & Unwin, 1977), p. 242.
13. *The Economist*, 21 April 1888, p. 500. This citation and the following one were brought to the author's attention by Richard C. Marston.
14. Ibid., 5 May 1888, pp. 570–1.
15. M. J. Gordon, 'Toward a Theory of Financial Distress', *Journal of Finance*, vol. 26 (May 1971), p. 348.
16. Carswell, *South Sea Bubble*, p. 170.
17. Sir John Clapham, *The Bank of England: a History* (Cambridge: Cambridge University Press, 1945), vol. 2, p. 257.
18. Edouard Rosenbaum and A. J. Sherman, *M. M. Warburg & Co., 1758–1938: Merchant Bankers of Hamburg* (New York: Holmes & Meier, 1979), p. 129.
19. D. P. O'Brien, ed., *The Correspondence of Lord Overstone* (Cambridge: Cambridge University Press, 1971), vol. 1, p. 368.
20. Michel Chevalier, *Lettres sur l'Amérique du Nord*, 3rd edn (Brussels: Société belge du librairie, 1838), vol. 1, p. 37.
21. Jean Bouvier, *Le krach de l'Union Générale* (Paris: Presses universitaires de France, 1960), pp. 129, 133, 137.
22. Wirth, *Handelskrisen.* p. 508.
23. D. Morier Evans, *The History of the Commercial Crisis, 1857–1858, and the Stock Exchange Panic of 1859* (1859; reprint edn, New York: Augustus M. Kelley, 1969), p. 203.
24. Testimony of Louis Adolphe Thiers, Ministère des Finances et al., *Enquête sur les principes et les faits généraux qui régissent la circulation monétaire et fiduciaire* (Paris: Imprimerie imperiale, 1867), vol. 3, p. 436.
25. Stephen A. Schuker, *The End of French Predominance in Europe, the Financial Crisis of 1924 and the Adoption of the Dawes Plan* (Chapel Hill: University of North Carolina Press, 1976), pp. 87, 104.
26. Arthur D. Gayer, W. W. Rostow, and Anna J. Schwartz, *The Growth and Fluctuation of the British Economy, 1790–1850* (Oxford: Oxford University Press, Clarendon Press, 1953), vol. 1, p. 190.
27. Ibid., p. 312.
28. Bouvier, *Le krach*, pp. 29, 130.
29. James S. Gibbons, *The Banks of New York, Their Dealers, the Clearing House, and the Panic of 1857* (New York: D. Appleton, 1859), p. 94.
30. See Clément Juglar, *Des crises commerciales et leur retour périodique en France, en Angleterre et aux Etats-Unis*, 2nd edn (1889; reprint edn, New York: Augustus M. Kelley, 1967), p. 427.
31. W. T. C. King, *History of the London Discount Market* (London: George Routledge & Sons, 1936), p. 232.
32. O. M. W. Sprague, *History of Crises under the National Banking System* (1910; reprint edn, New York: Augustus M. Kelley, 1968), p. 127.

R. Z. Aliber et al.

33. Ibid., p. 33.
34. Ibid., p. 36.
35. Bouvier, *Le krach*, p. 133.
36. Christina Stead may be referring to this episode in *The House of All Nations* (New York: Simon & Schuster, 1938), when she has one of her characters, Stewart, say: "'My first job. By jove we had fun. At one time they had a short position in Union Pacific which exceeded the floating supply. Were they ruined? Not that time. They came to terms with them ... they had to, otherwise a world panic would have resulted".'
37. Sprague, *History of Crises*, pp. 237–53.
38. See C. P. Kindleberger, 'Asset Inflation and Monetary Policy', *Banca Nazionale del Lavoro Quarterly Review*, no. 192 (March 1995), pp. 17–35.
39. Carswell, *South Sea Bubble*, pp. 136–7, 158.
40. Evans, *Commercial Crisis*, p. 13.
41. Gayer, Rostow, and Schwartz, *Growth and Fluctuation*, p. 307.
42. W. Jett Lauck, *The Causes of the Panic of 1893* (Boston: Houghton Mifflin, 1907), pp. 59–60.
43. Oskar Morgenstern, *International Financial Transactions and Business Cycles* (Princeton: Princeton University Press, 1959), p. 523.
44. Part of the reason Germany sold Russian bonds was political, as was the basis for German buying of Italian bonds. The French bought Russian bonds and sold Italian bonds. But Germany did float a Mexican loan of £10.5 million in 1888, so one cannot make the case that the domestic boom in Germany required capital that in nonpolitical circumstances would have gone abroad. See Fritz Stern, *Gold and Iron: Bismarck, Bleichröder, and the Building of the German Empire* (London: Allen & Unwin, 1977), pp. 427, 433, 442. Professor Stern has indicated that there is nothing in the Bleichröder correspondence that bears on German selling of Argentine securities.
45. Johan Åkerman, *Structure et cycles économiques* (Paris: Presses universitaires de France, 1955–57), vol. 2, p. 292.
46. E. Ray McCartney, *Crisis of 1873* (Minneapolis: Burgess Publishing Co., 1935), pp. 58, 71.
47. Wirth, *Handelskrisen*, p. 110.
48. George W. Van Vleck, *The Panic of 1857: an Analytical Study* (New York: Columbia University Press, 1943), p. 68.
49. H. S. Foxwell, introduction to Andréadès, *History of the Bank of England*, p. xvii.
50. E. Victor Morgan, *The Theory and Practice of Central Banking, 1797–1913* (Cambridge: Cambridge University Press, 1943), p. 109.
51. Elmer Wood, *English Theories of Central Banking Control, 1819–1858* (Cambridge, MA: Harvard University Press, 1939), p. 183.
52. R. G. Hawtrey, *Currency and Credit*, 3rd edn (New York: Longmans, Green, 1927), p. 28.
53. Clapham, *Bank of England*, vol. 2, p. 153.

54. Leone Levi, *History of British Commerce* (London: John Murray, 1872), p. 233.
55. Joan Edelman Spero, *The Failure of the Franklin National Bank: Challenge to the International Banking System* (New York: Columbia University Press, 1980), pp. 66, 71, 85, 91.
56. Milton Friedman and Anna J. Schwartz, *A Monetary History of the United States, 1867–1960* (Princeton: Princeton University Press, 1963), p. 339.
57. Lauck, *Causes of the Panic of 1893*, chap. 7.
58. Sprague, *History of Crises*, p. 253.
59. Thomas Joplin, *Case for Parliamentary Inquiry into the Circumstances of the Panic, in a Letter to Thomas Gisbourne, Esq. M.P.* (London: F. Ridgeway & Sons, n.d. [after 1832]), pp. 14–15.
60. Robert Baxter, *The Panic of 1866, with its Lessons on the Currency Act* (1866; reprint edn., New York: Burt Franklin, 1969), pp. 4, 26.
61. Clapham, *Bank of England*, vol. 2, p. 101.
62. Ibid., p. 100.
63. Rosenberg, *Weltwirtschaftskrise*, p. 118.
64. Van Vleck, *Panic of 1857*, p. 74.
65. Rosenberg, *Weltwirtschaftskrise*, p. 121.
66. Sprague, *History of Crises*, p. 113.
67. Alvin H. Hansen, *Cycles of Prosperity and Depression in the United States, Great Britain and Germany: a Study of Monthly Data, 1902–1908* (Madison: University of Wisconsin Press, 1921), p. 13.
68. H. S. Foxwell, 'The American Crisis of 1907', in *Papers in Current Finance* (London: Macmillan, 1919), pp. 202–3.

6

Bernie Madoff: Frauds, Swindles, and the Credit Cycle

Charlie Ponzi is the most famous banker in American history, immortalized in the term 'Ponzi scheme.' Ponzi owned a small firm that sold its own IOUs, sometimes called deposits, in one of the Boston suburbs in the early 1920s; he promised to pay the buyers of his IOUs 45 percent interest in months at a time when the traditional banks were paying two or three percent. Ponzi's operation was straightforward—he used the money that he received from the sale of deposits on Wednesday to pay the interest to those who had bought the deposits on Monday. The interest rate that Ponzi paid was so high that most of those who bought the deposits on Monday were happy to keep their money with Ponzi, so they could earn 'interest on the interest.'

Eventually some of the newly rich depositors decided to withdraw some of their money, and unfortunately, the money wasn't there. Ponzi went to jail. His scheme had flourished for eighteen months.

Bernie Madoff managed the largest Ponzi scheme in American history; at the time of its collapse in December 2008 the liabilities were reported to be $50 billion or $64 billion. Madoff's gimmick was that he had a 'split strike' options strategy—but the details are boring. Madoff differed from Ponzi in one important way—his investors earned rates of return of ten to twelve percent a year. (One measurement problem is deciding whether the estimate of losses should include only the amounts of the initial deposits that individuals made with Madoff, or whether these losses should also include the 'investment income' that they supposedly earned income over the years as Madoff increased the value of their accounts by the interest. Another involves

© The Author(s), under exclusive license to Springer Nature Switzerland AG 2023
R. Z. Aliber et al., *Manias, Panics, and Crashes*,
https://doi.org/10.1007/978-3-031-16008-0_6

whether the estimate of the losses should be adjusted downward to reflect the cash that some investors withdrew from their accounts.) Madoff had run the scheme for twenty years, so he may hold the world's record for both the largest and the most long-lived Ponzi scheme.

A 2022 update reveals an amazing outcome. Of the $20 billion in initial investments in the fund in 2008 (not counting the bogus investment returns) an very high fraction, 70%, has been returned by the court. The court not only sold Madoff's penthouse apartment in New York but has also doggedly pursued the many parties who took more money out of the scheme than they put in. Of course, the 70% takes no account of the time value of money, but it is still remarkable.

Every Ponzi scheme has a 'story'—an explanation for why the firm can afford to pay rates of return so much higher than its established competitors. Ponzi said he was arbitraging international postal reply coupons. (You don't really need to know the details.) Madoff said he had a 'split strike option strategy.'

Madoff's scheme differed from Ponzi's in one other important dimension—the rate of return on the funds entrusted to Madoff was in the range of 10 to 12 percent a year—a bit higher than stocks, and much higher than on bonds. Madoff's returns were steady but not spectacular.

Ponzi was flamboyant. Madoff in contrast was understated, and he created the impression that he accepted money to invest only from a few close friends and the close friends of his close friends. Subsequent investigation showed that he had more than 4500 'close friends.' and that he relied on at least four or five 'feeder firms' to bring him new money. The payment arrangements to these feeders varied, some appeared to get 1 percent of the money up front and then another 1 percent each year the money stayed with Madoff. Subsequently the attorneys responsible for cleaning up the mess indicated that some of these feeder firms received rates of return of 40 or 50 percent a year on their own money that they invested with Madoff.

Investigation by the court-appointed attorney to seek funds for Madoff's clients showed that Madoff rarely traded any securities. In 2008 clients withdrew $11 billion from their accounts, in part because the sharp decline in stock prices meant that they were reluctant to sell the stocks whose market prices had declined sharply. Madoff went out of business when he no longer had the cash to pay those who wanted to withdraw some of the money from their accounts. Most of the clients probably withdrew the money because they were losing money on most of their other investments.

Ponzi was in jail for about two years and then he moved to Florida to sell real estate during the mid-1920s bubble around Miami. Madoff was in jail until the end of his time on earth in 2021.

Ponzi and Madoff shared one attribute—they both traded on misinformation. Both lied about the rates of return that their clients would earn. Much of the corruption in financial markets involves misrepresentation about the values of inventories, the values of investments, and profit rates. But some corruption involves the theft of information and the efforts of outsiders to obtain information from insiders before that information is publicly available.

Sharp declines in the prices of securities always lead to the discovery of fraud and swindles. As long as the prices of securities increase, investors are content and often happy to borrow against the increase in their wealth if they need the money for their living expenses. When the prices of securities decline, some of them sell securities to get the cash for living expenses. And they generally sell their most liquid securities because they can't bear to take the large losses associated with selling illiquid securities.

Ponzi schemes tend to be personal, and the basic crime is that the promoters—Madoff excepted—almost always make promises about exceptionally high rates of returns from day one. Corporate chicanery involves false statements about the value of inventories and of other assets, and the profit rate with the difference that the fraud begins long after the firm has been established. Information is withheld or dissembled. Enron was the posterchild of corporate fraud in the 1990s dot.com boom. Enron had been in business for many years—basically a low-tech pipeline company and a high-tech company that traded electricity and commodities and securities. The fraud appears to have started in the mid-1990s, when Enron needed a massive amount of money to finance its expansion. Enron began its tumble into bankruptcy within a few months of the peak in US stock prices in 2000.

Measuring the supply of corruption is not rocket science. What is 'measured' is the corruption that rises to the surface; the corruption that remains undiscovered obviously cannot be measured. Corruption is discovered when money becomes tight and credit is less readily available, and when the prices of securities decline. Corruption increases in a pro-cyclical way, much like the supply of credit. Soon after a recession begins the firms that were fueling their growth with cheap credit find that they can no longer obtain as much credit as they would like because the lenders became more cautious. In the absence of more credit, the fraud sprouts from the corporate edifice like mushrooms under the logs in a soggy forest.

Most fraudulent behavior is illegal, but some hovers on a fuzzy legal borderline. Should the award of options to senior management and

employees be considered a cost, like wages, or should the award be buried in a footnote so that costs and profits are not affected? The answer affects how rapidly profits increase and presumably how rapidly the stock prices increase. Should Henry Blodgett and Mary Meeker and Jack Grubman, the gurus of the telecom firms and dot.coms in the 1990s, have been obliged to inform the investing public of the rationale for their forecasts for the increases in the prices of individual stocks, or was it sufficient for them to announce the price targets for these stocks six and twelve months into the future—more or less like touts at the racetrack? (See 'Shills, touts, and thieves' below.) Should the governmental authorities establish 'truth police' to prevent the investing public from being misled, or should the public be on its own in determining which statements made by the stock sales personnel are not strictly true? Certain business practices are legal, yet those engaged in such activities would be reluctant or embarrassed to have their transactions reported on the front pages of the *New York Times* or the *Wall Street Journal* or the *Chicago Tribune* or the London *Daily Telegraph,* because the sunshine would awaken the victims to the con. Consider Enron, MCIWorldCom, Adelphia, Tyco, HealthSouth, Global Crossing—the stars of some of the financial excesses of the 1990s stock price bubble. Much of the fraudulent behavior initially had occurred in the mania phase as stock prices were increasing but was obscured in the froth of the sharp increases in prices; the high-risk borrowers could readily refinance their maturing loans because the lenders were eager to increase their total loans. The investment banks believed in *caveat emptor*; in their view, customers old enough to vote should be capable of looking out for their own financial interests.

The Theft of Information and Insider Trading

Information is valuable, since it leads to changes in relative prices. After World War II, several US Congressmen got rich—or at least richer—because they just happened to buy some land near the sites where new exit and entry ramps would be built for the Interstate Highway System. Information about the size of the wheat crop—actually, projections of the information—lead to changes in the price of wheat, so the information about these projections before they become available to the public is valuable. Information about the quarterly earnings of firms, especially when the change is large, often lead to sharp changes in stock prices. Mergers of firms, especially the takeover or purchase of one firm by another, often lead to sharp increases in the prices of the shares of the firm that is in play.

Corruption is multi-faceted. One form involves breaking laws, perhaps with the connivance of government officials. A great deal of corruption involves the misuse of information; someone may provide misleading information about profits, dividends, and possible mergers. Information may be stolen, and there are laws against insider trading, where well-connected individuals seek to profit from information that is likely to lead to changes in the prices of securities before that information is available to the public.

Should Goldman Sachs have told a German bank that bought some of the mortgage-backed securities in 2006 and 2007 that the suggestions for the design of these securities had come from the firm that wanted to sell them short, or was the bank regarded as sufficiently knowledgeable to conclude that someone believed that the prices of these bonds would decline? (Goldman agreed to pay more than $500 million to the Securities and Exchange Commission to keep its name out of the newspapers—about $250 million will go to the German bank that bought these bonds.)

Large certified public accounting (CPA) firms were established to protect investors from miscounts of the numbers of beans and widgets that corporate firms report; the CPAs are there to verify the bean count. Arthur Andersen, at one time one of the 'Big Five' global accounting firms and the one with a reputation for paying exceptional attention to ethical issues, was 'captured' by several of the firms that it was auditing—the firms that were paying its bills—and colluded in misleading investors. Did the law firms that provided legal advice to Enron and MCIWorldCom and the other firms that provided misleading information discharge their obligations to investors as well as to their clients—or were the lawyers, who may have had billing rates of $800 an hour, also seduced by their clients?

The banks and the investment banks were on the front pages of the newspapers when property prices declined in 2007 and 2008. The Royal Bank of Scotland together with Santander Bank of Spain and Fortis of the Netherlands and Belgium bought ABN-AMRO for $100 billion in what has proved to be one of the most costly business acquisitions of the decade. (The smartest business decision of the decade was that ABN-AMRO agreed to sell the firm to these eager buyers.) While there was no obvious fraud, there was a lot of delusional grandiosity on the part of the buyers.

AIG (the acronym for the American International Group), then the world's largest insurance company, is the 'poster child' of the 2008 collapse because of the massive amount of financial assistance that it received from the US government to avoid bankruptcy. Most of its problems stemmed from the sale of credit default swaps (CDSs), which are a form of insurance purchased by the owners of bonds to protect themselves against loss if the firms that have

issued the bonds go bankrupt. (These swaps are similar to private mortgage insurance; the mortgage lenders may require that the borrowers with less than 20 percent of the cash needed for the traditional down payment buy insurance to protect themselves from loss if the borrowers default.) The buyers of the CDSs want the higher interest rates attached to the riskier securities but want to avoid the default risk attached to these securities.

A lot of the fraud in the mortgage market in the housing boom between 2003 and 2007 occurred at the 'retail level'—borrowers lied about their incomes and their credit histories, and the mortgage brokers knew that the borrowers were lying, but hey, 'It's business.' Several senior managers of Bear Stearns were indicted for misleading investors about the quality of the securities in the hedge funds that they managed—but the jury voted 'Not Guilty.'

Several bankers in Iceland were convicted by the government of trying to manipulate the prices of the shares of their banks. This practice occurred when these prices began to decline; the bankers lent a lot of money to a friend from one of the emirates so that he could buy shares in the bank and support the price—which would have also supported the family fortunes of the Icelandic bankers. The Icelandic courts got tough on the practices of the country's bankers, and dozens did jail time.

The Classes of Swindles and Corruption

Swindles, fraudulent behavior, defalcations, and elaborate hustles are part of life in market economies, more so in some countries than in others and more so at some times than at others. Many of the swindles involve supplying misleading information about inventories and profits. Occasionally the swindle involves the theft of information—when the presumption is that in a market economy each investor should have the same information at the same time—and it's a form of fraud if some individuals jump to the head of a queue.

Transparency International publishes an annual index of corruption; Finland has a lock on the number one position in terms of virtue and Iceland was close behind until the implosion of its massive stock price bubble in 2008. (A subsequent investigation revealed that the Icelandic banks had been looted by their owners.) For many years Bangladesh, the Democratic Republic of the Congo, and Nigeria were considered the most corrupt. The United States was much nearer the top of this hit parade although it may have slipped several places in the rankings because of the extensive fraud and

deception that occurred in corporate America during the stock price bubble of the 1990s and the real estate bubble ten years later.

Overstating the value of inventories is a traditional form of swindling lenders and investors. The McKesson Robbins scandal of the late 1930s involved the use of forged warehouse receipts as collateral for loans. Billie Sol Estes, the Texas plunger of the 1960s, used fertilizer tanks he had under lease as collateral for loans, but he exaggerated the number of tanks that he had under lease when he borrowed money from the banks. Tino De Angelis stung American Express and other large lenders by using tanks of 'salad oil' in the 1960s as collateral for loans; Tino knew that that salad oil was less dense than water and he floated a six-inch layer of salad oil on top of twenty feet of water.[1]

Swindles that involve falsified statements about the value of inventories eventually can be tested. Eventually the lenders wised up to Billie Sol Estes; someone counted the fertilizer tanks—which is what the CPAs are supposed to do. The lenders can be taken in by the falsified values of the collateral offered by the borrowers, and initially the lender's accountants may not catch the deception. Swindles in financial markets may involve statements about the growth of corporate earnings or about the 'warranted' prices of shares of individual firms. Corporations 'manage' their earnings so they appear less variable from one quarter to the next, because investors will pay higher prices for the stocks of firms with stable earnings. A typical statement is that the 'price of Amazon stock' will climb to $400 a share by 4 July; or the wording might be 'Our price target is $400 a share.' Another statement might be 'Corporate profits will increase at the rate of 15 percent a year for the next five years.' Some of the swindles in the financial markets involve 'excessive optimism' about the earnings of firms or stock prices three or six months from now that those making the statements know are not likely to be true.

Wall Street makes a lot of its money selling stocks, and it prospers by having 'stars' who are paid—very well paid—to make statements that the prices of the shares of individual firms will increase; they're like the shills in front of the sideshows at carnivals who persuade the public to buy tickets to see the sword swallowers and the hermaphrodites. Stocks increase in price twice as often as they fall, so that the odds are that the 'market strategists' will be right twice as often as they are wrong—although being right on the direction is different from making the right calls on the changes in the prices of stocks. The market strategists typically are reluctant to indicate that stock prices as a group will decline and very rarely suggest that the price of the stocks of individual firms will decline (because the top executives of those firms would become furious and threaten never to bring any underwriting

business to the investment bank that employed these market strategists). If share prices decline when the pitch has been that they will increase and the touts become an embarrassment to their employers, well they've been well paid and they're expendable and, hey, it's business. It's not hard to find replacements.

Corruption can't be measured unless an economy or a society has laws or norms or rules that distinguish permissible from illegal or immoral behavior. Anything would be permissible and acceptable in a society without rules or norms; corruption would not occur because there would be no perceptible boundary between acceptable and non-acceptable behavior. Virtually every society has rules or norms—these codes about what is and what isn't acceptable behavior were adopted to reduce the costs of doing business.

Laws about illegal practices and behavior differ among countries, practices that are legal in some countries may be illegal in others. Moreover, the laws and the norms about non-acceptable behavior within a country change over time; some financial practices that are now illegal were not illegal in the United States a hundred years earlier. Despite these differences across countries and over the years, there is a broader, more universal sense of acceptable financial behavior that is based on the Eighth Commandment: 'Thou shalt not steal.'

Corrupt behavior is part of virtually every economy. The number of transactions that appear to overstep both moral and legal norms increases in euphoric periods like the 1990s. Paradoxically, increases in personal wealth as the prices of stocks and real estate and commodities increase at 30 or 40 percent a year for several years seem to trigger an increase in fraudulent behavior by those who want even more rapid increases in their wealth. The Smiths wish to keep up with the Joneses, and they may blur the truth and cut a few corners. Some entrepreneurs and managers skate close to the edge of fraudulent behavior because of an apparent increase in the reward–risk ratio; the potential increase in their wealth from bending the rules and deceiving the public may seem extremely high relative to costs if one is caught and fined and exposed to public embarrassment. Some may calculate that they can achieve a massive fortune because the likelihood that they will be detected is low; but even if they are caught, they may keep half of the receipts. The odds on going to jail are low, and the prisons for white-collar crime are like modest country clubs with drab clothing and hard-surface tennis courts.

Crash and panic, with their motto of *sauve qui peut*, induce many to cheat in the effort to forestall bankruptcy or some other financial disaster. A little cheating today may avert a catastrophe tomorrow. When the boom ends and the losses become apparent, some individuals will make a big bet in the hope

that a successful outcome will provide an escape from what otherwise would be a disaster.

Nick Leeson was a modest functionary—one of five or six employees—in the Singapore office of Baring Brothers, the venerable London merchant bank. Leeson traded options on stocks and options on the Nikkei, the primary stock price index in Tokyo. The London office of Barings had set a limit on Leeson's positions, the maximum amount of the firm's capital that he could risk. Leeson bought and sold call-and-put options on the Nikkei; the purchase of a call option was a bet that the price of Japanese stocks would increase, and the purchase of a put option was a bet that this price would decline. The sale of a call option was a bet that the Nikkei would not increase significantly in price, and the sale of a put option was a bet that the Nikkei would not decrease significantly. When Leeson bought either call options or put options, he had to pay a premium to the sellers of the options who were acquiring the price risk; when he sold options, he earned the premium because he was acquiring the price risk.

Someone in Leeson's office apparently made an error in a transaction which led to a loss in his trading account. Rather than acknowledge the error to the head office of Barings in London, Leeson sold some put options on the Nikkei; his plan was to use the premium income to offset the trading loss. Unfortunately for Leeson, the Kobe earthquake led to a sharp decline in the price of Tokyo stocks, which meant that he incurred a loss on the options contract that was much larger than the premium income. Leeson then 'doubled his bet' in the hope that a profit on the new option contract would offset the previous losses, he would then close the position and no one in the head office would be wiser. But Leeson was unfortunate again, for he lost on the second bet. Each time that his position incurred a loss, he made another 'double up' bet in the hope that it was his turn to win. So it went, until the cumulative losses in his trading account were more or less equal to all of Baring's capital. Leeson probably made four or five losing bets in a row. Consider the probability that he could have made five successive losing calls on the traditional coin-flip—a run of five heads in a row is a 1 in 32 chance. If he had won just one of the bets, his misadventure would not have made the front pages of the newspapers and he would not have spent two years in a Singapore jail.

The gallery of rogue traders includes John Rusnak of the Baltimore office of the Allied Irish Bank who lost $750 million trading currencies before the head office in Dublin realized how large the losses were. Yasuo Hamanaka of the New York office of Sumitomo Bank lost several billion dollars trading

in the copper market. Five traders for the National Australia Bank in Sydney lost several hundred million dollars trading currencies.

Leeson and Rusnak and the Aussies made an extended series of losing bets before being discovered. Their problems made the headlines because they ran out of cash to pay off on the losing bets before they had one winning bet that would have enabled them to break even.

The likelihood is high—very high—that there have been other rogue traders who started like Leeson and Rusnak and incurred losses on two or three or four of their 'double or nothing' bets before winning again. The bank's capital was not affected and their illegal and fraudulent behavior went undetected.

The approach toward financial fraud in this chapter is descriptive and anecdotal. *Guinness World Records* does not yet have a chapter on the magnitude of financial swindles and fraud. Financial chicanery occurred in the US economic expansion following the Civil War, and fraud was widespread in the Gilded Age of the 1880s. In the late 1920s a few bankers continued to sell the bonds of several Latin American countries after they had been told that the countries had stopped paying interest.

BCCI—the Bank of Credit and Commerce International—was a major financial beneficiary of the oil price shocks of the 1970s. BCCI had been chartered in Pakistan; the firm established a network of branches and subsidiaries throughout the Middle East and in London and subsequently in some of the major cities in Europe and Africa. BCCI prospered following the surges in the oil prices in the 1970s; the Middle East was awash with money and some of its early depositors were wealthy sheikhs from the Persian Gulf. BCCI's subtle appeal was to Muslim depositors. BCCI made large loans to rulers for political reasons, which eased its regulatory problems and helped it expand.

BCCI may have been one of the largest-ever Ponzi schemes in the pre-Madoff days. Non-performing loans were refinanced, in effect delaying the recognition of losses. Some of BCCI's loans to a shipping magnate went sour, and the bank used fraudulent accounting to hide the losses; the auditors were bribed. BCCI dealt extensively in options to make good the loan losses, and the firm recognized 'in the money' options at their market value and valued 'out of the money' options, on which it had losses, at zero. BCCI—like Ponzi—continued to expand as long as it could sell its deposits to its 'captive clientele.'

When the bubble imploded in Japan at the beginning of the 1990s, the large banks headquartered in Tokyo and in Osaka incurred massive losses on the loans that they had made to finance the purchases of real estate and

stocks. Some of the regional banks in Japan had incurred even larger loan losses. Many of their loans for golf courses, hotels, and amusement parks were undertaken to promote local economies. The tradition that loans would be repaid was not well established in Japan; instead the practice was that the borrowers would use the cash from new loans to pay the interest on the outstanding loans so that their indebtedness would increase at the rate of interest. This practice of 'evergreen finance' was safe as long as the rate of increase in property values was higher than the interest rate.

Once real estate prices began to decline, some of the hanky-panky in the loan approval process became known. A woman who owned a small restaurant in Osaka had borrowed the yen equivalent of several billion dollars from the local branch of Sumitomo Bank; she had a 'friendly relationship' with the manager of the local branch. Some of the real estate appraisers for the banks had been bribed—or perhaps frightened—by the *yakuza*, who had concluded that the low-risk way to obtain money from the banks was to secure loans based on highly inflated appraisal values of the property that was pledged as collateral. The senior officers of several of the large regional banks made loans to real estate developers so that they could buy land that was owned by the bankers. Several senior officials of the august Ministry of Finance were entertained at a 'pantyless shabu-shabu restaurant' that had a mirrored floor; the suspicion was that these officials provided advance information to their hosts about impending changes in financial regulations.

When the real estate bubbles in Thailand and Malaysia and the other nearby Asian countries imploded and the banks incurred large losses, 'crony capitalism' suddenly appeared—favored treatment for certain borrowers that somehow had not been evident in the earlier years of exuberant economic growth. Indonesia had been a 'Suharto family business' for more than thirty years—and remarkably successful measured by the increase in the country's GDP. When Indonesia was doing well, the banks were happy to make loans to the business enterprises headed by President Suharto's children—indeed some of the banks were headed by his children. The banks were not especially concerned with whether the projects that would be financed with these loans would be profitable; they were confident that they would be repaid as long as the Suharto family managed the country.

One of the persistent US financial headlines in the early 1980s was the impending financial disaster of the US savings and loan associations and the US mutual savings banks—thrift institutions that had been established to help Americans of limited means finance the purchase of their first home. The thrifts used the funds obtained from the sale of deposits with short-term maturities to buy fixed interest rate mortgages with long-term maturities.

Because the maturity of the assets of the thrifts was much longer than the maturity of their liabilities, the thrifts had a 'transformation risk' (sometimes called 'duration risk') that short-term interest rates could increase relative to long-term interest rates and the excess of the interest rates they earned on their loans over the interest they paid on their deposits then would decline, and perhaps even become negative. The thrifts had lived with this risk for fifty years because the interest rates on short-term deposits had been regulated by US government agencies to limit 'excessive' price competition among the banks and thrifts for deposits. In the second half of the 1970s, however, interest rates on US dollar securities surged, and many individuals withdrew their money from the thrifts so they could buy US Treasury bills and money market funds that offered higher interest rates than the thrifts were allowed to pay.

The conundrum for the thrifts was that if they raised interest rates on their deposits to levels that were competitive with interest rates on US Treasury bills (assuming that they could get the regulators to raise the ceilings of the interest rates that they could pay on their deposits) then their interest payments would be higher than the interest income that they were earning on their mortgages and their capital would erode and eventually disappear. If instead they sold mortgages to reduce the excess of their interest payments over their interest income, they would incur large and immediate losses because the sale prices of the mortgages would be below—probably far below—the prices they had paid for them.

Most thrifts decided to pay the higher interest rates on deposits; slow death was preferable. Each thrift could estimate the monthly rate of depletion of its capital and project the date when its capital would be fully exhausted.

Hundreds, then thousands, of these thrift institutions failed. Initially a failed thrift was taken over by the Federal Savings and Loan Insurance Corporation or the Federal Deposit Insurance Corporation, the US government's deposit insurance guarantee agencies. These government agencies would sell the good loans of the failed thrifts and use the cash from these loan sales and their accumulated reserves to pay 100 cents for each dollar of deposits.

The accumulated reserves and the capital of both the FSLIC and the FDIC, which had been built up over nearly fifty years, soon were exhausted. Then the deposit insurance agencies could no longer afford to close those thrifts with negative net worth since they didn't have enough money to honor their deposit insurance guarantee; they needed a subterfuge to enable the failed thrifts to remain open. They discovered the policy of 'forbearance,' which allowed these bankrupt thrifts to continue in business.

Inevitably the losses of the FSLIC and the FDIC would have to be made good, either by a transfer of taxpayer money from the US Treasury or by increases in the deposit insurance premiums charged to the surviving banks and thrifts. These banks and thrifts were vehemently opposed—understandably—to paying higher premiums to cover the losses of their failed competitors.

Several members of the US Congress stalled the efforts of the FDIC and the FSLIC to obtain funds from the US Treasury that they could use to pay off the depositors and close the failed institutions; these elected officials wanted to use this financial disaster to force a deregulation of the financial services industry. Some of the failed thrifts were 're-capitalized' as 'phoenix institutions'; one failed thrift would acquire another and the asset side of the balance sheet of the acquiring institution would be credited with a large entry for 'good will' and there would be a corresponding increase in its capital. The idea—more precisely the hope—was that over the next twenty or thirty years the profits of the acquiring institution would be sufficient so it could amortize the good will and its negative net worth.

Some entrepreneurs had the bright idea that the way to save the failed thrifts was to help them rapidly increase their deposits and loans so that their profits on new mortgages and loans would be larger than their losses on the older, low-interest-rate mortgages. In 1982 the US Congress reduced the regulations applied to the thrifts; henceforth they would be allowed to buy almost any type of security. At the same time the ceiling on the maximum insured deposit that any individual might have in a single thrift was increased from $40,000 to $100,000. (However, individuals could easily circumvent this ceiling by acquiring deposits under slightly different versions of the same name; Mr. Jones might have an insured deposit of $100,000, Mrs. Jones might have an insured deposit of $100,000, and Mr. and Mrs. Jones together might have a joint, third insured account of $100,000. And the Jones family could buy separate deposit accounts for each child as well as a series of deposits in joint child accounts.)

These failed thrifts were eager to buy any loan or security that offered relatively high-interest rates—and so they became one of the 'natural markets' for junk bonds. Initially the supply of junk bonds had been limited to those of the 'fallen angels'; bonds that had lost their investment grade rating because the firms that had issued them had fallen on tough times. The loss of the investment grade rating meant that some financial institutions could no longer hold these bonds, and the interest rates on these bonds increased sharply when they lost their investment grade.

Michael Milken of Drexel Burnham Lambert developed some market innovations that greatly increased both the demand for and the supply of junk bonds. The decline in interest rates and the increase in the rate of US economic growth in the 1980s created an encouraging environment for the expansion of the junk bond market. The sales pitch was that the excess of the interest rates on the junk bonds over the interest rates on investment grade bonds was much larger than the losses the owners of its bonds would incur when one of these borrowers failed.

Milken provided the financing for some of his friends and associates to gain control of thrift institutions and insurance companies and other firms that would be 'natural' buyers of the junk bonds. Milken provided 'comfort letters' to entrepreneurs contemplating a takeover of an established firm, assuring them that Drexel could raise the money they would need to finance the takeover. Once his friends had ownership of one of these industrial companies, the firm would issue junk bonds that would be underwritten by Drexel, and Milken would place these bonds with the thrifts and the insurance companies that were controlled by his friends. Drexel established its own mutual funds that would buy the junk bonds that it had underwritten.

Milken had a money machine. Drexel earned underwriting fees when its client firms issued new junk bonds, fees for selling the bonds to the mutual funds, sales fees for selling the shares in the mutual funds to the American public, and management fees for operating the mutual funds.

Merrill Lynch—ubiquitous Merrill—began to broker deposits for thrifts; the thrifts in California and the Southwest began to offer much higher interest rates and Merrill's army of thousands of brokers became the channel for moving money from around the country to the thrifts controlled by Milken's friends. The deposits that the thrifts were selling were guaranteed by the US Treasury—which was all that the buyers of these deposits wanted to know.

Few of the corporate raiders financed by Milken had much industrial experience. They used Uncle Sam's money—money obtained from the sale of deposits guaranteed by the US government—to acquire more than fifty firms. They often 'overpaid' for these firms, but then they were paying with Sam's money.

Many of the firms acquired by Milken's buddies were unable to earn enough to pay the interest on the outstanding junk bonds. Not to worry, these firms issued some new securities that relieved them of the obligation to pay the interest on their outstanding bonds and the Milken-friendly thrifts bought these securities too. The money machine continued to work as long

as the junk bond market remained vibrant. (Is this reminiscent of Ponzi finance?).

The junk bond market collapsed at the end of the 1980s when junk ran out of buyers. It is easy to overstate the effect of a rule change by Federal regulators that prohibited thrifts from buying junk bonds. Well before the recession set in, a big issuer was in distress, banks refused to join a big deal, and there was a big liquidation by junk bond mutual fund shareholders. The liquidity disappeared from the junk bond market; the prices of these bonds declined sharply, and the bondholders incurred large losses. Most of the junk bonds that came to the market in the 1980s had been underwritten by Drexel, and about half of these junk bond issues went into default. Drexel incurred large losses on the junk bonds that it owned in its inventory waiting to be sold to the public and the firm went bankrupt in 1990.

The debacle of the thrifts cost the Federal government more than $100 billion. If the US Congress had supplied the deposit insurance agencies with the money to close the failed thrifts in the early 1980s when their capital was depleted, the cost to the American taxpayers would have been in the range of $20–$30 billion. A large part of the excess of the actual costs over the costs that would have been incurred if the failed thrifts had been closed in a timely manner resulted from the costs of closing down failed thrifts that had become major buyers of junk bonds.

Milken and his family became billionaires and he probably remained one even after paying a fine or penalty of $550 million and spending thirty months in a federal 'country club' (minimum-security prison).

Fact and Fiction About Junk Bonds

Corporate takeovers and junk bonds in the 1980s led to an interesting literature. Consider some of the titles of both fiction and non-fiction books. Tom Wolfe's *Bonfire of the Vanities* is a remarkable description of the values of New York's financial elite. *Predator's Ball* by Connie Bruck is a description of an annual party for the buyers and sellers of junk bonds. *Barbarians at the Gate*, by Bryan Burroughs and John Helyar, is a tale about the would-be takeover of RJR Nabisco; it is hard to decide whether the would-be acquirers or the target was less attractive. The title of James Stewart's *Den of Thieves* offers a clue to the story of Milken and his friends. Ben Stein's *A License to Steal* provides a record of large corporate failures in the 1980s and the 1990s and the number that had had their securities underwritten by Drexel Burnham Lambert. *Dodging Bullets: Changing U.S. Corporate Capital Structure in the 1980s and 1990s* by Robert McCauley, Judith Ruud and Frank Iacono provides a macrofinancial and legal overview.

Swindles and Theft in the 1990s

There was a bumper crop of scams, swindles, and frauds in the United States in the second half of the 1990s. Enron, as noted earlier, was at the top of the hit parade of firms involved in the fraud and chicanery associated with the stock market boom. Enron was born from the merger of two regulated natural gas pipelines. Enron had two 'arms'; 'Enron Heavy' made massive investments in an electrical generating plant in India and in water systems in Britain and in Mexico. 'Enron Light' began to expand rapidly in the production and trading of electricity and natural gas and broadband and anything else that could be traded in a wholesale market. The press hyped Enron as the single most important firm in the move to deregulate the market for electricity. The rapid expansion of both arms of Enron required large amounts of money for investment in plant and equipment, trading facilities, and software. Enron sold a lot of bonds and provided substantial revenues for its primary investment bankers, Merrill Lynch and Salomon Smith Barney. Enron's market capitalization peaked at $250 billion, the market value of its stock at $100 a share was over $200 billion and the market value of its publicly owned bonds was $40 billion.

Soon after US stock prices began to fall sharply in 2000, Enron—at one time touted (by its own public relations flacks) as the seventh largest firm in the United States and described by *Fortune* magazine as one of the most innovative firms in the country—filed for bankruptcy. The market value of the stock was zero, and the market value of the bonds declined sharply.

One intriguing issue is when the top managers at Enron came to the proverbial 'fork in the road' and started on their elaborate path of financial chicanery. A large part of the total compensation of the senior managers of Enron came from selling the stock options they had received from the company as incentives. The more rapid the rate of growth of Enron's profits, the higher the price of Enron stock; the more valuable the options, the wealthier the owners of the options. Enron's senior officers had a powerful reason to keep profits growing, since their individual wealth was geared to the stock price.

Enron was responding to the challenges presented by the stock market analysts on Wall Street. Quarter by quarter, the analysts predicted the earnings per share to the penny. There were plenty of examples of firms that failed to make their earnings estimates; their stock prices declined by 10 or 20 percent. The chief financial officers of Enron, as well as of other companies, had a strong incentive to 'smooth' earnings so they met the estimates of the Wall Street analysts.

Enron needed to manage the growth in earnings. The firm entered into sale-and-leaseback arrangements with Merrill Lynch and JP Morgan for some electrical generating barges in Nigeria. Merrill and Morgan paid above-market prices for the barges so that Enron could realize a profit from their sale, which would contribute to Enron's reported profits for the year. Merrill and Morgan are not charities; because they paid above-market prices for the barges, the annual lease payments that they were charging were correspondingly higher. From Enron's point of view, the increase in profits in year one would be at the expense of profits in the next few years.

Enron was scrambling to increase this year's profits regardless of the negative impact on next year's profits. Next year's problem in growing earnings could be solved next year.

Enron had placed very high market prices on some unique forward contracts that had maturities of five and ten years and were so specialized that they had no ready reference market prices. Enron increased the value placed on these contracts from one year to the next and the increase in these values contributed to Enron's reported profits, which was a sophisticated 1990s counterpart to Billie Sol Estes' exaggeration of the number of fertilizer tanks that he had leased.

Enron's financial finagling led to increases in its reported profits of more than $1 billion. At the same time, Enron was concealing substantial debt, which had been buried in off-balance sheet financing partnerships, so-called special financing facilities or vehicles (SFVs). Many banks and industrial firms used these SFVs to remove debt from their balance sheets so they would be better positioned to increase the amounts they could borrow. The accounting rules provided that these SFVs could be considered independent entities as long as 3 percent of the equity in the SFV was owned by 'unrelated individuals.' Enron owned 97 percent of the partnerships and some of the individuals who owned the remaining 3 percent were senior employees and some were the firm's bankers. (The likelihood that these individuals were unrelated seems trivially small.) These bankers were eager to invest in these partnerships and to lend to them because Enron was a source of large underwriting income. These partnerships had names taken from *Star Wars*—JEDI, Chewco, and so on. The partnerships would borrow from the banks and other lenders as if they were independent from Enron and then invest the funds with Enron. (What is the likelihood that these lenders knew that Enron was involved in a scam?)

Enron used some of the cash obtained from the SFV's borrowings to support the price of its own stock. That is more or less a Nick Leeson go-for-broke strategy; if the stock price should fall, then the value of the

partnerships would decline and they would be 'under water.' But that is the traditional practice and it had been used by American railroads in the nineteenth century.

The collapse of Enron led to the demise of Arthur Andersen, formerly the most respected of the large US accounting firms—although in the previous few years Andersen had been sued by the creditors of the Baptist Hospital of Arizona, Waste Management, and several other audit clients that had gone belly-up. Andersen was accused of shredding documents after the Securities and Exchange Commission had started its investigation into Enron's finances.

Andersen had been selling Enron $2 million a year of auditing services and $25 million of consulting services. The implication was that Andersen's desire to retain the consulting income clouded its judgment about the appropriateness of how Enron should measure its profits—and that's a charitable statement. Andersen was convicted of obstruction of justice in June 2002; hundreds of its clients did not want to be associated with a firm with a tarnished reputation, and the firm folded.

Andersen was only one of the outside groups that had been co-opted by Enron; its board of directors had multiple conflicts of interest since some members received consulting income from the firm. Enron had established several groups of advisers, usually from the media, on a $25,000 a year retainer for one meeting a year. Enron's chair, Kenneth Lay ('Kenny boy' in some political circles in Washington) was also a major contributor to politicians.

Criminal charges were filed against more than thirty Enron officials. There were three principal types of financial chicanery; the general thrust was to overstate income and understate the growth of indebtedness. Some of the top officials also under-reported their incomes to the Internal Revenue Service. Ken Lay and others were charged with providing misleading information about the financial well-being of the firm. Five were found guilty after trials and one was acquitted; fifteen pleaded guilty.

Jeffrey Skilling, the number two at Enron, was charged with thirty-five violations of the law, including conspiracy, securities fraud, wire fraud, and insider trading and received a long prison sentence (24 years 4 months) in 2006. Andrew Fastow, the chief financial officer, pleaded guilty to the conspiracy to commit securities fraud and was imprisoned for a minimum of ten years without the possibility of parole; Leah Fastow, his wife, pleaded guilty to tax fraud and was jailed for six months. Ben Glisan, the corporate treasurer, pleaded guilty to wire and securities fraud and received a five-year sentence. Michael Kopper, a finance executive, pleaded guilty to fraud and money laundering. The former directors of Enron agreed to a $168

million settlement of a lawsuit brought by the shareholders; $13 million of this amount came from their own pockets and the rest from the proceeds of an insurance policy. Lehman Brothers paid $222 million as part of this settlement and Bank of America paid $69 million.

WorldCom had been one of the most rapidly growing telecommunications firms in the 1990s, with more than sixty acquisitions. Bernie Ebbers, a Canadian-born former high school gym teacher and basketball coach in Jackson, Mississippi, was the maestro of its rapid expansion. The market's response to the rapid increase in WorldCom's earnings per share was that the price-earnings ratio of its stock was high, much higher than the same ratios of the firms that were being acquired. WorldCom paid for its acquisitions by exchanging newly issued shares in WorldCom for the shares in the firms being acquired.

WorldCom's earnings per share were increasing at a rapid rate because it was 'buying' the earnings of firms that had lower stock prices. (If WorldCom acquired a firm with a price-earnings ratio higher than its own, the rate of growth of its earnings would slow, unless the acquired firm was trivially small.) Ebbers was riding the proverbial tiger: to keep WorldCom's stock price high, the firm had to continue to acquire other firms that had lower stock prices. As these acquisitions led to an increase in the WorldCom's size, the only way it could maintain the rapid growth of earnings was to acquire larger and larger firms. The problem—the generic problem for firms that grow their earnings per share by acquisition—is that the number of firms that remained attractive takeover targets declined as WorldCom became larger.

WorldCom's last acquisition was MCI, one of the most innovative firms in the US telecommunications industry; MCI had developed a massive infrastructure of microwave towers that broke AT&T's monopoly on long-distance phone services. MCI was so large that the merged firm was re-named MCIWorldCom. In an effort to maintain the growth of its earnings, MCIWorldCom then attempted a merger with US Sprint, but this proposed acquisition was blocked by the US regulatory authorities.

Soon thereafter MCIWorldCom filed for bankruptcy—at the time the largest bankruptcy in US history. Subsequent investigation revealed that the chief financial officers in the firm had overstated earnings by claiming that $4.8 billion of everyday expenses were 'investments'—eventually the fudged numbers amounted to $10 billion. The major reason for this accounting fraud was to maintain the growth of earnings to support the stock price. Two of WorldCom's senior officials were arrested and charged, pleaded guilty, and went to prison.

Later it became known that MCI had lent Bernie Ebbers more than $400 million in off-the-books loans. Ebbers had used his WorldCom stock as collateral for the loan—and he used some of the cash obtained from the loan to buy more WorldCom stock. Ebbers flunked the first lesson in investing—diversification of assets.

Enron and WorldCom had become victims of their own success. The stock market analysts on Wall Street had developed the practice of forecasting each firm's quarterly earnings. If the firm failed to meet the earnings targets, the stock price would decline by 15 or 20 percent. A big hit. So the senior financial officials began to play the game in two ways. If the prospective earnings were likely to be much higher than anticipated, they had an incentive to prepay expenses or delay receipts, in effect postponing the recognition of earnings. The rationale was that the Wall Street analysts would raise the bar, and what might have been a one-time surge in earnings could become the new and higher benchmark. Conversely if earnings reported by the firm came in below estimates, they had a strong incentive to 'borrow' earnings from the future by delaying payments or advancing receipts. The problem would become more intense the next quarter—but someone would have to worry about that problem two or three months later.

Bernie Ebbers' trial on the charge of misleading the public about the financial condition of the firm began in January 2005. His lawyers claimed he was misinformed by Scott Sullivan, WorldCom's chief financial officer, and that Sullivan claimed that Ebbers directed the fraud to obtain a reduction in his own prison time. Ten of the former directors of WorldCom agreed to pay $18 million from their own funds as part of a $54 million settlement with the shareholders. Ebbers received a 25-year prison sentence.

Dennis Kozlowski, head of Tyco, a $200 billion conglomerate, and Mark Swartz, its chief financial officer, were accused by the Federal government of looting Tyco of hundreds of millions of dollars in two ways: they awarded themselves options to buy Tyco stock without the approval of Tyco's directors, and they tapped into Tyco's treasury to pay their personal living expenses. The Feds made a big deal of the $6000 shower curtain and the $2 million birthday party for the second Mrs Kozlowski in Sardinia; Tyco picked up 50 percent of the costs of the party. The press reported that one of the highlights of the party was an ice sculpture reproduction of Michelangelo's *David* that dispensed vodka from a vital lower body part.

Tyco had acquired several hundred firms in a wide variety of industries. The most frequent method of payment was its own shares, but occasionally Tyco paid with cash obtained by selling bonds and by borrowing from banks. Tyco massaged the earnings of the firms that it was about to acquire. After

these firms had agreed to the acquisition, their earnings would be squeezed or otherwise temporarily depressed; then earnings would surge when they were integrated into the Tyco family, which contributed to the rapid growth in Tyco's earnings.

Tyco was also sensitive about its costs and especially its taxes; the firm's operating headquarters was in New Hampshire (a state with neither an income tax nor a sales tax) and its legal headquarters was in Bermuda, which enabled the firm to avoid paying US corporate income taxes. The State of New York alleged that Kozlowski had failed to pay the appropriate sales tax of $1 million on paintings that he purchased in New York City by asserting that the paintings would be shipped to New Hampshire; the empty crates that had contained the paintings were shipped there after the paintings had been removed to Kozlowski's New York apartment.

Kozlowski's first trial ended with a hung jury. He was found guilty at a second trial. Tyco, unlike Enron and MCIWorldCom, did not go bankrupt; the fraud was personal, not corporate.

The Rigas family was charged by the Federal government with looting Adelphia Communications, the sixth largest cable system in the United States, of $2.3 billion; the family's transgressions combined elements of the misbehavior of both Enron and WorldCom. The family collected more than $3 billion in off-balance sheet loans; the company inflated capital expenses and hid debt. Adelphia had started as a small family-owned firm; and the boundary between personal accounts and business accounts is often blurred in such situations. Many of the borrowings by the firm were guaranteed by the family, and many of the Rigas family borrowings were guaranteed by the firm. The family borrowed in large part to use the cash to support the firm's stock. The former director of finance and the former vice president pleaded guilty. Two Rigas family members were convicted.

The founder and chair of HealthSouth, Richard Scrushy, was charged with an accounting fraud of nearly $3 billion. Scrushy was acquitted in the first trial began in January 2005, although there was agreement that fraud was committed. Scrushy claimed that the fraud was committed by his subordinates and that they suggested that he managed the fraud so their own prison time would be reduced. At a second trial he was found guilty on a range of charges and jailed; later, in a civil trial, he was ordered to pay a $2.86 billion penalty, perhaps the largest in US history, according to the *Wall Street Journal's* report.

Sam Waksal, the founder and promoter of ImClone, was committed to a federal prison after pleading guilty to six federal charges. Waksal had told his father and his daughter to sell their shares in the firm because an adverse

statement from the Food and Drug Administration would be released the next day and lead to a decline in the stock price.

Martha Stewart's five-month stay in a federal prison may have been related to Sam Waksal's decision to sell shares in ImClone. Stewart sold her shares but denied that she had received any information from Waksal. An interesting coincidence. The Federal government indicted Stewart on an 'obstruction of justice' charge. She was found guilty and went to jail.

Richard Grasso, the chairman and chief executive officer of the New York Stock Exchange, made it to the nation's front pages with the news that his retirement benefit package would be $150 million. The NYSE was before 2006 a not-for-profit institution, owned by its members; it provides its members with a trading floor and regulates their trading practices, and is the arbiter of permissible trading practices. Most of the directors of the exchange are senior officers of the firms that are regulated by the exchange— or perhaps more precisely, are supposed to be regulated by the exchange. Grasso's retirement compensation package seemed high—very high—relative to the revenues of the Exchange (a $28 million surplus the previous year) and to the retirement benefit packages of other leaders on Wall Street. The suspicion was that Grasso was soft on the regulatory front because he did not want to offend the directors who determined his salary and bonuses. After an uproar and pressure from pension fund investors Grasso resigned. Subsequently Grasso was sued in 2004 by the New York Attorney General over his compensation package.

Global Crossing swapped network capacity with other carriers to inflate its revenues. The company shredded documents and went bankrupt, but before it did, its founder and Chairman Gary Winnick received $800 million from the sales of his shares. He later paid substantial compensation in a class-action lawsuit by former shareholders, without, however, admitting wrongdoing.

Shell Oil agreed to pay a fine of $150 million to the US and the British regulatory authorities for overstating the volume of oil in its reserves in the ground. It's harder to quantify underground oil reserves than to count Billie Sol Este's fertilizer tanks. Several Shell officials were bounced from the firm, but none went to jail.

Mutual Fund Scandals of 2003

In 2003 a number of the large US mutual fund families—maybe half of the twenty largest firms that manage mutual funds—were accused of providing exceptional trading privileges to several hedge funds, which enabled them to earn large profits at the expense of the other owners of shares in these

same mutual funds. Some of these transactions were legal, most were not, and all violated the implicit contract between the mutual fund and its shareholders that each shareholder would be treated equally. Each US mutual fund is required to file a contract with the US Securities and Exchange Commission that stipulates its own rules for transactions—a description of what is permissible behavior and what isn't. A feature of most such contracts is that investors will not be allowed to make 'in-and-out' transactions—to sell the shares in the fund a day or two after the shares were purchased. The contract generally provides that if an investor does undertake an in-and-out transaction, the investor will be charged an additional 1 percent or the request to sell may be delayed. Another standard boiler-plate paragraph in the offering agreement is that the officers of the fund will not buy shares in a firm if the fund is buying shares in the same firm—or that if the officers buy shares in the firm, they will not 'front-run,' that is, buy the shares in a firm for their own private accounts before the mutual fund buys the shares in the same company. Moreover, the funds' standard practice was to disclose information about the securities that each fund owned only at the end of the quarter and not to provide any information on purchases and sales of individual securities between these end-of-quarter dates.

A number of hedge funds engaged in market-timing transactions with the mutual funds; the hedge funds would buy the shares in the mutual fund if they thought it likely that the news would lead to increases in the prices of the stocks owned by the mutual funds and increases in the funds' net asset value per share. The hedge funds would trade on 'stale prices,' like shooting fish in the proverbial barrel; the opportunity to trade on stale prices arose because some of the mutual funds owned foreign securities, and the markets in which these foreign securities were traded closed before the US market closed. For example, the Japanese market closed on Tuesday before the US market opened for trading on the same Tuesday. The mutual funds would inform some of the hedge funds about the stocks they were buying and selling during the quarter, although they would not provide the same information to other shareholders. Some mutual fund managers would trade the shares of their own funds on an in-and-out basis; some would front-run the purchases of the mutual fund.

Why did the mutual funds break their commitments to their shareholders?

Because a lot of business is quid pro quo, and the hedge funds might purchase shares in some mutual funds owned by one of the mutual fund management companies that needed a bit of a boost.

Canary Capital, a family-owned hedge fund, agreed to pay restitution of $20 million to the mutual funds and a penalty of $10 million to the Securities and Exchange Commission for its transgressions. Massachusetts Financial Services, the oldest US mutual fund, agreed to a $200 million settlement. Alliance Capital paid a $250 million penalty and agreed to cut its fees by $350

million over several years. The founder and the major owner of the Strong
Funds in Milwaukee resigned his management positions, sold his ownership
interest, and paid a penalty of tens of millions of dollars. Morgan Stanley
instructed its brokers to hustle its own mutual funds rather than funds in
general in a form of payola; the clients of Morgan Stanley were not made
aware that the advice of the brokers was not impartial.

Liar's Loans, Ninja Assets, and Too Big to Jail

There were two defining features of the boom and bust in the US real estate
market between 2003 and 2008—when was how extensive the fraud was and
the other was how few people were indicted, brought to trial, convicted, and
sent to jail. The 1990s featured Ken Lay and Jeffrey Skilling of Enron, Bernie
Ebbers of MCIWorldCom, Dennis Kozlowski and Mark Swartz of Tyco, and
John Rigas and his sons Timothy and Michael of Adelphia Communications.
It was as if all the fraud was at the retail level, and the suppliers of fraud were
too numerous and too low-level to be brought to trial.

Perhaps fifty people did jail time as a result of the fraud in the 1990s. And
the former head of Countrywide, Angelo Mozilo, was fined a record $67.5
million for securities fraud and insider trading in 2010, although without
admitting any wrongdoing.

Ninja Loans—Mortgage to Those with No Income and No Assets

Nearly ten years after the decline in real estate prices that began in 2007,
only a trivial number of bankers and lenders have been indicted or gone to
jail for fraud or some other indictable offense. But the US government has
collected more than $20 billion from banks and investment banks for fraud
in the mortgage market. The Bank of America has said that it will pay up to
$8.7 billion to settle the charges of predatory lending.

The increase in the number of swindles and the scope of fraudulent
behavior has attracted the economic theorists. Many of the swindles—often
the low-class ones—involve 'Ponzi finance,' a pattern of financial transac-
tions when a firm's interest payments are larger than its cash flows from
operations.[2] Another theorist noted that those borrowers who can set the

interest rates on their personal debts engage in Ponzi finance and use the cash obtained from new loans to make debt service payments on their outstanding loans.[3]

Most of the entrepreneurs who establish a Ponzi finance operation appear to know and understand what they are doing; they live high for a few months or years before the authorities catch up with them. Occasionally an innocent becomes involved and seems unable to understand the pattern of finance.

Shills, Touts, and Thieves

If you're at the carnival or the circus or the county fair, you know that the shill for the sideshow is likely to engage in some exaggeration about the attractions of those that you might see if you pay the six bucks entry fee. If you are at the racetrack, you know that the touts that want to sell you their list of winners are not likely to pass the boy scouts' code of honor when they describe how many winners they have picked in the last several days and the last week—somehow your intuition suggests that if they were half as successful as they claim they are, they would not be hustling their tip sheets. But what interpretation should you place on the statements of the touts for Merrill and Morgan Stanley and Credit Suisse when they indicate their price targets for the shares of individual firms?

In a good year in the late 1990s Henry Blodgett earned $10 million, Mary Meeker $15 million, and Jack Grubman $20 million. Henry, Mary, and Jack were the apostles of the dot.coms and the telecommunications firms in the bubble years of the 1990s. They earned these rock-star incomes because their public statements induced a lot of dentists in Peoria and undertakers in Kansas City to buy shares in the firms that they were hustling, and these firms brought a lot of underwriting and trading business to the Wall Street investment banks. There is no rule of thumb that relates their incomes to the profits they generated for their employers, but it's a safe bet that their employers had calculated that the profits they produced were at least eight to ten times larger than their incomes.

Henry Blodgett of Merrill Lynch became famous for setting price targets for the stocks of individual dot.com firms, and some of these targets were achieved; in the heyday of the bull market these achievements could be seen as testimony to his success as a forecaster, or to a self-fulfilling prophecy. Henry got a lot of attention because in some internal e-mails within Merrill he derided the attractiveness of some of the same stocks that he was promoting

to the American public. Henry agreed to leave the security business never to return. But he kept the money.

Jack Grubman of Salomon Smith Barney, then part of the Citigroup family, became infamous because he changed his recommendation on AT&T stock after a polite request from his boss Sandy Weill, the chief executive of Citi. The apparent *quid pro quo* was that Jack wanted Sandy's help in getting Jack's twin daughters admitted to the kindergarten class at the 92nd Street YMHA. About the same time Citigroup made a contribution of $1 million to the '92Y,' Jack left Salomon Smith Barney with a $20 million golden hand-shake. Jack paid a penalty of $20 million and agreed not to work in the securities business again.

Parmalat (the name combines that of the city of Parma, Italy, and *latte* or milk) the Italian dairy and food products company headquartered in Parma, used fabricated certificates of deposits to overstate its assets by $4 billion; the fraudulent CDs were prepared by superimposing one document on another in a copying machine. This fraud—the deception of the investing public and the investment banks—continued for more than ten years. It was an Italian version of Billie Sol Estes exaggerating the number of fertilizer tanks.

Boiler shops are another form of a swindle. Robert Brennan of First Jersey Securities operated a series of high-profile boiler shops. The sales brokers in these shops specialize in making cold calls to individuals about a stock, say Shazam Rockets. Shazam's share price is usually low, perhaps between $2 and $5 a share, and initially many of the shares in Shazam are owned by insiders—those who own the boiler shop. The insiders trade with each other and manage increases in the price of the stock say from $2 to $3 a share, and they then begin to make their cold calls, pointing to the 50 percent increase in the price of Shazam's stock in the last six weeks; they've learned that the gullible are much more willing to buy a stock whose price has increased rapidly. They also know that the unwashed investors have a preference for low-price stocks.

Swindles differ from ordinary robbery in that they abuse a trust. Daniel Defoe thought the stock-jobber cheat 10,000 times worse than the high-wayman because the swindler robbed people he knew—often his friends and relatives—and ran no physical 'risque.'[4]

Swindles should be distinguished from bribery, both of government offi-cials and of the employees of one business by those of another. These illegal and/or immoral transactions involve both misrepresentation and the viola-tion of an explicit or implicit trust between particular groups. Was Arthur Andersen corrupted by the $25 million a year in consulting fees from Enron? Was Bernie Ebbers bribed by Jack Grubman because Jack arranged for Bernie

to be able to buy shares in twenty or thirty firms on the days when these stocks would be sold to the public for the first time? In the bubble euphoria, the odds were extremely high that the share prices would double on the first day of trading. Or did Bernie bribe Jack Grubman with the implicit threat that unless he was provided with favored treatment in buying newly issued stock he would take WorldCom's underwriting business across the street to Merrill Lynch or Morgan Stanley? The rules of the stock exchanges and the rules of the futures exchanges are like a 'code of purity' designed to instill confidence in the public that everyone will be treated fairly—but the rules are really designed to protect some of the members of the exchanges from the adverse consequences for the industry of recognition of cheating by others.

The National Association of Security Dealers (NASD) pursues disciplinary actions against those of its members who have violated the rules. In recent years, hundreds of its members have been at the receiving end of disciplinary actions.

Corruption has been discussed historically by Jacob van Klaveren, who was especially interested in corruption as a form of market transaction that facilitated getting things done that were profitable but forbidden, as in black markets, or simply dishonest, such as the looting of India by Clive or Hastings.[5] Van Klaveren also discussed the systematic embezzlement from the Royal African Company and the East India Company by insiders who skimmed the profits due to stockholders through contracts with companies that they controlled. In a similar manner, the Credit Mobilier in the United States in 1873 diverted profits from Union Pacific stockholders to the inside group run by Oakes Ames, a congressman from Massachusetts, and his congressional and business cronies. Drew, Fisk, and Gould milked the Erie Railroad in similar fashion.[6]

Swindling in financial markets is many-faceted—the directors swindle the stockholders, the senior managers swindle the directors, the security underwriters swindle both the owners of the firms that they are bringing to the public and the stockholders, borrowers swindle their bank lenders, and one group of employees may swindle another. Some swindlers issue fraudulent bills of exchange to the cost of those who own these bills when the fraud is discovered and they only then realize that they are holding counterfeit securities.

The line separating moral from immoral acts is now less fuzzy than it once was. One way that modernity is distinguished from backwardness is morality. In early stages of economic development, codes provided for honor and trust only within the family. Nepotism was efficient in these circumstances since strangers virtually had a license to steal. In 1720 a firm could buy a man's

services but not his loyalty; to be a clerk was an invitation to start a new and competitive business at a time when embezzlement and fraudulent conversion were not regarded as crimes.[7] Lines between business and theft, commerce and piracy were not precise.[8] Hammond noted that it was not until 1799 that the borrowing of bank funds by bank officials was definitively ruled illegal,[9] although the 1720 House of Commons investigation of the South Sea Bubble ruled that the directors of the South Sea Company, having been guilty of a breach of trust in lending money of the company to buy its own stock, should use their own wealth to make good investor losses.[10]

A financial journalist writing a preface to a fictionalized biography of Ponzi drew a parallel between the 1920s and the 1970s and suggested that swindles were a product of inflation; his view was that when increases in the cost of living pinched family budgets, the heads of some households took additional risks to increase their incomes.[11] A somewhat different view held that destabilizing speculation in the absence of 'avoidable ignorance' is gambling, which provides utility to the participants even when they know they are likely to lose, in much the same way as participating in a lottery.[12]

Whether swindles should be included in the category of 'avoidable ignorance' is debatable. Cynics may share the belief of W. C. Fields that 'You can't cheat an honest man' and conclude that victims of swindles mainly have themselves to blame. *Mundus vult decipi—ergo decipitatur*: 'the world wants to be deceived, let it therefore be deceived.'[13] Some psychiatrists believe that the swindler and his victims are bound together in a symbiotic, love-hate relationship that provides satisfaction to both.

The Theft of Information

In 2009, Raj Rajaratnam, founder of the Galleon Fund group, was arrested by the FBI and indicted by the Securities and Exchange Commission for the use of 'inside information'—his fund traded on this information before it became available to the public and realized exceptional profits. Rajaratnam was charged with fourteen counts of securities fraud and pleaded not guilty; he asserted that the profits reflected his research. The government charged 26 people with illegal behavior; 21, including several who were traders for Galleon, have pleaded guilty. Some of the inside information involved corporate acquisitions, some involved large changes in corporate earnings.

Fraud and Euphoria

Fraudulent behavior increases in economic booms. Fortunes are made in a boom, individuals become greedy for a share of the increase in wealth and swindlers come forward to exploit that greed. The number of sheep waiting to be shorn increases in booms and an increasing number offers themselves as sacrifices to the swindlers. 'There's a sucker born every minute.' In Dickens' *Little Dorrit*, Ferdinand Barnacle of the Circumlocution Office tells Arthur Clennam, who had hoped that the exposure of Mr. Merdle's swindles would serve as a warning to dupes that 'the next man who has as large a capacity and as genuine a taste for swindling will succeed as well.'

Greed also induces some amateurs to commit fraud, embezzlement, defalcation, and similar misfeasance. The demise of Overend, Gurney and Company, the well-established 'Corner House,' in 1866, after the original partners had retired and the firm had gone public, was brought about by a pleasure-loving gallant inside the firm who had appointed an outsider as an adviser for £5000 a year, paid in advance and returned to the insider. D. W. Chapman, the insider, kept ten horses and entertained lavishly at Prince's Gate, Hyde Park. His outside adviser, Edward Watkins Edwards, a former accountant, recommended that many new activities be added to the bread-and-butter discount business: speculation in grain, production of iron, shipbuilding, shipping, and railroad finance. The firm became 'partners in every sort of lock-up and speculative business' and Edwards received a commissions on each of these activities. By the end of 1860 the firm was losing £500,000 a year net even though it was earning £200,000 a year on its discount business. The bubble was pricked by the failure of an unrelated firm of railway contractors, Watson, Overend, and Company.[14]

From the world of fiction—in this case, *Melmoth réconcilié*, by Honoré de Balzac—the comparable figure to Chapman is Castanier, a bank cashier, whose mistress, Mme Aquilinia de la Garde, has expensive tastes in silver, linen, crystal, and rugs, passions that prove his undoing. For a time he survives by issuing promissory notes. At the point of no return, when he finally calculates his debts, he might have been saved by leaving Mme de la Garde, but he cannot give her up. Finally, because of the impossibility of continuing his financial maneuvers, given the very large interest payments on his massive debts, it is clear that he is bankrupt. But he prefers fraud to honest bankruptcy and dips into the bank's till.[15]

Swindling increases in economic booms because greed appears to grow more rapidly than wealth; it's as if the increase in wealth triggers an increase in greed. Dennis Kozlowski was one of the richest people in America; yet the

money to pay for the $6000 shower curtain and the other furnishings in his apartment were taken from Tyco. Swindling also increases in times of financial distress as a result of a taut credit system which induces declines in asset prices; at that stage the fraudulent behavior is undertaken to avoid a financial disaster. Ponzi resisted the suggestions of his associates that he should take the money and run and they in their turn swindled him.[16] The London banker Henry Fauntleroy forged conveyances of estates to use as collateral for loans. These men served as models for Augustus Melmotte, the swindler of Trollope's *The Way We Live Now*, who forged both a conveyance and a deed when the price of his Mexican railroad stock declined and he could no longer sell stock to raise cash.[17] John Blunt of the South Sea Company, Eugène Bontoux of the Union Générale, Jacob Wasserman of the Darmstäderund Nationalbank (Danatbank), and the directors of the Credit Anstalt all bought the shares of their firms in the open market to support their prices in the hope that they might sell more shares at even higher prices at later dates. A bank that buys its own stock to keep the price high reduces its own liquidity since the ratio of its cash holdings to its deposits declines as it pays out cash to obtain the stock. In 1720 the Bank of England borrowed using its own stock as collateral. Clapham noted that the Bank of England did not penetrate into the far wilder and 'absolutely dishonest' finance of the South Sea Company.[18]

The revelation of a swindle or embezzlement increases distress which in turn often precipitates a crash and panic. In 1772 Alexander Fordyce absconded from London to the Continent, leaving his associates to meet obligations of £550,000, largely in dubious acceptances of the Ayr Bank, if they could—but they could not. Fordyce had personally been short of East India stock, whose price had risen enough to wipe him out.[19] On 24 August 1857, it became known that a cashier in the New York office of the Ohio Life Insurance and Trust Company had embezzled almost all the assets of that highly reputed enterprise to sustain his stock market transactions; the news triggered a series of failures that reverberated in Liverpool, London, Paris, Hamburg, and Stockholm.[20] A kind of mid-nineteenth-century version of Nick Leeson.

In September 1929 the Hatry empire in London, a set of investment trusts and operating companies in photographic supplies, cameras, slot machines, and small loans, collapsed. Clarence Hatry wanted to expand into the steel business, but was caught using fraudulent collateral in an attempt to borrow £8 million to buy United Steel; his failure led to tightening of the British money market, withdrawal of call loans from the New York market and contributed to the topping-out of prices on the stock market.

Bubbles and Swindles

Some bubbles are swindles, some are not. The Mississippi Bubble was not a swindle; the South Sea Bubble was. A bubble generally starts with an apparently legitimate or at least legal purpose. What became the Mississippi Bubble initially started as the Compagnie d'Occident, to which the Law system added the farming-out of national tax collections. John Law owned about one-third of the Place Vendôme and other valuable real estate in Paris, and at least a dozen magnificent country estates. His activities were not a swindle, but his financial demise reflected a mistake that was based on two fallacies: (1) that stocks and bonds were money, and (2) that issuing more money as demand increased was not inflationary.[21]

In the South Sea Bubble, the monopoly of trade in the South Atlantic was purely incidental.[22] Very quickly, the consolidation of British government debt overwhelmed the South Atlantic trade aspects of the enterprise, and stock-jobbing overwhelmed government debt shortly thereafter. John Blunt and his insiders sought to profit on stock issued to themselves against loans secured by the stock as collateral. As they realized the capital gains from the increases in the price of the stock that they owned and sold, they used the cash to buy estates; Blunt had six contracts to buy estates at the time of the collapse and a man named Surman had *four* contracts to buy real estate on which he owed £100,000. To get the cash that would be distributed as profits, the South Sea Company both needed to increase its capital and to have the price of its stock increase continuously. And it needed both increases at accelerating rates as in a chain letter or in a Ponzi scheme.[23]

History has given less immortality to certain of Ponzi's forerunners. The former Munich actress Spitzeder paid 20 percent a year interest on the funds received from Bavarian farmers. She received 3 million gulden from these farmers. She and her helpers drew long jail sentences at the end of 1872. Placht, a dismissed officer, promised to pay 40 percent a year and borrowed the pennies of 1600 widows and orphans to get the money to play the stock market. His stock purchases were not profitable and he spent six years in jail.[24]

As economic booms progress, greed mounts, and the excuses become thinner, more nearly gossamer bubbles. In 1720 and again in 1847 (two occasions when lists were compiled), such swindles were numerous, although they have been embroidered with hoaxes perpetrated by and on later historians.[25] In 1720, for example, there was one proposal for carrying on an undertaking of great advantage that would be revealed only in due time. The perpetrator charged two guineas a share and made off with £2000, keeping his secret

intact by failing to attend a meeting with the investors.[26] Another scheme was for the 'nitvender,' or selling of nothing.[27] In the late 1990s stock market boom, some firms were able to raise money from the public before they had any business plans.

A project of modest current interest offers a premature example of women's liberation:

> A proposal by several ladies and others to make, print and stain calicos in England and also fine linen as fine as any Holland to be made of British flax ... They were resolved as one man [sic] to admit no man but will themselves subscribe to a joint-stock to carry on said trade.[28]

In later periods, both historians and novelists noted that stock promotions had little connection with reality. 'Many companies were founded without undertaking operations, railroads with any right-of-way or traffic.'[29] 'Construction companies grew like mushrooms. Many of these companies speculated in building sites rather than in construction.'[30] 'Limehouse and Rotherhithe bridge ... It was not at all necessary for them that the bridge should ever be built; that, probably, was out of the question ... But if a committee of the House of Commons could be got to say that it ought to be built, they might safely calculate on selling out at a large profit.'[31]

Financial distress leads to fraud in the effort to dump the losses on others before they cascade into ever larger losses. If the market goes decisively the wrong way, for example, bucket-shop operators abscond. When new cash subscriptions failed to meet profits paid out to greedy insiders, Blunt borrowed the cash of the South Sea Company for his own use,[32] a preview of the story of the Rigas family and Adelphia. In 1861 Bleichröder characterized Bethel Henry Strousberg as 'clever but his manner of undertaking new ventures in order to mend old holes is dangerous, and if he should encounter a [sudden] obstacle his whole structure may collapse and under its ruins bury millions of gullible shareholders.'[33] Bleichröder was right. Another German financier, the Hamburg banker Gustav Goddefroy, lost heavily in railroad and mining shares in 1873 and then bled his overseas trading company to support his position in the stock market.[34]

These incurable optimists, who know they are going to win the first time, but lose, frequently try again, often doubling their bets and increasing their risks by transactions that either are of dubious morality or clearly illegal. In the late 1920s, when US banks were still allowed to underwrite securities (before the Glass-Steagall Act of 1932), Albert Wiggins of the Chase Bank and Charles Mitchell of National City continued to sell Chilean and Peruvian government bonds at the old prices even after they had learned by cable from

those governments that they had stopped paying interest.[35] Horace under-stood the position, if Sprague quotes and translates him accurately: 'Make money; make it honestly if you can; at all events, make money.'[36] Equally cynical is Jonathan Swift over the South Sea Bubble:

> Get money, money still
> And then let virtu follow, if she will.[37]

On this topic, Balzac has the last word: 'The most virtuous merchants tell you with the most candid air this word of the most unrestrained immorality: "One gets out of a bad affair as one can".'[38]

Noble Gamblers

The literature abounds in condemnation of noble gamblers and insiders, who might have been thought to regard financial obligations as debts of honor but are better at promising than at paying their subscriptions.[39] The Austrian nobility was worse than the Junkers, who at least ostensibly disdained money. Eduard Lasker maintained that 'when the dilettantes enter, they make it even worse than the professional swindlers.'[40] Daigremont in Zola's *L'Argent* sends Saccard to the Marquis de Bohain to help launch his Banque Universelle: 'If he wins, he pockets it; if he loses, he does not pay. That is known, people are resigned to it.'[41] Again in novels and in real life, nobles seek seats on boards of directors. Wirth enumerates Austrian princes, Landgrafs, counts, barons, Freiherren, and other nobles on the boards of railroads, banks, and other industrial firms 'for which they have no capacity.'[42] To control the accounts of the Banque Universelle, Saccard appoints a *sieur* Rousseau and a *sieur* Lavignière, the first completely subservient to the second, who is tall, blond, very polite, approving always, devoured by ambition to come on the board.[43] *L'Argent* is a *roman à clef* based on Eugène Bontoux and the Union Générale, whose subscribers included the Pretender, royalists, notables, and country squires.[44] In Britain *The Economist* in October 1848 included the nobility and aristocracy at the head of a list of dishonor:

> Present prostration and dejection is [sic] but a necessary retribution for the folly, the avarice, the insufferable arrogance, the headlong, desperate and unprincipled gambling and jobbing which disgraced nobility and aristocracy, polluted senators and senate houses, and traders of all kinds.[45]

Rosenberg claims that while the Austrian and French aristocracy led the other estates in pursuit of the golden calf, Berlin bureaucrats successfully opposed a similar movement in Prussia, noting an abortive attempt by Mevissen to get some counts on the board of a 50 million thaler bank. Junkers speculated in spirits and land products, he admits, but shied away from urban developments.[46] Perhaps this was so in 1857. In the following decade, the perception of money as evil had weakened. Railroad finance, both inside Germany and in Strousberg's maneuvers in Romania, was tinged with scandal, reaching up to the peaks of the aristocracy and virtually into the Prussian court itself.[47]

Venal Journalism

Speculation generally was helped by the press. Some members of the press were for sale, some were critical, and some were both. Daniel Defoe excoriated stockbrokers in November 1719 when the South Sea stock sold at 120 yet turned around to defend them at the peak of 1000 in August 1720.[48] He expressed his 'just contempt' for people who claimed he wrote for the Royal African Company, stating he had sold his stock; but a modern critic concluded that he either continued to hold the stock or was hired by the company to attack individual traders who competed with the monopoly.[49] The press was still in an underdeveloped stage in France in the early nineteenth century; in 1837 a journalist wrote: 'Give me 30,000 francs of advertising and I will take responsibility for placing all the shares of the worst possible company that it is possible to imagine.'[50] Laffitte financed newspapers.[51] Charles Savary of the Banque de Lyon et de la Loire had 500 journalists singing the praises of his operations, using releases, largely paid for, as if they were stories created by the journal's staff.[52] Journals often sought favor with banks, the stock exchange, and the public by whipping up the speculative fever.[53] Bleichröder was cautious in avoiding speculation and outright misrepresentation, but he owned general and financial newspapers and used journalists to hype his financial interests. In 1890–1891 he financed a trip to Mexico for one Paul Lindau, who wrote thirty-four articles and a book on the country without mentioning his connection with Bleichröder who then was selling Mexican bonds on the Berlin market.[54] A critical press developed slowly during the nineteenth century on the Continent.

In the 1890s in the United States, on the other hand, a financier closer to the line was pursued by the press and lived in fear of it; at least this is the inference from Theodore Dreiser's fictionalized biography of Charles Tyson Yerkes, the Chicago streetcar tycoon who operated along, and sometimes

over, the knife-edge that separates legitimate transactions from illegitimate ones. Yerkes needed favorable publicity to sell securities, which he sought and won through his gift of an observatory to the newly formed University of Chicago. The well-publicized gift helped restore his reputation and enabled him to sell his streetcar bonds in Europe.[55] But later the press drove him from Chicago.[56]

Tipping off friends before hawking a stock to the world in an investor column may be an old trick, but it is more readily detected today, along with all buying and selling of shares based on insider information. Suspicious trades in a stock and in options to buy and sell the stock before the news that affects its price is made public are now analyzed by computer programs. The technique led to the arrests of investment columnist R. Foster Winans of the *Wall Street Journal*, who fed his tips in advance to a friend, and of former Undersecretary of Defense William Thayer, who told a friend of forthcoming events in a company of which he was a director. (Thayer's friend speculated on the basis of the information; Winans capitalized on his experience by writing *Trading Secrets: Seduction and Scandal at the Wall Street Journal*, St. Martin's Press, 1986.) Similarly, a young Merrill Lynch broker in New London, Connecticut, bought information from the local printers of *Business Week* before the magazine appeared on the newsstands. Once the ease of tracing trading on insider information became known, some miscreants with advance information would call a broker in, say, Zurich, instead of their local broker. The Zurich bank would place a massive order in London or New York before brokerage houses there became wary and would delay execution for a couple of days to see if a large order was based on breaking news.

Most recently the internet has become the vehicle for manipulating stock prices. Jonathan Lebeck, aged seventeen, posted 'news' about particular thinly traded stocks (which he owned) on internet chat rooms. The stock prices would increase and Jonathan would sell his shares. The Securities and Exchange Commission made Jonathan pay a penalty of $500,000.

MSNBC is a business news TV channel. Many of the commentators on the programs promote the stocks that they own.

Dubious Practices

There are many forms of financial felony. In addition to stealing, misrepresentation, and lying, other dubious practices include diversion of funds from the stated use to another, paying dividends out of capital or with borrowed funds, dealing in company stock on inside knowledge, selling securities without full disclosure of new knowledge, using company funds for non-competitive purchases from or loans to insider interests, taking orders but not executing them, and altering the company's books.

George Hudson, who may have been the greatest figure in British railroad history, practiced nearly all of these at the same time in the 1846 railway mania.

At one time he was chairman of four railways, and he mistakenly believed he was above the law that applied to his less powerful competitors. His accounts were muddled, and he may not have understood that he had appropriated shares or funds belonging to the York and North Midland railway. As a private individual he made contracts with various companies of which he was an officer, in direct violation of the Companies Clauses Consolidation Act. He raised the dividend of the Eastern Counties railway from 2 to 6 percent just before preparing the financial statements and then altered the accounts to justify the payments. Dividends of the York and North Midland were paid out of capital. He defended his actions against similar accusations in the case of the Yorkshire, Newcastle, and Berwick by noting that he had personally advanced funds to the railway to extend its network. The risk was his, and he was entitled to the advantages that ultimately accrued from the expansion of the rail system. He embarked, on his own authority, on transactions that he deemed advantageous to the company, but that were nevertheless of doubtful legality. Still, he had a career of great brilliance that greatly benefited the British railway network.[57]

A less interesting and imposing character in the United States in the 1850s was Robert Schuyler, who was president of the New York and New Haven, the New York and Harlem, and for a time the Illinois Central Railroad. Called the 'genteel swindler' by one author, he absconded to Europe in 1854 with almost $2 million obtained from fraudulently selling New York and New Haven stock and keeping the proceeds. Van Vleck suggests that the crisis of 1857 in the United States was precipitated by British withdrawals of funds following the publication of the news of Schuyler's defalcation. Schuyler had resigned from the presidency of the Illinois Central in 1853, but his fraud perpetrated on the New York and New Haven led to a massive sale of Illinois Central stock and bonds. The price of its shares fell drastically, and the

bonds declined to 62 from 100 by August 1855. British investors had been looking for this opportunity and they bought large amounts of these bonds; by February 1856 the bonds were back to 90. European investors owned more than 40,000 shares of the stock and 85 percent of the $12 million in bonds.[58] Schuyler was connected with a panic in September 1854 but not with the one in 1857.[59]

The 1920s in the United States has been called 'the greatest era of crooked high finance the world has ever known'—but that was before the 1990s.[60] Notorious swindlers of the period include Harold Russell Snyder, who stole to extricate himself from losses incurred from the stock market crash (a precursor of the Rigas family, but on a smaller scale, even after adjusting for inflation). Arthur H. Montgomery paid the sincerest form of flattery to Ponzi by organizing a foreign-exchange investment scheme that promised a 400 percent return in sixty days. Charles V. Bob sought and obtained favorable publicity through a $100,000 gift to the Byrd Antarctic Polar Expedition and won the right to call the admiral 'Dick,' which presumably helped promote his aviation stocks, which enjoyed a boomlet after Lindbergh's 1927 flight to Paris.[61]

The 1930s produced many memorable examples of fraud and alleged fraud, led by the bankruptcies of the Bank of the United States, of Ivar Kreuger, and of Samuel Insull's Middle West Utilities holding company. In his riveting account of the New York stock market from 1929 to 1933, Barrie Wigmore observed that Insull's reputation was irreparably damaged when he fled the United States to escape trial before what he considered would be inflamed juries for crimes of which he was later acquitted. Wigmore asserted that Insull was a brilliant manager of operating utilities who went on a buying binge, acquiring badly run companies for multiples of their net worth. Insull's purchases burdened his holding company with a mountain of debt, and the interest payments on the debt wiped out the equity of those who owned the common stock when the utilities got into trouble in the 1930s depression.[62] Wigmore treads warily in assessing the marketing practices of New York banks and their security affiliates. Albert Wiggins of the Chase Bank had a reputation as 'the most popular man on Wall Street' but his reputation was shattered when a Senate investigation exposed a picture of self-dealing at the expense of his bank, its subsidiaries, and its clients. Charles E. Mitchell of the National City Bank and its security affiliate, the National City Company, also marketed securities intensely, even though he had the inside information that the profits of the companies concerned were declining rapidly.[63]

Corruption in the 1990s and 2000s

The amount of corruption seems greater in the 1980s and the 1990s than in the 1920s. One explanation is that there has been a decline in adherence to moral norms. A second is that the risk-reward trade-off has been skewed; stock options have provided a much greater payoff from financial success. Finance has been democratized. A third is the rise of certified public accountants, which can be traced to the legislation that led to the Securities and Exchange Commission of the 1930s. The initial role of the accounting firms was to protect the public from the financial chicanery of corporate managers who might have had a tendency to overstate the value of inventories and of accounts receivable. The accounting firms were paid to verify or certify the data on financial performance presented by the firms' financial managers. The accountants may have been the guardians of the public interest but the fees for their services were paid by the financial managers. Some of the firms being audited leaned on their accountants, who then were forced to choose between agreeing to the firm's demands or walking away from the account.

Securitization was a central feature of the bubble in US real estate between 2002 and 2007; the investment banks issued new bonds, which were claims on the interest income and principal of mortgages, credit card debt, and student loans that they had placed in a trust. Mortgage Backed Securities (MBSs) were the dominant new instrument, and were much more liquid than the individual mortgages that were placed in the trust, and so they sold for higher prices. The investment banks earned fees from securitization and their fee income soared. They then issued Asset-Backed Securities (ABSs), which were claims to the interest income and principal of the segments of the ABSs that had been deposited in the trust. They earned a second round of fees from creating these new instruments, which had been based on 'slicing and dicing' the MBSs into three, four, or five different tranches, which differed in terms of their risk characteristics—one set of trusts contained the tranches that had the first claim on the interest income of the MBSs and hence they were the least risky, while another set of trusts contained the tranches that had the last claim on the interest income of the MBSs, and they were the most risky. And some investment banks issued a third round of ABSs.

The investment banks relied on the credit rating agencies—Moody's, Standard and Poor's—to rank the securities that the investment banks were producing. (The credit rating agencies are like the CPA firms, established to provide 'objective' information. The CPA firms were paid by the firms that they were auditing and the credit rating agencies were paid by the firms that

issued bonds.) But these agencies were relying on the 'models' that the investment banks had provided for them. The investment banks had indicated to the credit rating agencies that if they could not get rankings that would help them sell these securities, they would take their business to one of the other firms that provided ratings.

Was this illegal? Who knows? Was it corrupt? You bet. Is anyone from a credit rating agency likely to go to jail? Are you kidding?

In the end there was some crude justice, since the investment banks were done in by the declines in the market value of their holdings of asset-backed securities that they could not sell. But some of the top honchos left with tens of millions of dollars before market forces led to the implosion of the house of cards.

The Temptation of Banks

There are no firm data that permit comparisons of financial chicanery and fraudulent behavior across several centuries. The development of journalism as a profession may mean that any untoward activities are much more likely to be exposed today (although the activities themselves may not have changed). Exposure is the risk side of the equation; the reward is that the gains in wealth can be much greater. Martin Mayer's *The Bankers* does not dwell on safeguards against defalcation in the same way that James S. Gibbons did in 1859: 'There is perhaps no record of a bank fraud extant of which the perpetrator was not honest yesterday.'[64] Gibbons added, with emphasis, 'It will occur to the reader that there is one peculiar feature running through the whole system; and that is *the apprehension of fraud*.'[65]

What Gibbons said in 1859 is still true. The tendency is to believe that the banks and the bankers are 'paragons of integrity' and perhaps some of them are. A large number of banks lent extensively to Long-Term Capital Management in the 1990s, at the time believed to be one of the most innovative of the 'hedge funds.' (The term 'hedge funds' is a Madison Avenue home run, since the impression conveyed is that the firm has arranged its portfolio to reduce risk while in fact these firms rely extensively on borrowed funds to increase the returns to their shareholders and investors.) LTCM had been remarkably profitable—at least until its collapse. The banks were eager to lend to LTCM because they hoped they would learn enough about its portfolio to be able to mimic its trades and profit accordingly. In the spring and summer of 1998, LTCM encountered financial difficulties.

The awkward handling of derivatives and unclaimed deposits by Bankers Trust and the money laundering for Russia by the Bank of New York suggest that standards are not much higher today than they were, say, in the 1920s.

In the boom years of the second half of the 1990s, everyone—well, nearly everyone—was getting rich. The major investment banks had very high incomes from the fees associated with underwriting new issues of stocks and bonds, especially those of firms associated with information technologies and bio-genetics. The traditional 'Chinese wall' between the investment banking activities of these firms and their asset management activities was supposed to be retained after the repeal of the Glass-Steagall Act, which had become law in the early 1930s to force the separation of the traditional commercial banking activities of firms from their investment banking activities. The law had been adopted in response to the abuses of the 1920s. The firms 'promised' that they would maintain a Chinese wall and that the statements made by their security analysts would not be influenced by the desire of their investment bankers to sell more securities.

But consider the scorecard of Merrill Lynch. The firm was extensively involved in brokering deposits to the rogue thrift institutions in the 1980s. Henry Blodgett hustled information that he knew was misleading. Blodgett's superiors almost certainly knew that Blodgett was involved in a con. Merrill helped Enron falsify its income by paying an above-market price for the Enron barges in Nigeria.

Consider the scorecard of Citibank/Citigroup. The tale of Jack Grubman's hustles for the telecom firms has been noted; Citibank/Citigroup paid a settlement of $150 million. Citibank was obliged to close its private banking activities in Tokyo because of the failure of bank officials to deal fairly with customers by repeatedly buying inappropriate securities for them after ignoring the warning from the Japanese authorities to stop the practice. Several of the top managers of Citibank 'resigned'—a Park Avenue euphemism for being fired. Citibank's traders in London dumped a lot of German government bonds on the market and caused the prices to dive; they then repurchased these bonds at much lower prices. Several of the managers of Citibank's mutual funds took rebates based on the revenues of the bank rather than of the funds.

What happens when a swindler is found out? Charles Blunt, the brother of John Blunt and himself an insider in the South Sea Company, in early September 1720 cut his throat 'upon some discontent', as contemporary newspapers put it; Charles Bouchard, the retired manager of LeClerc, a small Geneva bank that lost money in unauthorized real estate investments, was found dead in Lac Léman, an apparent suicide, in May 1977. Psychiatry

holds that suicide in these circumstances comes from an intolerable loss of self-esteem, stemming from the realization of the irrationality of past behavior. The picture of stockbrokers jumping from Wall Street windows in October 1929 as they faced bankruptcy is now believed to be a myth.[66] An upswing in suicides is also part of the legend of the Austrian *krach* of 1873.[67] Nonetheless, the response does occur: 'Thus died by his own hand [having taken poison on Hampton Heath], at the early age of forty-two, John Sadleir, one of the greatest, if not the greatest, and at the same time the most successful swindler that this [Britain] or any other country has produced.'[68] (Greatness and success seem curious as characterizations in the circumstances.) Denfert-Rocherau of 1888, and Ivar Kreuger, the 'match-king' of the 1920s, both committed suicide[69]; Clifford Baxter, one of the senior officials of Enron, took his own life. But suicide may be more usual in fiction. Mr. Merdle cut his throat in a public bath with a tortoiseshell penknife in Dickens' *Little Dorrit*, and Augustus Melmotte in Trollope's *The Way We Live Now* took prussic acid at his club.

Flight is a less final form of exit than suicide. The prize case is Robert Knight, who doctored the books of the South Sea Company and then escaped to the Continent, there to make another fortune in Paris after breaking out of an Antwerp jail.[70] Robert Vesco fled to Costa Rica and then Cuba with an embezzled fortune. Charles Savary, who swindled the Banque de Lyon et de la Loire, died in Canada. Eugène Bontoux returned to France after five years of self-imposed exile to take advantage of a loophole in French law that held that prison terms not begun within five years of sentencing had to be dropped.[71] The analogous case roughly a century earlier was that of Arend Joseph, whose failure in January 1763 initiated the financial distress that culminated in the bankruptcy of the brothers DeNeufville on 25 July, touching off the panic of the same year. Arend Joseph left Amsterdam with 600,000 guilders, in a coach-and-six, for the free city of Kruilenburg in Holland, where he was immune from further process. He left a debt of one million guilders in Amsterdam.[72]

Comparisons can be made across the cycles in terms of the number of individuals who were indicted and the number who did jail time. Consider several episodes, from the 1920s, the 1980s, and the 1990s. In the 1920s two individuals went to jail for hustling the purchases of securities in a market that already had turned bearish. Eight or ten of the participants in the junk bond transactions of the 1980s, including Michael Milken, Ivan Boesky, Dennis Levine, and Charles Keating, were jailed for crimes that included insider trading, 'parking' of securities, and collusion to defraud; among those who served the longest sentences were heads of the thrifts that had been

large buyers of junk bonds. The number of those who will have served jail sentences for their transgressions in the 1990s includes five individuals who had received pay-checks from Enron and two who had been involved with MCIWorldCom. Most of the Enron officers who have been indicted have gone to jail. Several of the individuals involved with HealthSouth have gone to jail. Two executives associated with Rite-Aid went to jail. Several members of the Rigas family went to jail. Sam Waksal and his good friend Martha Stewart have gone to jail. Very few Wall Street bankers have been jailed. Frank Quattrone, one of the star investment bankers for Credit Suisse First Boston, was found guilty in a second trial of obstruction of justice by destroying e-mails, but his appeal succeeded. One Arthur Andersen partner involved with the Enron account did jail time.

Hundreds of Andersen partners and former partners implicitly paid large fines when the firm was forced to close and the value of partnerships and former partnerships collapsed. (Thousands of Enron employees lost their pensions and much of their financial wealth as well as their jobs when the firm went bankrupt.)

The Milken family probably had $2 billion in the bank when Michael Milken was released from prison. It would be impossible to figure out how much of the fortune was earned legally from innovation and how much was earned from illegal behavior. But assume that half of the family fortune could be tracked to transactions that were illegal. Consider how Milken might answer the charge, 'You were in the jail for 1000 days, you graduated with $1 billion so were paid $100,000 for each day in the jail.'

Economists are not qualified to discuss the appropriate punishment for the white-collar crime of swindling. At the time of the South Sea Bubble, Molesworth, then a member of the House of Commons, suggested that parliament should declare the directors of the South Sea Company guilty of parricide and subject them to the ancient Roman punishment for that transgression—to be sewn into sacks, each with a monkey and a snake, and drowned.[73] The suggestion is echoed in Dreiser's novel *The Titan*: 'Here the punishment consists of strangling first, then being sewn into a sack, without company, and thrown into the Bosphorus, a punishment reserved for cheating girl friends.'[74] In Christina Stead's *House of All Nations*, written a quarter of a century later, a character suggests that old sultans used to punish a faithless wife by tying her into a sack with two wildcats and sinking the sack in the Bosphorus.[75] These suggested punishments seem excessively harsh. Still, those who commit white-collar crimes seem to get off lightly, and many keep most of their ill-earned fortunes. The fines paid by the Wall Street

firms are a tax on the wealth of their shareholders and not a real burden on the malfeasants except in as much as they are also shareholders.

Whether swindlers are punished or live out their days in indulgent luxury is a more appropriate topic for corporate governance and business ethics than financial history. The revelation of swindles, frauds, and defalcation, and the arrests and punishment of those who violate trust are important signals that economic euphoria has reached too high a pitch and that there will be significant social consequences.

Theranos and Wirecard Parallels

Corporate frauds Theranos and Wirecard both had CEOs that wore Steve Jobs style black turtleneck shirts and aspired to visionary speech. Both filled social needs: for a woman CEO of a possible unicorn—a billion-dollar IPO—in the first case and for a German high-tech firm in the second. Both were felled by journalists who published their first critical pieces in 2015 and worked under the threat of lawsuits or worse. John Carryrou of the *Wall Street Journal* exposed the blood testing firm that claimed to be able, but was utterly unable, to run full tests on drops of blood. His book is *Bad Blood: Secrets and Lies in a Silicon Valley Startup*. Dan McCrumb of the *Financial Times* exposed the latter as having made it into the German equity index, the Dax 30, on the basis of fabricated revenues and profits. The German authorities lent themselves to the effort to make the journalist out to be a conspirator with short-sellers, those who seek to profit from share crashes. The pushback was so successful that the collapse of Wirecard took until five years after McCrumb's initial reporting. His book is *Money Men: A Hot Startup, A Billion Dollar Fraud, A Fight for the Truth*.

Notes

1. See Norman C. Miller, *The Great Salad Oil Swindle* (New York: Coward, McCann, 1965).
2. Hyman P. Minsky, 'Financial Resources in a Fragile Financial Environment', *Challenge*, vol. 18 (July/August 1975), p. 65.
3. Martin F. Hellwig, 'A Model of Borrowing and Lending with Bankruptcy', Princeton University Econometric Research Program, Research Memorandum no. 177 (April 1975), p. 1.
4. Daniel Defoe, *The Anatomy of Change-Alley* (London: E. Smith, 1719), p. 8. See also the title of Jean Carper's book on fraud, *Not with a Gun* (New York: Grossman, 1973).

5. Jacob van Klaveren, 'Die historische Erscheinungen der Korruption', *Viertelsjahrschrift für Sozial-und Wirtschaftsgeschichte*, vol. 44 (December 1957), pp. 289–324; vol. 45 (December 1958), pp. 433–69, 469–504; vol. 46 (June 1959), pp. 204–31. See also idem, 'Fiskalismus – Mercantilismus – Korruption: Drei Aspecte der Finanz- und Wirtschaftspolitik während der Ancien Regime', ibid., vol. 47 (September 1960), pp. 333–53.
6. E. Ray McCartney, *The Crisis of 1873* (Minneapolis: Burgess, 1935), p. 15.
7. John Carswell, *The South Sea Bubble* (London: Cresset, 1960), p. 13.
8. Maximillian E. Novak, *Economics and the Fiction of Daniel Defoe* (Berkeley: University of California Press, 1962), p. 103.
9. Bray Hammond, *Banks and Politics in America from the Revolution to the Civil War* (Princeton: Princeton University Press, 1957), p. 268.
10. Carswell, *South Sea Bubble*, pp. 222–4.
11. William G. Shepheard, Wall Street editor of *Business Week*, in the preface to Donald H. Dunn, *Ponzi, the Boston Swindler* (New York: McGraw-Hill, 1975), p. x.
12. Milton Friedman, 'In Defense of Destabilizing Speculation', in *The Optimum Quantity of Money and Other Essays* (Chicago: Aldine, 1969), p. 290.
13. Quoted in Max Winkler, *Foreign Bonds, an Autopsy: a Study of Defaults and Repudiations of Government Obligations* (Philadelphia: Roland Swain, 1933), p. 103.
14. E. Victor Morgan, *The Theory and Practice of Central Banking, 1797–1913* (Cambridge: Cambridge University Press, 1943), p. 177.
15. Honoré de Balzac, *Melmoth réconcilié* (Geneva: Editions de Verbe, 1946), pp. 45–50.
16. Dunn, *Ponzi*, p. 188.
17. Introduction by Robert Tracey to Anthony Trollope, *The Way We Live Now* (1874–75; reprint edn, New York: Bobbs-Merrill, 1974), p. xxv.
18. Sir John Clapham, *The Bank of England: a History* (Cambridge: Cambridge University Press, 1945), vol. 1, p. 229.
19. Charles Wilson, *Anglo-Dutch Commerce and Finance in the Eighteenth Century* (Cambridge: Cambridge University Press, 1941), p. 170.
20. George W. Van Vleck, *The Panic of 1857: an Analytical Study* (New York: Columbia University Press, 1943), p. 65.
21. Earl J. Hamilton, 'The Political Economy of France at the Time of John Law', *History of Political Economy*, vol. 1 (Spring 1969), p. 146.
22. Jacob van Klaveren, 'Rue de Quincampoix und Exchange Alley: Die Spekulationsjähre 1719 und 1720 in Frankreich und England', *Vierteljahrschrift für Sozial- und Wirtschaftsgeschichte*, vol. 48 (October 1961), pp. 329ff.
23. Dunn, *Ponzi*, op. cit.
24. Max Wirth, *Geschichte der Handelskrisen*, 4th edn (1890; reprint edn, New York: Burt Franklin, 1968), p. 510.
25. William Robert Scott, *The Constitution and Finance of English, Scottish and Irish Joint-Stock Companies to 1720* (Cambridge: Cambridge University Press,

1911), vol. 3, pp. 449ff.; and D. Morier Evans, *The Commercial Crisis, 1847–48*, 2nd edn, rev. (1849; reprint edn, New York: Augustus M. Kelley, 1969), pp. 33–4. A separate list for the South Sea Bubble, prepared by a contemporary and less detailed, is set out in Wirth, *Handelskrisen*, pp. 67–79.

26. A. Andréadès, *History of the Bank of England* (London: P. S. King, 1909), p. 133.
27. Carswell, *South Sea Bubble*, p. 142.
28. Scott, *Joint-Stock Companies*, p. 450.
29. Hans Rosenberg, *Die Weltwirtschaftskrise von 1857–59* (Stuttgart: W. Kohlhammer, 1934), p. 103.
30. Wirth, *Handelskrisen*, p. 480.
31. Anthony Trollope, *The Three Clerks* (New York: Harper & Brothers, 1860), p. 346.
32. Carswell, *South Sea Bubble*, p. 177.
33. Fritz Stern, *Gold and Iron: Bismarck, Bleichröder, and the Building of the German Empire* (London: Allen & Unwin, 1977), p. 358.
34. Ibid., pp. 396–7.
35. US Senate, Committee on Finance, 72nd Cong., 1st sess., *Hearings on Sales of Foreign Bonds of Securities*, held 18 December 1931, to 10 February 1932 (Washington, DC: US Government Printing Office, 1932).
36. O. M. W. Sprague, *History of Crises under the National Banking System* (1910; reprint edn, New York: Augustus M. Kelley, 1968), p. 341.
37. Quoted in Wirth, *Handelskrisen*, p. 80.
38. Honoré de Balzac, *La maison Nucingen,* in *Oeuvres complètes* (Paris: Calmann Lévy, 1892), p. 68.
39. Carswell, *South Sea Bubble*, pp. 176, 181.
40. Wirth, *Handelskrisen*, p. 491.
41. Emile Zola, *L'Argent* (Paris: Livre de Poche, n.d.), p. 125.
42. Wirth, *Handelskrisen*, p. 491.
43. Zola, *L'Argent*, p. 161.
44. Jean Bouvier, *Le krach de l'Union Générale* (Paris: Presses universitaires de France, 1960), p. 36.
45. *The Economist*, 21 October 1848, pp. 1186–8, quoted in Arthur D. Gayer, W. W. Rostow and Anna J. Schwartz, *The Growth and Fluctuation of the British Economy, 1790–1850* (Oxford: Oxford University Press, Clarendon Press, 1953), p. 316.
46. Rosenberg, *Weltwirtschaftskrise*, p. 101.
47. Stern, *Gold and Iron*, chap. 10 ('Greed and Intrigue') and p. 364.
48. Novak, *Economics of Defoe*, pp. 14–15 and 160 n.35.
49. Ibid., p. 16, n.50.
50. Maurice Lévy-Leboyer, *Les banques européennes et l'industrialisation internationale dans la première moitié du XIXe siècle* (Paris: Presses universitaires de France, 1964), pp. 632–3.
51. Ibid., p. 503, n.90.

52. Bouvier, *Le krach*, p. 124.

53. Ibid., p. 161, n.50.

54. Stern, *Gold and Iron*, chap. 11.

55. Theodore Dreiser's *Trilogy of Desire* consists of three novels: *The Financier* (1912), *The Titan* (1914) and *The Stoic* (1947). See *The Titan* (New York: World, 1972), pp. 371–2.

56. Ibid., pp. 515–40.

57. Henry Grote Lewin, *The Railway Mania and Its Aftermath, 1845–1852* (1936; reprint edn, rev., New York: Augustus M. Kelley, 1968), pp. 262, 357–64.

58. See Paul W. Gates, *Illinois Central Railroad and Its Colonization Work* (1934; reprint edn, Cambridge, MA: Harvard University Press, 1968), pp. 66, 75–6; John L. Weller, *The New Haven Railroad: the Rise and Fall* (New York: Hastings House, 1969), p. 37n; Van Vleck, *Panic of 1857*, p. 58.

59. See Willard L. Thorp, *Business Annals* (New York: National Bureau of Economic Research, 1926), p. 126.

60. Watson Washburn and Edmund S. Delong, *High and Low Financiers: Some Notorious Swindlers and Their Abuses of our Modern Stock Selling System* (Indianapolis: Bobbs-Merrill, 1932), p. 13.

61. Ibid., pp. 85, 101, 144, 309.

62. Barrie A. Wigmore, *The Crash and Its Aftermath: a History of Security Markets in the United States, 1929–1933* (Westport: Greenwood, 1985), pp. 344–8.

63. Ibid., pp. 358–60.

64. Martin Mayer, *The Bankers* (New York: Ballantine Books, 1989); James S. Gibbons, *The Banks of New York, Their Dealers, the Clearing House, and the Panic of 1857* (New York: D. Appleton, 1859), p. 104.

65. Ibid., p. 277.

66. John Kenneth Galbraith, *The Great Crash, 1929*, 3rd edn (Boston: Houghton Mifflin, 1972), pp. 133–5.

67. David F. Good, *The Economic Rise of the Hapsburg Empire, 1750–1914* (Berkeley: University of California Press, 1984), p. 165.

68. D. Morier Evans, *Facts, Failures and Frauds* (1839; reprint edn, New York: Augustus M. Kelley, 1968), p. 235.

69. See Robert Shaplen, *Kreuger: Genius and Swindler* (New York: Knopf, 1960).

70. Carswell, *South Sea Bubble*, pp. 225, 265–6.

71. Bouvier, *Le krach*, pp. 211, 219.

72. Herbert I. Bloom, *The Economic Activities of the Jews of Amsterdam in the Seventeenth and Nineteenth Centuries* (Williamsport: Bayard Press, 1937), p. 199.

73. Carswell, *South Sea Bubble*, p. 210.

74. Dreiser, *The Titan*, p. 237.

75. Christina Stead, *House of All Nations* (New York: Simon & Schuster, 1938), p. 643.

7

Domestic Contagion: Twin Peaks?

Real estate and equity market manias often occur in parallel. Both higher property prices and share prices tend to drive up GDP growth, which in turn tends to lift both asset prices. But the manias for real estate and equity also feed each other through portfolio rebalancing and the credit mechanism.

One feedback loop from increases in real estate prices and stock prices to the more rapid growth of GDP is from the increases in household wealth to higher levels of household spending. Many households have savings or wealth objectives; as the surge in the prices of securities and real estate leads to higher levels of wealth they spend more on consumption goods—including conspicuous homes (The mirror of the increase in consumption spending is that the household saving rate declines). The second loop is from the increase in stock prices to higher levels of investment spending. Firms can raise cash from investors at lower cost and because of the decline in the cost of capital, and they undertake new projects that would have been less profitable if this cost had not declined. The 'cost of capital' to a firm varies inversely with the price of its stock; the higher stock prices are, the lower their cost of capital and the larger their new investments in plant and equipment. A parallel loop is from the increase in property prices to higher levels of investment spending as firms' property holdings boost collateral for bank loans.

The association of bubbles in stock markets and in property markets also arises from three portfolio connections. One is that in many countries, and especially smaller countries and those in the early stages of industrialization, the market value of real estate companies, construction companies, and of

© The Author(s), under exclusive license to Springer Nature Switzerland AG 2023
R. Z. Aliber et al., *Manias, Panics, and Crashes*,
https://doi.org/10.1007/978-3-031-16008-0_7

firms in other industries closely connected with real estate, including banks, accounts for a relatively large share of the aggregate stock market valuation. A second connection is that individuals whose net worth has increased sharply as a result of the increase in real estate values buy stocks to diversify their wealth; there aren't many other ways to diversify wealth. The third connection is the mirror image of the second; the individual investors who have profited extensively from the increase in stock market valuations buy larger and more expensive first homes and they also buy second homes. The changes in the prices of apartments in the Manhattan real estate market are closely tied to the bonuses on Wall Street.

Because of the links through both aggregate spending and portfolios, it makes sense that stock market and property prices track each other upward, reaching what Claudio Borio and Patrick McGuire call 'twin peaks.'[1] One might imagine that stock market and property prices would likewise track each other downward. After all, the relationship between changes in wealth and changes in spending is broadly symmetrical; when the prices of securities and real estate decline, economic activity slows. And the portfolio balancing works in reverse, too: a stock market decline leads to for sale signs, especially on second homes.

However, it turns out that what goes up together need not go down together. Stocks and property may share peaks, but their downslopes differ systematically. The Japanese stock and property bubbles of the late 1980s exemplify this regularity (U.S. residential property peaked in early 2006, six quarters before U.S. equities, but equity prices bottomed in early 2009, while the downslope of property prices extended into 2012). Let us start by considering the domestic contagion of asset prices in one of the earliest bubbles.

Tulipmania

The tulipmania is generally regarded as an isolated incident but it seems to have stimulated asset prices and construction. The price of Dutch tulips increased by several hundred percent in the autumn of 1636—and the increases in the prices of the more exotic species of bulbs were even larger. Some analysts, especially those with a strong commitment to rationality and market efficiency, have questioned whether the use of the term bubble is appropriate to describe the increases in tulip prices. Tulip bulbs are subject to a cobweb-like growth behavior; once planted, a bulb may develop for six

to eight months before it begins to bloom—and then each bulb produces many little baby bulbs.

Not only the exotic varieties of bulbs were affected; ordinary garden-variety tulips such as the Gouda, Switzer, or White Crown that were traded among simple folk at so-called colleges or public houses also soared in price.[2]

The excitement around tulips began in earnest after September 1636, when bulbs were no longer available for examination since they had been planted to bloom during the following spring. Some of the buyers committed to pay for the 'merchandise' that was buried in the ground and that they could not see at the time of purchase. The excited bidding of November and December 1636 and January 1637 was conducted without any specimens in evidence.

The down payments for the purchase of bulbs frequently involved a barter transaction.[3] Simon Schama, the historian, provided examples; in one case, for a pound of White Crowns (*Witte Croon* in Dutch, sold by weight because of its ordinariness) four cows were paid at the time of purchase and then 525 guilders were to be paid on delivery, presumably the next June. Other down payments consisted of tracts of land, houses, furniture, silver and gold vessels, paintings, a suit and a coat, and a coach and dapple-gray pair; and for a single Viceroy (rare), valued at 2500 guilders, two *lasts* (a measure that varied by commodity and locality) of wheat and four of rye, eight pigs, a dozen sheep, two oxheads of wine, four tons of butter, a thousand pounds of cheese, a bed, some clothing, and a silver beaker.[4]

The changes in the prices of tulips spurred share prices, house prices, and canal building. The Dutch economy had been depressed during the 1620s when war with Spain was resumed after a twelve-year truce, but recovered impressively in the 1630s. The prices of shares in the Amsterdam Chamber of the Dutch East India Company doubled between 1630 and 1639, mostly after early 1636, going from 229 in March 1636 to 412 in August 1639, and then increasing to 500 by 1640. House prices had fallen in the early 1630s but 'shot up' in the middle of the decade. Investment surged in drainage schemes, in the West Indies Company and in canals.[5] Jan de Vries wrote of the *trekschuit*, a system of horse-drawn passenger barge canals which got under way in 1636 and reached a 'fever' in 1640. Construction was undertaken between pairs of towns to make the travel of merchants and officials more reliable than by sailing ships, which depended on the wind. Two lines from Amsterdam to smaller towns were decided on in 1636, and one between Leiden and Delft. Building of the complex network reached a peak in 1659 and 1665, but de Vries connected the project to the tulipmania and to the explosive growth of the Dutch economy between 1622 and 1660.[6]

Jonathan Israel wrote that the tulipmania should be viewed against the background of the general boom and as a mania of 'small-town dealers, tavern-keepers and horticulturalists' while for the most part the wealthy made money in other ways.[7] This perspective undermines one of Peter Garber's points that there could have been no tulipmania because there was no depression once bulb prices declined.[8] The Dutch economy slowed in the 1640s before putting on a tremendous growth spurt from 1650 to 1672, which included luxury housing, civic buildings and paintings. However, the market for paintings collapsed with the French invasion of 1672.[9] At the height of the boom there was a 'mania' for clocks and clock towers. In Leiden a clock was installed in a tower at the top of the White Gate where at the *trekschuit* station passengers were loaded and unloaded, to assure the punctuality of the personal barges.[10]

The decline in the prices of tulip bulbs led to a decline in economic activity, and the causal connection was that households were less eager spenders as their wealth declined.

The Stock Market and Real Estate

Homer Hoyt's *One Hundred Years of Land Values in Chicago*[11] traced five cycles of boom and relapse in real estate prices to the growth of Chicago. The boom in the US stock market in 1928–1929 was linked to increases in prices of raw land, residential sites and to commercial buildings in both the central business district and in the suburbs. Hoyt quotes from a *Chicago Tribune* editorial of April 1890:

> In the ruin of all collapsed booms is to be found the work of men who bought property at prices they knew perfectly well were fictitious, but who were willing to pay such prices simply because they knew that some still greater fool could be depended on to take the property off their hands and leave them with a profit.[12]

Chicago's reputation for real estate booms was such that Berlin, overindulging in real estate speculation in the euphoria of victory over France in 1870–1871, was called 'Chicago on the [river] Spree.'[13] The booms in Berlin and Vienna in 1873 were related to the changes in prices on the New York stock market. One writer claimed that in Chicago in 1871, every other man and every fourth woman had an investment in house lots.[14] The bubbles expanded in parallel until the summer of 1873.

The spread of euphoria from one market to another reflects that when the prices of securities and real estate are increasing at a rapid rate, the widows and orphans climb on the bandwagon. Capital gains can be made without any special skill.

When the stock market collapses, shareholders, especially those that have bought with short-term margin loans, know they are in trouble and must reduce their indebtedness. Those investors who have high leverage recognize that their wealth is declining much more rapidly than stock prices and so they sell—or their positions are sold by their brokers and lenders.

Speculators in real estate initially feel no such compunction. Their debts are bank loans on extended terms, and not callable like day-to-day brokers' loans. They have real assets, not just paper claims. Most choose to wait for the recovery that they think is just over the horizon.

The economic downturn leads to a drying up of the demand for real estate investments. Taxes and interest on loans, however, continue without interruption. Hoyt wrote with great prescience in his 1933 book, that slowly but inexorably the speculators in real estate are ground down. The lenders to the real estate speculators, and especially the bank lenders, incur large loan losses. One hundred and sixty-three of 200 banks in Chicago in 1933 suspended payment. Real estate loans in default, not advances to stockbrokers, were the largest single element in the failure of 4800 banks from 1930 to 1933.[15]

Hoyt's analysis of the relation between the stock market and the real estate market can be readily applied to the aftermath of the New York stock market crash of October 19, 1987, Black Monday, and to the Japanese stock market crash of 1990 (in the next section). In New York, the stock market's troubles of October 1987 were cleared up brilliantly after the monetary authorities rapidly poured liquidity into banks and brokers to forestall a shortage of their credit to shareholders who had bought on borrowed money. Margin requirements of 50 percent for ordinary shareholders helped limit leverage; not so helpful was so-called portfolio insurance that guided pension funds and other institutional investors to act as if they were leveraged investors by dumping shares into the declining market. But the agony in real estate was drawn out. Construction slowed as buildings were completed, but new starts were abandoned or postponed. Vacancy rates in office buildings rose sharply, varying according to location, whether downtown, midtown or in the 'edge cities' built in the suburbs during the 1980s boom.

Rockefeller Center Properties, Inc., had a $1.3 billion mortgage on the Rockefeller Center in midtown Manhattan after the complex had been sold to a Mitsubishi entity. The mortgage was held in a Real Estate Investment Trust (REIT). In 1987 the trustees sought to increase the income of the trust

by using the cash from short-term loans to buy back bonds that were selling at a discount. The gains were paid out as dividends. In 1989 as the deterioration in the real estate market progressed, the trustees borrowed, using a letter of credit to get the cash to pay off the short-term debt. The president of the REIT said, 'It was a prudent thing to do at the time.'[16] To the contrary, Hoyt's analysis suggested that one might expect an extended downturn in real estate values following a stock market crash. After prolonged agony, the REIT crashed.

Japanese Shares, Real Estate, and Banks

The story of the collapse of the bubble in the Japanese real estate market in the 1990s begins in the early 1950s when GDP began to increase rapidly in both nominal and real terms from the sharply depressed values immediately after World War II (Japanese per capita income returned to the 1940 level in 1951). Exports increased rapidly, and the composition of exports shifted from cheap toys and textiles to bicycles and motorcycles and then to steel and automobiles and electronics. Banks' deposit rates were regulated and the big banks had their pick of the largest firms to lend to.

Real estate prices increased steadily, although with substantial year-on-year variability. Because of financial regulation, the nominal interest rate had been below the inflation rates in the 1950s, the 1960s, and the 1970s; the real rate of return on bank deposits and other fixed-price assets often was negative. The price index for residential real estate in six large cities started at 100 in 1955 and reached 4100 in the mid-1970s and 5800 in 1980; the owners of real estate were one of the few groups with a positive real rate of return. During the 1980s the price of real estate increased by a factor of five to six.[17] At its peak, the market value of real estate in Japan was twice the market value of US real estate and the ratio of the market value of real estate to GDP in Japan was four times higher.[18]

The Nikkei stock market index, which started at 100 in May 1949, reached 6000 by the early 1980s. Stock prices surged in the second half of the 1980s and nearly reached 40,000 at the end of 1989. The volume of shares traded did not quite keep pace, increasing from 120 billion shares in 1983 to 280 billion in 1989.[19]

There are two possible displacements that set off the bubble. By the early 1980s, the government, looking to finance large deficits, deregulated the bond market, which in turn allowed big firms to tap the corporate bond market. '[P]art of the reason why banks in Japan got into trouble is that they

lost many of their best borrowers in a very short period of time.'[20] Kazuo Ueda noted that the change in the financing pattern of large firms, along with the liberalization of deposit rates from 1985, 'forced banks to look for lending opportunities with low screening costs.'[21] The big banks pursued a strategy of moving down market, lending to smaller, more domestic firms on the collateral of readily analyzed land holdings. Big Japanese banks fatefully changed their business models through credit creation on a massive scale.

The other candidate for the displacement was the rise in the yen after 1985 and extensive efforts by the Bank of Japan to limit its appreciation in the second half of the 1980s.[22] The yen rose from almost 240 to the dollar in 1985 to 170 in 1986, 145 in 1987 and 128 in 1988. The Bank of Japan reduced its discount rate from 5.5 percent in 1982 to 5 percent in 1983, 3.5 percent at the beginning of 1986 and 2.5 percent a year later. The 1986 reduction was taken simultaneously—with similar action by the Federal Reserve and the Bundesbank. In reverse, however, the United States and Germany began raising rates in 1987, eased after the October crash, and resumed raising rates in 1988. The Bank of Japan raised its discount rate only in May 1989, and a new governor, Yasushi Mieno, took over in December 1989 and did the heavy lifting. The expectation of continued low interest rates led to somewhat rapid growth in the supply of money and very rapid growth in the supply of credit.

The increase in real estate prices fed the boom in stock prices through the portfolio and aggregate spending connections described above. Real estate companies and banks with real estate exposure were well represented on the Tokyo Stock Exchange. The boom in real estate prices and financial deregulation led to a surge in construction activity. For their part, high equity prices signaled a low cost of equity (often misapprehended as the very low dividend yield or convertible bond yield) to Japanese firms, and investment spending rose in relation to GDP. Many new golf courses were built.

In addition, unusual features of big Japanese banks' balance sheets magnified the credit links between real estate and stock prices. Big banks had moved their business models down market to lending to small firms and depended on their land collateral. As a result, increases in the value of real estate increased the value of their collateral and made banks eager to make more loans. Easy credit led firms to borrow to fund so-called 'zaitech' (financial technology) investments in shares and exotic assets as well as to fund real estate investments.

Higher equity prices directly increased the capacity of Japanese banks to lend through gains on so-called 'cross-held' shares. Big banks held over 100 percent of their own equity in the shares of affiliated firms, who reciprocated

by holding affiliated banks' shares. Higher share prices thus made Japanese banks richer, that is, increased their capital. Competition for market share and asset size meant that the Japanese banks put their capital to work. One way to compete for market share was by lending a higher share of the appraised value of real estate. Equivalently, banks could lend to nonbank lenders (eg, jusen) that appraised property generously. Thus, gains on Japanese banks' shareholdings increased the supply of credit, reinforcing the effect of higher collateral values from higher land prices.

This mutual reinforcement of real estate and share prices, on the one hand, and bank lending on the other hand leveraged Japan as perhaps no major economy has before or since. The debt of nonfinancial businesses and households in Japan rose much faster than buoyant Japanese GDP in the four years 1986 through 1989 (Fig. 7.1). In particular, the ratio of private debt to GDP rose by about 10 percent of GDP per year to a level of over twice GDP.

The rise in the ratio of private debt to GDP in Japan in the late 1980s was a mountain in relation to the US hill in the mid-2000s. From 2003 through 2007, the debt of US households and firms grew faster than GDP, to be sure. But the lead up to the Great Financial Crisis saw US private debt rise by 5 percent of GDP per year, half the rate in Japan in the late 1980s.

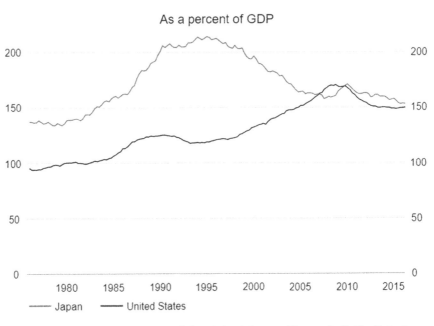

Fig. 7.1 Private credit in Japan and the United States (*Source* Refinitiv Datastream; Bank for International Settlements)

Given the powerfully magnified links through big banks' balance sheets, Japanese share prices and real estate prices rose sharply in tandem in the late 1980s, as shown in Fig. 7.2. So large a rise in so short a time was difficult for even top US economists to explain: Kenneth French and James Poterba answered their question 'Were Japanese Stock Prices Too High?' originally 'Are Japanese Stock Prices Too High,' in the affirmative.[23]

Stock prices peaked on the last trading day of 1989 and declined by 40 percent in 1990. Commercial land prices peaked two to four quarters later (the land price data in Fig. 7.2 peak in September 1990 but are semiannual March and September data that are interpolated for June and December). Borio and McGuire report a 5-quarter lag between the peak of share and residential real estate prices.[24]

Consistent with Hoyt's model, real estate prices fell gradually at first as longer term loans allowed investors to hang on in hope of a recovery. In the event, it took three to four years for the drop in real estate prices to catch up with share prices. The trough for stock prices and real estate prices occurred only in the 2000s. Real estate prices fell more slowly but more extensively.

Masaaki Shirakawa, later Governor of the Bank of Japan, shows losses on land of twice GDP in the 1990s and losses on equities of up to a half of GDP then.[25] Richard Koo contrasts such losses with Goldsmith's estimate

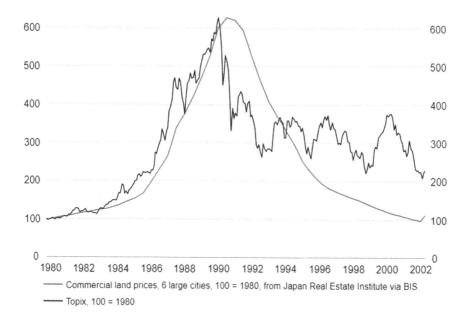

Fig. 7.2 Japanese commercial land prices and the Topix (*Source* Refinitiv Datastream; Bank for International Settlements)

of one-time GDP for the United States after 1929.[26] The decline in the prices of securities and real estate left many financial institutions with negative capital and they remained in business only because of the implicit support of the government. Only after a financial panic in 1997 did the government nationalize two big banks in 1998 and in 1999 inject capital in the rest.[27]

Economic growth slowed. The inflation rate began to fall and then ten years later the price level began to fall. The failures of firms meant that the banks took over title to the properties and sold them, which put further downward pressure on property prices which complicated the business plans of other firms. There was a downward spiral and concern about a debt deflation trap.[28]

Consumer Prices, Asset Prices, Credit, and Policy

The reduction in the Bank of Japan's discount rate, especially after 1986, one of the candidate displacements which touched off the bubble, was stimulated by pressures from the United States. But it was rationalized because the price level in Japan was more or less unchanged, in part because the increase in the price of the Japanese yen from 240 to the US dollar in 1985 to 130 in 1988 led to downward pressure on the goods price level.[29]

A major question is whether central bankers should be concerned with asset prices. Most central bankers choose the stability of the goods price level as the target of monetary policy. Most recently the policy mantra has been inflation targeting—central banks aim to achieve a consumer price inflation rate of 2 percent. If, however, the sharp decline in the prices of stocks and real estate leads to a significant decline in bank solvency, should the central banks more than keep an eye on asset prices?

In one view, asset prices should be incorporated into the general price level because, in a world of efficient markets, they forecast future prices and consumption.[30] But this view assumes that the prices of securities and real estate are determined by the economic fundamentals and are not affected by the surges in the supply of credit from domestic and foreign sources. The quadrupling of asset prices in Japan between 1985 and 1989 was not a useful forecast of the subsequent prices and spending.

Since the Great Financial Crisis, a consensus has formed that, however central banks respond to asset prices, they should be concerned with private credit that grows in a sustained fashion at a rate substantially higher than nominal GDP. In response to this consensus, the latest iteration of the Basel

capital standards for banks even provides for added capital requirement in response to such rapid credit growth.

Looking back, the first Basel Capital Accord was agreed in 1988, yet its higher bank capital requirement did not prevent or obviously limit the Japanese share and real estate bubble or the associated rapid credit growth. In principle, the new standard was to be phased in over several years, but financial market participants pushed Japanese banks to step up common stock issuance very markedly in the fiscal year to March 1988.[31] Between then and March 1990, the big Japanese banks almost doubled their prime 'tier 1' capital, while their risk-weighted assets rose by less than half.[32]

Nowadays this would be seen as a powerful tightening of so-called macroprudential policy—tightening bank capital requirements to restrain, or at least to defend banks' solvency against, very rapid credit growth amid buoyant asset prices. Did it fail in this important case?

Yes, but. The structure of the big Japanese banks' balance sheets made restraining the Japanese bubble a near impossible job.[33] Rising real estate prices inflated the collateral for many loans and spurred credit expansion. At the same time, the Nikkei bubble inflated the very foundation of the big Japanese banks' capacity for risk-taking and losses on a mark-to-market basis: their equity. Kazuo Ueda viewed it as 'destabilizing' that the Basel Committee allowed Japanese banks to count 45 percent of unrealized gains on equities in their second-tier capital.[34] However, Japanese banks sold (and immediately bought back) plenty of their cross-held shares in order to add their gains to declared income and to their tier-1 capital.[35] Thus, banks could and did drag hidden reserves onto their balance sheets, albeit at the expense of paying 55 percent of the gain away in income taxes. Indeed, without the benefit of the 45 percent of unrealized gains in secondary capital, big Japanese banks might have further weakened their financial strength by realizing even more capital gains on their equity holdings and paying even more tax.

Ultimately, the exposure of big Japanese banks' balance sheets and economic capital to the stock market posed the problem much more than its regulatory treatment. Banks that lived by share prices in the 1980s died by property prices in the 1990s. Death and near-death were delayed into the 1990s by both politics and Hoyt's lag of real estate prices to the share price crash. In the 2000s, Japanese policy sought directly to reduce banks' holdings of shares to promote financial stability.[36]

To conclude, contagion between manias in the stock and property markets leads to similar profiles of share and property prices on the way up. The manias reinforce each other domestically through macroeconomic, portfolio balancing, and credit channels. Differences in the time profile of lending

against shares and real estate result in a slower descent from the peak for property prices. Japan's tripling of asset prices in the latter 1980s, which stands out even measured against the US experience of the late 1920s or early 2000s, epitomized all these observations. What made for so extreme an outcome in Japan was that much contagion occurred within the big banks' balance sheets between property collateral and equity holdings. Such domestic contagion turbocharged credit in what Masaaki Shirakawa recently called, 'one of the largest [bubbles] the world has ever witnessed.'[37]

Acknowledgements Thanks are due to Masaaki Shirakawa and Kazuo Ueda for their comments on a draft of this chapter but they are not implicated in its limitations.

Notes

1. Claudio Borio and Patrick McGuire, 'Twin Peaks in Equity and Housing Prices?' *BIS Quarterly Review* (March 2004), pp. 79–93.
2. Peter M. Garber, 'Tulipmania', in Robert P. Flood and Peter M. Garber, eds., *Speculative Bubbles, Speculative Attacks, and Policy Switching* (Cambridge, MA: MIT Press, 1994), p. 72.
3. N. W. Posthumus, 'The Tulip Mania in Holland in the Years 1636 and 1637', *Journal of Business and Economic History*, vol. 1 (1928–29), reprinted in W. C. Scoville and J. C. LaForce, eds., *The Economic Development of Western Europe, vol. 2, The Sixteenth and Seventeenth Centuries* (Lexington: D.C. Heath, 1969), p. 169.
4. Simon Schama, *The Embarrassment of Riches: An Interpretation of Dutch Culture in the Golden Age* (New York: Knopf, 1987), p. 358. Schama's source is Krelage, *Bluemenspekulation.*
5. Jonathan I. Israel, *The Dutch Republic: Its Rise, Greatness and Fall, 1477–1806* (Oxford: Clarendon Press, 1995), p. 533. Jan de Vries and Ad van der Woude state that in the summer of 1636, speculation in commodity derivatives spread far beyond the circle of tulip fanciers, its flame being fanned by severe outbreaks of bubonic plague that released inhibitions (*The First Modern Economy: Success, Failure and Perseverance of the Dutch Economy, 1500–1815* [Cambridge: Cambridge University Press, 1997], pp. 150–1).
6. Jan de Vries, *Barges and Capitalism: Transportation in the Dutch Economy* (Wageningen: A. G. Bidragen, 1978), pp. 52ff.
7. Israel, *The Dutch Republic*, p. 533.
8. Garber, 'Tulipmania', pp. 71–2.
9. Israel, *The Dutch Republic*, Chap. 33.
10. Ibid., p. 869.

11. Homer Hoyt, *One Hundred Years of Land Values in Chicago: The Relationship of the Growth of Chicago to the Rise in Land Values, 1830–1933* (Chicago: University of Chicago Press, 1933).

12. Quoted in Hoyt, *Land Values*, p. 165. This suggests that the 'greater fool theory'—a speculator buying an asset he believes is overpriced because he thinks he can sell it to a greater fool, widely quoted today—goes back at least a century.

13. Fritz Stern, *Gold and Iron: Bismarck, Bleichröder, and the Building of the German Empire* (London: Allen & Unwin, 1977), p. 161.

14. Hoyt, *Land Values*, p. 102. One stimulus to the boom was the huge fire of 6 October 1871, which destroyed somewhat more than one-fourth of the 60,000 houses in the city.

15. Hoyt, *Land Values*, p. 401.

16. 'How to Ruin a Safe Bet: Did Rockefeller Center Financiers Reach Too Far?', *New York Times*, 5 October 1995, pp. D1, D11.

17. Keizai Koho Center, *Japan 1994: An International Comparison* (Tokyo, 1993), Chart 11–3, 'Increase in Land Prices in Japan', p. 83.

18. Koichi Hamada, 'Bubbles, Busts and Bailouts', in Mitsuaki Okabe, ed., *The Structure of the Japanese Economy* (London: Macmillan, 1995), pp. 263–86.

19. Masahiko Takeda and Philip Turner, 'The Liberalization of Japanese Financial Markets: Some Major Themes', *BIS Economic Papers*, no. 34 (November 1992), graph 8, p. 53.

20. Takeo Hoshi and Anil Kashyap, 'The Japanese Banking Crisis: Where Did It Come From and How Will It End?', in Ben Bernanke and Julio Rotemberg, eds., *NBER Macroeconomics Annual 1999*, vol. 14 (Cambridge: MIT Press, 1999), p. 144.

21. Kazua Ueda, 'The Japanese Banking Crisis in the 1990s', in *Strengthening the Banking System in China: Issues and Experience, BIS Policy Papers*, no. 7 (October 1999), p. 256.

22. William Sterling, 'The Leveraging of Japan', *International Economy* (May/June 1989), p. 69.

23. Kenneth R. French and James M. Poterba, 'Were Japanese Stock Prices Too High?' *Journal of Financial Economics*, vol. 29, no. 2 (October 1991), pp. 337–363. See also Kazuo Ueda, 'Are Japanese Stock Prices Too High?' *Journal of the Japanese and International Economies*, vol. 4, no. 4 (December 1990), pp. 351–370.

24. Borio and McGuire, 'Twin Peaks in Equity and Housing Prices?', p. 82.

25. Masaaki Shirakawa, 'Monetary Policy under the Zero Interest Rate Constraint and Balance Sheet Adjustment', *International Finance*, vol. 4 (2001), p. 471.

26. Richard Koo, *The Holy Grail of Macroeconomics: Lessons from Japan's Great Recession* (Singapore: Wiley, 2008), pp. 16–17.

27. Hiroshi Nakaso, *The Financial Crisis in Japan during the 1990s: How the Bank of Japan Responded and the Lessons Learnt*, BIS Papers, no. 6 (October 2001), pp. 12–15.
28. See Koo, *Holy Grail*; and Gauti Eggertsson and Paul Krugman, 'Debt, Deleveraging, and the Liquidity Trap: A Fisher-Minsky-Koo Approach', *Quarterly Journal of Economics*, vol. 127, 2012, pp. 1469–1513.
29. Keizai Koho Center, *Japan 1994*, Charts 5–0, pp. 52, and 4–19, p. 44.
30. See Armen A. Alchian and Benjamin Klein, 'On a Correct Measure of Inflation', *Journal of Money, Credit and Banking*, vol. 5, no. 1 (February 1973), pp. 172–91.
31. Robert McCauley, 'The Japanese Bubble and Bust: Lean and Clean Lessons', in Martin Wolfson and Gerald Epstein, eds., *The Oxford Handbook on the Political Economy of Financial Crises* (Oxford: Oxford University Press, 2013), Figure 29.2, p. 585.
32. Kunio Okina, Masaaki Shirakawa, and Shigenori Shiratsuka, 'The Asset Price Bubble and Monetary Policy: Japan's Experience in the late 1980s and the Lessons', *Bank of Japan Monetary and Economic Studies*, no. 19 (February 2001), p. 414.
33. See McCauley, 'The Japanese Bubble and Bust', pp. 578–601.
34. Ueda, 'The Japanese Banking Crisis in the 1990s', p. 260. See also Masaaki Shirakawa, *Tumultuous Times: Central Banks in an Era of Crisis* (New Haven: Yale University Press, 2021), the 45% rule 'was bound to have adverse consequences… [it] had the effect of further promoting Japanese banks' aggressive credit creation'.
35. Robert McCauley and Steven Zimmer, 'Bank Cost of Capital and International Competition', *Federal Reserve Bank of New York Quarterly Review*, vol. 15 (winter 1991), p. 40; McCauley, 'The Japanese Bubble and Bust', pp. 585–6, 588.
36. McCauley, 'The Japanese Bubble and Bust', p. 588.
37. Shirakawa, *Tumultuous Times*, p. 28.

8

International Contagion 1618–1933

Allocating the Blame for the Crisis

The tendency in every country is to believe that its crisis is imported because of wayward behavior in one of its trading partners. US President Herbert Hoover insisted that Europe was responsible for the 1930s depression because of its cartels and that the 'European statesmen [who] did not have the courage to face these issues.'[1] There was global overproduction of wheat, rubber, coffee, sugar, silver, zinc, and cotton. Hoover accepted some US responsibility for stock market speculation. Friedman and Schwartz asserted that the crisis originated in the United States, and that the gold-exchange standard rendered the international financial system and various US trading partners vulnerable to the US crisis. The initial climactic event—the October 1929 stock market crash—was American, and the developments that led to a decline in the US money supply in the late 1930 were predominantly domestic.[2] But what factors led to the surge in US stock prices that began in 1927?

In 1837 President Jackson placed the blame for that year's crisis on both Britain and the United States:

> It would seem impossible for sincere inquiries after the truth to resist the conviction that the causes of the revulsion in both countries have been substantially the same. Two nations, the most commercial in the world, enjoying but recently the highest degree of apparent prosperity, are suddenly, without any great national calamity, arrested in that career, and plunged into embarrassment and distress. In both countries have we witnessed the same redundancy

R. Z. Aliber et al., *Manias, Panics, and Crashes*,
https://doi.org/10.1007/978-3-031-16008-0_8

of paper money, and other facilities of credit, the same spirit of speculation, the same partial success, the same difficulties and reverses, and, at length, the same overwhelming catastrophe.[3]

Although observers in the 1850s called the panics of 1836–1837 the 'American panics' because they originated in and were confined to the banks in London that traded with the United States,[4] one twentieth-century economist concluded that it was 'futile to try to draw any hard-and-fast line assigning to either country causal primacy in the cycle as a whole or in its individual phases.'[5]

Friedman and Schwartz relied on the data on the pattern of gold movements to conclude that the United States was responsible for the recession of 1920–1921.[6] Another observer disagreed:

How was [the early postwar fall in economic activity] brought about? ... I think the answer must be: It was a deliberate policy inaugurated by the two economically dominating countries, the U.K. and the U.S.A. It is impossible to give priority to any of them. The earliest official statement of the policy was undoubtedly made by England. On the other hand, causally U.S.A.'s policy must have the greater weight.[7]

A few crises are purely national—the crisis involving the gold agio in the United States in 1869, the crisis involving the City of Glasgow Bank in 1878, and the crisis involving Union Générale in France in 1882. Similarly, the Canadian financial crises that occurred in 1879, 1887, and 1908 were related at most loosely to major financial currents that also affected Western Europe, Scandinavia, and the United States.[8] In these cases the issue of the geographical origination of the crisis does not arise.

Some countries may not be affected by international crises that impact their neighbors and for obvious reasons. France was not affected in 1873 because it had undergone severe deflation in 1871 and 1872 as it made the reparations payments to Prussia. The United States was insulated from the European potato disease and the tumultuous European wheat situation in 1847 because the US grain market was not yet closely tied to those in Europe; much closer links developed later after further expansion of the US railroad system.

Financial crises often ricochet from one country to another. Juglar,[9] Mitchell,[10] and Morgenstern[11] noted that financial crises tend to be international, and either affect a number of countries at the same time or alternatively spread from the centers where they originate to other countries.

One of the several links among countries is that arbitrage connects national commodity and financial markets; thus the Law of One Price is that the difference in the prices of identical or very similar goods in various countries cannot exceed the costs of transport and of trade barriers. Only a modest amount of trade is necessary to link the change in the prices in one commodity market with those in the markets in various foreign countries. When the price of cotton soared in the 1830s in one country, the price increased in all other countries, and the decline in the price of cotton after 1864 was worldwide. A decline in the price of a given commodity—especially a widely traded product like wheat or cotton—may produce bankruptcies and bank failures far from the source of the original shock to demand or supply that triggered the large price decline.

Similarly the financial markets in various countries are also closely linked, since the prices of internationally traded securities with similar attributes in terms of maturity and credit risk available in different national markets must be virtually identical after the conversion of prices into the same currency. The prices of internationally traded securities that are listed on the stock exchanges in several different countries increase and decrease together. The prices of domestic securities often move in a synchronous fashion with the prices of internationally traded securities as a result of psychological linkages or through impacts of changes in short-term interest rates that are result from cross-border investment flows.

When changes in stock prices are small, the correlations between the stock price movements in the various national markets are low. As the changes in stock prices become larger, the correlations become stronger.

In 1929 all stock markets crashed simultaneously and again in October 1987 virtually all of the stock markets except for the one in Japan declined at the same time. Changes in share prices in different countries were strongly correlated, even though national financial markets generally were believed to be more fully integrated in the 1980s and the 1990s than in earlier periods. Because of the strong correlations in the stock price movements in different countries, many of the investors who sought to reduce risk by diversification through ownership of stocks of firms headquartered in different national markets obtained smaller reductions in risk than they had anticipated.

The correlations among changes in stock prices in different countries are somewhat asymmetric in that changes in US stock prices have a much more powerful impact on prices in foreign countries than changes in stock prices in any one of these countries have had on the prices of US stocks. Thus US stock prices increased throughout the 1990s while stock prices in Tokyo were on a downward trend—but when US stock prices declined in 2001 stock prices

in Tokyo, London, and Frankfurt declined. The Mexican financial crisis of 1994–1995 impacted both Brazil and Argentina; US investors became more cautious about buying both Latin American bonds and stocks. The sharp decline in the price of the Thai baht in early July 1997 triggered the 'contagion effect' and induced similar declines in the prices of the currencies in nearby Asian countries in the following six months and then spread to Russia and Brazil, and eventually Argentina.

Transmission Mechanisms

Booms and panics are transmitted from one country to another in several different ways, including arbitrage in commodities and securities and movements of money in various forms (specie, bank deposits, bills of exchange), cooperation among monetary authorities and investor psychology.[12]

Cross-border investment inflows and outflows link the prices in the security markets in different countries. The US goods price inflation in the late 1960s and the early 1970s led to larger investment flows from the United States to Germany and Japan because investors anticipated that the price of the US dollar would decline and the increases in the monetary bases in these countries would lead to increases in their money supplies and their inflation rates.

Cross-border investment inflows may respond to structural shocks, including wars and revolutions, technical innovations and the opening of new markets and of new sources of raw materials, and to changes in the relationship among the growth rates in different countries. The privatization of government-owned firms in a country often induces investment inflows as foreign investors buy shares in these firms.

Consider the connections between the increase in the price of a currency and the decline in the prices of imports in that country's goods market (or the connections between the decline in the price of the country's currency and inflation in that country's goods market); the increase in the price of the currency leads to a decline in the prices of internationally traded goods. The increase in the price of the Japanese yen in the second half of the 1980s and the early 1990s put downward pressure on the prices of internationally traded goods in Japan. The declines in the prices of the Argentine, Uruguayan, Australian, and New Zealand currencies in the early 1930s contributed to the decline in wheat prices in the United States that in turn led to bankruptcies among farmers and to the failures of banks in Missouri, Indiana, Illinois, Iowa, Arkansas, and North Carolina.[13]

Booms and busts are connected internationally in several different ways. An economic boom in one country almost always attracts investments from abroad. Similarly, a boom in one country may reduce the flow of money to others; thus in 1872 Berlin and Vienna stopped lending to New York, while the US stock market boom in 1928 led to a sharp reduction in US purchases of German, Australian, and Latin American bonds. As a result, some of the countries in Latin America stopped pegging their currencies to gold when the US purchases of their bonds declined sharply. The collapse of the market in syndicated bank loans to Mexico, Brazil, and Argentina in 1982 brought depression in these countries and a sharp decline in the prices of their currencies.

Stock prices and real estate prices increased sharply in three of the Nordic countries in the late 1980s, with a threefold increase in Norway and five-fold increases in Sweden and Finland.[14]

The *Kipper- Und Wipperzeit*

This financial crisis occurred with metallic money; credit from banks or other lenders was not involved. Princes, abbots, bishops, even the Holy Roman Emperor, debased the subsidiary coinage used in daily transactions (but not the gold and silver coin of large denominations) by raising the denomination of existing coins, substituting base metals for precious metals in the coins, and reducing the metallic content of coins to extract more seignorage to prepare for the Thirty Years' War that began in 1618. Debasement was limited at first to the coins used in their own territories. Some entrepreneurial spirit then found that it was more profitable to take bad coins across the borders into neighboring principalities to exchange for good coins with ignorant common people; the good coins were brought home and debased. The territorial unit on which the original injury had been inflicted would debase its own coin in defense and turn to other neighbors to make good its losses and build its war chest. More and more mints were established to extract more seignorage.

Debasement accelerated until the subsidiary coins became practically worthless, and children played with them in the street, much as recounted in Leo Tolstoy's short story, 'Ivan the Fool.'

Some local sources suggest that the first invasion of debased money came from Italy and from there to southern Germany through the Bishop of Chur on Lake Constance. The same source at Ulm, however, claimed that the counterfeiting in the Upper Rhine Circle that included Strasbourg was especially outrageous. Beginning on a small scale around 1600, debasement slowly

picked up speed after 1618 and spread to Germany and Austria and to what became Hungary and Czechoslovakia and into Poland and, according to some sources, to the Near and Far East by way of Lvov in Russia.[15]

The South Sea and Mississippi Bubbles

Åkerman called the crisis of 1720 the first international crisis, because the speculation from 1717 to 1720 in France and in Britain affected the cities of the Netherlands, northern Italy, and Hamburg.[16] The South Sea and Mississippi bubbles were connected in several ways. As early as 1717 British investors began to follow trading in the shares of John Law's banks and companies on the Rue de Quincampoix in Paris. In May 1719 the British ambassador in Paris received letters from friends and relatives in Scotland begging him to buy stock for them in the Mississippi Compagnie des Indes. Thirty thousand foreigners, including British nobility, traveled to Paris to subscribe in person. In May, Ambassador Stair urged his government to do something to compete with John Law and slow the flow of money from London to Paris. As Law's system peaked in December 1719, some speculators, including the Duke of Chandos, sold South Sea stock and bought Mississippi stock.[17]

While British speculators were buying Mississippi stock in Paris, many continentals were buying South Sea stock in London. Sir Theodore Janssen had a long list of subscribers from Geneva, Paris, Amsterdam, and The Hague. One of the French investors was the banker Martin, who as already noted was recorded by Charles McKay as subscribing £500 with the remark: 'When the rest of the world are mad, we must imitate them in some measure.' When the early birds liquidated in July, the Canton of Berne, which had speculated with £200,000 of public funds, sold for a profit of £2 million.[18]

Amsterdam profited from its position between Paris and London. The Dutch sold their stock in Mississippi Compagnie des Indes at the right moment and lost little in the crash. In April 1720, a bit prematurely perhaps, David Leeuw liquidated his South Sea stock and bought Bank of England and East India Company stock. By the end of that month, the Dutch banker Crellius observed coolly that Exchange Alley resembled 'nothing so much as if all the Lunatics had escaped out of the Madhouse at once.'[19] In June and July there were twelve-hour relays by ship between Britain and Amsterdam, and on 16 July eighty Jews, Presbyterians, and Anabaptists, speculators from Exchange Alley, went to Holland and Hamburg to trade insurance stocks.[20] In the autumn of 1720 London and the Continent were sharing the financial

disaster. Samuel Bernard, a French banker, was sent to London to sell South Sea stock against gold, to be brought back to France in revulsion against Law's system. Dutch banks 'shortened sail, recalling advances, refusing further credit, selling stocks held as collateral.'[21] The price of the British pound in terms of the guilder in Amsterdam, which had risen from 35.4 guilders to the pound to 36.1 when the first increase in South Sea stock took place in April and 'France, Holland and to some extent Denmark, Spain and Portugal' were buying, declined to 33.9 on 1 September as 'foreigners lost their taste for English securities.' At the height of the panic it recovered to 35.2.[22]

South Sea Company or Intermediate Treasury Bond Fund?

The South Sea Company name misleads, suggesting an operating company engaged in international trade. The reality was an enterprise dominated by its holding of a UK Treasury intermediate bond paying 5 percent then 4 percent interest and callable at par after seven years. In modern terms, the best analogy is a closed-end government bond fund.

Like any closed-end fund, its price was set by demand and supply for a given pool of assets, so that the fund's market value could trade at a premium or discount to its net asset value. Less than two months into the scheme in early June 1720, the shares traded at a 270 percent premium to its net asset value, according to a sharp-penciled member of Parliament at the time, Archibald Hutchison. He correctly predicted 'a dreadful reckoning when "the present reigning madness should happen to cease."'* The shares would rise by another third by mid-summer.

A 270 percent premium on a closed-end bond fund is an amazing observation. A high-flying contemporary closed-end bond fund, Pimco's High Income Fund (PHK), has generally offered double-digit percentage distributions, but its premium over net asset value during the 10 years into 2022 averaged only 32 percent, albeit with a peak in 2012 about twice that level.**

At a 270 percent premium, the South Sea Company could only pay a dividend (without paying out its capital) of between 1 and 2 percent of its market value out of income. At the same time, market interest rates remained at 4 percent to 5 percent.*** And a call of its bonds by the UK Treasury any time after 1727 meant that even if market rates were to fall to 1 percent, the investors would benefit little.

Thomas Levenson emphasizes the innovation of the origin of this closed-end bond fund. The scheme converted or abstracted Britain's 'prior tangle of unmanageable obligations' into a single security, South Sea shares.**** This abstraction led eventually to the country's 'ability to conjure up money more or less at will out of little more than trust in the future.' Levenson likens this

abstraction to the one that allowed Isaac Newton to calculate the motion of the heavenly bodies.

Whether because of the incalculable madness of people, as Newton styled it, or because of the highly social fear of missing out goaded by a corrupt and corrupting promoter, South Sea company shares reached an unsustainable level and then crashed within months. What distinguished this mania from most others is that the scheme largely had known, limited, and low-risk future cash flows that should have kept the South Sea share price in bounds.

*Richard Dale, *The First Crash* (Princeton: Princeton University Press, 2004), p. 114.

**Closed-End Fund Center, Fund Selector, PHK, www.cefa.com, accessed May 1, 2022.

***Dale, *The First Crash*, pp. 134, 165.

****Thomas Levenson, *Money for Nothing* (London: Head of Zeus, 2020), p. 324.

1763 to 1819

The crisis of 1763 involved mainly Holland, Hamburg, Prussia, and Scandinavia, with repercussions on and help from London. France was not involved; the Seven Years' War had been directed against France. George Chalmers, a perceptive contemporary observer, claimed that speculation in land in the United States was a factor in the crisis although the statement is not supported by others.[23] Amsterdam had been the entrepôt center for the payment of money to British allies, and the Dutch had been expanding credit by buying British government stock and *Wisselruiti* (chains of accommodation bills) that led to a giddy credit edifice on a small base (the proverbial 'house of cards') with bills drawn on merchant houses in Stockholm, Hamburg, Bremen, Leipzig, Altona, Lubeck, Copenhagen, and St Petersburg. Bills of exchange drawn with the security of goods shipped also circulated in Amsterdam in addition to the accommodation paper. When prices of commodities fell after the war—especially sugar as imports from the French West Indies were resumed—the bills could not be paid.[24] Hamburg warned Amsterdam houses that they would suspend payment unless support was furnished to the DeNeufvilles. In one account, the letter arrived too late.[25] Another stated that a plan to save the firm failed because its reputation was too bad.[26] In the long run, the DeNeufvilles would have been able to pay 70 percent of their obligations, but their creditors settled for 60

percent before that became known. In the end, the Hamburg creditors had to wait thirty-six years to collect even that much.[27] The *coup de grâce* occurred when King Frederick II of Prussia, who had debased the silver coins in 1759 to help fight the war, recalled the old coins and had new ones minted in Amsterdam on the basis of credits from the Dutch bankers.[28] Withdrawing the old coins before issuing new ones meant the money supply declined and led to deflation.

London came to the rescue of Amsterdam and financed a considerable portion of Dutch trade and investment with Scandinavia and Russia. Very much against his will, King Frederick had to assist Berlin merchants that were caught in the crisis as their bills were protested.[29] Swedish houses complained early in the fall of 1762 that bills they drew were protested and not paid in Amsterdam while remittances sent to cover the bills were retained. Whether Amsterdam tried to save itself by selling British securities is debatable. Wilson claimed that in this way Amsterdam exported the crisis to London. Carter insisted she cannot find evidence of sales in the transfer books.[30]

The 1772 crisis spread from Scotland and London to Amsterdam and thence to Stockholm and St Petersburg. Large outflows of specie from Paris to London fed the canal and country bank mania during the Reign of Terror in 1792 that peaked with the guillotining of Louis XVI in January 1793; the direction of flow of precious metals was reversed in 1797 when monetary order had been more or less restored under the Consulate after the Assignats.

The British crisis of 1810 was localized: British exporters first overdid sales to Brazil and then were cut off from their Baltic outlets by the blockade. There were echoes of this crisis in Hamburg and in New York.

The international aspects of the crises of 1816 and 1819 reflected that the prospect of the end of the war in 1814 led to large British sales of manufactures on the Continent. Smart called this an exporting frenzy that soon broke, like the South Sea and Mississippi bubbles. When prices collapsed, the goods were sent to North America which led to the US tariff of 1816. The result was a deep depression without a panic or even a crisis.[31] In 1818 and 1819 there were panics on both sides of the Atlantic that were connected in a non-obvious way. The 1819 crisis in Britain followed the collapse of commodity speculation in 1818, the discredit and distress 'originating clearly in great previous overtrading.'[32] The year 1819 was marked by the resumption of specie payments and by the Peterloo massacre, when protesting Manchester workers and their families were charged by cavalry who killed at least eight individuals; Smart called it a 'disastrous year.'[33] In America, the Second Bank of the United States precipitated a panic by having its branches call on state banks to redeem large balances and notes that it owned. The purpose was to

assemble $4 million in specie to repay the borrowing undertaken in Europe in 1803 to pay for the Louisiana Purchase.[34] But the Second Bank itself was a bubble, having been re-established in 1817 after the dissolution of the First Bank in 1811. The bank was run by greedy and corrupt directors who accepted promissory notes in payment of stock, registered stock in different names to get around the law limiting concentration of ownership, voted loans on the security of bank stock, permitted other loans without collateral, and allowed accounts to be overdrawn. Hammond observed that the sober pace of eighteenth-century business had given way to a democratic passion to get rich quick, and that men imbued with this passion and unscrupulousness had gained control of the Second Bank.[35]

1825 to 1896

The 1825 crisis involved Britain and South America, although there was a distinct spillover to Paris that stretched until panic struck there in January 1828. With the panic in London in December 1825, continental sales halted, which impacted the banks in Paris, Lyon, Leipzig, and Vienna and obliged Italy and other markets that depended on these centers for finance to reduce their purchases. Distress from burdensome inventories in the textile-producing area of Alsace was general; firms were low on money and circulated between 9 million francs and 16 million francs of their own IOUs as a substitute for money. The London crisis that resulted from overtrading in South American stocks had arrived on the Continent when this edifice was toppled in December 1827 by the refusal of the banks in Paris to renew the Alsatian loans.[36]

Åkerman calls the crises of 1825 and 1836 'Anglo-American' in contrast to the one in 1847 that was Anglo-French.[37] The first two were Anglo-American in different ways: the 1825 crisis was Anglo-South American, and the 1836 crisis Anglo-United States.

In addition, the situation in 1836 was more complex than the one in 1825. As noted earlier, President Jackson considered that responsibility for the crisis of 1836 to 1839 should be divided between Britain and the United States, while Matthews thought it futile to assign causal primacy. Monetary expansion in the two countries was vastly different. Wildcat banking aided by silver imports had started in the United States while new joint-stock banks had been established in Britain following new legislation in 1826 and 1833. British speculation was in cotton, cotton textiles, and railroads; American speculation was in cotton and land, especially land that could grow cotton.

Moreover, Anglo-American banks in London financed British exports to the United States.

The crisis was not a purely Anglo-American affair, although it is often discussed in these terms with emphasis on its impact on the evolution of the Bank of England's discount policy.[38] Hawtrey states that it started in Britain in 1836 and 1837, spread to the United States, and then in May 1838, when Britain was recuperating, erupted in Belgium, France, and Germany to spread back to Britain and to the United States in 1839.[39] The crisis in the United States also affected France and Germany directly through the decline in the volume of imports, price declines, and financial connections. Lyon felt the loss of outlets for silk immediately. American purchases were important to the success of the fairs in Frankfurt and in Leipzig. American commission houses in Paris, which financed their purchases largely in London, and the American banker Samuel Welles, who also relied on London for finance, were threat-ened with failure as early as the spring of 1837.[40] The Maison Hottinguer, a French bank, helped Nicholas Biddle of the Bank of the United States under-write the corner in cotton, which strangled cotton spinners in Manchester, Rouen, and Alsace in the summer and fall of 1838 before the collapse of the corner in November of that year that followed from an Anglo-French boycott.[41] Moreover the Bank of France provided assistance to the Bank of England. By the 1830s, the financial world had complex transatlantic rela-tions in trade, commodity prices, and investment flows among Britain, the United States, and France.

In January 1847 distress developed in London in response to railroad calls and the crisis came late in the summer. Åkerman stated that the distress was Anglo-French, but it had echoes in British-Indian trade, in Amsterdam and the Low Countries, and also in Germany and even New York. Some sense of the spread of the crisis is evident from the number of bankruptcies collected by Evans but not the value of the assets of the failed banks and firms. The data are more complete for Britain than for other countries since Evans reported only the 'principal foreign failures.' Despite its serious deficiencies a table showing the monthly failures provides a useful impression of how the shock wave of the crisis spread. The British crisis is seen to have almost died away, except for London, when revolution in France and Germany produced the reactions of March and April 1848 that are probably under-recorded in Evans's data.[42]

The failure of the A. Schaaffhausen Bank of Cologne on 29 March 1848 played a role in the development of German banking. The Prussian govern-ment allowed the bank to be saved through its conversion into a joint-stock company, despite its standing policy of opposition to credit expansion; this

precedent paved the way for the substantial expansion of German banks in the 1850s with important consequences for German economic growth.[43] Since Cologne had been a Hanseatic city, the bank was probably tied into the merchant banking network of London-Antwerp-Hamburg-Bremen-Le Havre-Marseilles that Evans featured prominently. A local source claimed that Cologne was at the crossroads of trade between Holland, Brabant, France, and eastern and upper Germany and that the city suffered many bankruptcies as a consequence of the British crisis of 1825. The source admitted that apart from some financing of leather imports from South America, most banking finance was local and undertaken for heavy industry. Johann Wolter and Abraham Schaaffhausen got their start as leather merchants, purchasing South American hides from Spain, first through Amsterdam and then directly. Abraham, the son, was a merchant, commission agent, forwarder, and banker with international connections. The trouble in 1848, however, came largely from financing real estate investments in Cologne. Almost one-quarter of the portfolio of the bank consisted of land and loans to a single builder that together amounted to 1.6 million thalers compared to the bank's capital of 1.5 million. As social unrest increased and depositors sought cash, the bank first took on a Dutch partner and then received help from the Prussian Bank's branches in Cologne and Münster, the Prussian Seehandlung (another state financial agency), and the Prussian lottery. Permission for A. Schaaffhausen to convert into *A. Schaaffhausen'scher Bankverein* may have been related to the fact that joint-stock banks were forbidden to invest in building sites and all other forms of speculation.[44]

The boom leading up to the panic of 1857 was worldwide. Gold discoveries in California (1849) and Australia (1851) led to export spurts to those countries and enlarged the credit bases in Europe and the United States. The expansion of the credit bases was dampened because money in the form of silver coinage was flowing to India to finance its trade surplus. Both Europe and the United States had railroad and banking booms. Expansion also came from joint-stock banks in Britain and Germany and from the *Crédit Mobilier, Crédit Foncier*, and *Crédit Agricole* in France which made large loans to trade and industry. Scandinavia in particular had been stimulated by the boom in trade generated by the repeal of the British Corn Laws, timber duties, and Navigation Acts.[45] Bad harvests and the Crimean War, which cut off Russian exports, raised the price of grain for farmers worldwide. These were golden years for British farmers, despite the repeal of the Corn Laws in 1846. After the war, grain prices sank as Russian supplies came on the market, and railroad building declined. The dominoes started their collapse in Ohio—or, rather, the New York branch of an Ohio bank—and fell in New York, Ohio,

Pennsylvania, Maryland, Rhode Island, and Virginia, and then in Liverpool, London, Paris, Hamburg, Oslo, and Stockholm. Evans's data on bankruptcies for 1857 are sketchier than those for 1847 and the path of failures cannot be traced. The failure of the New York branch of the Ohio Life and Trust Company occurred around the same time as British withdrawals of funds from the United States in response to increases in interest rates in London (Table 8.1).

The concentrated nature of the crisis from the Ohio Life revelation on 24 August to the suspension of the Bank Act in London on 12 November through Hamburg's loan from Austria (the *Silberzug*) on 10 December is striking. Clapham observed that the crisis appeared at almost the same moment in the United States, Britain, and Central Europe and was felt in South America, South Africa, and the Far East.[46] Rosenberg calls it 'the first worldwide crisis.' The chamber of commerce of Elberfeld asserted: 'The world is a unit; industry and trade have made it so.'[47]

The crisis of 1866 is the tail end of one that began in 1864. Åkerman said that it parallels the 1857 crisis, insofar as it followed the Civil War as 1857 followed the Crimean War, and as the collapse of cotton in 1866 paralleled the collapse of wheat a decade earlier.[48] The inclusion of 1864 eliminates a general view that the crisis was strictly British.[49] The timing of the panic on Black Friday, 11 May 1866, was intimately tied to the Prussian-Austrian war, largely through stock market collapses attributable to rumors of war and then the advent of the war, and then to the *corso forzoso* of 11 May 1866, when the Italian government suspended convertibility of the lire into gold and in return for this privilege borrowed 250 million lire from the national bank.[50] Like the Overend, Gurney collapse, the *corso forzoso* had been triggered by an internal run on notes against gold, stimulated by money withdrawals toward Paris that in turn had suffered from sales of foreign securities. The London market was shaky in mid-April because of rumors of war. The Berlin bourse panicked on 2 May with mobilization and again on 12 May when war broke out. The Prussian Bank raised its discount rate to 9 percent on 11 May. The panic in London that same day was part of a general rush for liquidity against a vulnerable company at a time of acute financial distress. Alfred André, a Parisian banker with major interests in Egypt, spent 'an exhausting week' in London looking after the interests of his firm at the time of the Overend, Gurney crisis. He returned to Paris on 17 May, having concluded that the finance companies were ruined and that business was paralyzed in Italy, Prussia, Austria, and Russia, with France standing up pretty well, at least for a moment.[51]

Table 8.1 Reported failures in the crisis of 1847–1848, by cities (number of failures)

City	1847					1848								
	Aug	Sept	Oct	Nov	Dec	Jan	Feb	Mar	Apr	May	June	July	Aug	Oct–Dec
London	11	19	21	25	7	3	7	3	1	8	2	1	1	1
Liverpool	5	4	28	10	4		3						1	
Manchester		6	11	8	1				1	1				
Glasgow	2	4	6	9	7	6								
Other UK	2	4	16	7	7	2		1	1	2				1
Calcutta					1	11	5		1	2				1
Other British Empire														4
Paris		1				2	1	14	2		1	2	1	
Le Havre				1			1	5	2					
Marseilles		1			1	1		2	13					
Other France			2			1		1		1	1			
Amsterdam				3	1	1		14	4		1			
Other Low Countries			1					4		1	1	1		
Hamburg	1			2		1			7	4	3	1		
Frankfurt					3	1			1					
Berlin								3	4	1				
Other Germany		2			1		1		6					
Italy		3		7	1									

City	1847					1848								
	Aug	Sept	Oct	Nov	Dec	Jan	Feb	Mar	Apr	May	June	July	Aug	Oct–Dec
Other Europe	1	1		3	2	1	1		1	1				
New York	1	1		3	1	1	1		1	5				4
Other US														7
Elsewhere	1	1			1					2	1			2

Source Derived from names of firms and banks listed by D. Morier Evans, *The Commercial Crisis, 1847–48* (1849; reprint edn, New York: Augustus M. Kelley, 1969), pp. 69, 74, 91–2, 103–4, 105–6, 112–13, 118–20, 123, 127

There is no obvious connection between the US gold crisis of September 1869 and the Austrian crisis of the same month. Both currencies were floating. Both countries had had investment booms following their wars, although the devastation from the conflict had been much greater in the United States. Wirth prefaced his brief discussion of the 'great crash of 1869,' which preceded the real great crash of 1873, with remarks about German and Austrian investments in the United States, the invasion of European markets by US goods, and the extension of shipping and banking connections across the Atlantic.[52] Since Wirth did not mention the US gold crisis, however, it seems unlikely that he was suggesting a connection. The accounts of the 1869 gold crisis in the United States ignore Austria.[53] A possible link is through the price of wheat, which Jay Gould and Jim Fisk were trying to increase when they bid up the gold premium (for example, the discount on the greenback or paper dollar). The difficulties following the September 1869 'crash' were concentrated in Hungary, which was a wheat-growing country.[54] Gould states that the United States could sell wheat to Britain in competition with the low-priced labor and water transportation from the Mediterranean with the gold agio at 45, but the United States could not sell wheat with gold below 40.[55] The decline in the gold agio in the United States in September should have assisted Hungarian economic prospects.

The 1873 story begins with the Franco-Prussian indemnity that was one-tenth paid in gold in 1871 and led to substantial speculation in Germany which then spilled into Austria.[56] Jay Cooke, a latecomer to railroad finance and seeking capital for railroads in Europe, overextended himself with the Northern Pacific; he tried to borrow in Frankfurt but could not compete with the German and Austrian building booms.[57] Other shocks included the opening of the Suez Canal in 1869, the mistake of the German authorities in paying out new coin before withdrawing the old silver coins, the Chicago fire of 9 October 1871,[58] and especially the excitement generated by German unification under the leadership of Prussia's Bismarck. German acquisition of £90 million from the indemnity endangered stability in Britain because of the threat of conversion into gold. France deflated to pay the indemnity and was not affected by the inflation that occurred elsewhere in Europe.

A major question is the connection between the collapse in May 1873 in Austria and Germany after some months of distress and that in the United States in September. One link is through the changes in German investments in American railroads; initially German investors speculated in the railroads and western lands and then there was an abrupt halt to further investment. McCartney stated that 1873 is generally accepted as the first significant international crisis. The crisis erupted in Austria and Germany in May; spread to

Italy, Holland, and Belgium and then to the United States in September; and then later involved Britain, France, and Russia. A second panic hit Vienna on 1 November but was shortlived.[59] Morgenstern noted 'clear evidence of transmission throughout the year, extended to Amsterdam and Zurich' in his table of international stock market panics.[60] In the fall of 1875, Baron Carl Meyer von Rothschild wrote to Gerson von Bleichröder and commented on the low state of stock prices everywhere, noting that 'the whole world has become a city.'[61]

A series of less intimately related failures and panics followed, including the City of Glasgow in 1878, Union Générale in 1882, and the New York stock market in 1884; the European-wide stock market panics in 1887 over the threat of war between Russia and Turkey; the copper corner in 1888 in Paris with the failure of the Comptoir d'Escompte; and the Baring crisis of 1890, the Panama scandal of 1892, and the New York panic of 1893. Their propagation was studied in detail by Morgenstern[62] and Pressnell who focused especially on the Baring crisis and attached particular importance to its impact on the Bank of England's gold reserves.[63] The 1890 Baring crisis produced financial stringency rather than panic in New York as British investors sold good US stocks to carry bad Latin American loans.[64] One view is that the financial crisis in New York in October 1890 precipitated the Baring Brothers collapse in November by producing failures in London, which made it more difficult for Baring to continue. The Baring crisis, induced by difficulties in Argentina, brought a sharp decline in British lending worldwide and contributed strongly to economic crises in South Africa, Australia, and the United States for the next several years.[65]

1907

The US crisis of 1907 began several years earlier in Italy, which had participated in the upswing of the first several years of the century.[66] Speculation fed by credit had been rife. There were fictitious ventures and a steel trust that used funds ostensibly borrowed for real investment to speculate in its own securities; high dividends were paid with the cash from borrowings to stimulate investor interest. Distress set in in May 1905 with the collapse of many new companies. A second relapse occurred on the Genoa stock market in October 1906. By April and May 1907 lending from Paris and London had slowed and the distress became more acute. The Società Bancaria Italiana had started in 1898 with a capital of 4 million lire, which was raised to 5 million in 1899, 9 million in 1900, 20 million in 1904, 30 million

in 1905, and 50 million in March 1906. As the capital was increased, old and often troubled banks and new personnel were acquired.[67] The head office of the bank in Milan did not know the risks that had been acquired by its branch in Genoa.[68] In particular, the bank was deeply involved in advances on securities (*riporti*). Governor Stringher of the Banca d'Italia was worried because of the poor quality of its loans and the large amount it had borrowed from the central bank by December 1906. When Paris and London cut off new credits to Italy and to the United States in the spring of 1907, the upstart, marginal bank was doomed. Direct connections between Turin-Milan-Genoa and New York were limited. But Italian centers were connected to Paris; New York was connected mainly to London; and Paris and London to each other. Bonelli asserted that when Paris sold its British securities, and Paris and London both stopped lending, the colonial countries suddenly found themselves deprived of capital and were obliged to halt ongoing investment projects with consequent downward pressure on demand and output and employment and prices. The analogy between Italy in 1907 and a colonial territory is striking. Bonelli asserted that the Paris cut off of loans to Italy would have had much more serious consequences if it had not been for emigrant remittances, largely from the United States.[69] There was a direct connection across the Atlantic, largely New York to Naples. Bonelli's account focused on the narrow direct connections and contrasted with that of a Frank Vanderlip, a contemporary observer and New York banker in a paper called 'The Panic as a World Phenomenon.' Vanderlip asserted that the basic causes of the panic were the Boer War, the Russo-Japanese War, and the San Francisco earthquake. But after such a grandiose beginning, he discussed overtrading by newly formed trust companies and the need for an expansive currency.[70]

The International Ramifications of 1929

President Hoover stated that part of the real cause of the Great Depression was the expansion of production outside of Europe during World War I, which contributed to global oversupply when European production recovered after the war. In addition, there were the financial complications of reparations and war debts; an overvalued British pound and an undervalued French franc, and the recycling of German reparations after the Dawes Plan by American purchases of the bonds of German corporations and public bodies. Some blame attaches to the reduction of US interest rates in the summer of 1927 to assist Britain in maintaining the parity for the pound when US domestic

purposes would have been better served by higher interest rates. When US stock prices increased in March 1928 and especially after June, US purchases of foreign bonds came to a halt. For a time, Germany, the Latin American countries, and Australia borrowed at the short term. Germany responded to the reduced inflow of money by deflating its economy so it would have the cash to make reparations payments. The payments positions of Argentina, Australia, Uruguay, and Brazil turned sharply adverse. Unable to fund their accumulations of short-term indebtedness or to borrow more, the prices of their currencies declined sharply after the stock market crash of October 1929, as the prices of wheat, coffee, rubber, sugar, silk, and cotton fell sharply.

An open-market program undertaken by the Federal Reserve Bank of New York on its own initiative, over the protest of the Federal Reserve Board in Washington, alleviated the credit squeeze early in 1929. There was an increase in international lending in the first half of 1930; the volume of international lending in the April-June quarter was larger than in any other quarter in the 1920s. However, the lower level of prices and the loss of confidence in Germany, especially after the National Socialist gains in the September 1930 elections, meant that financial distress continued. Banks in Central Europe, largely in Austria and Germany, tried to improve their positions by bidding up the prices of their own stocks. Two private banks, the Banque Adam and the Banque Oustric, failed in Paris, the latter unleashed a scandal that implicated three government officials and led to the fall of the government. The deflationary Laval government came to power early in 1931. And then the deflation that rolled across countries started: the failure of the Credit Anstalt in Vienna in May, the failure of the Danatbank in Germany in July, the German standstill agreement of July, and withdrawals of money from London in August that culminated in the decision of the British in September 1931 to break the link between the pound and gold. The gold bloc of France, Belgium, the Netherlands, and Switzerland started buying gold and the shipment of gold from the United States reduced the reserves of US banks. Japan went off gold standard in December 1931. Deflation in the United States came from the decline in the price of the British pound and the currencies of the sterling area countries that remained pegged to the pound and from the reduction of bank reserves. In February 1932 the Glass-Steagall Act made it possible to reflate through open-market operations, but it was too late. Bank failures continued to spread in a positive feedback debt-deflation process of declining prices of goods, bankruptcies, and bank failures. The US economy reached the bottom at the time of the Bank Holiday that began in March 1933 and the decline in the price of the dollar in the spring of that year after the abandonment of the US gold parity of $20.67.

Two different financial events preceded the sharp decline in production, the surge in unemployment, and the monetary distress associated with the Great Depression. One was the sharp decline in stock prices that began in October 1929. The other was the rapid increase in the number of banks that failed. The decline in stock prices was associated with the reduction of industrial output. While many investors were on margin or had borrowed to buy stocks, the lenders were primarily the brokerage firms.

Several hundred banks had failed in each of the years of the 1920s; most of these banks were small and rural. Failures accelerated in 1931, especially in the second half of the year.

Despite a lot of chatter that many investors had bought stocks with down payments as low as 10 percent, bank credit had little to the financing of stock purchases by individuals. The banks began to fail in 1931 as a result of the declines in real estate prices and from the decline in prices of farm products.

History does not lead to the conclusion that the Great Depression of the 1930s originated in the United States.

Notes

1. Herbert Hoover, *The Memoirs of Herbert Hoover* (New York: Macmillan, 1952), vol. 3, pp. 61–2.
2. Milton Friedman and Anna J. Schwartz, *A Monetary History of the United States, 1867–1960* (Princeton: Princeton University Press, 1963), pp. 359–60.
3. Quoted in Leone Levi, *History of British Commerce* (London: John Murray, 1872), p. 234.
4. S. Saunders, quoted in D. Morier Evans, *The History of the Commercial Crisis, 1857–1858, and the Stock Exchange Panic of 1859* (1859; reprint edn, New York: Augustus M. Kelley, 1969), p. 13.
5. R. C. O. Matthews, *A Study in Trade-Cycle History: Economic Fluctuations in Great Britain, 1832– 1842* (Cambridge: Cambridge University Press, 1954), p. 69.
6. Friedman and Schwartz, *Monetary History*, p. 360.
7. Jørgen Pedersen, 'Some Notes on the Economic Policy of the United States during the Period 1919– 1932', in Hugo Hegelund, ed., *Money Growth and Methodology: Papers in Honor of Johan Åkerman* (Lund: Lund Social Science Studies, 1961), reprinted in J. Pedersen, *Essays in Monetary Theory and Related Subjects* (Copenhagen: Samfundsvienskabeligt Forlag, 1975), p. 189.
8. R. T. Naylor, *The History of Canadian Business, 1867–1914*, vol. 1, *The Banks and Finance Capital* (Toronto: James Lorimer & Co., 1975), p. 130.

9. Clément Juglar, *Des crises commerciales et leur retour périodique en France, en Angleterre et aux Etats-Unis*, 2nd edn (1889; reprint edn, New York: Augustus M. Kelley, 1967), pp. xiv, 17, 47, 149, and passim.
10. Wesley C. Mitchell, Introduction to Willard L. Thorp, *Business Annals* (New York: National Bureau of Economic Research, 1926), pp. 88–97.
11. Oskar Morgenstern, *International Financial Transactions and Business Cycles* (Princeton: Princeton University Press, 1959), chap. 1. esp. sec. 6; on international stock exchange panics from 1893 to 1931, see table 139, pp. 546–7, and chart 72, p. 548.
12. C. P. Kindleberger, 'The International (and Interregional) Aspects of Financial Crises', in Martin Feldstein, ed., *The Risk of Economic Crisis* (Chicago: University of Chicago Press, 1991), pp. 128–32.
13. Friedman and Schwartz, *Monetary History*, p. 308.
14. See C. E. V. Borio, N. Kennedy and S. D. Prowse, 'Exploring Aggregate Price Fluctuations across Countries: Measurement, Determinants, and Monetary Policy Implications', *BIS Economic Papers*, no. 40 (April 1994), Graph A.1, p. 74.
15. C. P. Kindleberger, 'The Economic Crisis of 1619 to 1623', *Journal of Economic History*, vol. 51, no. 1 (March 1991), esp., pp. 159–61.
16. Johan Åkerman, *Structure et cycles économiques* (Paris: Presses universitaires de France, 1957), vol. 2. pp. 247, 255.
17. John Carswell, *The South Sea Bubble* (London: Cresset Press, 1960), pp. 84, 94, 100, 101.
18. Ibid., pp. 151, 160–1, 166. There may be some doubt about this; P. G. M. Dickson maintains that the Canton of Berne still held £287,000 of South Sea annuities in 1750 (*The Financial Revolution in England: A Study in the Development of Public Credit, 1688–1756* [New York: St. Martin's Press, 1967], p. 90).
19. Charles Wilson, *Anglo-Dutch Commerce and Finance in the Eighteenth Century* (Cambridge: Cambridge University Press, 1941), pp. 103, 124.
20. Carswell, *South Sea Bubble*, p. 167.
21. Ibid., pp. 178, 199. In *The Great Mirror of Folly* [*Het Groote Tafereel der Dwaasheid*], *an Economic Bibliographical Study* (Boston: Baker Library, Harvard Graduate School of Business Administration, 1949), Arthur H. Cole observes that Holland had a full-scale bubble between April and October 1720, stimulated by the excitements of Paris and London. Forty new companies were floated in thirty mostly smaller towns, in the amount of 350 million guilders. Shares of the Dutch East India Company tripled in this period, and those of the West India Company went from 40 to 600 before the bubble burst (pp. 5, 6).
22. T. S. Ashton, *Economic Fluctuations in England, 1700–1800* (Oxford: Oxford University Press, Clarendon Press, 1959), p. 120.
23. George Chalmers, *The Comparative Strength of Great Britain* (London, 1782), p. 141, quoted in Ashton, *Economic Fluctuations*, p. 151.

24. E. E. de Jong-Keesing, *De Economische Crisis van 1763 te Amsterdam* (Amsterdam, 1939), pp. 216–17.

25. Wilson, *Anglo-Dutch Commerce*, p. 168.

26. De Jong-Keesing, *Economische Crisis van 1763*, p. 217.

27. Ernst Baasch, *Hollandische Wirtschaftsgeschichte* (Jena: Gustav Fischer, 1927).

28. Max Wirth, *Geschichte der Handelskrisen*, 4th edn (1890; reprint edn, New York: Burt Franklin, 1968), p. 87.

29. Stephan Skalweit, *Die Berliner Wirtschaftskrise von 1763 und ihre Hintergründe* (Stuttgart/Berlin: Verlag W. Kohlhammer, 1937), p. 50.

30. Wilson, *Anglo-Dutch Commerce*, p. 168; Alice Clare Carter, *Getting, Spending and Investing in Early Modern Times: Essays on Dutch, English and Huguenot Economic History* (Assen: Van Gorcum, 1975), p. 63.

31. William Smart, *Economic Annals of the Nineteenth Century*, vol. 1 (1911; reprint edn, New York: Augustus M. Kelley, 1964), pp. 529–30.

32. Arthur D. Gayer, W. W. Rostow and Anna J. Schwartz, *The Growth and Fluctuation of the British Economy, 1790–1850* (Oxford: Oxford University Press, Clarendon Press, 1953), vol. 1, p. 159.

33. Smart, *Economic Annals*, vol. 1, chap. 31.

34. Murray N. Rothbard, *The Panic of 1819: Reactions and Policies* (New York: Columbia University Press, 1962), p. 11.

35. Bray Hammond, *Banks and Politics in America from the Revolution to the Civil War* (Princeton: Princeton University Press, 1957), chap. 10, esp., pp. 253–62.

36. Maurice Lévy-Leboyer, *Les banques européennes et l'industrialisation internationale dans la première moitié du XIXe siècle* (Paris: Presses universitaires de France, 1964), pp. 464–79.

37. Åkerman, *Structure et cycles économiques*, p. 294.

38. Maurice Lévy-Leboyer, 'Central Banking and Foreign Trade: The Anglo-American Cycle in the 1830s', in C. P. Kindleberger and J.-P. Laffargue, eds, *Financial Crises: Theory, History and Policy* (Cambridge: Cambridge University Press, 1982), pp. 66–110.

39. R. G. Hawtrey, *Currency and Credit*, 3rd edn (New York: Longmans, Green, 1927), p. 177.

40. Lévy-Leboyer, *Banques européennes*, pp. 570–83.

41. Juglar, *Crises Commerciales*, p. 414.

42. D. Morier Evans, *The Commercial Crisis, 1847–48* (1849; reprint edn, New York: Augustus M. Kelley, 1969).

43. Richard Tilly, *Financial Institutions and Industrialization in the Rhineland, 1815–1870* (Madison: University of Wisconsin Press, 1970), p. 112.

44. Alfred Krüger, *Das Kölner Bankiergewerbe vom Ende des 18. Jahrhunderts bis 1875* (Essen: G. D. Baedeker Verlag, 1925), pp. 12–13, 35, 49, 55–6, 202–3. Reference courtesy of Professor Richard Tilly.

45. This is discussed in a Swedish study of the crisis of 1857: P. E. Bergfalk, *Bidrag till de under de sista hundrade aren inträffade handelskrisershistoria*

(Uppsala: Edquist, 1859), referred to in Theodore E. Burton, *Financial Crises and Periods of Industrial and Commercial Depression* (New York: Appleton, 1902), pp. 128–9.

46. Sir John Clapham, *The Bank of England: A History* (Cambridge: Cambridge University Press, 1945), vol. 2, p. 226.

47. Hans Rosenberg, *Die Weltwirtschaftskrise von 1857–1859* (Stuttgart: Verlag von W. Kohlhammer, 1934), p. 136.

48. Åkerman, *Structure et cycles économiques*, p. 323.

49. Clapham, *Bank of England*, vol. 2, p. 268. R. G. Hawtrey makes the point that the crisis was not isolated but a sequel to the Continental crisis of 1864. See *Currency and Credit*, p. 177.

50. Shepard B. Clough, *The Economic History of Modern Italy* (New York: Columbia University Press, 1964), p. 53.

51. David S. Landes, *Bankers and Pashas: International Finance and Economic Imperialism in Egypt* (Cambridge, MA: Harvard University Press, 1958), p. 287.

52. Wirth, *Handelskrisen*, pp. 462–3.

53. Larry T. Wimmer, 'The Gold Crisis of 1869: A Problem in Domestic Economic Policy and International Trade Theory' (PhD diss., University of Chicago, 1968); US Congress, House, *Gold Panic Investigation*, 41st Cong., 2nd sess., H. Rept. 31, 1 March 1870.

54. Wirth, *Handelskrisen*, p. 464.

55. US Congress, House, *Gold Panic Investigation*, p. 132.

56. C. P. Kindleberger, 'The Panic of 1873', paper presented to the NYU-Salomon Brothers Symposium on Financial Panics, reprinted in *Historical Economics: Art or Science?* (New York: Harvester/Wheatsheaf, 1990), pp. 310–25.

57. Henrietta M. Larson, *Jay Cooke, Private Banker* (Cambridge, MA: Harvard University Press, 1936).

58. Homer Hoyt, *One Hundred Years of Land Values in Chicago: The Relationship of the Growth of Chicago to the Rise in Land Values, 1830–1933* (Chicago: University of Chicago Press, 1933), pp. 101–2, 117.

59. R. Ray McCartney, *Crisis of 1873* (Minneapolis: Burgess, 1935), p. 85.

60. Morgenstern, *International Financial Transactions*, p. 546.

61. Fritz Stern, *Gold and Iron: Bismarck, Bleichröder, and the Building of the German Empire* (London: Allen & Unwin, 1977), p. 189.

62. Morgenstern, *International Financial Transactions*, p. 548.

63. L. S. Pressnell, 'The Sterling System and Financial Crises before 1914', in Kindleberger and Laffargue, eds, *Financial Crises*, pp. 148–64.

64. O. M. W. Sprague, *History of Crises under the National Banking System* (1910; reprint edn, New York: Augustus M. Kelley, 1968), p. 132.

65. C. P. Kindleberger, 'International Propagation of Financial Crises: The Experience of 1888–93', in idem, *Keynesianism vs. Monetarism and Other Essays in Financial History* (London: Allen & Unwin, 1985), pp. 226–39.

66. Franco Bonelli, 'The 1907 Financial Crisis in Italy: A Peculiar Case of the Lender of Last Resort in Action', in Kindleberger and Laffargue, eds, *Financial Crises*, pp. 51–65.

67. Franco Bonelli, *La crisi del 1907: una tappa dello sviluppo industriale in Italia* (Turin: Fondazione Luigi Einaudi, 1971), pp. 31–2.

68. Ibid., p. 34.

69. Ibid., pp. 42–3.

70. Frank Vanderlip, 'The Panic as a World Phenomenon', *Annals of the American Academy of Political and Social Science*, vol. 31 (January–June 1908), p. 303.

9

Bubble Contagion: Mexico City to Tokyo to Bangkok to New York, London, and Reykjavik

That four waves of surges in cross-border indebtedness and surges in prices of securities and of real estate have occurred in 50 years may set a record for global monetary instability. This succession of waves of financial crises might have been a coincidence; the alternative explanation is that one or several of these waves led to increases in cross-border investment inflows that led to increases in the prices of securities in other centers to levels that eventually became too high to be sustained. Obviously the first wave of surges in cross-border flows—which involved the rapid growth in loans from the major international banks to governments and government-owned firms in Mexico and ten other developing countries—did not follow from an earlier wave, even if its displacement was the growth of the eurodollar market in 1971–72. Was there a connection between the financial crises in these countries and the surge in the supply of bank loans in Japan in the last half of the 1980s? Similarly was there a connection between the implosion of the prices of securities and real estate in Tokyo at the beginning of the 1990s and the surge in the external indebtedness in Thailand and its neighbors in Southeast Asia in the mid-1990s as well as in the external indebtedness of Mexico, Russia, Brazil, and Argentina? Was there a link between the Asian Financial Crisis that began in mid-1997 and the sharp increase in US stock prices in the next thirty months? And were the sharp increases in the prices of real estate in the United States, Britain, Ireland, Spain, and Iceland between 2002 and 2007 related to these earlier events?

R. Z. Aliber et al., *Manias, Panics, and Crashes*, https://doi.org/10.1007/978-3-031-16008-0_9

Sharp increases in prices of securities and real estate in major industrial countries are infrequent. US stock prices had increased by a factor of three from the early 1950s to the late 1960s. US stock prices also had increased by a factor of three between January 1927 and October 1929. Japan had never previously had an asset price bubble and neither had the other Asian countries. Sharp increases in stock prices or real estate prices in three, four, or more countries at the same time is extraordinary and suggest a common cause—a Minsky-type displacement or shock that impacts several countries and probably one that was external to these countries because so many were similarly impacted at about the same time. The intuition is that four waves of financial crisis in 50 years suggest that the reversal in the direction of cross-border investment inflows that follows the implosion of one spike in prices of securities may contribute to the next wave as the external indebtedness of the second group of countries increases more rapidly.

Most surges in the supply of credit have led to increases in the prices of securities; every surge in the price of real estate has resulted from the rapid increase in the supply of credit. The loans from the major international banks to the governments and government-owned firms in Mexico and other developing countries surged in the 1970s in response to the supply of Eurodollars amid sharp increases in commodity prices and the acceleration of GDP growth in these countries. The sharp increases in prices of stocks and property in Japan in the second half of the 1980s resulted in part because the country had to adjust to the decline in net investment outflows, which required that adjustments were necessary to ensure that its trade surplus declined. Similarly the sharp increases in real estate and stock prices in Thailand, Malaysia, and the other Asian countries as well as in Mexico and other Latin American countries in the first half of the 1990s were responses to the increases in investment inflows. The increases in the prices of residential real estate in the United States, Britain, and a few other European countries after 2002 resulted from a massive increase in the supply of credit that partly followed from the securitization of mortgage loans as investment inflows to the United States increased.

One of the three essential components for the development of a surge in the external indebtedness of a country is that there is a large supply of credit that can be readily accessed to finance the growth of its indebtedness. A second component is a shock that leads to sharp increases in the anticipated rates of return—or to a significant reduction in risk—on loans to a particular group of borrowers in the country; the shock may involve a reduction in regulation that makes it easier for borrowers to access credit in a foreign financial center. A third component is a group of investors or banks that are willing to

extend more credit to the group of borrowers in a country. The large international banks often have been involved in cross-border investment inflows since the early 1970s.

The 1970s Surge in Bank Loans to Mexico Et Al.

The exceptional feature of the 1970s was the surge in the US and world inflation rates. The first episode of sharply rising prices in the twentieth century was during and after World War I, and the second episode was during and after World War II. The surge in the inflation rates in the 1970s followed in part from the large payments imbalances in the late 1960s and early 1970s, which led to a massive increase in the monetary base in the countries with the payments surpluses. While the prospect was that payments imbalances would decline after the move to floating currency arrangement early in 1973, the elimination of national 'anchors' for monetary policies meant that central banks no longer had a strong commitment to a low inflation rate and that central banks were no longer constrained from under-pricing their currencies.

One dramatic impact of the increase in the US inflation rate that began in the late 1960s was that interest rates on both short-term and long-term US dollar securities increased. The interest rates that banks in the United States could pay on their deposits bumped into the Regulation Q ceilings set by the Federal Reserve on US dollar deposits. The result was a large shift of US dollar-denominated deposits from US domestic banks to offshore banks (including the foreign branches of US banks) in London and other financial centers that were not subject to these ceilings.

The surge in demand that followed from the rapid increase in money supplies led to sharp increases in the prices of petroleum and other primary products. The price of petroleum increased by a factor of five in the autumn of 1973 following the Yom Kippur War and again by a factor of three in the late 1970s following the Iraq–Iran war; the payments surpluses of some of the oil-exporting countries surged, and their demand for US dollar securities increased rapidly.

The governments in the commodity-producing countries were more attractive to borrowers because the lenders anticipated that their fiscal revenues would increase more rapidly. US, British, Canadian, Japanese, and other foreign banks sourced the money for US dollar-denominated loans to Mexico and other developing countries from the banks in these offshore centers. Previously these borrowers had relied on US banks and on institutions like the World Bank for most of their external financing. The number

of lenders that were willing and able to increase their loans to these borrowers increased dramatically. These non-US banks could increase their loans much more rapidly than they could in their domestic economies. The US banks responded to the challenge of foreign banks entering 'their turf' in Latin America by cutting prices—reducing interest rates—to minimize the decline in their market share.

The borrowers in these developing countries were eager for the money, and the lenders believed that the credit risk was modest; a respected New York banker had announced that 'countries don't go bankrupt.' As long as the money available to the borrowers on new loans was several times larger than the interest payments on their indebtedness, these borrowers encountered no burden in making their debt service payments in a timely way. The chatter was that the major international banks were involved in 'petro-dollar recycling,' which enabled the oil-importing countries to finance much larger trade deficits. However, the increase in the indebtedness of oil-importing countries was much larger than the increase in the holdings of international reserve assets of the oil-exporting countries. The increase in the investment flows to borrowers in Mexico and other developing countries enabled them to finance larger trade and current account deficits, which meant that the industrial countries had significantly larger current account surpluses.

The external indebtedness of Mexico and other developing countries increased by 20 percent a year for a decade, while the interest rate on these loans averaged 8 percent a year, although these rates trended upward in the 1970s as the world inflation rate increased. The cash flows to the borrowers from new loans were significantly greater than their interest payments on the outstanding loans, which meant that the prices of the currencies of these countries increased in real terms and their trade deficits increased. Because their indebtedness was increasing more rapidly than their interest payments and their GDPs, the pattern of cross-border investment flows was non-sustainable, since it was inevitable that eventually one or several of the lenders would become more cautious. And it was also inevitable that when the cross-border indebtedness of these countries increased less rapidly, the prices of their currencies would decline.

The rapid increase in the external indebtedness of Mexico and other developing countries was punctured by the sharply contractive monetary policy that the Federal Reserve adopted in late October 1979. The ability of the developing countries to finance trade and current account deficits declined sharply—which meant that the trade surpluses of the industrial countries declined. Moreover, there was a rapid increase in the investment flows to the United States in response to the surge in interest rates on US dollar securities;

the price of the US dollar increased sharply, or what is the same thing, the prices of the German mark, the Japanese yen, and other currencies declined.

The prices of the US dollar continued to increase until the summer of 1985 and the US trade deficit increased until 1987. By the mid-1980s the incentives for foreign investors to buy US dollar securities had declined, in part because of the decline in interest rates on these securities and in part because the price of the US dollar was more likely to decline than increase further.

The 1980s Asset Price Bubble in Japan

During the first half of the 1980s there was a surge in investment outflows from Japan, the price of the Japanese yen declined, and Japan's exports increased modestly relative to its imports; the ratio of the country's trade surplus to its GDP increased by nearly two percentage points. The investment outflows from Japan declined about 1985, and the price of the Japanese yen increased in the second half of the 1980s. Hence the net investment outflows from Japan were declining. Because the price of the Japanese yen was floating, adjustments had to occur in Japan's domestic economy to ensure that its imports would increase relative to its exports so that the reduction in its current account surplus would correspond with the reduction in its capital account deficit. The rapid growth in the supplies of money and credit in Japan in the second half of the 1980s resulted from the reluctance of the Japanese authorities to allow market forces to determine the scope of the increase in the price of the Japanese yen because the country's trade surplus would decline, with negative impacts on profits and employment in the export industries. The Bank of Japan bought US dollars to dampen the upward pressure on the price of the yen, which led to a rapid increase in the reserves of the Japanese banks, who then increased their loans at a rapid rate. Regulations on bank loans for real estate investment and construction were relaxed in the belief that increased spending on real estate would contribute to economic growth and lead to increases in imports and dampen the tendency toward a higher price of the yen. Regulations that limited foreign investments by Japanese firms and banks also were relaxed in the belief that the larger investment outflows also would dampen upward pressure on the price of the yen.

The surge in real estate prices in Japan in the 1980s and especially in the second half of the decade was so massive that by 1989 the chatter in Tokyo was that the market value of the land under the Imperial Palace was greater

than the market value of all of the real estate in California. The land area in California is several billion times larger than the grounds of the Imperial Palace, which meant that the price per hectare was a million times higher than the price per hectare in California. Not that there had been an auction or even a pseudo-auction for the Imperial Palace grounds. The analyst who made this comparison estimated the value of the palace grounds by multiplying the hundred or so hectares by the recent price per hectare paid for a small plot of land in the nearby Ginza entertainment neighborhood, which was much the most valuable land in Tokyo. The value of Californian real estate was obtained from Federal Reserve data on US household wealth.

All of the financial values in Tokyo were sky-high at the end of the 1980s. The market value of Japanese stocks was twice the market value of US stocks, even though Japanese GDP was less than half of US GDP. The comparison between Japanese and US firms in terms of the ratios of the market value of stocks to profitability was even more skewed. The market value of Japanese real estate was twice the market value of US real estate, even though the land area in Japan is 5 percent that in the United States and 80 percent of Japan is mountainous. The market value of land per capita in Japan was more than four times that in the United States while per capita income in Japan was 60–70 percent of US per capita income.

The Japanese banks were at the top of the hit parade of the world's banks as measured by assets and by deposits (but not by profits); usually seven of the ten largest banks on this list were Japanese. The capital of Nomura, Japan's largest investment bank, was larger than the combined capital of the five largest US investment banks.

Japanese firms were acquiring trophy buildings in New York and London. The first chapter mentioned that the Mitsui Real Estate Company paid $625 million for the Exxon building on Sixth Avenue in New York City even though the asking price had been much lower. Mitsubishi Real Estate and a group related to Sumitomo Bank bought the Pebble Beach Golf Course in Northern California. Sony bought Columbia Records and then Columbia Pictures, and Matsushita, its dominant rival in the electronics industry, acquired MGM Universal.

By the 1980s Japan was the second leading industrial power. Toyota, Nissan, and Honda were leaders in the global automobile industry. Sony, Matsushita, and Sharp and a seemingly endless list of firms dominated the global electronics industry. Nikon and Canon 'owned' the world's photo-optics industry.

The mandarins in the Ministry of Finance maintained low interest-rate ceilings on both bank deposits and bank lending rates; the interest rates on

deposits often were below the inflation rates so households had to save a high proportion of their incomes or else their wealth would have declined. The demand for loans from business firms at these low-interest rates was much greater than the supply; government officials provided 'window guidance' to the banks identifying the firms that were to be given preference when they made loans. The real rates of return on both real estate and stocks were positive and high because of rapid increases in their prices.

Japanese banks owned large amounts of real estate and stocks; as the prices of these assets increased, their capital increased. They increased their loans, and some of the borrowers used the money to buy real estate. In the early 1980s the banks established a new set of intermediaries, '*jusen*,' to make housing loans, which Japanese banks had been reluctant to make. The *jusen* obtained the funds for housing loans by borrowing from the banks—seven of the large banks established these specialized lenders. About the same time the Ministry of Finance established public sector lending institutions that would also make housing loans. The banks then decided to make housing loans on their own.

In the first half of the 1980s Japan began liberalize its financial regulations, in part because of pressure from the Americans to 'open up' the markets in Tokyo so US firms would have access to clients and customers and trading opportunities in Japan comparable to those that Japanese firms had in New York. Interest rate ceilings on deposits and on loans were raised. Window guidance became less extensive. Moreover, the restrictions on the foreign investments of Japanese firms were relaxed and Japanese banks were permitted to increase their foreign branches and subsidiaries.

Financial liberalization meant that big firms funded themselves with bonds, leaving the banks to increase their loans to borrowers with land collateral or who wanted to buy real estate and to build new office buildings and apartment buildings and shopping centers, and golf courses. Real estate prices increased. Firms involved in the real estate business accounted for a significant proportion of the market value of all of the firms listed on the Tokyo Stock Exchange. These real estate holding companies were somewhat like mutual funds; when the prices of the properties they owned increased, investors rushed to buy more of their shares, and so the prices of the shares of the real estate companies increased. Increases in real estate prices led to a construction boom as new skyscrapers were constructed.

Japan had developed the financial equivalent of a 'perpetual motion machine.' The increases in real estate prices led to increases in stock prices; the increases in both real estate prices and stock prices led to increases in bank capital. As bank capital increased, banks could increase their loans, and

because of financial liberalization, they felt it necessary to increase their loans to groups that had been restricted in their ability to borrow in earlier periods. Because most bank loans were collateralized by real estate, bank loan losses were trivially small as long as real estate prices continued to increase. The profits of the firms that invested in real estate were increasing, and many of these firms borrowed more in their search for even larger profits.

The real estate loans were collateralized by property; traditionally banks would lend up to 70 percent of the appraised value of these properties. Some of the loans made by the *jusen* went to '*yakuza*,' organized criminal groups, who used their 'privileged connections' to secure exceptionally high appraisals for the values of the properties that they were purchasing. Since property prices were increasing by 30 percent a year, a modest 'error' made by an appraiser in putting too high a value on the property would soon be corrected by the market.

Real estate prices increased much more rapidly than rents, with the consequence that the rental rate of return declined significantly below the interest rate on the borrowed funds. Investors who had bought properties in the last several years of the 1980s had a negative cash flow—the rental income on their properties after the payment of the operating costs was below the interest payments due to the lenders—but because property prices were increasing so fast, they could raise cash to make the interest payments by increasing the amounts borrowed against properties that they had previously purchased.

As Japan's capital account deficit declined in the second half of the 1980s, adjustments had to ensure that the country's trade surplus also declined. Most of Japan's imports are primary products, which are not especially sensitive to changes in their price; rather the amount of imports increases as its GDP increases. Hence Japan needed a massive increase in household wealth to bring about a higher level of imports.

The rapid increases in real estate prices and stock prices led to a surge in household wealth—Japanese households owned currency and bank deposits, real estate, and stocks. While many of the stocks in Japanese firms were owned by other firms in the same '*Keiretsu*' (successors to the *Zaibatsu*), one-third of the stocks were owned by individuals. In effect each corporate firm combined an operating company that produced steel or glass or automobiles and a mutual fund that owned a lot of shares in other firms, especially those in the same *Keiretsu*.

The surge in property prices in Japan reached its crescendo at the end of 1989. Real estate prices seemed so high that the quip by the much-quoted baseball star Yogi Berra that 'It's so expensive that no one can afford

to live there' seemed applicable. Banks developed one hundred year, three-generation mortgages. The incoming governor of the Bank of Japan was concerned that high prices for homes would erode social harmony. A new central bank regulation instructed Japanese banks to limit the rate of growth of their real estate loans so that it would be no greater than the rate of growth of their total loans.

Once the rate of growth of bank loans slowed, some recent buyers of real estate developed a cash bind because their rental incomes were smaller than the interest payments on their mortgages. Since they could no longer obtain the cash needed to pay the interest on their outstanding loans from new bank loans, they became distress sellers of their properties. The combination of the sharp reduction in the rate of growth of credit for real estate and these distress sales led to a decline in real estate prices—and belied the cliché that the price of land always rises.

Stock prices began to decline at the beginning of 1990 and fell by 30 percent in 1990 and 30 percent again in 1991. The stock price trend in Japan was downward although there were four significant rallies. At the beginning of 2010, stock prices in Japan were in the same ballpark that they had been thirty years earlier.

Now the perpetual motion machine began to work in reverse. Property sales led to declines in prices. The decline in real estate prices and stock prices meant that bank capital was declining; banks were now much more constrained in making loans. Because the value of Japanese stocks was declining while that of US stocks was increasing, the global stock equity funds sold Japanese stocks and bought US stocks.

One of the stylized facts in monetary economics is that the sharp reduction in household wealth is deflationary, the flip-side of the economic boom that occurred during the expansion phase of the cycle as household wealth was soaring. Investment spending in Japan declined in part because the cost of capital had surged and the anticipated growth of profits had been revised downward, and in part because the splurge in investment spending during the expansion phase had resulted in significant excess capacity. Household spending increased more slowly as millions of families increased their savings from their earned incomes to compensate for the decline in their wealth that followed from the fall in stock prices and in real estate prices.

The recession in Japan in 1991 meant that import growth slowed markedly while exports surged; some Japanese firms greatly increased their efforts to sell abroad because the domestic markets for their products were growing less rapidly than the growth in their supply capabilities. The slowdown in the growth of imports and the surge in the growth of exports meant that Japan's

trade surplus increased, which contributed to the increase in the investment flow from Japan and led to higher prices for the yen, which became a handicap to export-oriented Japanese firms. Many increased their investments in China, Malaysia, and Thailand to take advantage of lower wage rates in these countries.

The East Asian Economic Miracle and the Bubble in Emerging Market Equities

Four innovations contributed to the surge in property prices and real estate prices in Mexico, Thailand, and other emerging market countries in the early 1990s. The funding of the overhang of bank loans into Brady bonds effectively removed these countries from their bankruptcy—and the countries were re-christened as emerging markets. With the discovery of 'emerging market equities as a new asset class,' index-based mutual funds and pension funds began to acquire these stocks. The expectation was that these countries would industrialize at a rapid rate, and corporate profits of industrial firms in these countries would surge. Privatization of government-owned firms in resource extraction, communications, manufacturing, and other industries led to a surge in investment inflows as investors purchased shares in these firms. The increase in the price of the Japanese yen following the sharp decline in prices of securities led to the 'hollowing out' of the Japanese economy and led firms to seek lower-cost production sites in Thailand, Malaysia, Indonesia, and their neighbors.

In 1992 the World Bank published *The East Asian Miracle*, an expressively descriptive title for the economic performance of the countries in the arc from Thailand to South Korea; the annual increases in the rates of growth of their GDPs were comparable to those in Japan in the 1950s and the 1960s. The Korean peninsula had been fractured in the war in the early 1950s; in the mid-1960s South Korea began a remarkable period of rapid economic growth. Singapore had been a fortified swamp in the 1950s but by the 1990s had achieved a first-world standard of living. The change in political leadership in China from Mao Zedong to Deng Xiaoping in 1978 led to a dramatic change from a self-contained, isolated country to one that was open and eager for international trade and international investment; the annual rate of growth averaged nearly 10 percent for more than twenty years and the increase was even more dramatic in the provinces that bordered the seacoast and in the major cities such as Beijing, Shanghai, and Shenzen. Hong Kong had evolved from an outpost for peeking into China in the 1950s, the 1960s,

and the 1970s into an entrepôt center for prepping goods produced in China for exports to foreign markets.

Thus the increases in the prices of securities in various countries in Asia followed from the decline in prices of stocks and real estate in Tokyo and the surge in the flow of money from Japan that started at the beginning of the 1990s. Much of the investment inflow to these countries was from Japan, which led to increases in the prices of their currencies if they were floating and to increases in their central bank holdings of international reserve assets if these currencies were pegged. The rates of growth of GDP in these countries increased in response to the increases in investment spending and in consumption spending that resulted from the increases in the prices of real estate and of stocks. The residents in these countries who sold their securities and assets to the Japanese and other foreign investors used most of their receipts to buy other domestic securities and real estate.

The Salinas government in Mexico adopted three sets of measures to prep the country to join the North American Free Trade Agreement with the United States and Canada. Several hundred government-owned firms were privatized. The central bank adopted a severely contractive monetary policy to reduce the inflation rate, which had been above 100 percent; as a result, the real interest rates on Mexican securities were extraordinarily high. Finally, many restraints on competitive business practices were relaxed or removed. The prospect was that Mexico would become a low-cost source of supply for the US and the Canadian markets. There was a massive surge in investment flows to Mexico, partly in response to the high real interest rates on securities denominated in the peso and partly to buy shares in some of the newly privatized firms.

These countries were re-labeled emerging market countries in the early 1990s after the overhang of past-due bank loans was funded into long-term bonds under the Brady plan. Some bright investment banker came up with the very profitable idea that emerging market equities were a new 'asset class.' Every pension fund and every mutual fund that followed an index fund approach toward developing a global portfolio believed it had to acquire stocks that were available in these countries; the sales spiel was that because these countries would grow more rapidly, the rates of return on their equities would be higher than the rates of return on equities of the firms headquartered in the industrial countries. And, moreover, the pattern of changes in the prices of equities of these countries was not correlated with those of equities of the firms headquartered in industrial countries, so their inclusion of the equities of the firms headquartered in the one of emerging market countries would reduce the risk of the global portfolios.

In Thailand, Malaysia, and Indonesia in the first half of the 1990s stock prices increased by between 300 and 500 percent and manufacturing activity surged. Stock prices doubled in most of the East Asian countries in 1993 and continued to increase in 1994. Real estate prices soared. The economies boomed. Trade deficits grew. Moreover, the increases in the prices of securities in these countries were pervasive despite marked differences in economic structures, per capita incomes, exchange rate arrangements, and whether they were international creditor countries like Singapore, Taiwan, and Hong Kong or international debtors like Thailand and Malaysia.

China, Thailand, and the other East Asian countries were on the receiving end of outsourcing by American, Japanese, and European firms that wanted cheaper sources of supply for established domestic markets. Rapid economic growth was both the result and the cause of the inflow of foreign money, especially from Japan. Japanese investment initially took the form of the construction of manufacturing plants to take advantage of lower labor costs; high valued-added components would be produced in Japan and shipped to the affiliated plants in the lower-wage countries for assembly. From there a large part of the production would be exported, some to the United States, some to Japan, and some to third countries. The direct foreign investment by Japanese firms attracted supplier firms and banks from Japan. The buzzword was export-led growth, which was almost always based on a low value for the country's currency. Many of these exports were produced by major firms headquartered in the United States, Japan, and Taiwan. Firms headquartered in South Korea began to invest in China and Indonesia because their wage rates were so much lower.

The surge in investment flows to Mexico in the early 1990s led to the increase in the price of the peso in real terms, and the Mexican trade deficit increased to 6 percent of the country's GDP. External debt was increasing much more rapidly than GDP. Several political incidents associated with the presidential election in 1994 led to a sharp decline in investment flows to Mexico; the Bank of Mexico drew on its holdings of US dollar securities to support the price of peso in the currency market as its ability to continue to support the peso was exhausted, and price of the peso declined sharply.

Investment flows to other countries in Latin America diminished in the 'Tequila Crisis.' Then in the winter of 1996 the consumer finance companies in Thailand—many of which had been established by the large Thai banks to circumvent the regulations that limited their ability to make consumer loans—began to experience large losses on their loans to those who had acquired credit cards. Foreign lenders to Thailand became increasingly concerned about the value of their loans to Thai borrowers, and the flow of

investment money to Thailand declined. The Bank of Thailand's ability to support the price of the baht at its existing value was quickly exhausted, and in early July 1997 the price of the baht fell sharply.

The decline in the price of the baht triggered the contagion effect and within six months the prices of each of the currencies on the Asian arc, with the exception of the Chinese yuan and the Hong Kong dollar, had fallen by 30 percent or more. Stock prices in these countries declined by 30–60 percent, partly because foreign investors were seeking to bring their money home, partly because the domestic firms were no longer profitable. Real estate prices declined sharply. Most banks, with the exception of those in Singapore and Hong Kong, failed. The closing of many banks in Indonesia triggered racial strife, and an immense run on the rupiah, whose price declined by more than two-thirds.

As the banking crises in these countries developed, the play script for market developments was a reprise of similar events in Japan in the first half of the 1990s. A new set of buzzwords—crony capitalism and spontaneous privatization—replaced the chatter about the East Asian miracle.

The sharp declines in the prices of the Thai baht, the Indonesian rupiah, and the other Asian currencies led to significant losses for the firms operating in these countries that had borrowed US dollars or Japanese yen or some other foreign currency, since the local currency counterpart of their liabilities denominated in a foreign currency increased. The banks that had lent to these firms also incurred losses and often toppled in bankruptcy because of the revaluation losses of the firms to whom they had made loans.

The decline in the price of the currencies of the Asian countries led to a reversal of their trade balances from large deficits to large surpluses. The counterpart of the large swings in the trade and current account balances of the Asian countries was a mirror image increase in the US trade deficit.

Irrational Exuberance and US Stock Prices in the Dot.Com Boom

Between 1982 and 1999 US stock prices increased by a factor of thirteen, the most remarkable run of annual increases in stock prices in the two hundred years of the American republic. In the very long run, US stock prices have declined every third year; in the last two decades of the last century, stock prices fell in only one year, and then only by 5 percent. The market value of US stocks increased from 60 percent of US GDP in 1982—an exceptionally low ratio—to 300 percent of GDP in 1999, an extraordinarily high ratio.

The increase in US real estate prices during this period was modest on a national basis, although there were significant increases in those regions that experienced large increases in per capita income or in the number of employed individuals, including Silicon Valley and the broader San Francisco Bay area, Washington, DC, and Boston and New York.

The US economy boomed in the 1990s. The inflation rate declined from above 6 percent at the beginning of the decade to less than 2 percent at the end, the unemployment rate declined from 8 percent to less than 4 percent, the rate of economic growth increased from 2.5 percent to 3.5 percent, and there was a remarkable increase in US productivity. The US Treasury's annual fiscal balance changed by more than 5 percent—from a deficit of nearly $300 billion at the beginning of the 1990s to a surplus of nearly $200 billion at the end of the decade.

One of the 'negatives' in terms of US economic performance was that the annual US trade deficit surged to $500 billion. Another was that the household saving rate declined to a new low.

The remarkable aspect of the boom was the focus on the 'new economy' and especially the role of information technology, the computer, dot.coms, and the firms that provided both the hardware and the software or exploited these developments to serve traditional needs. These technological developments led to sharp declines in the cost of sending and storing information. Ebay provided a nationwide auction market for tens of thousands of different products. Amazon developed the technology for the sale of books and electronic products. Peapod allowed individuals to shop for their groceries at home. Millions of accounts were established at the discount broker Charles Schwab and at its competitors. Firms were established that enabled investors to trade stocks using the computer at extremely low transaction costs. 'Day traders' emerged: individuals who quit their regular jobs to trade stocks either from their computers at home or from desks in specially designed shops. A new group of online firms enabled airlines and hotels to sell seats and rooms at sharply discounted prices.

Entrepreneurs were able to get the cash to develop these ideas from venture capitalists (VCs) who provided seed money. The VCs developed a portfolio of investments in different firms in the hope that within three to five years they would be able to sell these shares—and secure their profits—when the firms made their first public offerings of stock. The VCs' rates of return would depend on whether the firms in which they had invested were successful in their technological challenges and on the selling prices of their shares and the lengths of the holding periods.

As stock prices increased, the high rates of return earned by the VCs attracted lots of money, and the capital available to the VCs as a group surged by a factor of five. No investors wanted to be left behind. The money was there, so a large number of ideas were funded; money was chasing ideas and concepts. Three or four years on, the new firms would have an Initial Public Offering (IPO). The IPO would follow the traditional road-show, when the investment banks would parade the company to asset managers around the country seeking to induce them to buy its shares.

At the end of the road-show, the investment bankers would estimate the amount of the shares that they might sell at the IPO, and set both the price and the quantity. In 99.46 percent of the cases, the share price at the end of the first day of trading was significantly higher than the IPO price, and those fortunate enough to buy at the initial offering price would make a significant capital gain.

One impact of this price pop was that more and more investors clamored to buy at the IPO price. The second impact was that the demonstration of the strength of the demand meant that more and more people wanted to get a 'piece of the action'—the entrepreneurs were attracted to the immense wealth they might earn with a successful innovation, the VCs were attracted to the large profits they could gain by identifying the entrepreneurs that were likely to be successful, and the investment bankers wanted the fees from bringing a large number of these successful firms to the public. The investors wanted the large capital gains associated with the pop between the IPO price and the price of the same shares at the end of the first day of trading, the first week of trading, and the first month of trading.

The size of the price pop was like dynamite or nitroglycerine or maybe even a nuclear explosion. The investment bankers appeared to set the price for the IPOs so as to maximize the price pop on the first day of trading—rather than to maximize the cash received by the shareholders who were selling. From this point of view, a lower price for the IPO might be preferable to a higher price, for the demand for the stock would increase—at least for a while—as the pop increased. The entrepreneurs sold only a small part of their total shares at the IPO; they calculated that the larger the pop, the greater their wealth. They appeared to be more interested in the apparent value of the shares they owned at the end of the first day's trading than they were with the amount of cash they might obtain from the IPO.

On some IPO days the number of shares traded was three or four times the number of shares that had been sold at the IPO. Since many of the buyers at the IPO had been told to hold their shares, the float was much smaller than

the number of shares sold, and so these shares in the float might have been traded five or six times in the course of the first day of trading.

The United States seemed to have its own perpetual motion machine, one designed to enrich the fortunes of hundreds of thousands of families. The larger the price pop on the first day of trading, the greater the number of investors that were attracted to IPOs. The stronger the demand for IPOs, the larger the number of venture capitalists that were willing to back the entrepreneurs. The more capital that the entrepreneurs were willing to put in play, the larger the number of entrepreneurs that would seek their fortunes by breaking away from established firms.

In December 1996 Chairman Greenspan of the Federal Reserve Board used the term 'irrational exuberance' to describe the increases in stock prices; the Dow Jones was at 6400 and change and the NASDAQ was at 1300. Greenspan was cautious and careful with data; it seems highly unlikely that he would have commented on the level of stock prices unless he believed they were then overvalued by at least of 15 or 20 percent. At the end of December 1999 the Dow Jones was at 11,700 and the NASDAQ was at 5400, and the market value of NASDAQ stocks was 80 percent of the market value of stocks traded on the New York Stock Exchange.

In the late 1990s the prices of stocks representing the new economy— the dot. coms, e-commerce, fiber optics, servers, chips, software, IT, and telecoms—which were traded on the NASDAQ had increased much more rapidly than the prices of old-economy stocks, like GE and GM, AT&T and Time-Life, that were traded on the New York Stock Exchange. But there was more than a spillover effect, for the enthusiasm about the future that was characterizing the new-economy stocks was infectious and also led to increases in the prices of the old-economy stocks.

It seemed as though developments in information technology were driving finance. Computers were becoming much more powerful and less expensive. The costs of transmitting and storing information and data were declining rapidly. Moore's Law came into play, and the cost of a unit of computing power continued to decline by 30 percent a year. The World Wide Web was developing rapidly, and markets in separate centers were becoming linked. Computers were replacing humans in trading stocks. Individuals could order their airline tickets over the web. Fiber optics were linking the US east and west coasts and the prices of long-distance phone calls were declining to the level of local calls. Servers were big, and so was their storage capacity. Thousands—tens of thousands—of new firms had been established to move information or data or to store information or data, and the profits earned by the venture capitalists that had funded these firms were so high that more

money flooded in from pension funds, university and charitable endowments, and wealthy families. The demand for newly issued shares at the IPO prices was much larger than the supply, which led the investment bankers to engage in the process of 'spinning'—of allocating a goodly number of shares to the heads of the major firms that would bring them more investment banking business. The investment bankers became rich; they had a lot of product to sell and a public convinced that share ownership would bring them large profits.

There is no easy answer to the question of when rational exuberance morphed into irrational exuberance. The idea that there might be an asset price bubble in US stocks occurred to different investors at different dates. The first date for the onset of the bubble in US stocks is the spring of 1995, eighteen or twenty months before Greenspan's 'irrational exuberance' comment. Stock prices had increased at an annual rate of 34 percent in 1995, and at 25 percent a year in the first eleven months of 1996.

The surge in stock prices in 1995 and 1996 can be attributed to two different aspects of the Mexican financial crisis of 1994; one was direct and one was indirect. The direct effect was the sharp decline in the price of the Mexican peso which resulted in a sudden shift in the Mexican trade balance from a deficit of $20 billion in 1994 to a surplus of $7 billion in the next year. The mirror image was that the US trade deficit increased by $25 billion, since the United States was by far the largest trading partner for Mexico. The counterpart of this change in the Mexican trade balance was that there was an investment flow to the United States (a modest preview of the events that would occur in 1997 following the Asian Financial Crisis and the massive turnaround in the trade balances of the Asian countries). In effect the increase in the investment flow from Mexico to the United States led to an increase in the price of US securities and an increase in the price of the US dollar. The second aspect was that the Federal Reserve eased its monetary policy and reversed its tightening policy of 1994.

An alternative starting date for the onset of the bubble is the summer of 1998, following the Asian Financial Crisis, the financial debacle in Moscow, and the collapse of Long-Term Capital Management, the largest and the most sophisticated of the US hedge funds. The sharp decline in the price of the Asian currencies led to an increase in the US trade deficit of more than $150 billion a year—more or less the mirror of the increase in the exports of the Asian countries relative to their imports. Moreover, the Federal Reserve again eased policy, partly because of concern with the fragility of the monetary arrangements following the debacle in Long-Term Capital Management.

In the twelve months after the end of June 1998 the market value of the stocks traded on the New York Stock Exchange increased by 40 percent, from $9,005 billion to $12,671 billion. The market value of NASDAQ stocks increased by 90 percent.

The surge in the investment flows to the United States had the same impact that the increase in investment flows had on other currencies; the price of US dollar increased and the US trade deficit increased. The investment inflows led to higher prices for US securities, both bonds and stocks; household wealth and consumption spending and investment spending increased while the domestic saving rate declined sharply.

Those who moved funds to the United States then bought US dollar securities, which led to increases in their prices; US financial wealth surged. The Americans who sold some of the securities they had owned to foreign investors then had to decide what to do with the money they received from the sale; they used most of the money to buy more securities from other Americans, but they also increased their purchases of US goods as their wealth objectives were achieved. The decline in the US saving rate and the increase in the US trade deficit were inevitable outcomes of the increase in the investment flows to the United States.

The data suggest that between 95 and 97 percent of the increase in US household wealth that followed from the increase in the investment flow from other countries to the United States was used to buy other US securities and 3–5 percent was used to buy consumption goods. Yet to the extent each of the sellers of the securities spent some of the money receipts on consumption goods, the domestic saving rate declined.

The spending on consumption goods is like a 'leakage.' The smaller the amount spent on consumption goods, the larger the amount spent to buy securities and real assets and hence the larger the increase in their prices.

During 1999 the Federal Reserve, the banks, and the country at large became obsessed with the Y2K problem—a neurosis that the US economy would break down because some computers would not be able to change the date when the year changed to 2000. Precautionary behavior by the Federal Reserve led to an expansion of bank liquidity. Once again banks increased their loans in response to the increase in liquidity.

The increase in stock prices attracted European investors, and the price of the euro declined. Because of the decline in US import prices and the surge in US imports, inflationary pressures declined in the United States. Consequently, the Federal Reserve felt no need to adopt more contractive monetary policies even as the economy boomed.

With the advent of the new millennium, the Fed began to withdraw liquidity. Stock prices began to decline and fell by 40 percent between 2000 and 2003, the decline in the market value of stocks traded on the NASDAQ was 80 percent. The cost of capital to US firms increased as US stock prices declined; similarly, household spending declined as household wealth fell. Once again the implosion of a stock price bubble was followed by a recession, which was dated from the beginning of 2002. Because the surge in the prices of securities had not been based on increases in credit, the subsequent decline in stock prices had no significant impact on the banks.

The Global Bubble in Real Estate

The remarkable feature of the first years of the third millennium is that there significant increases in real estate prices in the United States, Britain, Ireland, Spain, Iceland, South Africa, Australia, and New Zealand, which began in about 2002. The price increases in the United States were in sixteen states that account for about half of the country's GDP. Most of these states were in the South and along both the Atlantic and Pacific coasts, and were among those that were growing most rapidly—but not all of the high growth states experienced significant increases in real estate prices. Spain and Ireland no longer had their own currencies because they were members of the European Monetary Union.

Each of these countries had a current account deficit; each experienced an increase in investment inflows and the prices of the currencies of most of these countries increased. One exception was that the price of the US dollar declined, hence the increase in investment flows to the United States dampened the increase in the price of the euro that was underway after the implosion of the stock price bubble of the late 1990s.

The ratio of the increase in household wealth to GDP was much larger in Iceland than in any of the other countries that experienced sharp increases in security prices. Moreover, the ratio of the increase in the investment inflow to GDP was much higher for Iceland than for any other country. The unique feature of the surge in prices of securities in Iceland was that the increase in stock prices was three to four times larger than the increase in real estate prices. The annual flow of investments to Iceland during several years reached nearly 20 percent of the country's GDP. The price of the Icelandic krona increased by more than 30 percent. The balance of payments accounting identity is that the changes in the value of a country's capital account balance and changes in the value of its current account balance were necessarily equal

as long as its currency was floating. Thus the autonomous increase in the foreign demand for Icelandic securities led to increases in the price of the Icelandic krona and to increases in the prices of securities in Iceland to ensure that the country's imports would increase relative to its exports so that the induced increase in the country's current account deficit corresponded with the increase in its capital account surplus.

The Bubble in US Housing

After the implosion of the real estate bubble in the United States, and prices of homes and commercial real estate began to decline, and banks and other financial institutions began to collapse, the press chatter turned to the cause or causes of the bubble. The list is long and varied and includes excessively high leverage, the repeal of the Glass-Steagall Act, the corruption of the credit rating agencies, compensation based on increases in revenues rather than on increases in profits after adjustment for loan losses, 'derivatives,' the opacity of the over-the-counter market in derivatives, the inflow of money from China, the proclivity of Chairman Greenspan to keep interest rates too low for too long, and so on.

This list is US-centric, and ignores the sharp increases in prices of real estate in Britain, Ireland, Spain, and Iceland and several other countries that occurred at about the same time.

Sloshing Money and Surges in Prices of Real Estate and Securities

Water flows downhill in response to gravity, investment flows across national borders toward higher anticipated rates of return. Perhaps there are examples where the 'law of gravity' has been repealed or suspended and water flows uphill. But there are episodes when investment has moved from countries with high rates of return to countries with lower rates of return. Both increases in stock prices in a country and increases in the price of its currency attract investments from abroad. The surge in investment flows to the United States following the Asian Financial Crisis illustrates that the change in the pattern of cross-border investment flows links one wave of surges in the prices of securities to the next.

The surges in investment inflows in four spasms in forty years reflect that there had been a sharp increase in the size of the pool of global money as a

result of the large payments imbalances that developed in the late 1960s and continued into the 1970s and the next several decades. Major international banks can access the funds that they might want to fund loans by selling their IOUs in this market (Moreover, the floating currency arrangement meant that asset prices in a country would increase in response to an increase in money inflows). The efforts of banks headquartered in different countries to grow their loans contributed to the increase in the supplies of credit available to borrowers in various countries. Each wave of surges in prices of securities and real estate began when the lenders become more willing to extend credit to a group of borrowers, perhaps because their incomes or anticipated incomes had been revised upward, or because the regulatory environment had become less restrictive and the lenders were no longer prohibited from extending credit to these borrowers. Alternatively, the change in the regulations enabled borrowers to reduce their anticipated costs of credit by selling their IOUs in a foreign financial center.

The second feature of the period since the early 1970s is that the differences in interest rates and in anticipated rates of return on similar securities denominated in different currencies have become much larger because countries were no longer committed to parities for their currencies. The divergences in national inflation rates were larger—although the departure from the Bretton Woods system of adjustable parities occurred because of differences between the United States, and Germany and several other European countries on the maximum acceptable inflation rate. Cross-border investment flows occur when the differences in the anticipated rates of return on similar securities available in different countries differ significantly from the anticipated rates of change in the price of the country's currency. In the long run, these cross-border investment flows reduce the differences in anticipated returns in various countries. However, because there may be an almost immediate feedback from investment inflows to increases in anticipated rates of growth of income in the destination country, the investment inflows often lead to a surge in prices of securities—and the extension of credit can become self-fulfilling, at least in the short run, because higher rates of growth led to higher anticipated rates of return.

The impacts of a surge in cross-border investment inflow is illustrated by the Iceland experience in 2002. Rates of return on Icelandic krona securities were high and attractive to foreign investors at a time when interest rates were relatively low in most industrial countries. The increase in investment flows to Iceland led to both an increase in the price of the Icelandic krona and an increase in the prices of krona securities, the feedback from the increase in investment inflows to the price of the krona was almost immediate

because the market for the krona was thin. Hence the investment inflows of an amount that was trivial relative to the supply in the global market led to an increase in the price of the krona and an increase in the price of Icelandic securities.

The prices of the currencies of most of the countries that experienced a surge in investment inflows increased in response to an increase in investment inflows; the major exception was that the prices of the euro and the Swiss franc and other currencies increased in 2002 and the next several years even as investment inflows to the United States increased (The surge in stock prices in Tokyo in the second half of the 1980s attracted investment inflows, but the Japanese purchases of foreign securities were larger than the investment inflows and the price of the yen increased as the Japanese trade surplus increased). The increase in asset prices in each country as the price of its currency increased was an integral part of the adjustment process that ensured that the increase in the country's trade deficit would correspond with the increase in investment inflows.

The increases in the external indebtedness of the countries involved in the first, third, and fourth waves were more rapid than the increases in their GDPs; similarly the increases in investment inflows were much higher than the interest payments on the indebtedness. Hence it was inevitable that the prices of these currencies would decline when the investment inflows would slow. Similarly it was inevitable that the growth of credit for the purchase of real estate in Japan would slow, and that some of the recent buyers of real estate would encounter cash flow problems because their interest payments would be larger than their rental incomes. The increase in the domestic indebtedness of those who bought real estate in Japan in the 1980s was more rapid than the increase in their incomes, and it was inevitable that the lenders would become more cautious in the extension of credit.

The increases in the supplies of credit often have been so rapid that the less creditworthy borrowers become attractive to the lenders. Often new or recent entrants lenders may cut prices to increase market share, and then the larger, more established lenders may respond by reducing price—that is, the interest rate markups over the costs of funds.

The first wave of credit bubbles involved sharp increases in the loans from the international banks to governments and government-owned firms in Mexico and other developing countries at a time when the world inflation rate was accelerating. The demand inflation led to rapid increases in commodity prices and in the anticipated growth rates in the countries that produced petroleum and other primary products. Moreover, the pool of global savings surged as a result of large payments imbalances, the rapid

growth in deposits in the offshore market, and the large payments surpluses of Saudi Arabia, Kuwait, and several other oil-exporting countries.

The link between the banking crises in the developing countries and the surge in prices of securities in Japan was the slowdown in investment outflows from Japan in the second half of the 1980s; the Japanese capital account deficit declined, which led to an increase in the price of the Japanese yen. The Bank of Japan bought dollars to dampen the increase in the price of the yen. Moreover, the restrictions that had limited bond sales by big firms were relaxed and banks turned to lending to smaller firms with real estate collateral and for the purchase of real estate, and the rapid increase in these loans led to a surge in real estate prices, a boom, and euphoria.

The price of the Japanese yen continued to increase in the first several years of the 1990s, even as the prices of domestic securities were declining. The increase in the price of the resulted from the decline in imports and an increase in exports as the growth rate slowed. Japanese firms then increased their investments in Thailand and other emerging market countries to supplement and replace factories in Japan as sources of supply in response to the 'hollowing out' of the Japanese economy. About the same time, four regulatory changes contributed to the increase in the demand for securities available in these countries. The discovery of 'emerging market equities as a new asset class' followed from the remarkable increase in stock prices in Japan in the 1980s. Moreover, the Brady bond initiative of 1988 funded the overhang of bank loans to the developing countries into long-term bonds, and these countries became 'bankable.' The privatization of government-owned firms, both in the industrial countries and in the emerging market countries, led to a flow of money to Mexico, Brazil, Argentina, and other countries to purchase these firms and shares in these firms. One factor was Mexico-specific and involved the policy initiatives to stabilize the economy to prepare it for entry into the North American Free Trade Agreement; an extremely tight monetary policy adopted to reduce the monthly inflation rate led to high real interest rates on short-term peso securities that attracted investment inflows from the United States.

Banks headquartered in Thailand, Malaysia, South Korea, and Indonesia increased the amounts borrowed in the offshore money market as their creditworthiness increased because the interest rates were lower than those in their domestic markets, although the offshore borrowing meant that the banks were incurring a currency risk indirectly as they lent to domestic borrowers in the foreign currency.

When the prices of real estate and securities in Thailand and Malaysia began to decline in the second half of 1997, the prices of their currencies

declined, and there was a surge in the investment flows to the United States as they repaid loans. The Federal Reserve reduced interest rates three times within several months to dampen the deflationary effect of the Asian financial crisis—which contributed to the increase in the prices of US stocks.

The implosion of the bubble in US stocks led to a reduction in the flow of money to the United States and many foreign currencies—the euro, the Swiss franc, the Japanese yen—appreciated, which led to a reduction in the US trade deficit and contributed to an increase in the profit rate in US manufacturing. At about the same time, an autonomous event—an increase in the Chinese trade surplus—led to increases in the US trade deficit and the trade deficits of other industrial countries. The money flows from China went to the countries with the most attractive security markets.

The pattern is that the implosion of a bubble leads to a change in cross-border money flows. The implosion of the credit bubble in Mexico and other developing countries in the early 1980s would have led to an appreciation of the currencies of the industrial countries; the desire of the Japanese to dampen the strengthening of the yen led to an increase in the money supply and the credit available for the purchase of real estate. The increase in the flow of money from Japan in the early 1990s contributed to the increase in asset prices in various emerging market countries; similarly the flow of money from these countries contributed to the bubble in the United States.

The meltdown in the prices of securities and real estate in Japan led to an increase in the price of the yen and the increase in anticipated profit rates in manufacturing in Thailand and Malaysia; the implosion of these other three waves led to a depreciation of the currencies because money flows to these countries diminished.

One feature of the last fifty years is that large international banks can access funds in the international market that they can then lend to the borrowers in various countries. The real estate boom in Ireland that ended abruptly in 2008 was financed by the banks headquartered in Dublin, who obtained the funds by borrowing from foreign banks. Similarly the building boom in Spain at about the same time was financed by the Spanish banks who obtained the funds by borrowing in the international markets. There is a large—an increasingly large—volume of money that can be accessed to finance loans to borrowers in various countries at a relatively low cost. Another feature is a succession of shocks, including policy shocks like the shift from a pegged currency arrangement to a floating currency arrangement or the relaxation of regulations that limited corporate bonds in Japan or the relaxation on borrowing abroad by banks headquartered in one of the countries in Southeast Asia. The increase in investment inflows to a country leads to an increase

in its growth rate, and attracts more money, at least for a while; the price of its currency and the price of securities in the country increase. Then the lenders conclude that the borrowers are too extensively indebted, and the slowdown in cross-border investment leads to a reduction in the price of its currency and to prices of securities. Banks often fail. Implosion of several of the bubbles induced a change in the pattern of cross-border money flows and contributed to the increase in asset prices in the countries that experienced an increase in these inflows.

10

Policy Responses: Benign Neglect, Exhortation, and Bank Holidays

If many financial crises have a stylized form, should there be a standard policy response? Assume plethora, speculation, panic; what then? Should the government authorities intervene to cope with a crisis and if so when? Should they seek to forestall increases in real estate prices and stock prices as their price increases expand so the subsequent crash will be less severe? Should they prick the bubble once it is evident that the prices of property and corporate shares are so high that it is extremely unlikely that increases in rents and in corporate earnings could be sufficiently rapid and large to 'ratify' these lofty prices? When the prices of securities begin to fall, should the authorities adopt measures to dampen the decline and ameliorate the consequences?

Virtually every country has established a central bank to prevent or minimize shortages of liquidity, especially during a banking crisis. Many countries have a deposit insurance arrangement to reduce the likelihood of runs on their banks by small depositors and to forestall what otherwise could be a self-fulfilling prophecy that a shortage of liquidity would cascade into a solvency crisis as firms eager to boost their holdings of cash sold securities, whose price would then decline. Even when there is no formal insurance for bank deposits, individuals in many countries believe that their governments will ensure that they will not incur losses if the banks should fail—in effect, the banks will be nationalized and the government will become the owner of the banks.

Chairman Greenspan of the Federal Reserve initially took the view that the Fed should focus monetary policy on the achievement of a stable price

© The Author(s), under exclusive license to Springer Nature Switzerland AG 2023
R. Z. Aliber et al., *Manias, Panics, and Crashes*,
https://doi.org/10.1007/978-3-031-16008-0_10

level for goods and services—or at least a low inflation rate—and the macro-employment objectives. Then, as the US financial system imploded in the last few months of 2008, he seemed more open to the idea that the Fed should have paid more attention to increases in real estate prices that had been ongoing since 2002.

The management of financial crises is the focus of this chapter, which first deals with regulatory measures that might be adopted to reduce the susceptibility of financial arrangements to manias and then with the approach to panics. The next chapter focuses on the domestic lender of last resort and the following two on the lender of last resort in an international context.

The Austrian view is that the best remedy—the most efficient response—for a panic is to 'leave it alone'—to let it run its course, and to allow the economy to adjust to the decline in household wealth, the de-capitalization of the banks, and the slowdown in household and business spending that follow from the declines in the prices of real estate, stocks, and commodities.

The moral hazard argument is the primary rationale for non-interference by the government; the proposition is that the more interventionist the authorities are in the current crisis, the more intense the next mania will be because some of the lenders and investors will extend credit in the belief that they will be bailed out if the prices of securities and real estate should decline sharply. The argument is that government intervention to dampen the sharp decline in prices of securities skews the risk and reward trade-off in the minds of many investors—both the shareholders in banks and perhaps some of the creditors of the banks, including those who own bonds or other fixed price claims on the banks—by reducing both the likelihood and scope of future losses. A second rationale for this view—essentially the Austrian position—is that if the adjustments to the imbalances created by the sharp decline in the prices of securities and real estate are delayed, the subsequent economic recovery will be slower than it would have been if the government had not intervened.

The moral hazard argument usually does not distinguish between those who own shares in a bank and those who own the bonds that are claims on the bank. Shareholders in Lehman Brothers and Fannie Mae and Freddie Mac lost virtually all their money when these firms failed, as did the shareholders of the Icelandic banks. The shareholders of Northern Rock, the Royal Bank of Scotland, and Lloyds TSB lost most of their money—probably 90–95 percent. Similarly the shareholders of AIG and Bear Stearns lost more than 90 percent of their money. Moreover, a substantial part of the personal wealth of the employees of both Lehman and Bear was in the shares of their

firms and in options to buy more shares; some senior management officials lost 60 or 70 percent or more of their personal wealth.

At times the concern about moral hazard is expanded beyond the shareholders to include the creditors of the financial firms, including both the bondholders and those who have short-term claims on the banks; unlike the shareholders, these creditors have no significant upside gain if the banks' strategies prove immensely profitable. The returns of these creditors are skewed—if the banks fail, these creditors will incur substantial losses and if the banks are successful, the creditors do not share in these gains. Creditors may be lulled into complacency about potential losses because they believe that the banks will not be allowed to fail—but the failure of a bank is not an unambiguous event. If the shareholders lose 90 or 95 percent of their money before the government provides financial assistance to 'save the bank,' has the bank failed? Most of the shareholders are unlikely to agree with the statement that they have been bailed out if they have lost 90 or 95 percent of their wealth. The bondholders may receive somewhat higher interest rates because the managers of the banks believe that they are 'too big to fail' and undertake somewhat riskier investments—and the banks will be able to pay higher interest rates to the bondholders, at least for a while. The 'too big to fail' doctrine may have the same impact as deposit insurance—unless the authorities reduce the value of the claims of the creditors below their face value if the banks are closed and re-organized with government assistance. Thereafter the owners of the deposits that are much larger than the amounts covered by insurance may withdraw their money whenever there is modest skepticism that the bank is solvent.

The choice for each country is whether to design a system that would allow large institutions to fail, with losses to those who own shares in the bank and losses to those who own the bonds sold by the bank, and losses to those involved with counterparty risk or instead to provide some form of effective insurance for all of those with claims on the banks to reduce the likelihood of runs during periods of distress. And then who should pay the insurance premiums, either explicitly or implicitly?

Financial Reform: Bank Regulation and Supervision

Can financial crises be forestalled by strict regulation and supervision? Some observers advocate more comprehensive regulation. Most of the rules for sound banking are already incorporated in the regulations or are implicit in

banking tradition. Many of these rules are ignored by both the banks and the regulators. Banks are supposed to 'mark to market,' that is, to value their loans and investments each day (or each week or month) at the prices that they would realize if they sold these securities today rather than at their historic costs. Reserves should be established against 'problem loans' and write-offs against 'doubtful' ones. As a bank's loan losses increase and its capital declines, a bank might be required to raise more capital or be closed under the traditional rules. As an illustration of the unusual character of banks following these rules, the press was full of the news in the spring of 1987 when Citicorp wrote down the value of its loans to borrowers in the developing countries and the Federal Savings and Loan Insurance Corporation (FSLIC) allowed 500 insolvent banks to remain open in the hope that they would become sufficiently profitable to rebuild their capital. The FSLIC was concerned that if it closed these banks, the amount of losses that it would have to make good would be larger than its assets. As part of the regulation process, the Federal Reserve began to collaborate with other central banks in the Group of Ten countries to strengthen bank structures worldwide by applying the same risk-based capital requirements to banks headquartered in each country.

The emphasis that bank regulators attached to capital requirements as a percentage of assets or bank liabilities led some banks to develop 'off-balance sheet' operations, which generate fees and commissions and interest income for the bank, but the assets and liabilities are contingent and are shown only as a footnote on the bank's balance sheet. The banks established special investment vehicles (SIVs) that circumvented formal capital requirements; hence the SIVs enabled the banks to increase their effective leverage. The demand for the IOUs of each SIV depended on the reputational capital of the bank that had established the SIV. These off-balance sheet transactions include interest rate and currency swaps, futures contracts, options, underwriting risks, 'repos' (sales of securities with a guarantee to repurchase them at a later date), and note-issuing facilities. Each of these positions can be valued as an option and included among the bank's assets when calculating its appropriate required capital.[1]

A strong case can be made for stricter regulations and supervision of banks to forestall lending in euphoric periods that may morph into a banking crisis. Responsibility for bank examination in the United States was divided among the Comptroller of the Currency, the Federal Reserve Banks, and the state banking commissions. In one view there was competition in regulation rather than in deregulation.[2] 'Divided responsibility,' said a famous German banker-politician, 'is no responsibility.'[3] The astute examination personnel needed when the prices of securities tumble are unwilling to submit to the boredom

of long periods of calm between crises. The mismanagement of a bank is often hard to detect before a crisis. In booms, entropy in regulation and supervision permits the build-up of vulnerable positions that burst only after the prices of securities decline. If the bank's capital declines below the required minimum, the regulatory authorities then have to decide whether to close the bank, or arrange for the bank to be sold. or to stall and hope for a miracle.

The paradox is that although banks have been regulated for more than three hundred years, the universal response to failure or near failure of banks is that more regulation or more effective regulation is needed. The problems of Bear Stearns, Lehman Brothers, and other US investment banks have been attributed to the decision of the US Securities and Exchange Commission to relax the restraints on the capital requirements or the leverage of the investment banks. At times the collapse of an investment bank has been attributed to the repeal of the Glass-Steagall Act—which conveniently neglects the failures of hundreds of financial firms in the 1980s and the failures of banks in Britain, Iceland, Ireland, and many other countries.

Regulation imposes costs. History shows that increases in regulations applied to established institutions create incentives to develop new institutions that are outside the scope of regulations—and yet they are similar to regulated firms. A universe of 'shadow banks' was established to circumvent regulation—and the costs of regulation. Money market funds were developed as a way to pay interest on demand deposits when the banks were prohibited from paying interest on deposits; the deposits in the money market funds are not guaranteed by the US government. The offshore market in bank deposits developed to avoid the costs that domestic banks incur in the form of reserve requirement and deposit insurance premiums; the offshore branches of US banks could pay higher interest rates on their deposit IOUs than the domestic branches of these banks could pay on their IOUs.

Manias are macro phenomena and result from the excessively rapid growth of credit. Regulation is generally a micro phenomenon. Since the Great Financial Crisis of 2008, bank regulators have come to a consensus that bank regulation should take a macro perspective and aim at slowing down very rapid credit growth. The details of this new 'macro-prudential' approach need not detain us. A key feature that national authorities in country A determine when credit growth is so rapid as to call for higher required capital for banks under their supervision. To make sure that business does not just migrate to foreign banks, supervisors in country B, C and D agree to require the same higher capital of their banks in their lending to borrowers in country A. Such a regulatory approach might affect whether a mania develops. But even if it

does not, it could make it more likely that banks are more resilient and able better to survive the crisis and panic.

Benign Neglect

Many economists believe that the panic will work its own cure, and that 'the fire can be left to burn itself out.'[4] 'Cool if not very imaginative heads in the Bank [of England] parlour thought it in the nature of panics to exhaust themselves.'[5] Lord Overstone maintained that support of the financial system in crisis is not really necessary because the resources of the system are so great that even in times of the utmost stringency, those that offer a sufficiently high rate of interest could borrow a large amount of money.[6] In 1847, an increase in the discount rate to 10 and 12 percent in London stopped the flow of gold to the United States; a small sloop was sent to overtake a ship that had already sailed for New York and got it to turn around and unload £100,000 in gold.[7] Testifying before the 1865 French *Enquête* (inquiry) into monetary circulation, Baron James de Rothschild stated that increases in interest rates could be relied upon to reduce speculation in commodities and in securities. He added: 'If speculators could find unlimited credit, one can't tell what crises would ensue.'[8]

The moral hazard dilemma is that policy measures undertaken to provide stability to the system during the current crisis may encourage much more speculation during the next expansion by those who seek exceptionally high returns and who have become convinced that there is a strong likelihood that the government will adopt measures to prevent the economy from imploding—and so their losses on the downside will be limited. A 'free lunch' for the speculators today means that they are likely to be less prudent in the future. Hence the next several financial crises could be more severe because the lenders would have taken on riskier positions during the boom years. The moral hazard problem is a strong argument for non-intervention as a financial crisis develops to reduce both the likelihood and the severity of future crises. Will the policymakers be able to devise approaches that penalize individual speculators while minimizing the adverse impacts of their imprudent behavior on the rest of the economy? Even then the cost–benefit question is whether the benefit to the economy from not allowing the panic to run its course is worthwhile in terms of the undeserved reward to the speculators.

The losses incurred by shareholders of Bear Stearns, Fannie Mae and Freddie Mac, AIG, Citicorp, and Bank of America were immense. Moreover, the leadership and directors of these institutions were replaced. The

top management was replaced, and many of the top officers lost most of their wealth. Each of these firms continued in business, but for all practical purposes they failed. Individuals who invested on the assumption that these institutions were 'too big to fail' incurred large losses. The major beneficiaries of government intervention have been the bondholders and those with counterparty positions.

The view that a panic should be allowed to pursue its course has two elements. One element takes pleasure in the troubles—or enjoys *schadenfreude*—that the investors or speculators encounter as retribution for their excesses; this puritanical view welcomes hellfire as the just deserts for the excessively greedy. The other sees panic as a thunderstorm 'in a mephitic and unhealthy tropical atmosphere' that clears the air. 'It purified the commercial and financial elements, and tended to restore vitality and health, alike conducive to regular trade, sound progress and permanent prosperity.'[9] One powerful statement of this position was made by Herbert Hoover as he characterized—without approval—the view of Andrew Mellon:

> The 'leave-it-alone liquidationists' headed by Secretary of the Treasury Mellon felt that government must keep its hands off and let the slump liquidate itself. Mr. Mellon had only one formula: 'Liquidate labor, liquidate stocks, liquidate the farmers, liquidate real estate.' He insisted that when the people get an inflationary brainstorm, the only way to get it out of their blood is to let it collapse. He held that even panic was not altogether a bad thing. He said: 'It will purge the rottenness out of the system. High costs of living and high living will come down. People will work harder, live a moral life. Values will be adjusted, and enterprising people will pickup the wrecks from less competent people.'[10]

The neo-Austrian economic historian Murray Rothbard added: 'While phrased somewhat luridly, this was the sound and proper course for the administration to follow.'[11] The conservative historian Paul Johnson commented: 'It was the only sensible advice Hoover received during his presidency.'[12]

The opposing view conceded that while it is desirable to purge the system of bubbles and manic investments there is a grave risk if the government does not intervene to staunch the crisis. Then a deflationary panic could spread and wipe out sound investments by conservative investors who would not be able to obtain the credit they need.

One feature of many liquidity crises is that interest rates seem extremely high for private borrowers, especially because they are expressed as annual percentage rates, they are really premiums for liquidity for one, two, or at

most a few days. The more fundamental question is whether money is available at these high-interest rates or whether the credit market is cleared by non-price rationing. The evidence from many crises is that it is difficult and sometimes impossible to borrow in a panic and that the quoted interest rates are irrelevant because credit is not available.

- After first Arend Joseph and then DeNeufville failed in 1763, and panic broke out on 22 July, a succinct, not very informative or convincing report commented: 'Panic even on securities and on goods, no money was to be had.'[13]
- The statement in 1825 was: 'A panic seized upon the public, such as had never been witnessed before: everybody begging for money—money—but money was hardly on any condition to be had. "It was not the character of the security," observes the *Times*, "that was considered, but the impossibility of producing money at all".'[14]
- The interrogation of Thomas Tooke before the Select Committee on the Commercial Crisis in 1847: Question 5421: 'For several days, if not some weeks, the Bank of England was the only establishment that was discounting?' Answer: 'Yes.' Question 5472: 'The Governor of the Bank of England said he could not sell £1 million of stock [English government bonds] in the week after October 14, if there had been no letter. Do you think it possible?' Answer: 'No, perfectly impossible, taking the word impossible to signify with the exception of such a reduction in price as could not be contemplated.'[15]
- The evidence of Mr. Glyn in the same inquiry: Question: 'Are you aware that it was the opinion of the Bank broker that a very large sum might have been sold without materially affecting the prices of Consols [English perpetual bonds]?' Answer: 'I was not aware that the Bank broker had stated that. I should say, from what I saw at the time, that a sale of a million or two million, which were the figures talked of, would have been almost impossible without knocking down the funds to such a price as would have created a further panic.'
- Mr. Browne, MP, did not think such sales could have been effected, unless at a great sacrifice, adding that 'if the panic had been equal to what we might suppose it might have been, under such circumstances, I doubt whether they could have been sold at all.'[16]
- Then in 1857, 'At one stage during the crisis it was impossible to negotiate paper at all, the charge under the most favorable circumstances being 12 and 15 percent.'[17]

- A letter from Liverpool: 'Bills of exchange of the first Quality in themselves, and to which this and other Banks were willing to add their Endorsement, were absolutely inconvertible into Cash, and it is my Belief that many Houses, who were not merely solvent but able to pay 40s and 60s to the Pound, must have stopped had not the Government letter been issued.'[18]
- 'Commercial confidence in Hamburg is entirely at an end. Bills of only three or four of the first houses are negotiable at the highest rate of interest … A government bond advance of 15 million marks banco payable by banks failed to help. The panic was so great that government bonds could not be discounted, and on no security whatsoever would capitalists part with their money … When it was known on December 12 that assistance would help all, the panic ceased. Government bonds which had not been discountable at 15 percent on the first of the month were readily taken at 2 and 3 percent.'[19]
- Edward Clark in New York wrote to Jay Cooke in Philadelphia before Cooke left Clark's firm to start his own firm: 'Money is *not tight* — *it is not to be had at all*. There is no money, no confidence & value to anything. A week more of such times and the Bks [sic] will fail.'[20]
- Then in 1866 'The Bank court raised the discount rate to 9 percent and intimated that loans on Government securities were available at 10 percent. Before that announcement it was impossible to sell either Consols or Exchequer bills. Jobbers in other securities refused to deal.'[21]
- During the 1873 crisis in New York the 'National Trust Company of New York had eight hundred thousand dollars worth of government securities in its vaults, but not a dollar could be borrowed on them; and it suspended.'[22]
- And finally, in 1883, 'The growing demand for money finally led to a money famine. Time loans were unobtainable, call loans were 72 percent in June, 72 percent on July 28, 51 percent on August 4. First-class commercial paper was quoted 8–12 percent nominal, with a very small amount of money available.'[23]

The evidence is not unambiguous, since the sale of government bonds is somewhat qualified by such remarks as 'with the exception of such a reduction in price [i.e., increase in the rate of interest] as could not be contemplated.' Moreover, there is occasional information on the other side of the argument, especially in the United States under the national banking system, in which a lender of last resort was unavailable. In 1884:

> To add further to the discomfiture of dealers, money became exceedingly stringent, and at one time commanded as much as 4 percent for 24 hours' use. This caused a further sacrifice of stocks since few could afford to pay the high rate

asked. The exorbitant charge was, of course, the direct result of the distrust prevailing, since there was no actual scarcity ... It was to ... the desire to realize and obtain cash that the large decline on Thursday and Friday of nearly 7 percent on United States Government bonds is to be attributed. There was no loss in confidence in these, nor was there in good railroad bonds and stocks.

One result of the phenomenal and temporary rise in rates for money was to bring a vast amount of foreign capital to the market. Some of it was sent here to buy stocks at their depressed prices, and more to loan on stocks or on any other good securities at the high rates of interest. The effect of this was to completely turn the foreign exchanges which had been running so heavily against the US.[24]

This statement in its turn is not unambiguous, since the panic started before an acute liquidity shortage had developed.

The International Monetary Fund acted as a lender of last resort in the Asian crisis of 1997—although long after the prices of the Thai baht, the Indonesian rupiah, and other currencies had declined sharply—and insisted that the government in each of the Asian countries balance its budget and that the central bank in each country increase interest rates. Some economists objected to these contractive measures because they would lead to an increase in unemployment, especially among the poor, while the financial problems had been set in motion by comfortable officials and well-to-do bankers.

Some support for orthodoxy, however, came from the Japanese experience in the 1990s when the combination of an expansive monetary policy and the decline in the price of the yen produced a 'liquidity trap.' Both Japanese interest rates and bank loans decreased after the declines in stock prices and real estate prices, and the inference was that there was a 'credit crunch.' Banks were reluctant to lend because their loan losses had eroded their capital and firms were reluctant to borrow because of uncomfortably high leverage as well as the sluggish growth in the demand for their products.

The decline in short-term interest rates in Tokyo to 1 percent and below led to a surge in the 'carry-trade'; US hedge funds borrowed yen, which they sold to buy US dollars which were used to buy US dollar securities that yielded 3 or 4 percent. The 'carry-trade' transactions led to an increase in the flow of funds from Tokyo to New York and to a decline in the price of the yen that in turn led to an increase in the Japanese trade surplus and increases in Japanese output and employment. The increase in the Japanese trade surplus was a useful response to the liquidity trap and an effective supplement to expansive Japanese fiscal and monetary policies. The carry-trade transactions would remain profitable for the US hedge funds as long as any increase in the

price of the yen was smaller than the excess of the interest rates on US dollar securities over the interest rates on yen loans.

Moral Suasion and Other Exhortatory Devices

The dominant argument against the a priori view that panics can be cured by being left alone is that they almost never *are* left alone. The authorities intervene to forestall further decline in the prices of securities. In panic after panic, crash after crash, crisis after crisis, the authorities or some 'responsible citizens' try to halt the panic by one measure or another. The authorities may be unduly alarmed and the position might correct itself without serious harm. The authorities may be stupid and unable to learn. (The Chicago School assumes that the market participants are always more intelligent than the authorities, in large part because the authorities are motivated by short-term political objectives.) The uneven distribution of intelligence cannot be tested against crisis management because the authorities and leading figures in the marketplace both exert themselves to halt the spread of declines in the prices of securities, bankruptcy, and bank failures. If there is a learning process at work—and the assumption of rationality requires one—the lesson has been that a lender of last resort is more desirable and less costly than relying exclusively on the competitive forces of the market.

One insight from the historical record is that there are many examples when the authorities initially were resolved not to intervene but eventually did so reluctantly. Lord Liverpool threatened to resign as Chancellor of the Exchequer in December 1825 if an issue of Exchequer bills was provided to rescue the market after he had warned against excessive speculation six months earlier.[25] William Lidderdale, Governor of the Bank of England at the time of the Baring crisis, refused categorically to accept a 'letter of indemnity' to permit the Bank to exceed its lending limit.[26] On both occasions, face was saved by finding some other approach to avert the panic. The initial strong stand not to intervene was reversed on many other occasions as the panic escalated. These included the intervention of Frederick II in the Berlin crisis of 1763,[27] the Bank of England's refusal to discount for the 'W banks,'[28] and the US Treasury's decision in 1869.[29]

The view of the US authorities in September 2008 was that Lehman Brothers should be allowed to fail, even though the government had blessed JPMorgan Chase's purchase of Bear Stearns and the conservatorship of Fannie Mae and Freddie Mac. One explanation is that the then Secretary of the Treasury, Henry Paulson, did not want to become known as 'Mr Bailout.' A day

after Lehman closed, the 'policy' was reversed in response to the massive run on AIG. In effect a new policy of 100 percent deposit insurance was implicitly provided to all large financial firms.

Stalling

In a run, each depositor rushes to get his or her money from the bank before the doors are closed because the bank's money holdings are likely to be too small relative to the demand of the depositors who want their money. Banks are often reluctant to pay the depositors that want their money because the banks' holdings of cash or money are much smaller than their short-term deposit liabilities. During the Great Depression, banks took their time to pay off depositors, hoping like Micawber for something to turn up. The technique goes back to the eighteenth century.

Macleod's *Theory and Practice of Banking* describes how the Bank of England defended itself in September 1720 against a run brought on by its reversal of a promise to absorb the securities of the South Sea Company at £400. The Bank organized its friends in the front of the line of depositors that wanted their money and paid them slowly in sixpence coins. These friends brought the coins back to the Bank through another door. The money was deposited, again slowly counted, and then again paid out. The run was staved off until the feast of Michaelmas (29 September). When the holiday was over, so was the run, and the Bank remained open.[30]

A second story, which may well have the same origin and is likely to be more accurate, is that the Sword Blade Bank, a supporter of the South Sea Company, resisted attempts to redeem its paper with silver coins. When the run started on 19 September, the bank brought up wagonloads of silver that it paid out 'slowly in small change.' One depositor is reported to have received £8000 in shillings and sixpences before the bank closed its doors on Saturday 24 September.[31] The circumstances suggest one story; the dates, two. Since the Sword Blade Bank and the Bank of England were mortal enemies, it is unlikely that they cooperated.

The lessons of 1720 were not lost on the Bank of England a quarter century later. The Young Pretender (Charles Edward, grandson of James II) landed in Scotland in July 1745, unfurled his banner in September, invaded England in November, arrived in Carlisle on 15 November, and reached Derby on 4 December. Panic broke out on Black Friday, 5 December 1745. British Consols fell to 45, the lowest price on record, and a run began on the Bank of England. The Bank resisted, partly by paying off its notes in

sixpence coins; the Bank used the time gained to induce London merchants to proclaim their loyalty and readiness to accept Bank of England notes. The second half of the prescription, collecting pledges of faith in notes, was used again in similar circumstances when the French landed at Fishguard in 1797. On that occasion, 1140 signatures of merchants and investors in government securities were collected in a single day.[32] The time gained in 1745 by both the slow payout and the petition of support enabled the government to organize the army that defeated the Young Pretender at Culloden in April 1746.

Complete Shutdowns and Bank Holidays

One way to stop a panic is to close the market so trading stops. Trading on the New York Stock Exchange was halted in 1873, and in London and many other centers at the outbreak of war in 1914. In both cases, the motivation was to stop a run by providing the market participants with more time to think about whether it was necessary or desirable to sell their securities at depressed prices.

However, closing the market may drive the trading underground and intensify the panic. Moreover, short-run and long-run goals are in conflict. Closing the stock market during one panic may exacerbate the next, as investors sell their stocks or withdraw their money from the call money market because they are fearful that trading soon will be halted. A financial editor suggested that fear that trading on the New York Stock Exchange might be halted in October 1929 hastened the withdrawal of call money by out-of-town banks and other market participants, who were aware that the market had been closed in 1873.[33] The closing of stock exchanges in Pittsburgh and New Orleans for two months in 1873 had fewer serious consequences, since they traded only the securities of local firms.[34]

The New York Stock Exchange and the other US stock exchanges were closed for a week after the bombing of the World Trade Center towers on 11 September 2001 because the communications and the technical support systems were inoperative. Many of the same securities could have been traded on the regional stock exchanges in the United States, although these exchanges would have been overwhelmed by the volume of trading.

The declaration of a legal holiday by the government is another technique for closing the market, which was used during the panic of 1907 in Oklahoma, Nevada, Washington, Oregon, and California.[35] The declaration of bank holidays started in various US states in the autumn of 1932 and then

was adopted at the national level on 3 March 1933, the day that Franklin D. Roosevelt was inaugurated as president. (A bank holiday closes only the banks, while all businesses are closed on a legal holiday.)

Another device is to suspend the publication of bank statements, as in 1873, in the hope that 'what you don't know won't hurt you.' The technique was designed to hide the large losses of a few banks since the fear was that accurate news would reduce depositor confidence further.[36]

Some commodity and financial markets set daily limits on the maximum change in prices; when the limit is reached, trading is suspended for the rest of the day. Specialists in individual stocks often have taken a 'time out' whenever the imbalance between the buy orders and the sell orders has been exceptionally large. This 'circuit breaker' was recommended for US stock markets after the meltdown of Black Monday, 19 October 1987. The proposal for the New York Stock Exchange was to postpone trading for a stated interval—such as twenty minutes—in those stocks whose prices increased above or declined below the limit.

Time has been gained by moratoriums on payment of all debts or on particular types of obligations, such as bills of exchange that have less than two weeks until they mature. The most ubiquitous measure of this sort is that the bank examiners ignore the bad loans that banks own as long as they can—an implicit moratorium on marking the loans to their market value. Regulatory forbearance was used in the US savings and loan debacle in the 1980s. The International Monetary Fund and the World Bank continued to allow the indebtedness of many African countries to increase by the amounts of the interest that were due; if the Fund or the Bank had declared the loans in default, they would have had to recognize the losses on their loans to these countries. The banks that were the lenders to the Real Estate Investment Trusts (REITs), landlords of mortgaged shopping centers, and the owners of mothballed Boeing 747s allowed the interest on their bank loans to compound because they wanted to delay the recognition of the loan losses to a more propitious moment when their own capital would be larger. But the lenders need forbearance from the bank examiners.

Official moratoriums may be less effective than informal ones, however. A moratorium on the settlement of differences in payments due on the 1873 Vienna Stock Exchange lasted a week, from the stock market collapse to 15 May. A guarantee fund of 20 million gulden was put together by the Austrian National Bank and the commercial banks.[37] Another moratorium was noted in Paris after the July Monarchy when the municipal council decreed that all bills payable in Paris between 25 July and 15 August should be extended

by ten days. This moratorium sterilized the commercial paper in banking portfolios and but it did not discourage a run by holders of notes.[38]

Clearinghouse Certificates

The major device used in the United States to cope with bank runs prior to the establishment of the Federal Reserve System was the clearinghouse certificate, which was a near-money substitute that was the liability of a group of large banks in each city. A bank subject to a run could meet the demands of depositors that wanted their money with these certificates rather than with currency or coin. The New York Clearing House was established in 1853, and the one in Philadelphia a year after the panic of 1857. During the panic of 1857, New York banks failed to cooperate to halt the run. The Mercantile Agency of New York took the position that if four or five of the strongest banks had come to the assistance of the Ohio Life and Trust Company so that it could meet its obligations, the business and the credit of the country would have been preserved.[39] By 1873 the New York banks were ready to accept Clearing House certificates as payment on cleared checks. The advantage of these certificates was that they reduced the incentive for any bank to bid deposits away from its competitors. Sprague insisted that this system had to be accompanied by an agreement to pool bank reserves; otherwise, a bank that was not subject to a net drain might be forced to suspend payments after it paid cash to its own depositors if it had not received cash in settlements from other banks.[40] In 1873 reserves were pooled.

One serious drawback of clearinghouse certificates was that they were acceptable only in the local area—New York, Philadelphia, Baltimore. Thus these certificates helped maintain domestic payments such as payrolls and retail sales within a city but they dampened the effective flow of payments between cities. In the 1907 panic, 60 of the 160 clearinghouses in the United States used these certificates to facilitate local payments. Nevertheless, Sprague claimed that the dislocations of the domestic exchanges were as large and disruptive as they had been on previous occasions. The prices of New York funds in Boston, Philadelphia, Chicago, St Louis, Cincinnati, Kansas City, and New Orleans between 26 October and 15 December 1907 varied from a discount of 1.25 percent in Chicago on 2 November to a 7 percent premium in St Louis on 26 November, an increase from 1.5 percent the previous week.[41] In December 1907 Jacob H. Schiff wrote: 'The one lesson we should learn from recent experience is that the issuing of clearing-house certificates in the different bank centers has also worked considerable

harm. It has broken down domestic exchange and paralyzed to a large extent the business of the country.'[42]

Other devices of the same general character were clearinghouse checks and certified checks that were close substitutes for money and increased the means of payment in circulation.

Non-bank groups have also organized to mitigate a panic. Consider, for example, the stock market consortium. On 24 October 1907, a bankers' pool, headed by JP Morgan, loaned $25 million at 10 percent in call money in an attempt to stem the collapse of the stock market.[43] Twenty-two years to the day later, on Black Thursday in 1929, Richard Whitney went from post to post on the floor of the New York Stock Exchange and placed bids to buy stocks on behalf of a syndicate headed by JP Morgan and Company.[44]

Bank Cooperation

Banks have also collaborated through rescue committees (as in Vienna in May 1873 and earlier), loan funds, funds for guarantees of liabilities, arranged mergers of weak banks and firms, and other devices whereby the strong banks support the weak and failing banks.[45] Three examples include the role of the Paris banks in the 1828 crisis in Alsace, various devices employed by Hamburg in meeting the difficulties of 1857, and the Baring Brothers loan guarantee of 1890.

The Alsatian Crisis of 1828

Three firms in the textiles industry in Mulhouse failed in December 1827. The Paris banks then refused to accept any Alsatian paper, and the Bank of France set a limit of 6 million francs on the amount it would support, a figure that was 'scarcely the fortune of two Alsatian houses.' The Bank of France then decided against accepting any paper with Mulhouse or Basel endorsements and that decision precipitated a panic. On 19 January, two more Mulhouse merchants failed. On 22 January in Paris there were rumors of the failure of two Schlumberger firms. The Paris banks sent Jacques Laffitte as an emissary to Mulhouse; he arrived on 26 January and offered to lend 1 million francs on the consignment of merchandise. Before he came, however, two textile merchants, Nicholas Koechlin and Jean Dollfuss, had left Mulhouse for Paris. To raise cash, these merchants had been selling inventories of goods at discounts of 30–40 percent below their traditional market prices. Nine houses failed from 26 January to 15 February. Lévy-Leboyer wrote that it

could have been worse. At the last minute a syndicate of twenty-six Paris banks, presided over by J.C. Davillier, extended a credit of 5 million francs to Koechlin and Dollfuss, who returned to Alsace on 3 February and distributed 1 million francs to those of their colleagues who offered guarantees and kept 4 million for themselves. Another 1.3 million francs was scraped up in Basel. These measures restored confidence.[46] Those who qualified for neither the Koechlin-Dollfuss fund nor the Basel money failed.[47]

The Hamburg Crisis of 1857

The background of the crisis of 1857 in Hamburg was that trade had expanded, particularly because the Crimean War had led to an expansion of credit. Hamburg was the 'all-English' city of Germany, but had close relations with the United States in sugar, tobacco, coffee, and cotton, and with Scandinavia. When the deflationary tidal wave swept across the Atlantic, Hamburg was inundated. The panic touched off by the failure of Ohio Life on 24 August arrived in Hamburg three months later (following price declines of 30 percent) with the suspension of Winterhoff and Piper, a firm that was engaged in the American trade.[48] Daily dispatches from the British consulate in Hamburg by date tell the story:

21 November: Some of the leading merchant houses and two banks plan for relief.

23 November: Two major houses engaged in the London trade fail, and the Discount Guarantee Association grows more cautious in endorsing Hamburg bills.[49] On one authority the Discount Guarantee Association is exhausted in three days.[50]

24 November: A Discount Guarantee Association (Garantie-Diskontverein) is formed, initially with a capital of 10 million marks banco, later raised to 13 million (about £1 million), of which the sum of 1 million marks is to be paid in immediately.

28 November: The chamber of commerce and leading merchants induce the Senate to call parliament (Burgerschaft) to arrange to issue government bonds in order to lend 50 to 66 2/3rds percent of the value of hypothecated goods, bonds, and shares to merchants in distress.

1 December: With the suspension of Ullberg and Cremer, ten to twelve houses in the Sweden trade have gone down. The Discount Guarantee Association will not issue any more guarantees. Business is at a standstill.

2 December: A suggestion is made to change the laws of bankruptcy to enable creditors to share in attachment of goods.

7 December: A proposal is made to establish a state bank for discounting good bills to the amount of 30 million marks banco (about £2.4 million). Parliament rejects this, wanting instead to issue 30 million marks banco of paper currency as legal tender. The senate rejects this, insisting on clinging to the silver standard.

In the end, a compromise was reached for a State Loan Institute fund of 15 million marks that included 5 million marks banco of Hamburg government bonds and 10 million in silver to be borrowed in foreign financial centers.[51] The story of the silver train (*Silberzug*) is recounted in Chapter 12 as an early example of an international lender of last resort.

One observer totaled the sums available for rescue operations to 35 million marks banco, which included 15 million in the Discount Guarantee Association, 15 million in the State Loan Institute, and 5 million from the chamber of commerce. He compared this amount with 100 million marks banco of protested bills and noted that if merchants speculated with capital equal only to one-sixth the value of their goods, a 17 percent decline in prices of these goods would be sufficient to wipe out their capital position. To the suggestion that the senate was 300 years behind the times, he reported with approval the senate's answer: The merchants have been 300 years ahead of the times in issuing debt. State help in these cases, he insisted, merely means assistance for speculation and perpetuation of higher prices at a cost to the consumer.[52]

Guarantees of Liabilities: The Baring Crisis

The most famous guarantee of liabilities was that worked out by William Lidderdale when he was Governor of the Bank of England during the Baring crisis of 1890. Similar guarantees had occurred earlier in Britain. In December 1836 the private bank Esdailes, Grenfell, Thomas and Company, which served as London agents for seventy-two country banks, was in financial difficulty. The view was that this firm could not be allowed to fail because of its relationships with the country banks; moreover, its paper included all the best names in the City. The assets of the bank far exceeded its liabilities, and the London bankers offered guarantees. The Bank of England led the list with £150,000. Esdailes survived, but only for two years.[53]

The guarantee was worked out as an alternative to a letter of indemnity that permitted suspension of the Bank Act of 1844. The letter was offered by the Chancellor of the Exchequer, Lord Goschen, to Lidderdale, who refused on the ground that 'reliance on such letters was the cause of a great deal of bad banking in England.'

While Lidderdale refused to quiet the market by the usual means that had been employed in 1847, 1857, and 1866, he did not 'let the market take its medicine.' In August 1890, he warned Baring Brothers that the firm would have to moderate its acceptances for its Argentine agent, S. B. Hales. Baring Brothers revealed its acute distress to Lidderdale on Saturday 8 November. Fearful of a panic when Barings' condition was made public, the Bank of England met with the Exchequer on Monday 10 November, turned down the letter of indemnity, prepared for the problem by seeking assistance from foreign countries (a subject for Chapter 12), and formed a committee headed by Lord Rothschild to address the question of the large overhang of Argentinean securities.

As the days passed, the rumors circulated and Barings' bills were increasingly discounted at the Bank of England. By Wednesday, Lidderdale had learned that although Baring was solvent it would need £8–9 million of financial assistance. On Friday John Daniell, the leading man at Mullens and Co., used by the Bank of England in open-market operations, came to Lidderdale, crying 'Can't you do something, or say something, to relieve people's minds: they have made up their minds that something awful is up, and they are talking of the *very highest* names — the very highest!'.[54]

On 14 November Lidderdale met with two cabinet ministers who represented the Exchequer, Lords Smith and Salisbury. They agreed that the British government would increase its balance at the Bank of England immediately and that the government would share with the Bank in any losses suffered on Baring Brothers' paper discounted by the Bank between 2 pm Friday and 2 pm Saturday. On the basis of this agreement, Lidderdale met with eleven private banks to get them to contribute to a fund that would guarantee Barings' liabilities, and he got the State Bank of Russia to agree not to withdraw its £2.4 million deposit at Barings. The private banks as a group contributed £3,250,000, which included £1 million from the Bank of England as well as £500,000 from each of the three lenders, Glyn, Mills & Co., Currie and Co., and Rothschild. Lidderdale then used these commitments to obtain the agreement of the five London joint-stock banks to join the guarantee fund for another £3,250,000. On the basis of these assurances, *The Times* of 15 November announced that Baring Brothers would fail but that no creditor of Barings would incur a loss. The work of the guarantee fund continued on Saturday because the directors of the joint-stock banks had to meet to approve their subscriptions, which was done by 11am. Then other banks and financial institutions raised the fund from £7.5 million in the morning to £10 million by 4 pm; the guarantee fund eventually reached

£17 million and was taken as a measure of the strength of the London financial system. Martin's Bank was in distress over its loans to Barings and to Murriettas, another bank involved in Argentina. Martin's Bank joined the guarantee fund for £100,000 on 18 November (Tuesday), too late to afford much help to Barings, but early enough to demonstrate its own strength.[55] In summarizing the episode, Powell stated: 'The Bank is not a single combatant who must fight or retire, but the leader of the most colossal agglomeration of financial power which the world has so far witnessed.'[56]

On 25 November a new firm, Baring Brothers and Co, Ltd was formed as a joint-stock company with a capital of £1 million. The form of the guarantee may be of interest.

Guarantee Fund
Bank of England, November, 1890
In consideration of advances which the Bank of England have agreed to make to Messrs. Baring Brothers and Co., to enable them to discharge at maturity their liabilities existing on the night of the 15th of November, 1890, or arising out of business initiated on or prior to the 15th of November, 1890.

We, the undersigned, hereby agree, each individual, firm, or company, for himself or themselves alone, and to the amount only set opposite to his or their names respectively, to make good to the Bank of England any loss which may appear whenever the Bank of England shall determine that the final liquidation of the liabilities of Messrs. Baring Brothers and Co. has been completed so far in the opinion of the Governors as practicable.

All the guarantors shall contribute rateably, and no one individual, firm, or company, shall be called on for his or their contribution without the like call being made on the others.

The maximum period over which the liquidation may extend is three years, commencing the 15th of November, 1890.[57]

The rescue of Long-Term Capital Management in September 1998 provides a parallel and contrast to the rescue of Barings. William McDonough, the president of the Federal Reserve Bank of New York, convened fourteen large commercial banks and investment banks, including Merrill Lynch, Morgan Stanley Dean Witter, J.P. Morgan, Chase Manhattan Bank, and the Union Bank of Switzerland. They agreed to provide $3.6 billion of capital to prevent the collapse of LTCM in exchange for 90 percent of LTCM's equity.[58] The Federal Reserve poured the coffee but did not provide capital. These firms were creditors of LTCM, so the 'bailout' to some extent involved a change in

the legal nature of their claim on LTCM. The Federal Reserve was concerned that if LTCM failed the markets would be paralyzed by the need to unwind its massive position in futures and options contracts and other types of derivatives.

Deposit Insurance

Since 1934, federal deposit insurance in the United States has prevented bank runs by providing an *ex ante* guarantee of deposits in insured banks. Initially the deposits were guaranteed up to $5000 but gradually the ceiling on deposits was raised in stages and eventually reached $100,000—and then $250,000 during the 2008 crisis. When large banks got into trouble, the FDIC deliberately removed all limits on the amounts of deposits covered by the guarantee to halt imminent runs and in practice it established that banks with significant deposits over $100,000 were 'too big to fail' (although the shareholders of these banks would probably lose most or all of their money). Similarly, the owners of the subordinated debt of these banks might lose much or all of their money. The deposits of the foreign branches of these banks had implicitly become insured even though the banks had not paid insurance premiums on these deposits. Although deposit insurance was designed to prevent bank runs by taking care of the 'little man,' this ceiling had in practice been raised to the sky—although owners of deposits over the ceilings have taken haircuts.[59]

When the limit on deposit insurance was $100,000, brokers in Merrill Lynch and other large brokerage firms arranged for the placement of larger amounts of money in guaranteed deposits. John Doe could have an insured deposit of $100,000, his wife Jane also could have an insured deposit of $100,000, and together John and Jane could have a third insured deposit of the same amount. And the Does could follow the same strategy with the bank across the street.

This innovation provided a guarantee to wealthy individuals and was an end run around one purpose of the ceiling to limit the insurance coverage to those with modest wealth. Moreover, the innovation encouraged banks to make riskier loans since they were confident that they were protected against runs by the owners of the larger deposits—if these riskier loans proved profitable, the owners of the banks would benefit and if the loans went into default, the owners would not have to worry about bank runs (although the market value of their own shares might decline and even become worthless).

The fall in the prices of stocks and of real estate in Japan that began in 1990 caused the value of the loans of the banks headquartered in Tokyo and Osaka and various regional centers to decline sharply below the value of their liabilities. Nevertheless, there were no bank runs; the Japanese depositors (as opposed to the non-Japanese depositors) were confident that they would be made whole by the Japanese government if any of the banks was closed.

Deposit insurance has limited both bank runs and contagion in the runs from one troubled bank to other banks in a neighborhood. How can the reluctance to provide insurance at an earlier date be explained?

In the long tradition of the United States, free banking, even wildcat banking, was the rule. Anyone could start a bank, and many did. Risks were large, turnover among bankers rapid. A guarantee of bankers' deposits would have constituted a license to speculate, if not embezzle, and would have removed the threat of withdrawal of deposits that was the major check on the irresponsibility of bankers. Deposit guarantees were rejected as conducive to bad banking as late as 2 March 1933, when the Board of Governors of the Federal Reserve was not prepared to recommend such a guarantee, or any other measures, on the eve of the national bank holiday.[60]

The Federal Deposit Insurance Corporation had an excellent financial record until the 1970s in that the insurance premiums that it collected from the insured banks were much larger than the amount it paid to make good the losses when a bank failed. From the beginning in 1934 through 1970, only one bank with deposits of more than $50 million failed, and most banks that failed had deposits of less than $5 million. In most cases, the FDIC arranged for the takeover of a failed bank so that individuals and firms with deposits above the maximum insured amounts did not incur losses.

Beginning in the late 1970s, the financial problems of the FDIC and those of the FSLIC increased sharply as more and more banks and thrifts were closed. The FDIC rescued a large number of banks including two giants, the Continental Illinois Bank of Chicago and the First Republic Bank of Dallas; honoring the deposit insurance guarantee cost these agencies billions of dollars. The usual operating procedure was to close the bank or the thrift institution when its capital had been depleted, and then to carve a 'good bank' from the rescued institution while the remaining assets of the failed institution would be retained for eventual sale by another newly created government agency, the Resolution Trust Corporation (RTC). Both insurance agencies incurred such large losses in honoring their guarantees that their capital and reserves were exhausted; they then borrowed from the US Treasury. In the early 1990s, the estimates were that the losses to the US taxpayers would amount to $150 billion but the increase in the US growth rate meant that

the RTC received more money than anticipated from the sale of real estate and bad loans so the losses totaled slightly more than \$100 billion.[61] There was some question whether a portion of this cost to the taxpayers could be reduced by increasing the insurance premiums on bank deposits — a suggestion that the sound banks resoundingly opposed.[62]

During the 2008 crisis the US Treasury extended deposit insurance to the money market funds because of the fear that the shareholders of these funds would transfer their money to banks whose deposits were guaranteed by the FDIC. The money market funds then would be obliged to shrink and to sell securities, which would depress their prices. More money market funds then would 'break the buck'; the net asset value per share would decline below \$1.00—which would trigger a massive, self-justifying run.

During the 2008 crisis, the FDIC also guaranteed newly issued bonds of insured banks and bank holding companies. Many governments around the world through various agencies also provided such guarantees at the time. Also, the FDIC provided for a time unlimited insurance for non-interest-bearing transaction deposits. The FDIC pocketed \$9 billion from the fees for the two guarantees net of payouts.

Exchequer Bills

One ancient device short of lending money to a firm in trouble was to issue marketable securities to the firm against appropriate collateral. (Of course, when markets break down, even the most liquid securities may not be sold readily.) The securities have been private and public; both types were part of the complex package put together by Hamburg in 1857. In 1763 and 1799, in an equally complex and jerry-built system of support, admiralty bills were an integral feature.[63] The widest development, however, concerned the Exchequer bills issued in Britain in 1793, 1799, and (without enthusiasm) 1811, but sternly rejected in 1825.

The Exchequer bill was widely thought to have been the idea of Sir John Sinclair, although it may have originated with the Bank of England. On 22 April 1793, City leaders met with the Prime Minister, William Pitt, to devise means to combat the crisis that arose from the failure of 100 of the 300 country banks and the calamitous decline in commodity prices. The next day, eleven members of this group met at the Mansion House to formulate a scheme for state assistance. According to Clapham, there was no clear guide to what should be done. Then the idea emerged of having the government

issue £3 million in Exchequer bills, a total that was later raised by parliament to £5 million, to be issued to merchants on the collateral of goods that they would deposit in the customs houses. An additional feature of the plan was to issue £5 notes—the previous minimum was £10—to economize on the use of gold and silver coin. The Exchequer bills were issued by special commissioners rather than the Bank of England; £70,000 of these bills was immediately sent to Manchester and an equal amount to Glasgow. The device worked like a charm, according to MacPherson. Three hundred and thirty-eight firms applied for £3 million of the total amount. A total of £2.2 million was granted to 228 firms, only two of which subsequently went bankrupt. Applications for more than £1.2 million were withdrawn after the panic abated.[64]

In 1799, the panic in Hamburg had an echo in Liverpool, and Exchequer bills again were used. Parliament provided £500,000 in Exchequer bills, used solely in Liverpool, against £2 million of goods stored in warehouses.[65]

In 1811, the question arose again. A Select Committee on the State of Commercial Credit was appointed. Among its members were Henry Thornton, Sir John Sinclair, Sir Thomas Baring, and Alexander Baring. The committee's report, completed in a week, recorded the distress of exporters to and importers from the West Indies and South America, as well as the piles of goods bound for the Baltic that had been cut off and stored in London warehouses, and recommended a new issue of £6 million of Exchequer bills. Support was moderate in the House of Commons because of the overtrading in South America; the opposition, while sympathetic to the distress, doubted the wisdom of bailing out the speculators. William Huskisson, who later made his mark as the president of the Board of Trade, claimed that the evil came from too easy credit:

> Did gentlemen not see that the race of old English merchants, who never could persuade themselves to go beyond their capital, was superseded by a set of mad and extravagant speculators, who never stopped so long as they could get credit, and that persons of notoriously small capital had now eclipsed those of the greatest consequence; so that speculations now took place even in the lowest articles of commerce ... If the relief given was used for further speculation, it would only aggravate the evil — and he feared that this might be done — in which case the present measure would go only to add six million to the circulation and to raise the prices of all our commodities.[66]

Smart gave the fullest account of the debate and noted that many criticized the measure, though few were bold enough to deny it. In the end the proposal passed, but few applications were made and only £2 million was advanced.

'Not many of those who were in embarrassed circumstances were able to furnish the desired security, and it is difficult to see what remedy there was in being enabled, by advances, to produce more goods when the radical evil was that there was no market for them.'[67]

Luck: A Tailpiece

Lady Luck once worked effectively to assist a bank in distress. Wirth wrote that the Brothers Kauffmann in Hamburg was failing during the crisis of 1799 when one of the brothers sent his bride a Hamburg city lottery ticket, which carried a first prize of 100,000 marks banco. She bought the same number in another lottery in the Duchy of Mecklenburg, the prize for which was an estate worth 50,000 Prussian thalers, then equal to 100,000 marks banco. She won both, and the Brothers Kauffmann was fully rehabilitated.[68] The odds at Las Vegas may be higher for the solution to a global crisis.

Notes

1. Ian Giddy, 'Regulation of Off-Balance Sheet Banking', in *The Search for Financial Stability: the Past Fifty Years* (San Francisco: Federal Reserve Bank of San Francisco, 1985), pp. 165–77.
2. Edward J. Kane, 'Competitive Financial Reregulation: an International Perspective', in R. Portes and A. Swoboda, eds, *Threats to International Financial Stability* (Cambridge: Cambridge University Press, 1987), pp. 111–45.
3. Stanley Zucker, *Ludwig Bamberger: German Liberal Politician and Social Critic, 1823–1899* (Pittsburgh: University of Pittsburgh Press, 1975), p. 78.
4. Thomas Joplin, *Case for Parliamentary Inquiry into the Circumstances of the Panic, in a Letter to Thomas Gisborne, Esq., M. P.* (London: James Ridgeway & Sons, n.d. [after 1832]), p. 10 (apropos the panic of 1825).
5. Sir John Clapham, *The Bank of England: a History* (Cambridge: Cambridge University Press, 1945), vol. 2, p. 236 (apropos the panic of 1847).
6. E. Victor Morgan, *The Theory and Practice of Central Banking, 1797–1913* (Cambridge: Cambridge University Press, 1943), p. 133.
7. The episode is noted in A. Andréadès, *History of the Bank of England* (London: P. S. King, 1909), p. 334. For an extended discussion, see Rudiger Dornbusch and Jacob Frenkel, 'The Gold Standard and the Bank of England in the Crisis of 1847', in Michael Bordo and Anna J. Schwartz, eds, *A Retrospective on the Classical Gold Standard, 1821–1931* (Chicago: University of Chicago Press, 1984), pp. 233–64.

8. Ministère des Finances et al., *Enquête sur les principes et les faits géneraux qui régissent la circulation monétaire et fiduciare* (Paris: Imprimerie impériale, 1867), vol. 1, p. 456.

9. 'The Revulsion of 1857—Its Causes and Results', *New York Herald*, n.d., quoted in D. Morier Evans, *The History of the Commercial Crisis, 1857–1858, and the Stock Exchange Panic of 1859* (1859; reprint edn, New York: Augustus M. Kelley, 1969), p. 121.

10. Herbert Hoover, *The Memoirs of Herbert Hoover* (New York: Macmillan & Co., 1952), vol. 3, p. 30.

11. Murray N. Rothbard, *America's Great Depression*, 3rd edn (Kansas City: Sheed & Ward, 1975), p. 187.

12. Paul Johnson, *Modern Times: the World from the Twenties to the Eighties* (New York: Harper & Row, 1983), p. 244.

13. Ernst Baasch, *Holländische Wirtschaftsgeschichte* (Jena: Gustav Fischer, 1927), p. 238.

14. Joplin, *Parliamentary Inquiry*, pp. 14–15.

15. Great Britain, *Parliamentary Papers, Monetary Policy, Commercial Distress* (1857; Shannon: Irish University Press, 1969), vol. 1, pp. 427, 431.

16. D. Morier Evans, *The Commercial Crisis, 1847–1848*, 2nd edn (1849; reprint edn, New York: Augustus M. Kelley, 1969), p. 89n.

17. Evans, *Commercial Crisis*, p. 181.

18. Parliamentary Papers, *Commercial Distress*, p. xii.

19. Ibid., vol. 4, appendix 20; *Foreign Communications Relative to the Commercial Crisis of 1857*, Hamburg consular circular no. 76, November 23, 1857, pp. 435, 440, 441.

20. Henrietta M. Larson, *Jay Cooke, Private Banker* (Cambridge, MA: Harvard University Press, 1936), p. 80.

21. W. C. T. King, *History of the London Discount Market* (London: George Routledge & Sons, 1936), p. 243.

22. Theodore Dreiser, *The Financier* (1912), in *Trilogy of Desire* (New York: World Publishing, 1972), p. 491.

23. W. Jett Lauck, *The Causes of the Panic of 1893* (Boston: Houghton, Mifflin, 1907), p. 102.

24. *The Commercial and Financial Chronicle*, 16 May 1884, p. 589, quoted in O. M. W. Sprague, *History of Crises under the National Banking System* (1910; reprint edn, New York: Augustus M. Kelley, 1968), p. 112.

25. W. R. Brock, *Lord Liverpool and Liberal Toryism, 1820–1827* (Cambridge: Cambridge University Press, 1941), pp. 209–10 (cited by Clapham, *Bank of England*, vol. 2, p. 108).

26. Clapham, *Bank of England*, vol. 2, p. 332.

27. Stephan Skalweit, *Die Berliner Wirtschaftskrise von 1763 und ihre Hintergründe* (Stuttgart: Verlag W. Kohlhammer, 1937), pp. 49–73.

28. Arthur D. Gayer, W. W. Rostow, and Anna J. Schwartz, *The Growth and Fluctuation of the British Economy, 1790–1850* (Oxford: Oxford University Press, Clarendon Press, 1953), vol. 1, p. 272.

29. Larry T. Wimmer, 'The Gold Crisis of 1869: a Problem in Domestic Economic Policy and International Trade Theory' (PhD diss., University of Chicago, 1968), p. 79.

30. Andréadès, *Bank of England*, p. 137, citing Henry D. McLeod, *Theory and Practice of Banking*, 3rd edn (London: Longman Green, Reader & Dyer, 1879), p. 428.

31. John Carswell, *The South Sea Bubble* (London: Cresset Press, 1960), p. 184.

32. Andréadès, *Bank of England*, p. 151.

33. Alexander Dana Noyes, *The Market Place: Reminiscences of a Financial Editor* (Boston: Little, Brown, 1938), p. 333.

34. Sprague, *History of Crises*, p. 259.

35. Ibid.

36. Ibid., p. 181.

37. Max Wirth, *Geschichte der Handelskrisen*, 4th edn (1890; reprint edn, New York: Burt Franklin, 1968), p. 521.

38. Maurice Lévy-Leboyer, *Les banques européennes et l'industrialisation internationale dans la première moitié du XIXe siècle* (Paris: Presses universitaires de France, 1964), p. 480, text and note 5.

39. George W. Van Vleck, *The Panic of 1857: An Analytical Study* (New York: Columbia University Press, 1943), p. 80.

40. Sprague, *History of Crises*, pp. 120, 182–3.

41. Ibid., pp. 75, 291–2.

42. Jacob H. Schiff, 'Relation of a Central Bank to the Elasticity of the Currency', *Annals of the American Academy of Political and Social Science*, vol. 31 (January–June 1908), p. 375. For a more contemporary account, see Jean Strouse, 'The Brilliant Bailout', *New Yorker* (23 November 1998), pp. 62–77.

43. Myron T. Herrick, 'The Panic of 1907 and Some of Its Lessons', *Annals of the American Academy of Political and Social Science*, vol. 31 (January–June 1908), p. 309.

44. John Kenneth Galbraith, *The Great Crash, 1929*, 3rd edn (Boston: Houghton Mifflin, 1972), pp. 107–8.

45. For a discussion of the rescue committee (*Aufhilfsfonds*) in Vienna, see Eduard März, *Österreich Industrie- und Bankpolitik* in *der Zeit Franz Josephs I: Am Beispiel der k.k. priv. Österreichischen Credit-Anstalt für Handel und Gewerbe* (Vienna: Europa Verlag, 1968), pp. 177–82. März notes (p. 179) that the best account of the crisis is that of Josef Neuwirth, *Bank und Valuta in Österreich*, vol. 2, *Die Spekulationskrisis van 1873* (no publishing data given).

46. Lévy-Leboyer, *Banques européennes*, pp. 470–1.

47. Bertrand Gille, *La banque en France au XIXe siècle* (Paris: Droz, 1970), p. 93.

48. Parliamentary Papers, *Commercial Distress*, vol. 4, appendix, consular dispatch from Hamburg, no. 75. p. 434.

49. Ibid., p. 435.

50. Hans Rosenberg, *Die Weltwirtschaftskrise von 1857–1859* (Stuttgart/Berlin: Verlag von W. Kohlhammer, 1934), p. 129.

51. Parliamentary Paper, *Commercial Distress*, vol. 4, appendix, consular dispatches from Hamburg, nos. 77, 80, 81, 82, 84, 86, pp. 435–7.

52. Albert E. Fr. Schäffle, 'Die Handelskrise von 1857 in Hamburg, mit besonderer Rücksicht auf das Bankwesen', in *Gesammelte Aufsätze* (Tübingen: H. Raupp'schen, 1885), vol. 2, pp. 44, 45, 52, 53.

53. Clapham, *Bank of England*, vol. 2, p. 156.

54. Ibid., p. 331. For more detailed accounts of the Baring crisis and rescue, see L. S. Pressnell, 'Gold Reserves, Banking Reserves and the Baring Crisis of 1890', in C. R. Whittlesey and J. S. G. Wilson, eds, *Essays in Money and Banking in Honour of R. S. Sayers* (Oxford: Clarendon Press, 1968), pp. 67–228; and idem, 'The Sterling System and Financial Crises Before 1914', in C. P. Kindleberger and J.-P. Laffargue, eds, *Financial Crises: Theory, History and Policy* (Cambridge: Cambridge University Press, 1982), pp. 148–64.

55. Diary of John Biddulph Martin, in George Chandler, *Four Centuries of Banking* (London: B. J. Batsford, 1964), vol. 1, p. 330.

56. Ellis T. Powell, *The Evolution of the Money Market (1384–1915): an Historical and Analytical Study of the Rise and Development of Finance as a Central Coordinated Force* (1915: reprint edn, New York: Augustus M. Kelley, 1966), p. 528.

57. Ibid., p. 525.

58. 'New York Fed Assists Hedge Fund Bailout', *New York Times*, 24 September 1998, pp. A1, C11.

59. There are some purists or masochists who think that bank runs are an optimal response of depositors, and good for the system, with panic as a form of monitoring. 'If depositors believe that there are some underperforming banks, but cannot decide which ones may become insolvent, they may force out all the undesirable ones by a systemwide panic.' This is from Charles W. Calomoris and Gary Gorton, 'The Origins of Banking Panics: Models, Facts and Bank Regulation', in R. Glenn Hubbard, ed., *Financial Markets and Financial Crises* (Chicago: University of Chicago Press, 1991), pp. 120–1.

60. Hoover, *Memoirs*, vol. 3, pp. 211–12.

61. 'Bank Board Doubles Texas Cost Estimate', *New York Times*, 8 July 1988, sec. D.

62. 'Treasury Says Savings Aid Should Not Tax the Taxpayer', *New York Times*, 3 August 1988, sec. D.

63. Wirth, *Handelskrisen*, p. 100.

64. Andréadès, *Bank of England*, pp. 187–9; Clapham, *Bank of England*, vol. 1, pp. 263–5.

65. Gayer, Rostow, and Schwartz, *Growth and Fluctuation*, vol. 1, p. 34.

66. William Smart, *Economic Annals of the Nineteenth Century* (1911; reprint edn, New York: Augustus M. Kelley, 1964), vol. 1, pp. 267–8.
67. Ibid., p. 271.
68. Wirth, *Handelskrisen*, pp. 110–11.

11

The Domestic Lender of Last Resort

The hallmark in the development of 'the Art of Central Banking' over the last two hundred years has been the evolution of the concept of 'a lender of last resort.' The expression comes from the French *dernier ressort*, and centers on the last legal jurisdiction to which a petitioner can take an appeal. The term has become thoroughly anglicized, and now the emphasis is on the responsibilities of the lender rather than the rights of the borrower.

The idea is that the lender of last resort can and should forestall a run by depositors and other investors from real assets and illiquid securities into money by supplying the amount of money that is needed to satisfy the demand; the concept is of an 'elastic supply of money' that increases to meet the demand in panics. Otherwise, if the supply of money is fixed, then individual lenders will seek to increase their money holdings by selling securities—the identity of the firms that own the money has changed but the supply remains unchanged while the price of securities has declined. How much money? To whom? On what terms? When?

The dilemma for the lender of last resort—the moral hazard argument—is that if owners and managers of banks believe that their firms will be supported in moments of distress, they will be less cautious in making risky loans during the next boom. The moral hazard storyline is that the public good that more credit will be available from the lender of last resort to cope with a crisis weakens the responsibility of private lenders to ensure that they make 'sound' loans. If, however, in a panic the rush from the securities and commodities into money cannot be halted, the fallacy of composition takes

center stage. The sale of these securities by investors leads to declines in their prices with the consequence that a large number of firms that previously were solvent and well-capitalized may be dragged into bankruptcy as the prices of the assets in their portfolios declines.

The opposition to a lender of last resort has been continuous. Napoleon's minister of the public treasury, François Nicholas Mollien, wrote strongly against the interventionist instincts of his mentor, who wanted to save the failing manufacturers damaged by the Continental System (blockade); he asserted that a start in this direction would only get the Treasury in deeper and deeper.[1] Louis Antoine Garnier-Pagès, French minister of finance in 1848, claimed later that it was useful to precipitate a crisis to render it less durable: 'Do nothing to save the *rente*, clean out stocks; sell merchandise.' The policy, he asserted, contributed to the brilliance of the French recovery from 1850 to 1852.[2] Murray Rothbard asserted that 'any propping up of shaky positions postpones liquidation and aggravates unsound conditions.'[3] The most trenchant formulation is that of Herbert Spencer: 'The ultimate result of shielding man from the effects of folly is to people the world with fools.'[4]

An understandable view in a Darwinian age.

Origin of the Concept

The development of the lender of last resort evolved from the practice of the market. Ashton asserted that the Bank of England was already the lender of last resort in the eighteenth century,[5] although this statement does not seem consistent with his statement that 'long before the rules for the treatment of crises were laid down by economists, it was recognized that the remedy [for a financial crisis] was for the monetary authority (the Bank of England or the British government) to make an emergency issue of some kind of paper which bankers, merchants and the general public would accept. When this was done the panic was allayed.'[6]

The indecision about whether the central bank or the government was the final monetary authority remains to this day and qualifies the statement that the Bank of England emerged as the lender of last resort in the 1700s. E. V. Morgan maintained that the Bank of England's realization of its responsibility was delayed by the government's action in issuing Exchequer bills in 1793, 1799, and 1811 and that the Bank assumed the role as lender of last resort only gradually during the first half of the nineteenth century 'in spite of the opposition of theorists.'[7] The same evolutionary process can be seen in the Bank of France. In 1833, the majority of the Conseil General overrode

Hottinguer's idea for a policy on the English model as well as Odier's plea for an entirely new policy and concluded that the major function of the Bank of France was to defend the French franc. Capital outflows were not to be feared. Interest rates should not be held artificially low or speculation will be encouraged and crises intensified. When a crisis occurred, however, the Bank should provide abundant and cheap discounts to moderate its intensity and shorten its duration.[8]

The role of the lender of last resort was not respectable among theorists until Bagehot's *Lombard Street* appeared in 1873, although Sir Francis Baring called attention to the idea at the end of the eighteenth century[9] and Thornton's classic, *Paper Credit*, developed both the doctrine and the counter-arguments in his discussion of the financial problems of the English country banks.[10] Bagehot traced the origin of the doctrine to David Ricardo in his statement before the Parliamentary Select Committee on Banks of Issue in 1875: 'The orthodox doctrine laid down by Ricardo is that there is a period in a panic at which restrictions upon the issue of legal tender must be removed.'[11] Bagehot had articulated the doctrine in his first published article, written in 1848, when he commented on the suspension of the 1844 Bank Act in the panic of 1847:

> It is a great defect of a purely metallic circulation that the quantity of it cannot be readily suited to any sudden demand ... Now as paper money can be supplied in unlimited quantities, however sudden the demand may be, it does not appear to us that there is any objection on principle to sudden issues of paper money to meet sudden and large extensions of demand ... This power of issuing notes is one excessively liable to abuse ... It should only be used in rare and exceptional cases.[12]

Some analysts continue to reject the doctrine and powerful minds have argued both sides of the issue. Should one worry about the present panic or the next boom, the condition, or the principle? 'There are times when rules and precedents cannot be broken; others when they cannot be adhered to with safety.'[13] The dilemma is that breaking the rule creates a new precedent and a new rule. Lord Overstone, the distinguished Currency School theorist, strongly opposed expansion of the money supply in a crisis but reluctantly admitted that a panic may require 'that power, which all governments must necessarily possess, of exercising special interference in cases of unforeseen emergency and great state necessity.'[14] On one occasion he produced a ringing metaphoric defense: 'There is an old Eastern proverb which says, you may stop with a bodkin a fountain, which if suffered to flow, will

sweep away whole cities in its course.'[15] Friedman and Schwartz similarly and metaphorically flirted with lender of last resort doctrine:

> The detailed story of every banking crisis in our history shows how much depends on the presence of one or more outstanding individuals willing to assume responsibility and leadership ... Economic collapse often has the characteristics of a cumulative process. Let it go beyond a certain point, and it will tend for a time to gain strength from its own development ... Because no great strength would be required to hold back the rock that starts a landslide, it does not follow that the landslide will not be of major proportions.[16]

The paradox is equivalent to the prisoner's dilemma. Central banks should lend freely to halt the panic, but leave the market to its own devices to reduce the likelihood of future panics. A dilemma: actuality inevitably dominates contingency, today wins over tomorrow.

The Bank Act of 1844 represented a victory for the Currency School, which stood for a fixed supply of money, over the Banking School, which thought it useful for the money supply to grow as output and trade increased. Both schools were concerned with the long run rather than with the short run, and neither approved of increasing the money supply as a temporary expedient to meet a crisis. When the Bank Act was being considered, the idea that the government has the power to suspend its provisions in an emergency was rejected. After 1847 and again after 1857, when it proved necessary to suspend the Bank Act and issue more money as a last resort, parliament conducted inquiries to determine whether there was a need to change the legislation. Both inquiries concluded that it was not desirable to have built-in provision for suspending the act even though the suspension had been useful and necessary. To limit precedent-setting, the bill brokers who had been sudden borrowers 'wanting incalculable advances in 1857 were told not to expect the like again.'[17] The principle of having a rule but breaking it if one had to was so widely accepted that after the suspension in 1866 there was no demand for a new investigation.

In the 1850s, Jellico and Chapman had proposed rules for adjusting the discount rate of the Bank of England to the state of its reserves by a mathematical formula written into the legislation. Wood criticized them as having no real grasp of Bank transactions and methods of procedure.[18] Robert Love, Chancellor of the Exchequer in June 1875, introduced a bill that would authorize a temporary increase in Bank of England notes in exchange for securities (under certain contingencies, including panic), a bank rate above 12 percent, and a favorable position in the currency market. The bill was tabled and given a first reading on 12 June but it never received a second

reading and was withdrawn in July.[19] Hard-and-fast rules were agreed not to be workable. *The Economist* and Bagehot thought it proper that the Bank of England, rather than the banks, should hold the reserves necessary to get the country through a panic. Mr. Hankey, a former governor of the Bank, called this 'the most mischievous doctrine ever broached in the monetary or banking world in this country; viz. that is the proper function of the Bank of England to keep money available at all times to supply the demands of bankers who have rendered their own assets unavailable.'[20] The public, however, sided with Bagehot and practice against Hankey and theory. If the expansion of credit in boom periods cannot be controlled, then measures should be adopted to halt the contraction of credit in crisis.

Who Is the Lender of Last Resort?

The lack of clear agreement in Britain about whether the Treasury should relieve panics through the issue of Exchequer bills or whether instead the Bank of England should discount freely at a penalty rate, even if it is necessary to suspend the limits imposed by the Bank Act of 1844, has already been noted. Uncertainty about the answers to these questions may be optimal, along with the question of whether the government authorities should rescue firms in distress and whether the money will arrive in time. Thus, there was no explicit provision for a lender of last resort in Britain and no fixed rule as to which agency should fill this role. In 1825, the Exchequer was not the selected agency. The task was given resolutely to the Bank of England whose reluctant acceptance was 'the sulky answer of driven men.'[21] In 1890, guarantees were used rather than the Bank or the Exchequer. Gradually the responsibility devolved on the Bank, which led Alfred Marshall to write that 'its directorate came to be regarded at home and abroad as a committee of safety of English business generally.'[22]

By the 1830s, the Bank of France had agreed that it had responsibilities in a crisis, but it thought it had other responsibilities as well, such as to ensure monopoly of the bank note circulation, which permitted it to let the regional banks fail in 1848 and then to convert them into subsidiaries (*comptoirs*). The provinces feared Paris; their concern was that in a crisis Paris would take care of its own needs first at the expense of the regions and hence they wanted the privilege of note issue. But after Le Havre had acquired its own bank which then needed assistance because it had made too many illiquid industrial loans including some to shipyards and some to importers of cotton, the Banque du Havre went to Paris in 1848 seeking financial help. 'The return was not

glorious. The Bank of France had been impitiable.'[23] It refused to lend on mortgages, saying: 'The statutes forbid it, and you have refused to accept a *comptoir*.'[24]

The Bank of France wavered over this question even as it wanted to destroy the regional banks. From America, Chevalier observed that the Bank of France had discounted freely in 1810, 1818, and 1826, with Jacques Laffitte as governor for the first two years—making great efforts to sustain commerce; but it lacked the same courage in the crisis of 1831–1832.[25] In 1830, after the revolution, the task was left to local authorities. A regional bank, conducted with honesty but not prudence, threatened a provincial crisis. The local receiver-general undertook to discount its doubtful paper, apparently after consulting Paris, where, Thiers testified, after 'mature reflection the public interest was put above that of the Finance Minister, M. Louis,' 'with happy results,' that is, the avoidance of the collapse of the bank and a resultant disturbance.[26]

After the Bank of France achieved its monopoly of the note issue and the conversion of the banks in the regions into its branches, the Bank began to act as a lender of last resort. Its statutes required that it discount only three-name paper; the task became one of producing acceptable names. Sixty *comptoirs d'escompte* were established throughout France, as well as a number of *sous-comptoirs* organized by various branches of trade to hold stocks of goods and issue IOUs using them as collateral. With the names of the merchant, the *sous-comptoir*, and a *comptoir*, the Bank of France could discount the paper and relieve liquidity crises. Louis Raphael Bischoffsheim of Bischoffsheim & Goldschmidt mocked the requirement of three names: 'The number is not important. With bad signatures one can collect 10 instead of three. I prefer one good to 20 bad.'[27] After the end of the crisis, a number of the *comptoirs* were taken over by bankers, merchants, and industrialists and became regular banks. The most famous of this group, the Comptoir d'Escompte de Paris, took its place among the leading banks in the country.[28]

The Crédit Mobilier of the Pereire brothers was not saved in 1868; the Bank of France refused to discount its paper, which might be interpreted as the revenge of the establishment on an outsider as punishment for not conceding the Banque de Savoie note issue to the Bank of France when the Pereires took over the Savoy bank after the region had been ceded to France by Italy in 1860.[29] The alternative explanation was that this was the entirely normal refusal of a lender of last resort to bail out an insolvent institution.[30] Cameron accuses the Bank of France of conducting guerrilla warfare against the Pereire brothers because of a quarrel between Rothschild and the Pereires that went back to the 1830s.[31]

The Bank of France and Paris bankers did not come to the rescue of the Union Générale in 1882 but seven years later they rescued the Comptoir d'Escompte de Paris. Critics of the Bank of France ascribe the difference in outcomes to venality. A less emotional position asserts that a second large bank failure in seven years might have completely destroyed the French banking system and that, on this account, Rouvier, the minister of finance, took the necessary measures to have the Bank of France and the Paris banks advance 140 million francs to the Comptoir d'Escompte.[32] In the Union Générale operation, as was noted in an earlier chapter, the Paris banks withdrew from the speculative activity when it began to peak in August 1881 and advanced 18.1 million francs to the Union Générale after the crash the following January to permit a more orderly liquidation of the bank rather than to save it.[33] Led by Rothschild and Hottinguer, and including the Comptoir d'Escompte and the Société Générale (but not the Lyons rival of Bontoux, the Crédit Lyonnais), the consortium represented the establishment, in which it was not really necessary to distinguish the Bank of France from the leading private banks (*hautes banques*) and deposit banks.

In Prussia in 1763, the king was the lender of last resort. In 1848, various state agencies including the Prussian Bank, the Seehandlung, and the Prussian lottery tried to help the Cologne bank, A. Schaaffhausen, before it was allowed to reorganize as a joint-stock bank. In the absence of a central bank in 1763, 1799, and 1857, the Hamburg city government, the chamber of commerce, and the banks—any and all leading agencies—took part in the rescue operation.

The US experience is especially relevant about the identity of the lender of last resort. There was some ambiguity as to whether the First Bank of the United States and then the Second Bank of the United States were lenders of last resort despite the designation of the Bank in each case as the chosen instrument. On various occasions, the US Treasury assisted the banks by accepting customs receipts in post-dated thirty-day notes (1792), by making special deposits of government funds in the banks that were in trouble (1801, 1818, and 1819), and by relaxing the requirement that a commercial bank pay the Bank of the United States in specie (1801).[34] After the failure to renew the charter of the Second Bank of the United States in 1833, the US Treasury was even busier, both before and after the passage of the 1845 law that required that the Treasury keep its funds out of the banks. In times of crisis and in periods of credit stringency caused by crop movements, the US Treasury would pay interest or principal on its debt in advance, make deposits in banks, and offer to accept securities other than government bonds as collateral for deposits of government funds. Banks began to look to the Secretary

of the Treasury for help in emergencies and to relieve seasonal tightness in the supply of credit. In the autumn of 1872, Secretary of the Treasury George S. Boutwell served as a lender of last resort by reissuing retired greenbacks—which may have been illegal. His successor, William A. Richardson, did the same thing a year later.[35]

The US Treasury could absorb money in deposits and pay out surplus cash that it had previously acquired, but apart from the greenback period, it could not create money. Thus the Treasury was unsatisfactory as a lender of last resort unless it had previously built up its holdings of cash from budget surpluses. In 1907, when its cash holdings were low, the Treasury issued new bonds—$50 million of Panama Canal bonds, which were eligible for collateral for national bank notes, and $100 million of 3 percent certificates of indebtedness—that it hoped would entice existing cash and specie from hoards. In the end, the crisis was averted by a flow of more than $100 million of gold from Britain.[36] Moreover, the devices used to cope with a crisis were ad hoc. An analysis of the crisis of 1857 suggested that the Federal government was incapable of intervening effectively and that the public, including the banks, was left without guidance to stem the crisis.[37] In fact, intervention proved to be too much and too early.

The complex record of involvement by the US Treasury raises the question of whether the market should have regulated itself and, if so, how. O. M. W. Sprague, the historian of crises under the National Banking System for the 1910 Aldrich Commission, believed that the banks should have taken responsibility to ensure that they had enough reserves to meet all needs.[38] But Sprague was vague on which banks should take this responsibility or why the duty fell on them in the absence of responsibility embodied in legislation. Noblesse oblige? Duty? Several statements by Sprague indicate that a limited number of New York banks had the obligation to stabilize the system and behave differently from other banks:

> During the period before the crisis of 1873 some 15 of the 50 New York banks held practically all the bankers' deposits in the city, and 7 of them held between 70 and 80 percent of these deposits. These 7 banks were directly responsible for the satisfactory working of the credit machinery of the country. (From the New York Clearing House report of 11 November 1873; p. 15)

> It must always be remembered that in the absence of any important central institution, such as exists in other commercial nations, the associated banks are the last resort in this country, in times of financial extremity, and upon their stability and sound conduct, the national prosperity greatly depends. (p. 95)

The fundamental characteristic of our banking system was illustrated [in 1890], that for any extraordinary cash requirements the reserves of the country banks are an unused asset. Evidence was again given which should have brought home to city institutions the heavy responsibility which they have incurred in attracting the reserves of other banks. (p. 147)

The New York banks did not normally maintain the large reserves which the responsibilities of their position demanded. (p. 153)

... there was the possibility that the contraction of loans by outside banks, trust companies, and foreign lenders might come together, creating a situation ... well nigh impossible if in normal times the important clearing house banks failed to exercise great caution and maintain large reserves. (p. 230)

The failure of the banks holding the ultimate reserve of the country to live up to the responsibilities of their positions is evident in still another direction. While the exact moment of the outbreak of the crisis of 1907 could not be foreseen, the imminence of a period of trade reaction had for many months been so probable that precautionary measures might reasonably have been expected from these banks if not from banks and the public in general. (pp. 236–7)

The outside banks feel no responsibility for the course of the market. They will naturally withdraw from it when affairs at home require more of their funds or when they come to distrust future developments in the market. It therefore becomes necessary for the local banks to be able at all times to shoulder at least a part of the loans that may be liquidated by outside banks, and also to supply the cash which they thus secure the power to draw away. (p. 239)

It is certainly an element of weakness in our central money market that influential credit institutions should have to be dragooned into doing what is after all in their own interest as well as to the general advantage. (p. 255)

... feeling common among New York bankers that they cannot reasonably be expected to remit funds which are the proceeds of loans made in the New York money market by outside banks and liquidated in an emergency ... It should be remembered, however, that responsibilities are incurred in return for the advantages which accrue to the New York banks from their peculiar position. London holds its commanding position because it is known that money lent there can be instantly recalled. Similarly, New York is not meeting the obligations of its position as our domestic money center, to say nothing of living up to future international responsibilities, so long as it is unable or

unwilling to respond to any demand, however unreasonable, that can lawfully be made upon it for cash. (pp. 273–4)

Sprague believed that the market needed a stabilizer and that the banks could not depend on the US Treasury to help supply the seasonal needs for cash, but he also did not believe that the biggest and most profitable US banks should take on that responsibility. These banks should be aware of seasonal currency requirements, the prospect that the out-of-town banks may withdraw deposits, and the state of the international balance of payments. Sprague believed that the New York banks that should take on this responsibility were only those that charged interest on out-of-town deposits, or the largest, or those with intimate connections with the stock exchange, or the leading members of the New York Clearing House.

The leading bankers in New York drew a different conclusion; they believed that the difficulties arose from the lack of elasticity of the money supply and thus they fell into the trap of the Banking School. This was the real bills doctrine, the idea that the money supply should expand and contract on the basis of changes in the supply of trade bills, which represented goods moving in domestic trade and in foreign trade. Thus increases in the money supply would not be inflationary as long as they corresponded to the increases in the supply of goods, and would have the necessary elasticity as long as they were discounted at banks and rediscounted at the central bank. There could be no doubt about it: 'The laws of finance are as well known, and as sure in their operation as the laws of physics.'[39] The lesson that Frank Vanderlip, Myron T. Herrick, William Barret Ridgely, George E. Roberts, Isaac N. Seligman, and Jacob H. Schiff drew from the panic of 1907 was that there should be a central bank that could respond to increases in demand for currency by producing more currency.[40]

Some ambiguity as to the location of ultimate responsibility for changes in the supply of currency may be helpful because it leaves some uncertainty so that the bankers are more self-reliant—provided there is not so much uncertainty that the market is disoriented. In London, it was vaguely understood that there should be no formal provision for a lender of last resort but that there should be one in time of crisis. The intuitive politicians in the British government and the merchant bankers who ran the Bank of England thought it best to give the power to grant relief neither wholly to the Bank nor wholly to the government but to leave it uncertain.[41] If giving relief were formally within the power of either the Bank or the government, it would be difficult to resist the pressure from the public.[42]

No one would bear the responsibility in too large a group. If only one entity were responsible, pressure for action might become irresistible. The

optimum may be a small number of actors, closely attuned to one another in an oligarchic relation, like-minded, who apply strong pressure to keep down the chiselers and free-riders and who are prepared ultimately to accept responsibility. To give a more up-to-date example, tension in 1975 and 1976 among New York City officials, the unions, bankers, the State of New York, and the Federal government as to who would be the lender of last resort for New York City may have ensured uncertainty at a high level, and to have encouraged Yonkers, Buffalo, Boston, Philadelphia, and other heavily indebted cities not to slacken in their efforts to reduce their deficits; yet action to save New York was eventually taken.

During the early stages of the 2008 crisis, the New York Fed provided credit to facilitate the acquisition of Bear Stearns by JPMorgan Chase, which took $1 billion in first loss on a $30 billion portfolio of toxic assets bought by the Fed. Ten years later, the facility was wound up, at a profit of $2.5 billion for the Fed. In between, Congress prohibited such Fed rescues for single firms.

Bonelli's statements about the 1907 crisis in Italy offer a moving account of a muddle. The Società Bancaria Italiana was failing, and dragging down a host of small financial, mercantile, and industrial firms. A consortium of the larger banks put together a support fund. The Bank of Italy was involved early and deeply, and almost became too heavily committed. The Italian Treasury finally came to the rescue, at the insistence of Bonaldo Stringher, governor of the Bank of Italy, and paid the interest on the national debt early and thus relieved the liquidity crisis. Bonelli saw that the episode inevitably involved both the Bank of Italy and the government and suggested that this indecision might develop when the economy worked for more than ten years with no one in charge.[43] Part of the difficulty may reflect the lack of sufficient cohesion among Turin, Genoa, Milan, and Rome and the resulting uncertainty, buck-passing, and indecision.

Some uncertainty was inevitable because, as a House of Commons committee noted in 1846, 'looking to the impossibility of foreseeing what the precise character of the circumstances might be'; it was thus 'more expedient to leave to those with whom the responsibility of government might rest at the time, to adopt such measures as might appear to them best suited to the emergency.'[44] Consider Sir Robert Peel's statement on the Bank Bill on 4 June 1844:

My Confidence is unshaken that we have taken all the Precautions which legislation can prudently take against the Recurrence of a pecuniary Crisis. It may occur in spite of our Precautions; and if it be necessary to assume a

grave Responsibility, I dare say Men will be found willing to assume such a Responsibility.[45]

George Harrison, the president of the Federal Reserve Bank of New York in the late 1920s, opened the discount window wide during the October 1929 stock market crash and then was criticized by the Board of Governors in Washington when the New York Fed bought $160 million in government bonds on the open market in October and another $210 million in November. The Board of Governors resented the New York bank because of the earlier high-handed dominance of the system by Benjamin Strong (who had died in 1928) and had little compunction in reining in Harrison when he tried to emulate Strong's penchant for filling a power vacuum by strong leadership. Ambiguity as to whether there will be a lender of last resort and who it will be may be optimal in a close-knit society. The division in experience and outlook between Washington and New York handicapped more effective action in coping with the collapse of stock prices in 1929.

There was no hint of criticism or second-guessing when the Federal Reserve Board, six months after Alan Greenspan became the chairman, set about expansive open-market operations immediately after the 19 October 1987 crash, and poured in high-powered money 'right and left,' to use Bagehot's expression. The Fed under Greenspan provided liquidity to cope with the Asian Financial Crisis in 1997, and then, in the summer of 1998, more liquidity in response to the debacle in the Russian ruble and the failure of the banks in Moscow, and the collapse of Long-Term Capital Management. Moreover, the Greenspan Fed also provided abundant liquidity both in anticipation of the Y2K crisis in the last few months of 1999 and in response to the sharp decline in stock prices in 2000 and 2001.

The Federal Reserve under the chairmanship of Ben Bernanke was slow to recognize the magnitude of the housing bubble and the impacts of the subsequent decline in real estate prices on the capital of the banks, the tone of the financial markets, and the economy. The Fed opened 'all of its windows' only after the panic triggered by the failure of Lehman Brothers in mid-September 2008. The Fed was willing to accept many different types of collateral for loans at the discount window, and the window was opened to nonbanks. The Fed became a direct lender to business and the Fed's assets nearly tripled in a year.

To Whom on What?

The rule laid down by Bagehot was that loans should be granted to all comers on the basis of sound collateral 'as largely as the public asks for them.'[46] But in his testimony before the 1875 inquiry, two years after the publication of *Lombard Street*, Bagehot resisted the suggestion that last resort lending be turned over to a body of commissioners appointed by the government on the grounds that they might make loans to 'improper persons.' They would be subject to political pressure while the Bank of England is 'a body withdrawn from the political world and not subject to political pressures.'[47]

Bagehot's suggestion that central banks are immune from political pressure seems naive. The dilemma about collateral is that its soundness depends on when and whether the panic is stopped; the longer the panic continues, the sharper the decline in the prices of securities and real estate and bills of exchange and commodities and, hence, the less sound the collateral. In this case, it becomes necessary to look at the character of the borrowers, something that J.P. Morgan was reported to consider exclusively. Here, the dilemma relates to the wry comment that bankers lend money only to those that do not need it.

Central banks typically have rules.[48] When the rules cannot be easily broken—as in the Federal Reserve Act of 1913, which permitted only gold and negotiable bills of exchange, but not government securities, to be held as a reserve against Federal Reserve notes and demand deposits—there is frequently trouble. There is also trouble when rules are too readily broken. The beauty of the Chancellor of the Exchequer's letter of indemnity was that it preserved the rule while violating it and did not create a precedent, at least not for a while. The Bank of France and the Reichsbank occasionally discounted only three-name paper. But discretion to reject paper because it was 'unsound,' or the borrower because of his character, gave the lender of last resort a life-or-death power that might not always be used with complete objectivity. The literature is full of accusations of venality on the part of the directors of central banks. Protestant and Jewish directors of the Bank of France were alleged to have punished the Catholic (and worse-off) supporters of the Union Générale in 1882 while saving the insider Comptoir d'Escompte in 1888.[49] In the crisis of 1772, the Bank of England's issuance of new regulations about discounting and refusal to discount doubtful paper were interpreted as an attempt to break the Jewish houses in Amsterdam that had been most involved in speculation. Then there was the Bank's decision to refuse the bills of Scottish banks, and finally to stop discounting altogether, which was probably 'a step taken quite deliberately to break up a group of

Dutch speculators.'[50] Outsiders particularly suffered. The Bank of the United States was allowed to fail in New York in December 1930 by a syndicate of banks amid accusations that the Bank was being punished for its pushy ways.[51]

The rule of discounting for everyone with good paper evolved slowly in Britain. For a time 'the invariable practice' to discount bills was respectable London names on paper with no more than two months until the maturity date; but this description of 1793 is accompanied by a statement that while a request from Manchester had been turned down (along with one from Chichester, which helped bring a bank down), £40,000 had been advanced to banks in Liverpool. Only in July 1816 did the Bank, breaking a rigid precedent, agree to accept 'country securities of undoubted respectability if the firm cannot get enough London names.'[52]

The Bank of England made advances on a wide range of different types of securities much beyond two-name paper. In 1816, the Bank broke its rule against lending on mortgages, undertaking a 'Transaction quite out of the ordinary course of Business' to relieve the distress of poor people in the Black Country. The Bank resolved to lend only in the old way 'on notes of respectable parties' but a few years later the Bank began a regular mortgage business on the ground that the volume of discounts and, especially, the income from discounts had collapsed—a private rather than a public purpose.[53] At one stage, the Bank made loans on the security of a mortgage on a plantation in the West Indies (ultimately the Bank foreclosed on this loan[54]) and on unimproved land in England. The land was unencumbered by a mortgage but belonged to a duke, an indication that collateral and the character (or status) of the borrower were not unrelated. Loans were not made on land in Scotland and Ireland.[55]

With the growth of railroads, the discounts of the Bank of England were made on the collateral of railroad debentures. In 1842, as the second railway mania got underway, the Bank voted to make occasional loans to firms in difficulty and to well-tried firms for development.[56] The Bank of France began lending to a railroad syndicate in 1852; in fact, it was accused of supporting, if not starting the feverish speculation in railroads.[57] Bagehot thought the Bank of England was mistaken for not lending on railroad debentures when it did so on Consols and Indian securities; Bagehot stated that a railway was less liable to unforeseen accidents than the Empire of India.[58] But Indian securities were guaranteed by the Colonial Office and in effect were British government obligations.

Exchequer bills were issued on the collateral of goods, as were Admiralty bills in Hamburg. Clapham observed that many of the Bank's advances in

1825 were not actually on goods but rather on personal security[59]; the Bank loaned freely and was not 'over-nice.'[60] In a few weeks in 1847, the Bank advanced £2.25 million in both usual and unusual ways, including the securities of the Company of Copper Miners, through which it involuntarily acquired a copper works.[61]

The rule is that there is no rule. One does not lend to insolvent banks, except to avoid the mischief that would occur if the Lord Mayor of London were to go bankrupt (1793),[62] or to maintain for a time a payroll in Newcastle, a town used to banking disasters.[63] The Bank of France had never discounted as much as 4 million francs for anyone but Jacques Laffitte when Samuel Welles, an American banker, applied in 1837; he proved to be an exception.[64] (The Laffitte transaction had also been exceptional, with a political motivation.) The Conseil General could not abandon such an important bank, so the bank received a line of credit of 15 million francs.[65] In the crisis of 1830 the Bank of France discounted royal and municipal bonds, customs receipts, woodcutting receipts, obligations of the city of Paris, and canal bonds repayable by lottery.[66]

Some of the decisions that the lender of last resort must make are easy, such as whether to discount Treasury bills. Some are difficult, such as whether to discount shaky collateral from shaky banks. The record is full of firms that were refused help, failed, and paid off 20 shillings to the pound, and of banks that were helped in one crisis and failed in the next. The 241-page appendix to Evans's book on the commercial crisis of 1857 was devoted to court records of bankruptcies in Britain between 1849 and 1858. The reading is doleful. G. T. Braine, who was refused accommodation by the Bank of England in 1848, paid 20 shillings to the pound and finished with a surplus that was twice that originally estimated. One also finds petitions in bankruptcy brought by the Bank, such as that against Cruickshank, Melville and Co., for the unpaid residue of a bill it drew on another bankrupt firm that had paid only 12s. 6d. on the pound.[67]

Even the judgment of history is not always helpful. The Bank of England first refused to help the three American 'W banks' (Wiggins, Wilsons, and Wildes) in the autumn of 1836, and then relented and advanced them credit in March 1837. Andréadès noted that the Bank took a bold step and had no occasion to regret its courage.[68] Clapham held, on the contrary, that the Bank lent most reluctantly and was not surprised when Wilsons and Wiggins failed at the end of May and Wildes thereafter and the consequence was 'a long, dreary tale of debt lasting 14 years.'[69] To Matthews, the Bank of England's aid to the three banks 'in the vain hope of avoiding their suspending was a

matter of faulty judgment but the principle on which they operated was a sound one.'[70]

When and How Much?

'Too little, and too late' is one of the saddest phrases in the lexicon of central banking. But how much is enough? When is the right time?

Bagehot's rule is to lend freely at a penalty rate. 'Freely' means only to solvent borrowers and with good collateral, subject to the inevitable exceptions. It means rejecting the expedients that various central banks are tempted to indulge in crises. Early in 1772, the Bank of England tried to apply the brakes to overtrading by selective limitation of discounts and was criticized.[71] In 1797, the Bank began to pro-rate discounts, and Foxwell thought that might have been undertaken again in 1809.[72] Another technique when a central bank feels it is getting overcommitted is to tighten eligibility requirements for collateral, shortening the maturity of eligible bills from 95 or 90 days to 65 or 60 days, or adding to the number of names required. In May 1783, the Bank of England had discounted so heavily for its own clients that it departed from its regular practice and refused to make advances on subscriptions to government bonds issued that year. Clapham commented that, fortunately, no public or private catastrophe of the sort that starts a panic occurred that summer since the Bank had limited its capacity to meet one.[73] In this case, the Bank was behaving like a private bank worried about its own safety rather than a public institution with the responsibility to provide for the stability of the system.

The lender of last resort might supply funds to the system through open-market purchases rather than through the discount mechanism. How much should the central bank expand the money supply? Were the $160 million of advances by the New York Fed in October 1929 and the additional $210 million through November 1929 adequate? The Federal Reserve Bank of New York believed that these advances were not large enough. The New York Fed was operating under a directive from the Board of Governors that permitted it to buy $25 million of government bonds each week. It violated this rule in October by buying $160 million worth, and on 12 November recommended to the Board that the limit of $25 million a week be removed and that the Open Market Investment Committee be authorized to buy $200 million of bonds for the system. After considerable negotiation, the Board reluctantly approved this request on 27 November, and $155 million of bonds was purchased between 27 November and 1 January 1930. By this time, discounts

were running off rapidly, interest rates had fallen sharply, and the need for a lender of last resort—to accommodate the liquidation of call loans in the market—was over.[74]

Some monetarists seem ambivalent on the role of the lender of last resort. Friedman and Schwartz quoted Bagehot approvingly on not starving a panic.[75] They asserted that the action taken by the Federal Reserve Bank of New York in buying $160 million in October 1929 was 'timely and effective' although they were gently skeptical about Harrison's claim that the open-market purchases kept the New York stock exchange open.[76] Friedman was opposed to all discounting.[77] An ultra-monetarist view maintains that the open-market operations of the period constituted a renewal of the credit inflation of the 1920s.[78] But most monetarists believe that there is no need to have a lender of last resort as long as the money supply increases at a constant rate. In retrospect, the open-market operations were woefully inadequate in the weeks from mid-October to the end of November 1929. They enabled the New York banks to take over the call loans of out-of-town banks but at the cost of reducing the amount of credit available for purchases of stocks, commodities, and real estate, which led to declines in their prices and contributed to the subsequent depression.[79]

The timing of the Federal Reserve Board in providing abundant liquidity in response to the Black Monday crash of October 1987 was impeccable, as was the help for the US capital market when Long-Term Capital Management collapsed in September 1998.

Timing presents a special problem. As the boom mounts to a crescendo, it must be slowed without precipitating a panic. After a crash has occurred, it is important to wait long enough for the insolvent firms to fail, but not so long as to let the crisis spread to the solvent firms that need liquidity—'delaying the death of the strong swimmers,' as Clapham put it.[80] In a speech during the debate on the indemnity bill on 4 December 1857, Disraeli quoted the leader of an unnamed 'greatest discount house in Lombard Street' who said that 'had it not been for some private information which reached him, to the effect that in case of extreme pressure there would be an interference on the part of the Government, he should at that moment have given up the idea of struggling any further, and [that] it was only on that tacit understanding that he went on with his business.'[81] Questions could be raised about the equity of private information and of tacit understandings for insiders but not outsiders. Still, the remark underlines the importance of timing. Whether too soon too much is worse than too little and too late is difficult to answer.

In 1857, the US Treasury came to the rescue of the market too early and helped it inflate still further. In 1873, the response was too slow; no steps were

taken during the first part of the year.[82] Sprague refers to 'the unfortunate delay of the Clearing House,' that is, the slowness of any authority to respond to the 1907 crisis, in which as in no other crisis since the Civil War, things were allowed to drag on too long.[83]

If the need for a lender of last resort is accepted after a speculative boom and it is believed that restrictive measures are not likely to slow the boom without precipitating a collapse, the lender of last resort faces dilemmas both of amount and timing. The dilemmas are more serious with open-market operations than with a system of discounts. In the latter case, Bagehot specified the right amount: all the market will take—through solvent houses offering sound collateral—at a penalty interest rate. With open-market operations, the decision for the authorities is more difficult, but Bagehot was right not to starve the market. Given a seizure of credit in the system, more is safer than less since the excess can be mopped up later.

Timing is an art. That says nothing—and everything.

Bagehot and assistance to insolvent banks

The Bagehot doctrine is that the central bank should lend freely to solvent banks but at a penalty interest rate—an interest rate higher than the one the banks earn on their loans. The rationale is that if a central bank does not lend freely, then one or several lenders will sell securities and the inevitable decline in their prices will mean that some of the banks that previously had been solvent will be likely to fail because of the decline in the market value of their assets.

Bagehot did not want the central bank to extend credit to an insolvent institution. If a bank is insolvent, the courts will require that the administrator of its estate sell its securities and assets to obtain the cash for payment to its creditors and depositors. This sale will depress the prices of securities and assets in the same way that the sale of securities and assets by a solvent and illiquid bank would have led to a decline in the prices of these securities. The buyers of these securities and assets will not know whether they were sold by a solvent or by an insolvent bank.

The Bagehot doctrine distinguishes between providing support for solvent banks but not for insolvent ones. Part of the problem is operational, since whether a bank is insolvent depends on the prices of securities that it owns and the prices of securities owned by its competitors. During a crisis, there is a massive shift toward the securities of public sector borrowers from private sector borrowers because the former can never fail, since the central bank will be obliged to buy government securities. The shift away from the bonds and IOUs of private borrowers means their prices will decline and perhaps

sharply; the prices of these securities will be extraordinarily low relative to their prospective interest income. The role of the lender of last resort can dampen the decline in the prices of these securities, but some cautious intermediaries will sell some of these securities because they are less than 100 percent confident that these IOUs of various private borrowers are no more risky than the IOUs of public borrowers. Hence, when economic activity slows, it is normal for the prices of riskier securities to decline relative to the price of government bonds. The lender of last resort will not be able to determine in advance which banks are likely to survive; thus a bank that was solvent on 1 January may be insolvent a month later even in the absence of a shortage of liquidity. Hence, the lender of last resort must choose between being too cautious in providing more liquidity because it is not fully confident that various banks are not insolvent, and too eager to provide credit because the concept and the measure of solvency are fuzzy when the prices of securities and assets are declining rapidly.

Notes

1. François Nicholas Mollien, *Mémoires d'un Ministre du Trésor Public, 1780–1815* (Paris: Fournier, 1845), vol. 2, pp. 298ff.
2. Ministère des Finances et al., *Enquête sur les principes et les faits généraux qui régissent la circulation monétaire et fiduciaire* (Paris: Imprimerie impériale, 1867), vol. 2, pp. 31–2.
3. Murray N. Rothbard, *America's Great Depression*, 3rd edn (Kansas City: Sheed & Ward, 1975), p. 167.
4. Herbert Spencer, from 'State Tampering with Money and Banks', in *Essays: Scientific, Political and Speculative* (London: Williams & Norgate, 1891), vol. 3, p. 354, quoted by Charles Lipson, *Standing Guard: Protecting Foreign Capital in the Nineteenth and Twentieth Centuries* (Berkeley: University of California Press, 1985), p. 45.
5. T. S. Ashton, *Economic Fluctuations in England, 1700–1800* (Oxford: Oxford University Press, Clarendon Press, 1959), p. 112.
6. Ibid., p. 111.
7. E. Victor Morgan, *The Theory and Practice of Central Banking, 1797–1913* (Cambridge: Cambridge University Press, 1943), p. 240.
8. Maurice Lévy-Leboyer, *Les banques européennes et l'industrialisation internationale dans la première moitié du XIXe siècle* (Paris: Presses universitaires de France, 1964), p. 490.

9. See F. A. Hayek's introduction to Henry Thornton, *An Enquiry into the Nature and Effect of the Paper Credit of Great Britain* (1802; London: Allen & Unwin, 1939; reprint, London: Frank Cass, 1962), p. 38.

10. Thornton, *Paper Credit*, pp. 187–8.

11. *The Collected Works of Walter Bagehot*, ed. Norman St John Stevas (London: The Economist, 1978), vol. 11, p. 149.

12. Ibid., vol. 9, p. 267.

13. Thomas Joplin, *Case for Parliamentary Inquiry into the Circumstances of the Panic, in a Letter to Thomas Gisborne, Esq., M. P.* (London: James Ridgeway & Sons, n.d. [after 1832]), p. 29.

14. Jacob Viner, *Studies in the Theory of International Trade* (New York: Harper & Bros., 1937), p. 233.

15. D. P. O'Brien, 'Overstone's Thought', in D. P. O'Brien, ed., *The Correspondence of Lord Overstone* (Cambridge: Cambridge University Press, 1971), vol. 1, p. 95. (A bodkin is a dagger, stiletto, ornamental hairpin, or a blunt needle with a large eye.)

16. Milton Friedman and Anna J. Schwartz, *A Monetary History of the United States, 1867–1960* (Princeton: Princeton University Press, 1963), pp. 418–9. The metaphor of an avalanche is also used by Alfred Marshall in stating that prompt action by the Bank of England in regard to the rate of discount often checks unreasonable expansions of credit, 'which might otherwise grow, *after the manner of a fall of snow on a steep mountain side*' and become an avalanche (Marshall's emphasis). See Marshall, *Money, Credit, and Commerce* (1923; reprint edn, New York: Augustus M. Kelley, 1965), pp. 258–9.

17. Walter Bagehot, *Lombard Street: a Description of the Money Market* (1873; reprint edn, London: John Murray, 1917), p. 160.

18. Elmer Wood, *English Theories of Central Banking Control, 1819–1858* (Cambridge, MA: Harvard University Press, 1939), p. 147.

19. J. H. Clapham, *The Bank of England: a History* (Cambridge: Cambridge University Press, 1945), vol. 2, p. 289.

20. Bagehot, *Lombard Street*, pp. 161–2.

21. Clapham, *Bank of England*, vol. 2, p. 108.

22. Marshall, *Money, Credit, and Commerce*, p. 307. In their concluding chapter on the Dutch Republic, Jan de Vries and Ad van der Woude note that in 1780 the Dutch international banking sector lacked but one critical feature: effective credit-creating institutions to maintain liquidity in time of crisis (*The First Modern Economy* [Cambridge: Cambridge University Press, 1997], p. 683).

23. Bertrand Gille, *La banque en France au XIXᵉ siècle: Recherches historiques* (Geneva: Librairie Droz, 1970), p. 32.

24. Bertrand Gille, *La Banque et le crédit en France de 1815 à 1848* (Paris: Presses universitaires de France, 1959), p. 367.

25. Michel Chevalier, *Lettres sur l'Amérique du Nord*, 3rd edn (Paris: Charles Gosselin, 1838), p. 37, note 1.

26. Ministère des Finances et al., *Enquête*, vol. 3, pp. 411–2.

27. Ibid., vol. 2, pp. 129–30.

28. Jean Bouvier, *Un siècle de banque française* (Paris: Hachette Littérature, 1973), pp. 83–4.

29. See Rondo Cameron, *France and the Economic Development of Europe, 1800–1914* (Princeton: Princeton University Press, 1961), pp. 191ff.

30. Maurice Lévy-Leboyer, *Histoire économique et sociale de la France depuis 1848* (Paris: Les Cours de Droit, Institut d'Etudes Politiques, 1951–52), p. 121.

31. Cameron, *France and Europe*, p. 117.

32. Alfred Pose, *La monnaie et ses insitutions* (Paris: Presses universitaires de France, 1942), p. 215.

33. Jean Bouvier, *Le krach de l'Union Générale, 1878–1885* (Paris: Presses universitaires de France, 1960), pp. 150, 152–3.

34. Esther Rogoff Taus, *Central Banking Functions of the United States Treasury, 1789–1941* (New York: Columbia University Press, 1943), pp. 22, 23, 29.

35. Ibid., pp. 39–131.

36. C. A. E. Goodhart, *The New York Money Market and the Finance of Trade, 1900–1913* (Cambridge, MA: Harvard University Press, 1969), p. 120.

37. George W. Van Vleck, *The Panic of 1857: an Analytical Study* (New York: Columbia University Press, 1943), p. 106.

38. O. M. W. Sprague, *History of Crises Under the National Banking System* (1910; reprint edn, New York: Augustus M. Kelley, 1968).

39. Myron T. Herrick, 'The Panic of 1907 and Some of Its Lessons', *Annals of the American Academy of Political and Social Science*, vol. 31 (January–June 1908), p. 324.

40. Ridgely's essay in *Annals* was more narrowly entitled 'An Elastic Credit Currency as a Preventive for Panics', but the papers of the others, except for Seligman, were unqualified in their advocacy of central bank currency elasticity.

41. Note Bagehot's characterization of the character of the then members of the court of the Bank of England: 'A board of plain, sensible prosperous English merchants; and they have both done and left undone what such a board might be expected to do and not to do. Nobody could expect great attainments in economical science from such a board; laborious study is for the most part foreign to the habits of English merchants' (Walter Bagehot, *Lombard Street: a Description of the Money Market* [1873; reprint edn, London: John Murray, 1917], p. 166). Later he is more critical: 'Unluckily … directors of the Bank of England were neither acquainted with the right principles, nor were they protected by a judicious routine. They could not be expected themselves to discover such principles. The abstract thinking of the world is never to be expected from people in high places … No doubt when men's own fortunes are at stake, the insight of the trader does somehow anticipate the conclusions of the closet' (p. 169).

42. Wood, *English Central Banking Control*, pp. 169–70.

43. Franco Bonelli, *La crisi del 1907: una tappa dello sviluppo industriale in Italia* (Turin: Fondazione Luigi Einaudi, 1971), passim and esp. p. 165.

44. Leone Levi, *History of British Commerce, 1763–1870*, 2nd edn (London: John Murray, 1872), pp. 311–2.

45. Great Britain, *Parliamentary Papers, Monetary Policy, Commercial Distress* (1857; Shannon: Irish University Press, 1969), vol. 3, p. xxix.

46. *Collected Works of Walter Bagehot*, vol. 9, p. 147.

47. Ibid., vol. 11, pp. 149–50.

48. See C. P. Kindleberger, 'Rules vs. Men: Lessons from a Century of Monetary Policy', in Christoph Buchheim, Michael Hutter, and Harold James, eds, *Zerrissene Zwischenkriegsheit: Wirtschaftshistorische Beiträge: Knut Borchardt zum 65. Geburstag*, reprinted in C. P. Kindleberger, *The World Economy and National Finance in Historical Perspective* (Ann Arbor: University of Michigan Press, 1995), pp. 181–200.

49. Bouvier, *Le krach*, chap. 5.

50. Charles Wilson, *Anglo-Dutch Commerce and Finance in the Eighteenth Century* (Cambridge: Cambridge University Press, 1941), pp. 176–7.

51. Friedman and Schwartz, Monetary *History*, p. 309 and esp. pp. 309–10n; Peter Temin, *Did Monetary Forces Cause the Great Depression?* (New York: W. W. Norton, 1976).

52. Clapham, *Bank of England*, vol. 1, p. 261; vol. 2, p. 58.

53. Ibid., vol. 2, pp. 59–60.

54. Ibid., vol. 1, p. 249.

55. Ibid., vol. 2, pp. 82–4.

56. Ibid., p. 145.

57. Alain Plessis, *La Politique de la Banque de France de 1851 à 1870* (Geneva: Droz, 1985), pp. 89, 99, 107. The Banque also loaned on Paris bonds, but not on those of Marseilles or Bordeaux; ibid., pp. 105–6.

58. Bagehot, *Lombard Street*, p. 195.

59. Clapham, *Bank of England*, vol. 2, p. 59.

60. W. C. T. King, *History of the London Discount Market* (London: George Routledge & Sons, 1936), p. 36.

61. Clapham, *Bank of England*, vol. 2, pp. 206–7.

62. Ibid., vol. 1, p. 261.

63. D. Morier Evans, *The History of the Commercial Crisis, 1857–1858, and the Stock Exchange Panic of 1859* (1859; reprint edn, New York: Augustus M. Kelley, 1969), p. 80.

64. Lévy-Leboyer, *Banques européennes*, p. 559.

65. Ibid., p. 647.

66. Ibid., p. 492.

67. Evans, *Commercial Crisis*, pp. i–ii, vi–xviii.

68. A. Andréadès, *History of the Bank of England* (London: P. S. King, 1909), p. 266.

69. Clapham, *Bank of England*, vol. 2, p. 157. He refers to it later as 'the long drawn out W bank affair' (ibid., p. 337).
70. R. C. O. Matthews, *A Study in Trade-Cycle History: Economic Fluctuations in Great Britain, 1832–1842* (Cambridge: Cambridge University Press, 1954), p. 173.
71. Clapham, *Bank of England*, vol. 1, p. 245.
72. H. S. Foxwell, preface to Andréadès, *Bank of England*, p. xvii.
73. Clapham, *Bank of England*, vol. 1, p. 256.
74. See Friedman and Schwartz, *Monetary History*, pp. 339, 363–7.
75. Ibid., p. 395.
76. Ibid., p. 339.
77. See Milton Friedman, 'Rediscounting', in *A Program for Monetary Stability* (New York: Fordham University Press, 1960), pp. 35–6.
78. Paul Johnson, *Modern Times: the World from the Twenties to the Eighties* (New York: Harper & Row, 1983), p. 244.
79. Friedman and Schwartz, *Monetary History*, pp. 334–5.
80. Clapham, *Bank of England*, vol. 2, p. 102.
81. Evans, *Commercial Crisis*, p. 207.
82. Taus, *Central Banking*, pp. 55, 70.
83. Sprague, *History of Crises*, p. 256.

12

The International Lender of Last Resort Before 2000

It follows from the international propagation of financial crises, from the efficacy under certain circumstances of lending in the last resort, and from the historical record about to be unfolded that a case can be made for an international lender of last resort. With no world government, no world central bank, and only weak international law, the question of where last resort lending comes from is a crucial one. The historical record points to the country that serves as the world's leading financial center, often assisted by other countries. It suggests further that when there is no such lender, as in 1873, 1890, and 1931, the depression following the financial crisis is long and drawn out—this, in contrast to episodes when there is one and crisis passes like a summer storm.

A Historical View of International Financial Crises

Often analysts have distinguished an internal drain that involved an increase in the domestic demand for currency or gold from an external drain that in the form of a flow of gold to a foreign country. An external drain could generally be reversed by an increase in interest rates; hence the quip that an increase in the Bank of England's discount rate of 1 percent would 'draw gold from the moon,' although often there was a lag before the higher interest rates would lead to the gold inflow. If investors viewed the increase in the discount rate as a sign of weakness and sold more of the country's currency, the external

© The Author(s), under exclusive license to Springer Nature
Switzerland AG 2023
R. Z. Aliber et al., *Manias, Panics, and Crashes*,
https://doi.org/10.1007/978-3-031-16008-0_12

drain would increase, and the central bank would need to increase interest rates further. At times, the increase in interest rates would not be adequate to correct the imbalances—perhaps because the lags were long and the time limited—and the central bank would need to intervene to avoid a sharp decline in the price of its currency. If the central bank's holdings of international reserve assets are too small to support its currency, it might borrow from other central banks, perhaps by activating a swap line.

What is the appropriate public policy to reduce the likelihood of international financial crises and to ameliorate their impacts? During the financial crisis of 1846–1848, when bond prices all over Europe were plummeting, some by as much as 75 percent, and the Rothschild banks in Paris, Vienna, and Frankfurt were threatened with bankruptcy, Nathan Rothschild in London, with the help of Auguste Belmont, his bank's representative in New York, helped privately. Belmont shipped silver from New York to London that was then shared among the Rothschild brothers. Central banks helped by keeping interest rates low, but Nathan, as the effective lender of last resort, saved the day with this assistance from New York.[1] In the 1930s, Paul and Felix Warburg of Kuhn, Loeb in New York served in the same capacity for their brother, Max Warburg, then in Hamburg, with a credit of more than $9 million.[2]

Last resort lending focuses on central banks as the providers of their own currency or cash. In 1694, the Bank of England borrowed 2 million guilders from the States General in Holland to assist the British Exchequer in remitting funds to the Continent to support British troops and allies during the Nine Years' War.[3]

In the years that followed (1695–1697), Amsterdam assisted the Bank of England by taking over its protested bills of exchange on the Continent; the Dutch charged an interest rate of 10 percent for the service—a penalty rate in Bagehot terms, but it was, after all, business rather than the provision of a public good.[4]

In the crisis of 1763, the Bank of England and London private bankers rescued their Dutch correspondents by granting, in distress, credits larger than those previously given in periods of prosperity. Five consignments of gold were shipped in August and two in September. In addition, the Bank of England and other banks delayed presenting bills for payment. Wilson comments that none of this was pure altruism. Instead, it represented a practical policy based on the knowledge that British prosperity was intimately associated with Dutch prosperity and that the intensification of the Dutch crisis would cut off a source of money for Britain.[5]

As the 1772 crisis reached a peak in January 1773, Anglo-Dutch trade was paralyzed. Amsterdam was helpless because of a shortage of credit, and only the Bank of England, Wilson says, could rescue the city. On 10 January, a Sunday, the Bank opened its windows and allowed specie to be drawn against the presentation of notes and government bonds. Loads of bullion were sent on the first packet boat, and one Dutch banker was said to have drawn £500,000. At the same time, the Bank refused to discount doubtful paper, which had the effect of breaking many Jewish-owned banks in Amsterdam.[6] Catherine the Great of Russia helped her best customers, the British merchants, in this same crisis, the first of a number of crises when czarist Russia assisted Western Europe.[7]

In the crisis of 1825, there was a rumor that the Bank of France was trying to add to the Bank of England's difficulties. Clapham insisted that instead France participated in an early example of international financial cooperation by shipping gold to London in exchange for silver.[8] That the price of gold in terms of silver was higher in London than in Paris (15.2 to 1 compared with 14.625 to 1) favored the exchange,[9] but the arrival via the Rothschild banks of £400,000 (mostly in sovereigns) from Paris on Monday 19 December 1825 helped because the Bank of England coffers were virtually empty after the run on the previous Saturday.

Twice during the extended crisis of 1836–1839, the Bank of England sought help from the Bank of France and the city of Hamburg to maintain its liquidity. The first time, the Bank of England drew bills on Paris for £400,000. In 1838, the Bank of England arranged for a line of credit and in 1839 drew on this line for £2 million, using Baring Brothers and ten Paris banks as intermediaries. A similar line of credit with Hamburg brought in £900,000 of gold, an arrangement possibly designed also to help Hamburg, which needed silver.[10] In 1838, the Bank of England, not the most usual of gold dealers, sent nearly 700,000 sovereigns to the United States. Clapham said the operation was without precedent, and damaging insofar as it encouraged American bankers to issue more securities in the British markets in 1838 and 1839, but he acknowledged that the Bank was wise to recognize the interlocking interests of Britain and the United States.[11]

The Bank of France borrowed 25 million francs from British capitalists in the second half of 1846, according to French sources[12]; a British source states that the sum was borrowed from the Bank of England in January 1847.[13] At that point, the emperor of Russia offered to buy 50 million francs of the French 3 percent *rente* to assist in financing the imports of wheat that France and Britain needed. Britain benefited since the French used half the money to repay the British advance.[14] Palmer, then governor of the Bank

of England, testified before the Select Committee of Parliament that it was preferable to have an understanding with the principal banks in the United States, Hamburg, Amsterdam, and Paris than to ship gold.[15]

Central bank cooperation was not universally applauded. Viner wrote that the Bank of England in 1836 found itself obliged to appeal to France for help 'no doubt reluctantly' and added that the necessity was regarded in Britain as humiliating because it came at a time when relations between the two countries were not particularly cordial, 'especially as it was reported that the followers of M. Thiers were boasting of the generosity of Frenchmen … while recommending that under no circumstances should such liberality be repeated in future.'[16] Thomas Tooke thought the loan a 'discreditable expedient,' a 'circumstance of almost national humiliation.'[17] The Bank of France was criticized in Paris by some who thought it irresponsible to profit from the British arrangement rather than aid those at home who sought its help.[18]

In the 1850s, there was less international cooperation in crisis periods. Clapham wrote that the Bank of England contemplated joint action with the Bank of France in November 1857, but he did not indicate what the action was and said little beyond that 'nothing came of it.'[19] Perhaps the most interesting operation was the December *Silberzug* in Hamburg, which was at the end of the line of the rolling crisis that swept from Ohio to New York to Liverpool and then to the Continent, particularly to Scandinavia. On 4 December, the Hamburg Senate voted a 15 million mark banco fund composed of 5 million in Hamburg bonds and 10 million in silver that would be obtained by borrowing in one or several foreign centers. The next task was to borrow the money. Appeals for a loan were made to Rothschild, Baring, and Hambros in London, to Fould in Paris, and to various political and financial bodies in Amsterdam, Copenhagen, Brussels, Berlin, Dresden, and Hanover. Each request was turned down. From Fould came this answer: 'Your message is not sufficiently clear.' From Berlin: 'Bruck and the Kaiser are not financially ambitious.' On 8 December, when every bank in Hamburg except Heine's was threatened with bankruptcy, and when captains of ships were unwilling to unload their cargoes because they were concerned that they would not be paid, word came from Vienna that it would provide all the money that was needed. The train the carried the silver, the *Silberzug*, arrived shortly.[20]

The silver was removed from the train, and loans in silver were made to Merck, Godeffroy, and Berenburg, Gossler and Co., among the leading bankers, plus five smaller ones. The panic ended on 12 December when it became known that there was enough silver. Some firms, like Donner & Co., which had initially been allotted 700,000 marks banco, turned out

not to need any when confidence was restored. Böhme, who gave the most detailed account of the crisis, said that for years the episode kept coming up whenever Hamburgers and non-Hamburgers talked about currencies.[21] The political aspects of the rescue operation were revealed in British diplomatic dispatches. The British consul in Hamburg noted that it was fortunate for Britain that Austria and not Prussia had brought the aid since there would then be no pressure on Hamburg to join the Zollverein.[22] From Berlin, on 29 December, came a dispatch with a translation of Baron Manteuffel's statement to Hamburg that explained why Berlin had been unable to help. Lack of ambition gave way to a series of lame explanations that underlined that Berlin had 'missed an opportunity.'[23]

The distress in Scandinavia was relieved as the panic in Hamburg subsided. A positive item of international official aid, however, was a loan on 18 December by the Bank of England on promissory notes of the Norwegian government in support of overdue bills the bank held from Norwegian houses.[24]

At the outbreak of the Civil War in November 1861, a panic in New York drew specie from Paris and London. French reluctance to raise the discount rate and the increasing departure of the French gold-silver ratio from the ratio in the market led France to exchange £2 million in silver for £2 million in gold with the Bank of England. The funds made available by this transaction failed to remedy the situation, so in 1861 the French bought gold in London at a price above the export point. The Bank of France then arranged through Rothschild and Baring to draw £2 million of bills on London.[25]

There was no international cooperation during the crisis of 1873 but there were two aspects that underline the sensitive political nature of central bank transactions. In the letter books for 1872–1873, the Bank of England refers to and denies a 'ridiculous rumor' that it had thought of applying for a loan from the Bank of France. And in the second week of November, the governor of the Bank of Prussia—a predecessor of the Reichsbank, which was not established until 1875—wrote a letter to the Bank of England offering a loan in gold at that time or at any future time. (Clapham commented earlier that Germany was half drunk with victory and that Berlin had swelled up like Aesop's frog.) The Bank of England politely but curtly declined the offer: 'The Bank is not, nor has it been in want of such aid and need not avail itself of the arrangement you so kindly suggest.' Clapham adds that this suggestion from the nouveau riche would have seemed impertinent to the Governor.[26]

In 1890, William Lidderdale, then the Governor of the Bank of England, prepared on two fronts for the crisis that would follow the revelation of Barings' weakened position. In addition to the domestic guarantee, he

arranged for the Russian government not to draw its £2.4 million deposit from Barings, and for loans of £3 million from the Bank of France and £1.5 million from the State Bank of Russia, both in gold. Lidderdale told the Governor of the Bank of France that the ordinary operations of bank rate would have brought the gold in time and that there was nothing discreditable in using exceptional measures to meet an unusually sudden storm. Nonetheless, Lidderdale and the City were uneasy about asking the French and the Russians for help. Clapham put it this way: 'Suppose for some political-financial reason they had been unwilling to oblige?'[27]

The sensitive character of such international assistance prior to World War I is revealed in the 1906–1907 incidents, when much discussion was devoted not to whether the Bank of France helped the Bank of England—which it clearly did—but to whether the Bank of England had asked for such help or, if it did not, whether the steps taken by the Bank of France were largely in its own interest. In Sayers' account of the Bank from 1890 to 1914, in a chapter titled 'Supposed Continental Support of the Bank,' he concluded that the Bank of England did not ask for help. Sayers quotes *The Economist* in September 1906:

> Some talk of the Bank of France helping the Bank of England cope with the American demand for gold … but it would not for a minute be supposed that the Bank would really put itself in so humiliating a position merely in order to permit American speculators getting gold here on easy terms.

Again in the autumn of 1907, the Bank of France forwarded 80 million francs in US gold eagles to London. The Bank of France report for 1907 refers to both incidents in its decisions. French journals cite the alleged reason: to relieve the Bank of England of the need to raise its discount rate, which implies that the Bank of England requested help. British sources emphasize that there was no announcement on the British side, as there was in 1890, and that the French did not want the Bank to increase its discount rate. Hartley Withers, financial editor of *The Times*, wrote later:

> The determination it [the Bank of England] showed finally compelled the Bank of France to take some share in the international burden, and to send three millions of its gold, not to America but to London, whence it knew it could rely on getting it back. It is commonly supposed the Bank of England asked it to carry out this operation, but this is quite untrue.[28]

Another view is that when the Bank of France entered into transactions in sterling bills in London in 1906, 1907, 1909, and 1910, it was involved in open-market operations, which it did not undertake in Paris until 1938.[29]

London vs. Paris as the World Financial Center

The general view among Anglo-Saxon students of economic history is that London was the world's financial center from the beginning of the nineteenth century until 1914 and that Paris, Berlin, Frankfurt, New York, and Milan were satellites.

According to a German observer, 'England had a monopoly of capital exports to 1850. Then France moved in, largely for *gloire*, undertaking capital exports in the service of national policies, expansionary commercial interests, and the opening of new markets.'[30] In the 1850s, Paris had a central role in international monetary relationships. Van Vleck wrote about the panic of 1857: 'Just as France was the political nerve center of Europe during the first half of the nineteenth century, so during the years from 1850 to 1857, it was the center from which fluctuations in the economic cycle radiated.'[31]

The center for the economic cycle is not necessarily the pivot of the international financial system. Between 1820 and 1840 Paris assisted in clearing London's foreign payments in the Baltic, Russia, China, Latin America, and the United States and then between 1850 and 1870 became the 'first place in Europe for foreign exchange.'[32] If this view were correct, the situation was changed by the Franco-Prussian War. According to Bagehot:

> Since the Franco-German war, we may be said to keep the European reserves
> … All great communities have at times to pay large sums in cash, and of that
> cash a great store must be kept somewhere. Formerly there were two such stores
> in Europe; one was the Bank of France, and the other the Bank of England.
> But since the suspension of specie payments by the Bank of France, its use
> as a reservoir of specie is at an end. No one can draw a cheque on it and be
> sure of getting gold or silver for that cheque. Accordingly the whole liability
> for such international payments in cash is thrown on the Bank of England
> … all exchange operations are centering more and more in London. Formerly
> for many purposes, Paris was a European settling-house, but now it has ceased
> to be so … Accordingly London has become the sole great settling-house in
> Europe, instead of being formerly one of two. And this pre-eminence London
> will probably maintain, for it is a natural pre-eminence … The pre-eminence
> of Paris partly arose from a distribution of political power, which is already
> disturbed; but that of London depends on the regular course of commerce,
> which is singularly stable and hard to change.[33]

Sprague echoed this view from the United States in 1910 when he explained that the Bank of England raised its discount rate in 1907 to secure payment from other countries of money they owed the United States rather than to check the flow of gold to New York. London was the central money market in the world and its interest rates were increased to avoid having to finance all the payments flowing to the United States.[34]

In contrast, Bonelli asserted that Paris was the center that regulated world liquidity when he discussed Italy's links to the 1907 crisis.[35] One of the most penetrating students of pre-World War I finance stated that 'Paris emerges in this study as the *strongest* [italics in original] financial center in the world before 1914, if the fact that its short-term rate was relatively the lowest is an indication of strength. This conclusion seems to contradict the generally held opinion that London was the world's money center.' Morgenstern attempted to reconcile these statements by distinguishing the abundance of funds in Paris and the 'machinery' in London for setting funds into motion.[36] This distinction seems forced. Each center had its own particular clients: thus Paris had Italy and Russia and London had the United States and the British colonies. Belgium, the Netherlands, and Germany were more closely linked to London than to Paris. Moreover, London lent on a worldwide basis while Paris lent funds to a smaller number of countries.

The Lender of Last Resort After World War I

There was no international lender of last resort in the 1920–1921 crisis. Part of the slack was taken up by the decline in the prices of the various European currencies. In a crisis caused by balance of payments weakness and money outflows, the decline in the price of a country's currency leads to increases in the domestic prices of tradable goods (those goods and services that are exported and imported, and those capable of being exported, and those that compete with imports). A sharp inflationary shock may produce another kind of crisis—out of money into goods—leading to hyperinflation, as happened in 1923 in the newly independent countries in Eastern and Central Europe that were coping with new boundaries and the lack of mechanisms for the collection of taxes.[37] The scenario is similar to that of Paul Erdman's thriller *The Crash of '79*, where the financial crisis was handled by printing massive amounts of currency and letting the US dollar float, which led to a surge in the demand for goods.[38]

Most governments in Western Europe in the early 1920s sought to stabilize the prices of their currencies at their 1914 gold parities because of tradition—restoring the status quo *ante bellum*. These countries often used stabilization loans, which were similar but not identical to loans from a lender of last resort, to dampen the declines in the prices of their currencies. There was a speculative attack on the French franc in 1924; many foreigners bought francs as the price of the franc declined in 1919–1920 in anticipation of large revaluation gains from the subsequent increase in its price toward its pre-war parity—but they eventually gave up and sold.[39] Speculators in Amsterdam, Vienna, and Berlin (perhaps stimulated by the German government) sold francs in anticipation that they would be able to purchase them later at much lower prices.[40] The story was that speculators who had profited from their short positions in the German mark as its price fell sharply in the hyperinflation of 1923–1924 then turned their attention to the French franc. Hundreds of thousands of Frenchmen with liquid securities denominated in the franc watched signals like the advances from the Bank of France to the French government approach the legal ceiling.

A panic began on 4 March 1924; the franc, which had been 98 to the pound on 17 February and 104 on 28 February, went to 107. The French government and the Bank of France met in emergency sessions. JP Morgan & Co. was willing to help if certain conditions were satisfied. The loan, a six-month revolving credit, would be for $100 million, not $50 million, which the bank, represented by Thomas W. Lamont, judged too small. The Bank of France resisted pledging its gold as collateral and yielded only after a face-saving formula was found. In turn, the Bank regents, including Rothschild and de Wendel, exacted a conservative financial program from the government. The program was worked out on Sunday 9 March and within three days the rout of the speculators began. The price of the franc increased from 123 francs to the pound to 78 by 24 March. The Bank of France then intervened to limit further increases in the price of the franc. The squeeze against the speculators was successful.[41] Lamont wrote that 'there has never been an operation that has given us more satisfaction.'[42]

Success was short-lived; there was another speculative attack on the franc in 1926, and the price declined to 240 francs to the pound in July 1926. Subsequently, the price of the franc increased to 125 in response to conservative Poincaré reforms and a surge in interest rates that was designed to reassure the French holders of wealth and induce them to bring their money back to Paris.

The League of Nations arranged stabilization loans in the 1920s for Austria and Hungary and for a number of new central banks in Eastern Europe under

arrangements with lenders in London, Paris, and New York. The most widely known were the Dawes and Young loans undertaken to recycle German reparations. The Dawes loan stimulated US purchases of foreign bonds. During the 1930s, the suggestion was frequently put forward, with only partial irony, that what France needed was a stabilization loan in gold, since the French franc and the currencies of the other gold bloc countries had become overvalued as a consequence of successive declines in the prices of the British pound, the Japanese yen, and the US dollar, and the imposition of exchange controls on foreign payments by both Germany and Austria. The gold, it was said, should be mounted in a vehicle like a glass hearse and paraded through the streets of every town and village in France to convince the people that the authorities had an abundance of gold and thereby encourage them to dishoard from the *bas de laine* (wool sock) in which they kept their *louis d'or*.

The rolling deflation of 1931 underlines the need for an international lender of last resort in a way that differs in scale and, therefore, in kind from previous episodes. The issues involved included the need for loans of the appropriate magnitude, the political character of the transactions, and the need for some country or group of countries to accept responsibility for the stability of the system.[43] Those who wrote along similar lines included Jørgen Pedersen and R. G. Hawtrey and other British economists whose advice to their government set out in Susan Howson and Donald Winch's *The Economic Advisory Council 1930–1939*.

Hawtrey presented a cogent analysis:

> The crisis of 1931 differed from earlier crises in its international character. Earlier crises were international in that the fall of prices and forced sales affected world markets. But only an unimportant part of debts were due to foreign creditors. In 1931, the outstanding characteristic of the panic was that foreign creditors of Germany and Eastern European debtors feared that the foreign exchange market would break down *even if the debtors remained solvent*. Against a panic-stricken withdrawal of foreign balances from London, it [raising Bank rate] was too tardy a remedy. Such a panic-stricken withdrawal *had never occurred before* … the underlying cause of the trouble has been *monetary instability*. The industrial depression, the insolvencies, the bank failures, budget deficits, and defaults are all the natural outcome of a falling price level … The need arises for an *international lender of last resort*. Perhaps someday the Bank for International Settlements … But as things are, the function can only be undertaken by a foreign central bank or by a group of foreign central banks in cooperation.[44]

Hawtrey's theoretical insight into the wisdom of limits on these stabilization loans was penetrating:

As a general rule, if credits are to be granted to a central bank in difficulties at all, they should be granted up to the full amount needed. There should be no limit. If the amount is inadequate and the exchange gives way after all, the sums lent are completely wasted … It can be argued in favor of unlimited credits, that if they *had* been granted, there would have been no withdrawal of funds at all … either no credits to the Bank of England or unlimited. But there is some risk. Unlimited credits would have enabled the country to remain on the gold standard, prolonging conditions that were rapidly becoming intolerable … the lesson: if the country can maintain the monetary standard without undue strain, then grant unlimited credits; but if the effort of maintaining parity is excessive, no credits and allow the currency to depreciate.[45]

Howson and Winch set out a series of reports written by British economists to their government in the 1930s, including one from a Committee of Economists chaired by J. M. Keynes that included Hubert Henderson, Alfred Pigou, Lionel Robbins, and Sir Josiah Stamp as members, with Hemming and Richard Kahn as secretaries. The reports advocated cooperation among central banks, preferably through the Bank for International Settlements, both to fund short-term claims and to form a pool of currencies for loans that could be used to prevent currency debacles like those experienced in the early 1920s, and to restore 'confidence in the financial stability of those many countries which are now the subject of distrust.'[46]

In July 1932, after Britain had gone off gold but before the World Economic Conference of 1933, the Cabinet Committee on Economic Information chaired by Stamp and including Citrine, Cole, Keynes, Sir Alfred Lewis, and Sir Frederick Leith-Ross as members, with Henderson and Hemming as secretaries, issued a report that discussed the 'international financial crisis.' The document quoted Bagehot, cited the crises of 1825 and 1847, and noted that Britain could no longer act as a lender of last resort; the report recommended that this function be performed by the Bank for International Settlements by the issue of 'paper gold,' to be called International Certificates.[47]

The first opportunity to halt the international disintermediation came in May 1931 with the collapse of Credit Anstalt, the leading Austrian bank. The Austrian central bank had maintained high interest rates to keep money in Vienna, which in turn contributed to the softness in the economy and large losses as the prices of securities and assets declined. The publication of the Credit Anstalt's statement on 11 May revealed that it had lost 140 million schillings, about three-fourths of its capital. The Austrian government asked the League of Nations for financial assistance because the League had organized the stabilization loans in the 1920s and the League turned to the Bank

for International Settlements that had been established under the Young Plan of 1930 to assist in the transfer of German reparations. The Austrian government wanted to borrow 150 million schillings ($21 million). During the last two weeks of May, the BIS arranged for a loan of 100 million schillings from eleven central banks. By 5 June the money from the loan was exhausted, and the Austrian National Bank requested another loan which was arranged by 14 June, subject to the condition that the Austrian government get a two- to three-year loan of 150 million schillings. The French demanded that the Austrian government renounce its customs union agreement with Germany that had been announced two months earlier, but the Austrian government refused and fell. The Bank of England then offered a loan of 50 million schillings ($7 million) for a week. The price of the schilling declined sharply after the Austrian government stopped pegging the currency to gold.

The run shifted to Germany. The German banking position was weakened by excessive speculation, large loan write-offs, fraud, quarrels among the bankers, banks that had been buying their own shares, and depleted liquid reserves—the full range of classic troubles.[48] The outsider was Jacob Goldschmidt of the Danatbank,[49] the product of the merger of the Darmstädter and the National banks. Other bankers, including Oskar Wasserman of the Deutsche Bank, detested Goldschmidt and his aggressive tactics. In 1927, the Berlin Handelsgesellschaft had stopped making loans to the Norddeutsche-Wolkämmerei (Nordwolle), an aggressive firm in the wool industry. The Danatbank took on Nordwolle as a client. Nordwolle's failure, on 17 June 1931, brought down Danatbank; other bankers were unwilling to provide support because of their dislike of Goldschmidt. There were political complications, and the internal financial turmoil led to massive withdrawals that were only briefly interrupted by the Hoover moratorium. On 25 June a loan for $100 million was arranged, including $25 million each from the Bank of England, the Bank of France, the Federal Reserve Bank of New York, and the Bank for International Settlements, for the period to 16 July. Hans Luther, president of the Reichsbank, had wanted a larger loan and had asked that its exact amount not be revealed, so the communiqué said only that a sufficient amount of discount facilities had been arranged. When the amount of the loan became known and the Reichsbank's statement of 23 June showed that its reserve cover was at 40.4 percent, just above the minimum requirement of 40 percent, the motto became 'Devil take the hindmost.'[50]

New loans were discussed but were not forthcoming. The Germans wanted to borrow $1 billion. The French were willing to consider a loan of $500 million, but they wanted to impose political conditions. The US government was worried about its prospective budget deficit of $1.6 billion and thought it

highly unlikely that the US Congress would approve lending more money to Germany. The US government was willing to consider the renewal of existing loans to Germany, which the Reichsbank wanted as well as a further loan. In Britain, the foreign secretary, Arthur Henderson, was attracted to the idea of a loan but Montagu Norman, then the Governor of the Bank of England, held that the Bank had 'already lent quite as much as is entirely convenient.'[51] One argument against foreign loans was that the crisis was believed to have been caused by a flight of domestic capital rather than by withdrawals of funds by foreign investors. By 20 July, the idea of a loan had been tacitly abandoned, 'brushed aside as impractical.'[52] Instead, the Germans relied on internal measures to halt the run on the domestic banks and on a Stand-still Agreement, imposed upon reluctant foreign bankers, to halt the external drain.

The speculative pressure then turned to Britain. The run began in mid-July 1931, stimulated partly by losses on the Continent, but also fed by the May and Macmillan reports of the large prospective domestic budget deficits and the unexpectedly high estimate of foreign money in London that might be withdrawn. Since 1927, the Bank of France had converted British pounds to gold by a roundabout device; it sold the British pounds in the spot foreign-exchange market, bought them in the forward foreign-exchange market, and then asked for gold on the dates when the forward exchange contracts matured.[53] The idea was to make it seem that the Bank of France was converting only its newly acquired British pound balances into gold, not its previously acquired balances. In the summer of 1931, the Bank of France cooperated fully and did not sell any of its British pound deposits or securities. At the end of July, the Federal Reserve Bank of New York and the Bank of France each loaned $125 million to the Bank of England. When these funds were depleted, the British government contemplated a one-year loan from the New York and Paris markets. The Bank of England reported that foreign bankers would not lend funds to Britain while it had such a large budget deficit. The British trade unions opposed a reduction in relief payments to the unemployed and withdrew support from the Labour government, which fell on 24 August. Four days later, after the formation of a new 'national govern-ment' with Ramsay MacDonald again Prime Minister and Philip Snowden as Chancellor of the Exchequer, $200 million was borrowed from a syndicate in New York led by Morgan and another $200 million from a French syndi-cate. On one showing, the bankers held up the British government; their own explanation, echoing the Morgan statements to the French in the 1920s, was that they were not imposing political conditions but instead indicating the

economic circumstances in which they felt they were justified in risking their own and their depositors' money.

On 5 August 1931, Keynes wrote to Prime Minister MacDonald, at the latter's request, to present a series of proposals for a decline in the price of the British pound and for the formation of a gold-based, fixed exchange currency unit at least 25 percent below the current parity, which all member countries of the British Empire, together with South America, Asia, Central Europe, Italy, and Spain—in fact, all countries—would be invited to join. The letter pointed out that if the British pound could not be successfully defended, it would be foolish to continue to borrow foreign currencies to support it.[54]

Loans of $400 million in addition to the $250 million were not enough, and the British stopped supporting the pound on 21 September. The Bank of France did not show the restraint toward the United States that it had shown to the British, and together with other members of the gold bloc, converted $750 million of US dollar deposits into gold. The deflationary pressure exerted by this reduction in US gold holdings, and by the decline in the price of the British pound and of the currencies pegged to the pound, weakened the US banking system. The New York Fed did not ask for help or even for forbearance in the conversion of US dollar deposits into gold. The code of the central banker calls for a stiff upper lip, reminiscent of Walter Mitty refusing the blindfold before the firing squad. In 1929, when Harrison asked Norman whether the pounds that the Federal Reserve Bank of New York had bought would be convertible into gold, he received the curt reply: 'Of course, the sterling is repayable in gold. This is the gold standard.'[55] In 1931, Harrison in turn offered to assist Moreau in converting any or all of the Bank of France's dollars into gold.[56]

Five aspects of the 1931 story are especially striking: (1) the inability of Britain to act as a lender of last resort; (2) the unwillingness of the United States to act as a lender of last resort apart from the (inadequate) loan to Britain (the country of the 'special relationship'); (3) the desire of France to advance its political objectives with respect to Austria and Germany; (4) the paranoia of Germany after 1923, preferring anything to a hint of inflation; and (5) the irresponsibility of the smaller countries.

This analysis has been questioned by several observers. One analyst thought that something more far-reaching was required to restore stability to the world economy after World War I, perhaps something on the order of the Marshall Plan after World War II.[57] Another considered that the German economy could not have been righted by a lender of last resort in 1931 since the authorities were determined to undo the Versailles Treaty and especially its reparations clauses.[58]

Bretton Woods and the International Monetary Arrangements

There was an extended debate in the early 1940s about the design of multilateral economic institutions that would provide for greater economic stability than in the twenty years after World War I. An international credit institution that became the International Monetary Fund was established to help countries finance short-term balance of payments deficits. A long-term lending agency that became the International Bank for Reconstruction and Development (IBRD or World Bank) was established to help war-torn countries finance their economic rebuilding; subsequently, its focus became economic development of low-income countries. An international trade organization would be established to resolve trade disputes and provide a forum for the reduction of tariffs and other trade barriers. The advent of the planned international trade organization was long delayed, but its preamble, the General Agreement on Tariffs and Trade (GATT), provided the basis for an organization to deal with trade policy issues in a less ambitious way. More than fifty years later, the GATT morphed into the World Trade Organization (WTO).

The debate about the key features of the international credit institution that would help countries finance their short-term payments deficits was primarily between the British and the Americans, who held different views about both its financial structure and its financial resources. The 'Keynes plan' presented by the British called for an institution that would have its own money or unit of account. Each country would be endowed with a deposit in this institution when it became a member, which it could transfer to other countries to finance its payments deficit. The American view, the 'White plan,' was that each member country would finance its payments deficit by the transfer of US dollars or some other currency to the country with the payments surplus; the country with the deficit would use its own currency to purchase the US dollar or some other currency from the Fund. Each member country would have a quota based on the volume of its trade and its gold holdings; each member's quota would determine its capital subscription and the amounts of gold and of its own currency that it would transfer to the Fund as part of this subscription. The amount of US dollars and other foreign currencies that a member country might obtain from the Fund would depend on its quota. Each country's quota was divided into four tranches; a country might draw on no more than one tranche in a given twelve-month period. Drawing on the first tranche was more or less automatic. Thereafter, access to credit was a matter of grace on the part of the IMF rather than a matter of right.

The US view prevailed because the Americans had all the money. The British got the Americans to agree to double the initial capital of the Fund.

The Fund's Articles of Agreement contained a set of rules for the management of the prices or parities of the currencies of the member countries. Each member country would be required to state a parity for its currency in terms of either gold or the US dollar; each would be required to limit the variation in the price of its currency to a narrow band around its parity. Moreover, each country would be required to obtain the approval of the IMF before changing its parity by more than 10 percent relative to its initial parity.

The structure of the Fund meant that its loans to a member country were limited in amount because it did not have its own money or unit of account. (Even if the Fund had had its own money, its constitution might limit its loans or credits to a member and, as well, its total loans.) Thus, the limit to its lending was set by the amount of currencies that it had obtained from countries when they became members and the amount of currencies that the Fund might borrow from its members. In the immediate years after the Second World War, the US dollar was the major currency that a country might buy from the IMF. Countries could retain exchange controls to limit capital flows that might complicate their ability to retain their parities. Loans from the IMF would have to be repaid.

During the first fifteen years after the end of the Second World War, the Fund and the World Bank were on the sidelines because most of the finance for economic reconstruction was provided under the Marshall Plan, and primarily in the form of grant aid. The Bretton Woods system did not come into full operation until 1958, after the British pound became convertible into other currencies on capital account, and restrictions on cross-border investment flows were largely abandoned by industrial countries.

Even as capital controls were retained, firms and investors began to increase their demand for securities and deposits in foreign currencies, which meant that countries needed much larger holdings of international reserve assets. Large money transfers could take place through changes in the 'leads and lags'; that is, changes in the timing of payments associated with both exports and with imports. A country might experience a sharp decline in its holdings of international reserve assets if its importers who previously had received three months' credit before paying for their purchases were suddenly asked to pay cash. One implication was that many countries wanted much larger holdings of international reserve assets; another was the amount of foreign currencies owned by the IMF was too small relative to the amounts that some countries might want to borrow to finance part of their payments deficits.

In 1960, the General Arrangements to Borrow (GAB) was adopted to increase the funds available to the IMF; ten large countries, the Group of Ten, pledged a total of $6 billion that the Fund could use to help members finance their payments deficits. Many countries still believed the Fund resources would be too small.

Moreover, the IMF's decision-making was ponderous and time-consuming. Decisions were made by the weighted voting of its directors, many of whom represented more than one country. To frame a proposal, obtain instructions and arrive at a decision to help a country in crisis could take three weeks.

Cross-border investment flows increased in the late 1950s and the 1960s. Economic distance was declining because of technological developments and the sharp declines in the costs of communication and storing information. Richard Cooper emphasized this development:

> A crude quantitative indicator of these developments is provided by contrasting the maximum daily speculation of under $100 million against the pound sterling, in the 'massive' run of August 1947, with the maximum daily speculation of over $1.5 billion in favor of the German mark in May 1969, and the movement of over $1 billion into Germany in less than an hour in May 1971. Moreover, as the barriers of ignorance fall further, there is no reason why $1.5 billion should not rise to $15 billion, or even $50 billion a day.[59]

The daily turnover in the currency market had reached $1 trillion by the late 1990s and $7.5 trillion in 2022. The increase in the transactions in the currencies of the emerging market economies was even more rapid.[60]

The increase in international investment flows in the second half of the 1960s challenged the ability of central banks to retain the parities for their currencies. Some central banks experimented by selling their currencies in the forward foreign-exchange market, which enabled them to maintain their parities without depleting their reserves—at least not until the forward exchange contracts matured. And on those dates, the central banks might 'roll over' or renew their forward foreign-exchange contracts. A few observers believed that these forward exchange transactions would relieve central banks of the need to hold international reserve assets or at least reduce the amount of reserves they would hold. The experience of the Bank of England from 1964 to 1967 suggests the limits to this view; by late 1967, its commitments to deliver US dollars in the spot foreign exchange market on the dates that the forward exchange contracts matured were several times larger than its holdings of international reserve assets, and market participants became increasingly reluctant to renew maturing forward exchange contracts. In

1964, the British were able to postpone the decline in the price of the British pound, which occurred in November 1967.

One of the major international financial innovations in the 1960s was the network of currency swaps among central banks worked out at the Bank for International Settlements in Basel, Switzerland. The United States had taken a leadership role in the development of this network, which was a series of bilateral credit lines between pairs of central banks. When the lines were activated, each central bank wrote up an asset in the form of a specified amount of the currency of the foreign central bank participating in the swap, and a liability in the form of an equivalent amount of its own currency that was an asset of the foreign central bank. Once the swap lines had been established, the foreign currency could be made immediately available, although the money drawn under the swap lines would have to be repaid. The first swap of US$50 million in March 1962 was between the Bank of France and the Federal Reserve Bank of New York. In June, the New York Fed entered into swaps of US$50 million with both the Dutch and the Belgian central banks and a US$250 million swap with the Bank of Canada. In July, the New York Fed established a US$250 million swap line with the Swiss National Bank. By October 1963, the swap network had been increased to a total of US$2 billion, by March 1968 to US$4.5 billion, and by July 1973 to US$18 billion.[61]

In 1961, when the British pound was under speculative attack, representatives of the major central banks at a meeting of the Bank for International Settlements committed a total of US$1 billion for credits. Charles Coombs, a senior vice president of the Federal Reserve Bank of New York, called this development a major breakthrough in international postwar finance.[62] The number was large enough to convince speculators that they could not break the parity of a currency. Most of the loan would be repaid with the funds obtained from the repatriation of flight capital.

The money available under the swap lines would be a country's first line of defense after the use of its own holdings of international reserve assets; the second line would be access to money from the IMF. A number of countries used their swap lines: Canada used more than US$1 billion in June 1962; Italy US$1 billion in March 1963; and Britain US$2 billion in the autumn of 1964. A US$1.3 billion package was available for France in July 1968, which would have been extended to US$2 billion in November for the defense of the devalued franc.[63] The French decision not to help the British in September 1965 has been characterized as a 'shocking repudiation of the central banking free masonry.' The pressure to conform to the club, and the

will to be different as a matter of foreign policy, were both intense. 'It cut no ice. The British got the support they wanted.'[64]

The proximate cause of the breakdown of the Bretton Woods arrangements was that the Federal Reserve and the Bundesbank began to follow divergent monetary policies, even though their money markets were closely linked through the market in offshore deposits. Any effort to follow divergent monetary policies would lead to a massive investment flow from New York to Frankfurt or from Frankfurt to New York. The Federal Reserve embarked on a policy of monetary expansion eight months before the US presidential election of 1972, while the Bundesbank maintained high interest rates. The result was that funds poured out of the United States into Eurodollars and into German mark securities. The Bundesbank was forced to lower its interest rates, but not before billions of dollars had spilled out on the world.

The decline in interest rates on US dollar securities led to the relaxation of lending standards, as in 1825, 1853, 1871, and 1885. Banks headquartered in New York, London, Tokyo, and other financial centers began to lend freely to Mexico, Brazil, Argentina, and other developing countries as well as to the Soviet Union and its neighbors in the Eastern bloc.

The great hemorrhaging of dollars over the world made it impossible to sustain the adjustable parity arrangement. The United States made no effort to defend the new parity for the US dollar that had been set in the Smithsonian Agreement. By February 1973, speculation that the price of the German mark would be increased led to an increasingly large investment flow to Frankfurt; the Bundesbank stopped buying the US dollar, and the price of the German mark immediately increased. Most other central banks in Europe followed the German initiative.

Most economists had thought that the adoption of a floating exchange rate arrangement would severely dampen the movement of interest-sensitive investments and that, once currencies were floating, central banks would be able to follow independent monetary policies without any untoward external effects. Economists differed about whether speculative money movements would be stabilizing or occasionally destabilizing in a serious way; the general view was that the fear of currency losses would deter cross-border investment flows. That view proved mistaken; many banks regarded currencies as a new asset class that they could profitably trade.

Initially, an international lender of last resort did not appear to be needed when currencies were floating. If the residents of a country increased their demand for foreign goods or foreign securities, the country would not experience an increase in its payments deficit but, instead, the price of its currency

would decline. The anticipation of changes in the prices of currencies encouraged investors, including some who worked for banks, to seek to profit from these changes. The Herstatt Bank of Cologne and the Franklin National Bank of New York lost money trading currencies and each failed in June 1974. The German authorities closed Herstatt in the middle of the trading day, which created a new problem because Herstatt had collected the money due to it on currency transactions but was closed before it had paid out the German mark counterpart that was due to the other banks. For a time, the consortium that guaranteed its liabilities was interested only in domestic German obligations and was prepared to let the sums due to foreign banks go unrequited. Second thoughts prevailed, however, and the foreign banks that owned Herstatt liabilities were made whole. The Federal Deposit Insurance Corporation took over Franklin National deposits up to the limit of $40,000, and the Federal Reserve System, acting as lender of last resort, in effect ensured that the owners of its remaining liabilities did not incur losses.

The arrangements worked out at the Bank for International Settlements in the Basel Protocol of March 1975 were supposed to settle the issue of national responsibility about the settlement of claims when a bank failed. A new problem developed in 1982 when the Luxembourg subsidiary of the Banco Ambrosiano of Milan defaulted on $400 million of liabilities to other European banks. The Bank of Italy refused to make good on these liabilities on the legal ground that the Luxembourg unit of Ambrosiano was incorporated under Luxembourg law and its assets and liabilities were distinct from those of the bank's head office in Milan. This interpretation placed the Basel Protocol under a cloud.

The sharp increases in the price of petroleum in 1973 and again in 1979 led to a surge in the export earnings of the oil-producing countries and in their holdings of international reserve assets. The export earnings of the developing countries as a group increased sharply, and their GDP growth rates trended up. Loans from the major international banks headquartered in one of the industrial countries to the governments and government-owned firms in Mexico, Brazil, Argentina, and other developing countries surged.

The combination of the increase in oil production in the North Sea and Mexico and elsewhere and the decline in demand due to the global recession in the early 1980s led to reductions in oil prices. By mid-1982, Mexico and many of the smaller oil-producing countries were in financial difficulty.

One method of international lender of last resort lending consists of the swap arrangements worked out at the Bank for International Settlements in March 1961. A country suffering a foreign-exchange crisis swaps its currency for those it needs to meet the drain. If the crisis subsides and the country

regains foreign exchange, the swaps are undone, usually, at the end of some specified period, say, six months. If the crisis has not been overcome, the country that has been helped is expected to fund unrepaid amounts at the International Monetary Fund. In extremis, it might issue long-term debt denominated in foreign exchange to its partners. Swaps rest less on contract than on trust. As standing arrangements, they were normally limited to the leading financial countries, the so-called Group of Ten, plus Switzerland. They were not generally available to Latin American countries because these had defaulted frequently on their foreign debts in the past, notably in the 1820s, 1850s, 1870s, 1890s, and 1920s. As a consequence, developing countries have had to turn to other devices during a financial crisis.

The arrangement for Mexico set the pattern of a package of official and private financing centered on conditional credits from the IMF. The presumption was that the problem was more a short-term liquidity problem than a solvency problem. Already in the spring of 1982, Mexico was making 'window-dressing' drawings on a swap line with the Federal Reserve Bank of New York, i.e., borrowing the funds, counting it toward otherwise dangerously low foreign-exchange reserves, and leaving the funds with the Fed. At the May monthly meeting at the BIS, Chairman Paul Volcker had warned central bankers that Mexico and other developing countries were on thin ice. On 4 August, the Mexicans really drew down the full amount of the $700 million swap, promising to go to the IMF if it could not repay it. Mexico closed its foreign-exchange market on August 12, and the Volcker plan took shape in the weekend and weeks that followed.

Governments and central banks would extend 'bridge' loans, while the developing country government negotiated a loan with the IMF with policy conditions attached. Thus, central bank swaps played an ad hoc role, attempting to somehow reconcile the need for immediate funding help with often contentious policy conditions. In some cases, drawing on even the bridge loans required agreement with the IMF on economic policies, such as tighter monetary and fiscal policies. For Mexico, the bridge loans included the US Treasury pre-paying $1 billion for oil for future delivery to the US Strategic Petroleum Reserve. Commercial banks accepted a stand-still on maturing loans, but continued to receive interest, and agreed to reschedule loans coming due over a period of initially a year, but later several years.

However, with interest rates in double digits, merely refinancing maturing loans left large interest bills to be paid. To pay these bills in full would have required the developing countries to run large trade surpluses by draconian cuts in public spending or heavy tax increases or the IMF to make larger

commitments than were readily available. The circle was squared by officials requiring the commercial banks to stump up 'new money' loans, for example, a sum equivalent to 7 percent of their outstanding medium-term credits. As might be imagined, the banks were not keen to do so, although the big banks with the largest exposure understood that their own solvency depended on keeping the developing countries paying rather than defaulting. Smaller banks that had signed up for broadly syndicated loans wanted out. It took much moral suasion, from not only the IMF but also from the major central banks, to keep a critical mass in the game. This was not easy given that officials had insisted that the banks lower the spread on their loans to Libor plus 13/16, barely covering banks' funding cost. In short, officials from the creditor countries not only funded the IMF loans to the developing countries but also managed commercial bank lending to prevent their suddenly cutting off the flow of new lending.

These improvisations enabled the governments of Mexico, Brazil, Argentina, the Philippines, and others to muddle through and avoid default. The debtors liked this arrangement because otherwise they would have been cutoff from international capital markets for a generation (if indications from history were any guide) and because they wanted more foreign capital to enhance their rates of economic growth. The creditors liked these arrangements because, otherwise, defaults by the borrowers would force them to recognize large loan losses. Whereas default in earlier periods was generally less of a concern to the credit system of developed countries since it affected bonds held by individuals and not loans extended by banks, default on Third World debt in the 1980s might have led to runs on some of the major international banks because of concern about the adequacy of their capital.

Conditionality

The populist view is that the IMF has been excessively restrictive about the choice of monetary policies and fiscal policies by the emerging market countries. Most lenders, both domestic and international, stipulate conditions on their loans. Some French analysts were irked by the requirements laid down by JP Morgan & Co. in its 1924 stabilization loan,[65] although the standard response is that the lenders have an obligation to their depositors and their creditors to ensure that their loans will be repaid. French conditions for loans to Austria and Germany in 1931 were political. American and French loans to Britain later that summer were regarded by the Labour Party as a

'bankers' ramp' (in American, 'racket') as the lenders thought that the recommendations of the British May Committee to balance the budget and reduce unemployment benefits should be carried out.

Conditions have not been attached to the credits extended under swaps although there are 'understandings.' When the Bank for International Settlements makes a loan to Hungary under a swap, it knows that Hungary will obtain the funds to repay the loan from access to credit at the IMF. Conditions will be attached to that loan. When a G-7 member borrows from the IMF, as Britain did in 1976, conditions also apply.[66]

The Mexican Crisis of 1994–1995

The Mexican financial crisis of 1994–1995 began with a peasant revolt in January in the southernmost province of the country and the assassination of the leading presidential candidate of the dominant political party several months later. The cross-border investment inflows slowed dramatically, and the Bank of Mexico intervened to support the price of the peso in the currency market to finance the country's large current account deficit; as a result, its holdings of international reserve assets rapidly declined.[67] In April 1994, the United States and Canada came to the rescue, largely because of the 'special relationship' involved in the North American Free Trade Agreement Act of November 1993. A credit line of $6.7 billion was arranged, with $6 billion from the United States and $700 million from Canada. Mexican troubles continued. There was another attack on the peso in December 1994, partly the flight of Mexican money and partly the withdrawal of money by disenchanted American and other foreign investors. In January 1995, the US Treasury organized a $50 billion rescue fund including $20 billion from the US Treasury's Exchange Stabilization Fund, $18 billion from the IMF, $10 billion from central banks organized by the BIS, and $2 billion from Canada.[68] The amount proved persuasive. The investment outflows stopped and then were reversed. Only $12.5 billion of the US credit line was drawn, and, in the fall of 1995, repayment started with the help of money loans placed privately.

Several questions remain about the Mexican rescue operation in 1994–1995. One is whether the loans made in the early 1980s led the Mexicans to believe that they would be helped if they again encountered difficulties—the moral hazard question. Another is whether the large amounts of credit created a precedent that would lead to future problems. Holders of short-term Mexican government dollar-linked bills paying high yields escaped without

loss. Moreover, did the financial authorities forestall contagion and prevent the crisis from spreading to Brazil and Argentina, as contagion had spread from Austria in May 1931?

Bagehot enunciated the prescription that a lender of last resort should lend freely because low limits excite. An official loan package summarized by a big number that seems beyond any possible need can be seen as lending freely. Yet, the window-dressing swap organized at the BIS for Mexico would not work so well when one was announced for Thailand a couple of years later.

The East Asian Crisis of 1997

The financial crisis in East Asia that started in July 1997 involved euphoric lenders in developed countries keen on diversifying their portfolios, and developing country borrowers that wanted to increase their investments and their growth rates and that had been asked by the industrial countries to deregulate their financial markets. Other factors included crony capitalism in Indonesia, a weak government in Thailand, and enormous conglomerates (*chaebol*) in South Korea. Moreover, many loans by the domestic banks in these countries had become non-performing. The catatonic state of economic policy meant that Japan was no longer a source of strong demand, and the expansion of Japanese direct investment into lower-wage countries and of Japanese bank loans contributed to the increases in the current account deficits of Thailand and its neighbors. The rates of economic growth in these countries were high; in 1992, the World Bank published *The East Asian Miracle*. European banks also increased their loans to the banks headquartered in these countries. These countries developed large trade deficits in response to these investment inflows, and their economies became vulnerable to any shock that might lead to a decline in investment inflows, much like the shock that impacted Mexico in 1994.

The sharp decline in the price of the Thai baht in early July 1997 triggered the contagion effect, and the cross-border investment inflows to other Asian countries slowed and then were reversed. The President of Malaysia, Dr. Mahathir, blamed foreign speculators and specifically George Soros in the United States, who in turn asserted that he had not sold the ringgit short while Malaysia was constructing two new buildings taller than any other buildings in the world. Malaysia did not seek loans from the IMF but instead imposed controls on investment outflows and on interest payments to foreign creditors. Thailand, Indonesia, and South Korea borrowed from the IMF. The

Table 12.1 Official finance commitments (last resort lending) ($US billions)

Country	IMF	World Bank	Asian Development Bank	Bilateral commitments	Total
Thailand	3.9	1.9	2.2	12.1	20.1
Indonesia	10.1	4.5	3.5	22.0[a]	40.0
South Korea	21.0	10.0	4.0	22.0	57.0
Total	35.0	16.4	9.7	56.1	107.1
Memo item					
Mexico	*17.8*	*1.5*	*1.3[b]*	*21.0 [c]*	*41.6*

[a]Including the use of a $5 billion Indonesian contingency reserve
[b]InterAmerican Development Bank
[c]In addition, there was a credit facility of up to $10 billion with G-10 central banks, which was never activated

amounts of these loans and those to Mexico in 1994–1995 are set forth in Table 12.1 from the Bank for International Settlements.[69]

The report of the Bank for International Settlements noted that the $50 billion credit lines for Mexico had a

> ... psychological impact on the markets [halting] the erosion of foreign confidence. How large a package needs to be to do this is difficult to judge. International official support offered to the Asian countries was not large enough to cover all their short-term foreign obligations as had the Mexican package, a difference that did not pass unnoticed in the markets.[70]

In this case, evident limits excited. In the event, on Christmas Eve 1997, the major central banks returned in the case of Korea to a standstill on repayments of short-term bank credits and their managed rollover. In short, when the 'shock and awe' of piling up official commitments proved ineffective, the lender of last resort operation returned to moral suasion as in the 1980s: leaning on commercial banks to roll over their claims on Korea.

These credit commitments by the IMF were large by IMF standards and they depleted the funds available for rescue operations in the future. At the end of 1998, the US Congress agreed to the proposal of the Clinton administration to increase the IMF's capital and member country quotas. The IMF helped Brazil when it needed assistance after its currency crisis.

A world central bank would be a more efficient lender of last resort than the IMF, but the likelihood that many countries would agree to establish a world central bank seems low. Most large countries outside the European Monetary Union regard the issue and control of money as a mark of sovereignty; in the United States, these functions are enshrined in the Constitution.

Notes

1. Niall Ferguson, *The House of Rothschild: Money's Prophets, 1798–1847* (New York: Viking, 1998), chap. 16, Table 16a on p. 461, shows the course of bond prices in Vienna, Paris, Rome, and London. Ferguson states that 'the London house was not the lender of last resort at all'; but Alphonse, Nathan's grandson, was sent to New York to turn Belmont away from preoccupation with the Mexican indemnity and focus on Europe (pp. 466–70).

2. Ron Chernow, *The Warburgs: the Twentieth-Century Odyssey of a Remarkable Jewish Family* (New York: Random House, 1993), p. 328.

3. R. D. Richards, 'The First Fifty Years of the Bank of England, 1694–1744', in *History of the Principal Public Banks*, compiled by J. G. van Dillen (The Hague: Martinus Nijhoff, 1934), p. 234.

4. Violet Barbour, *Capitalism and Amsterdam in the 17th Century* (1950; reprint edn, Ann Arbor: University of Michigan Press, 1966), p. 125.

5. Charles Wilson, *Anglo-Dutch Commerce and Finance in the Eighteenth Century* (Cambridge: Cambridge University Press, 1941), pp. 168–9.

6. Ibid., p. 176.

7. Sir John Clapham, *The Bank of England: a History* (Cambridge: Cambridge University Press, 1945), vol. 1, p. 249.

8. Alain Plessis, *La Politique de la Banque de France de 1850 à 1870* (Geneva: Droz, 1985), chap. 4, esp. pp. 241–5.

9. Knut Wicksell, *Lectures on Political Economy* (New York: Macmillan, 1935), vol. 2, pp. 37–8.

10. Jacob Viner, *Studies in the Theory of International Trade* (New York: Harper & Bros., 1937), p. 273; Clapham, *Bank of England*, vol. 2, p. 169.

11. Clapham, *Bank of England*, vol. 2, pp. 164–5.

12. Clément Juglar, *Des crises commerciales et leur retour périodiques en France, en Angleterre et aux Etats-Unis*, 2nd edn (1889; reprint edn, New York: Augustus M. Kelley, 1967), p. 417.

13. E. Victor Morgan, *The Theory and Practice of Central Banking, 1797–1913* (Cambridge: Cambridge University Press, 1943), p. 148.

14. Arthur D. Gayer, W. W. Rostow, and Anna J. Schwartz, *The Growth and Fluctuation of the British Economy, 1790–1850* (Oxford: Oxford University Press, Clarendon Press, 1953), vol. 1, p. 333.

15. British Parliamentary Papers, *Causes of Commercial Distress: Monetary Policy* (Shannon: Irish University Press, 1969), vol. 1, p. 153, question 2018.

16. Viner, *Studies in International Trade*, p. 273.

17. Clapham, *Bank of England*, vol. 2, p. 170.

18. Bertrand Gille, *La Banque et le crédit en France de 1818 à 1848* (Paris: Presses universitaires de France, 1959), p. 377.

19. Clapham, *Bank of England*, vol. 2, p. 229.

20. Helmut Böhme, *Frankfurt und Hamburg: Des Deutsches Reiches Silber und Goldloch und die Allerenglishte Stadt des Kontinents* (Frankfurt-am-Main: Europaïsche Verlagsanstalt, 1968), pp. 255–68.

21. Ibid., pp. 267–74.

22. Parliamentary Papers, *Commercial Distress*, vol. 4, appendix 20, consular dispatch no. 7, January 27, 1858, p. 441.

23. Ibid., dispatch no. 393 from Berlin, December 29, 1857, pp. 450–1.

24. Clapham, *Bank of England*, vol. 2, p. 234.

25. Morgan, *Theory and Practice of Central Banking*, p. 176.

26. Clapham, *Bank of England*, vol. 2, pp. 291–4.

27. Ibid., pp. 329–30, 344.

28. Quoted from Hartley Withers, *The Meaning of Money* (1909) in R. S. Sayers, *Bank of England Operations 1890–1914* (London: P. S. King, 1936), p. 111.

29. J.-L. Billoret, 'Système bancaire et dynamique économique dans un pays à monnaie stable: France, 1896–1914', thesis, Faculty of Law and Economic Science, Nancy, 1969, quoted in Jean Bouvier, *Un siècle de banque française* (Paris: Hachette Littérature, 1973), p. 240.

30. Hans Rosenberg, *Die Weltwirtschaftskrise von 1857–1859* (Stuttgart: Verlag von W. Kohlhammer, 1934), p. 38.

31. George W. Van Vleck, *The Panic of 1857: an Analytical Study* (New York: Columbia University Press, 1943), p. 42.

32. Billoret, 'Système bancaire', as quoted in Bouvier, *Un siècle de banque française*, p. 238.

33. Walter Bagehot, *Lombard Street: a Description of the Money Market* (1873; reprint edn, London: John Murray, 1917), pp. 32–4.

34. O. M. W. Sprague, *History of Crises under the National Banking System* (1910; reprint edn, New York: Augustus M. Kelley, 1968), pp. 248–85.

35. Franco Bonelli, *La crisi del 1907: una tappa dello sviluppo industriale in Italia* (Turin: Fondazione Luigi Einaudi, 1971), p. 42.

36. Oskar Morgenstern, *International Financial Transactions and Business Cycles* (Princeton: Princeton University Press, 1959), pp. 128–37.

37. See League of Nations, *The Course and Control of Inflation After World War I* (Princeton: League of Nations, 1945).

38. Paul E. Erdman, *The Crash of '79* (New York: Simon & Schuster, 1976).

39. Stephen A. Schuker, *The End of French Predominance in Europe, the Financial Crisis of 1924 and the Adoption of the Dawes Plan* (Chapel Hill: University of North Carolina Press, 1976), p. 67.

40. J. N. Jeanneney, 'De la Spéculation financière comme arme diplomatique: a propos de la première bataille de franc (november 1923–mars 1924)', *Relations internationales*, no. 13 (Spring 1978), pp. 9–15, is persuaded that the German government organized the bear raid on the franc. Schuker is skeptical: *The End of French Predominance*, p. 56. Jean-Claude Debeir, 'La crise du franc de 1924: Une exemple de la spéculation "internationale"', *Relations Internationales*, no. 13 (Spring 1978), p. 35, lays considerable blame for

financing the attacks on American banks but states that the French did most of the speculation.

41. Schuker, *The End of French Predominance*, chap. 4.

42. Ibid., p. 111.

43. C. P. Kindleberger. *The World in Depression, 1929–1939*, 2nd edn (Berkeley: University of California Press, 1986), esp. chaps 7, 14.

44. R. G. Hawtrey, *The Art of Central Banking* (London: Longmans, Green, 1932), pp. 220–4; all italics are in the original. Hawtrey is prescient to a degree. Since the International Monetary Fund takes time to make credit decisions as a lender of last resort, and the Bank for International Settlements can act quickly, the latter has operated in a number of recent financial crises by providing 'bridge loans', that is, short-term finance (though limited in amounts) to countries with immediate needs. These loans would then be repaid with funds from credits from the International Monetary Fund. See Harold James, *International Monetary Cooperation since Bretton Woods* (Washington, DC: International Monetary Fund, 1995; New York and Oxford: Oxford University Press, 1996), pp. 361–2, 389, 557, 562, 592.

45. Hawtrey, *The Art of Central Banking*, pp. 229–32; italics are in the original.

46. Susan Howson and Donald Winch, *The Economic Advisory Council, 1930–1939: a Study in Economic Advice during Depression and Recovery* (Cambridge: Cambridge University Press, 1977), pp. 188–9. The personnel of the various committees are given in ibid., appendix 1, pp. 354–70.

47. Ibid., pp. 272–81.

48. This discussion is largely based on Karl Erich Born, *Die deustsche Bankenkrise, 1931: Finanzen und Politik* (Munich: R. Piper & Co. Verlag, 1967).

49. Ibid., p. 86.

50. Ibid., p. 83.

51. Norman to Harrison, cable, 3 July 1931, in Federal Reserve Bank of New York files.

52. Stephen V. O. Clarke, *Central Bank Cooperation, 1924–31* (New York: Federal Reserve Bank of New York, 1967), p. 44. This was after discussion by both sides, with the British and Americans saying no (Kindleberger, *World in Depression*, p. 153). The Germans for their part were debating a plan of Wilhelm Lautenbach of the Economics Ministry, which called for suspending service on foreign debt and expanding spending (ibid., p. 171, n.5). The Lautenbach plan came up again after the British pound went off gold in September 1931. See Knut Borchardt and Hans Otto Schöltz, eds, *Wirtschaftspolitik in der Krise* (Baden-Baden: Nomos, 1931 [1991]). This is a transcript of the riveting debate in the Reichsbank among German officials and economists.

53. Clarke, *Central Bank Cooperation*, pp. 121, 148.

54. Howson and Winch, *Economic Advisory Council*, pp. 88–9.

55. Ibid., p. 162.

56. Kindleberger, *World in Depression*, pp. 168, 184.

57. D. E. Moggridge, 'Policy in the Crises of 1920 and 1929', in C. P. Kindle-berger and J.-P. Laffargue, eds, *Financial Crises: Theory, History and Policy* (Cambridge: Cambridge University Press, 1982), pp. 171–87.

58. Stephen A. Schuker, *American 'Reparations' to Germany, 1919–33: Implications for the Third-World Debt Crisis*, Princeton Studies in International Finance no. 61 (Princeton: International Finance Section, Princeton University Press, 1988).

59. Richard N. Cooper, 'Economic Interdependence and Foreign Policy in the Seventies', *World Politics*, vol. 24 (January 1972), p. 167.

60. See Bank for International Settlements, *Annual Report* no. 63 to 31 March 1993, p. 196; and no. 64 to 31 March 1994. World turnover rose from $10 billion to $20 billion a day in 1973, to $80 billion in 1983, before soaring to over $1 trillion a day in 1995: *The Economist*, vol. 337, no. 7936 (14 October 1995), p. 10. For emerging markets and the European Monetary Union, see Bank for International Settlements, 68th *Annual Report* to 31 March 1998, p. 11, and chart p. 115.

61. Charles A. Coombs, *The Arena of International Finance* (New York: Wiley), pp. 77, 79, 81, 83, 195, 202, 292.

62. Coombs, *Arena*, p. 37.

63. Ibid., pp. 81, 85, 111, 121, 127, 134, 181, 185.

64. Susan Strange, 'International Monetary Relations', in Andrew Schonfield, ed., *International Economic Relations of the Western World, 1959–71* (Oxford: Oxford University Press, for the Royal Institute of International Affairs, 1976), vol. 2, p. 136.

65. See Debeir, 'La crise du franc du 1924'.

66. Kathleen Burk and Alec Cairncross, *'Goodbye Great Britain': the 1976 IMF Crisis* (New Haven: Yale University Press, 1992).

67. For background, see the paper on Mexico by Ernesto Zedillo in Donald R. Lessard and John Williamson, eds, *Capital Flight and Third World Debt* (Washington, DC: Institute for International Economics, 1987), pp. 174–85. The crisis itself is discussed at length in the *New York Times* issues from 21 to 29 December 1994.

68. 'President Clinton Sidesteps Congress Using Emergency Authority', *New York Times*, 1 February 1995, p. A1.

69. Bank for International Settlements, *Annual Report*, no. 68, p. 134.

70. Ibid.

13

The Twenty-First Century International Lender of Last Resort

'The great merit of the Basle agreement [on swaps between central banks] ...is the availability of unlimited amounts of assistance through rediscounting in a period of crisis... Lines of credit must be unlimited...'[1] So wrote Charles Kindleberger in 1967. Forty-one years later, unlimited credits between central banks made the transition from academic prescription to operational reality. This was a Kindleberger moment. Thus, the international lender of last resort changed so much in the twenty-first century that it merits a separate chapter in this edition.

In the Great Financial Crisis (GFC) of 2008, central bank swaps came to play a role almost without precedent, under circumstances without precedent, and in a size without precedent. The Fed's motive is often said to be the financial stability goal of making good the lost dollar funding of non-US banks. But the Fed's extension of dollar credit to non-US banks through its swaps with central banks served both to fix the transmission of the Fed's monetary policy to key dollar borrowing rates and to counter the runs on non-US banks.

Central bank swaps during the acute phase of the pandemic crisis in March 2020 confirmed their role as backstops to global dollar banking. Again, they succeeded in reversing a rise in the dollar London interbank rate (Libor) and relieving dollar funding shortages for non-US banks.

In addition, the Fed in the spring of 2020 played a new role, well beyond what Perry Mehrling calls the dealer of last resort.[2] The Fed's role as buyer of last resort in the US bond market backstopped the global market for

dollar bonds, including those issued outside the United States by non-US borrowers. Last resort buying extended from the money market to the capital market and ramified globally.

The previous chapter identified the central bank swap network as an important innovation in the international lender of last resort. Central bank technicians meeting at the Bank for International Settlements (BIS) in Basel or talking over the telephone could agree to provide each other with their respective key currencies with speed, in size, and without policy conditions. By contrast, credit from the International Monetary Fund (IMF), with its almost universal membership, board meetings, and voting rules, takes time, is rule-bound in scale, and comes with policy conditions attached.

These differences underlay the division of labor between central bank swaps and IMF credit, as described in the previous chapter. While swaps could speedily provide credit, they were to be repaid in months. Failing that, the borrower needed to turn to fully multilateral credit from the IMF to refinance the short-term swaps over the medium term.

The use of central bank swaps in this century continues an evolution in their purposes since their origins in the 1960s. The swap network started out as one of the multiple devices to keep the fixed exchange rate system going.[3] When that system broke down with the beginning of generalized floating of major exchange rates in 1973, the swap network not only survived but expanded to support the management of major exchange rates through the 1970s. Then from 1982 through 1998, central bank swaps served at times as temporary bridges to IMF loans to developing (later called emerging market) economies that were experiencing difficulty in managing their external debt. In short, swaps morphed from major exchange rate management tool under first fixed then floating exchange rates to short-term bridge credit to IMF medium-term credit to Latin American and Asian debtors to banks.

The central bank swaps of 2008 and 2020 made for a new chapter in this evolution. They did not serve the purpose of intervention in the foreign-exchange market. Nor did they bridge to IMF credit. Instead, along with other emergency measures of the Fed, the swaps kept dollar funding going to non-US banks.

As sketched in the following section on global dollar banking, the dollar played an outsized global role and non-US banks predominated in dollar intermediation outside the United States. This had three key consequences for the Fed's global last resort lending.

First, it proved to be very large. In 2007–2008, the Fed advanced dollars to first a narrow and then a broad circle of central banks and ratcheted up the agreed amounts into the fall of 2008. In October, the Fed's agreed to extend

credit to five central banks without ex ante limits and the aggregate amounts advanced reached almost $600 billion. It took most of a trillion dollars to backstop just 5 percent of the dollar liabilities of non-US banks. In 2020, the amounts quickly reached almost $500 billion. This was another Kindleberger moment.

Second, such a scale broke the link between central bank swaps and potential IMF credit. Available IMF credit fell well short of the swaps. The Fed reassured the US Congress that the partner central bank took the risk of (secured) lending to the borrowing non-US banks, but in lending without limit the Fed's trust in the partner central bank was complete. Nor was there in general a backstop at the national level. For instance, the maximum swap to the ECB well exceeded the foreign-exchange reserves of the ECB and the Eurosystem's national central banks. Central bank swaps stood on their own feet as never before.

Finally, the international last resort lending in 2008 overwhelmingly took the form of dollars, and thus it centered on the Fed. In the 1960s and 1970s, the Fed had been both lender and borrower in the reciprocal network of swaps; intra-European swaps were at times very sizeable from the 1960s until the introduction of the euro.[4] In 2008, the ECB and Swiss National Bank (SNB) also extended swaps to some European central banks to backstop, for example, respectively, Swedish banks' funding of euro mortgages in Latvia and Polish banks' funding of Swiss franc mortgages. But these regional operations were not large. Dollar predominance in private international banking made the Fed the global lender of last resort.

Non-US Banks in Global Dollar Intermediation

To understand the Fed as a global dollar lender of last resort, some perspective on the role of non-US banks in global dollar intermediation is useful. In the 50 years to 2008, the dollar's domain had extended from the United States to Western Europe and then across the world. In the rest of the world, firms borrowed dollars from banks to finance trade, inventories, and their capital stock, governments borrowed to fund their debts and in some places, households even took on dollar-denominated home mortgages. On the eve of the GFC, nonbanks outside the United States had borrowed almost $4 trillion from banks (Fig. 13.1, left panel). This was about double the sum of euro-denominated loans to nonbanks outside the euro area. As a currency for international borrowing, the dollar stood head and shoulders above its nearest rival.

Banks headquartered outside the United States did the bulk of this dollar lending to the rest of the world. To fund these and other dollar assets, non-US banks had by 2008 accumulated $13 trillion of dollar liabilities, almost $10 trillion of which from nonbanks (Fig. 13.1, right panel).[5] European and Japanese banks were the most prominent among the non-US banks. These banks actively managed these liabilities, depending on short-term funding to a considerable extent.

Although the overwhelming share of the dollar liabilities of non-US banks was raised outside the United States, their biggest single source of dollar funding in 2008 was US dollar money market funds (MMFs). US dollar MMFs lent non-US banks at least $1.2 trillion, or at least an eighth of their nonbank funding.[6]

Despite three decades of generally stable operation, MMFs were fragile by design. They operated without capital at the level of the fund, although losses could be covered by the fund sponsor. Despite the absence of capital, the US Securities and Exchange Commission allowed them to redeem their shares within limits as if they were worth $1 par. Calling these intermediaries shadow banks, as is often done, is at most half-right, however. These intermediaries to a considerable extent simply bundled together funding from firms and households to buy the IOUs of non-US banks. Shadow bank suggests

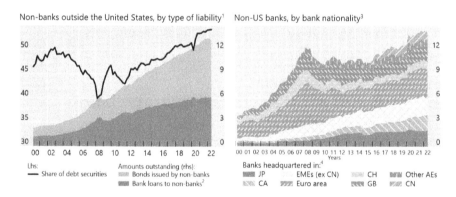

Fig. 13.1 On-balance sheet US dollar liabilities of non-banks outside of the United States and non-US banks. Amounts outstanding, in USD trillions. (1) Non-banks comprise non-bank financials, non-financial corporations, governments, households and international organisations. (2) Loans by LBS-reporting banks to non-bank borrowers, including non-bank financial entities, comprise cross-border plus local loans. (3) Non-US banks' US dollar-denominated liabilities raised in any of the 47 BIS reporting countries (including the United States). Excludes intragroup positions but includes liabilities to other (unaffiliated) banks. From end-2015, includes positions reported by China and Russia (*Sources* Dealogic; Euroclear; Thomson Reuters; Xtrakter; BIS locational banking statistics; BIS calculations)

an intermediary that competes with banks, not an intermediary that interacts symbiotically with certain banks.

In addition, non-US banks in effect borrowed dollars at generally short maturities invisibly in the foreign-exchange swap market. For instance, a German bank could take a euro deposit and exchange it for dollars with a forward purchase of the euros against the dollars, in effect borrowing dollars against euro collateral. Then the bank could use the dollars to fund a dollar loan or a dollar bond holding. The amounts could only be roughly estimated, but banks had used such swaps to fund themselves in dollars on the order of a trillion dollars.[7]

In the foreign-exchange swap market, big non-US banks mostly served as intermediaries, putting their balance sheets between those lending and borrowing dollars against other currencies. Among their most important counterparties are insurance companies and pension funds outside the United States who hold US dollar bonds and US equities on a hedged basis. For such institutional investors, the hedge would typically consist of a short-term forward sale of dollars against the home currency. These would be rolled at maturity as long as necessary. As a result, there tends to be a mismatch between the long-term dollar security that is being hedged and the hedge.

In sum, by the twenty-first century the dollar had come to play an outsized role in international banking in a competitive market in which the winners were non-US banks. These depended on unsecured and secured short-term dollar funding markets and the ability to borrow dollars against other currencies. Both sources of dollars proved vulnerabilities.

The Fed as Global Dollar Backstop: The 1960s Precedents

Shortly after non-US banks began to borrow and lend dollars outside the United States, funding strains emerged. Year-end window-dressing, financial turbulence, and war could all put up pressure on dollar funding and lead to unwelcome rises in offshore dollar yields. Recent archival work with Catherine Schenk has brought to light the use of dollar swaps to counter these offshore dollar funding strains in the 1960s. Thus, the international lender of last resort operations of 2007–2008 had important precedents 40 plus years before.[8] These formed an important part of the Basel-based central bank cooperaton that inspired Kindleberger to prescribe unlimited swaps.

As described in the last chapter, in the mid-1960s, Charles Coombs, head of foreign-exchange operations at the Federal Reserve Bank of New York,

persuaded European central banks to enter into swap arrangements mostly as a means to defend the dollar's fixed exchange rates. But right from the start, the New York Fed and the BIS agreed to a separate swap line designed to provide dollars to the BIS. The intention was precisely to manage strains in the fast-growing offshore dollar market. The operations that used this swap line lasted only a few years, but they anticipated the use of swaps in the present century, and also point to a more multilateral approach.

From 1965 through 1968, dollar funding strains could appear with end-year window-dressing operations, as Swiss banks, in particular, sought temporarily to replace somewhat mysterious dollar assets with solid Swiss franc assets to be reported in their annual reports. In addition, surprising events like the Six Day War or the devaluation of the pound sterling later in 1967 could disturb dollar funding markets. In retrospect, these were mild strains, but they could put upward pressure on dollar rates in London and other offshore banking centers if left untreated. Higher dollar rates in London could in turn disturb the US domestic dollar market, sending signals regarding dollar interest rates at odds with Fed policy.

To reduce such pressure, the New York Fed extended its operations abroad to match the spread of dollar markets across the Atlantic Ocean. The Fed advanced dollars to the BIS, and then money market dealers at this central bank condominium placed unsecured term deposits with mostly European banks offshore. The BIS played not just a coordinating role, as Saleem Bahaj and Ricardo Reis describe it, but acted as a principal, taking the risk of lending on an unsecured basis to the commercial banks.[9] In some cases, the SNB was involved as well. In this manner, central banks sought to restrain the rise of dollar yields.

The precedent for the twenty-first century lender of last resort is clear. In the mid-1960s, Federal Reserve credit flowed abroad to stabilize the funding of mostly non-US banks in the offshore dollar market. One difference from 2007 to 2008 was that a multilateral central banking organization served as intermediary between the Fed and the private banks that ultimately received the Fed credit.

Backstopping Global Dollar Banking, 2007–2008

To the vast offshore dollar intermediation described above, non-US banks in the 2000s added investments in US private mortgage-backed securities. They did so in manifold ways, as discussed in Chapter 2. They borrowed dollars in the United States to fund 'production line' and 'warehouse' holdings in their

US securities affiliates. They borrowed in the United States to fund holdings in their offshore offices. And they borrowed dollars offshore to fund holdings at offshore offices.[10] Non-US banks' exposure to risky privately packaged mortgages drove the foreign-held share of such securities to over 40 percent.

As US house prices peaked in 2006 and fell in 2007, the US real estate mania passed into distress. Bankers uneasily wondered at each others' holdings of, and prospective losses on, fiendishly complicated securities backed by US mortgages.

Central bank reserve managers began in the latter half of 2007 to withdraw some of the $600 billion in liquid dollar reserves held in offshore deposits at what had been the best-rated banks. These credit-conscious reserve managers responded to news indicating that such seemingly strong non-US banks had sizeable exposures to highly leveraged US mortgages. In the latter half of 2007, they reduced deposits with Swiss banks and proceeded subsequently to reduce deposits with most other European banks.[11] It was a slow run, by the standards of the later run after the Lehman failure on MMFs, and in turn their run on non-US banks.

Unease turned into distress on 9 August 2007. BNP Paribas chillingly announced the suspension of redemptions from funds holding US private mortgage-backed securities that were hedged into euro, citing 'the complete evaporation of liquidity in certain market segments of the US securitization market [that] has made it impossible to value certain assets fairly, regardless of their quality or credit rating.'[12] The ECB quickly extended €95 billion to banks in an attempt to keep the interbank market working. The Fed cut its discount rate on bilateral loans, but banks avoided one by one approaches to the discount window, lest they bear the stigma of needing such central bank credit.

Recall that European banks had a large structural need to borrow dollars, and did much at short maturity relative to the maturity of their dollar assets. If they, like the BNP Paribas funds, were holding unknown amounts of private mortgage-backed securities that were impossible to value, how could they roll over trillions of dollars in short-term dollar funding?

The Fed ultimately supported the dollar funding of non-US banks in three ways. First, the Fed set up a stigma-free version of its discount window, on which non-US banks drew heavily, and supplemented it with parallel dollar provision in Europe funded with swaps with the ECB and SNB. Second, the Fed used its emergency powers to stop the run on MMFs that heavily funded non-US banks and to support commercial paper. And, third, breaking the link to the discount window, the Fed swapped dollars with its partner central

banks in ultimately unlimited amounts so that they could provide dollars offshore to non-US banks.

In September 2007, as the Fed considered proposals to turn its discount window into a broad auction facility (similar to the usual ECB facilities), discussions began on a central bank swap between the Fed and the ECB. As later recalled by Fed and Treasury officials, 'The ECB initially sought to strike a posture that it was merely supporting the Fed's efforts to counter US-centric and dollar-centric stresses, rather than embracing its role as the Fed's full partner in fighting a crisis that was centered in the United States but that had truly global dimensions.'[13] If the Fed were to auction off 28-day discount window credit (in the Term Auction Facility or TAF), then the ECB would be happy to join the operation, in effect serving as the 13th Federal Reserve Bank, in the phrase of Francesco Papadia, then head of ECB operations.[14] In December 2007, the Fed and ECB agreed on a swap that would allow the latter, in coordination with the TAF operations, to lend up to $20 billion to banks in Europe against euro-denominated collateral. The Fed and the SNB agreed $4 billion.

Until the failure of Lehman Brothers in September 2008, non-US banks obtained more dollars from the TAF, using their US assets as collateral for Fed credit at the discount window, than from the ECB and SNB, using European collateral. TAF borrowers did not know that Bloomberg and Fox News would eventually succeed in 2011 in a freedom of information request for full disclosure of the TAF transactions: names, amounts, dates, etc. As a result, we know that, on the eve of the Lehman failure, the Fed had extended most of the TAF credit of $150 billion to foreign banks' US operations,[15] while the ECB swap line had risen to $55 billion and the SNB to $6 billion.[16] The discount window at the Second District Federal Reserve Bank of New York was doing the heavy lifting until September 2008.

Lehman's failure set off a run on non-US banks' most important single dollar source, MMFs. One of the oldest MMFs, the Reserve Primary Fund, 'broke the buck,' showing a net asset value below a dollar as it accounted for losses on Lehman commercial paper. The fund had no deep-pocketed sponsor that could make up the credit loss, as had been done before and after under these circumstances. Institutional investors redeemed shares in other MMFs holding bank and corporate paper. Within days, non-US banks had lost at least $175 billion of MMF funding, despite a rapid succession of policy measures.[17] This was a fast run.

The resulting 'dollar shortage' implied a rise in dollar interest rates payable in the rest of the world, in both cash markets and the foreign exchange

forward market. Non-US banks bid up Libor, the London benchmark short-term dollar interest rate for (increasingly scarce) unsecured funding. The rate payable by those borrowing dollars against the euro and other currencies soared in the foreign-exchange swap market. These borrowed dollars became the marginal financing for dollar assets held by banks. And as the premium on dollars rose, it boosted the cost of hedging trillions of dollars of dollar bonds and US equities held by institutional investors outside the United States. Punishing dollar rates for the rest of the world thus not only threatened tighter financing terms for firms and governments that had borrowed $4 trillion from banks. Such rates also risked banks' and institutional investors' liquidating dollar assets in fire sales.

The US authorities took emergency measures to stop the run on MMFs, and thereby stop their run on non-US banks. The policies included a Treasury guarantee the par value of MMFs, and Fed facilities to buy and underwrite commercial paper, both of which would reduce the rollover risk of holding such paper. In the first instance, these were domestic lender of last resort operations that sought to stabilize MMFs. But these policy interventions to support MMFs and the commercial paper market served at one remove as international lender of last resort operations: ending runs on the riskier MMFs ended their liquidation of claims on non-US banks.

After the Lehman failure, central banks expanded their swap lines to replace the private dollar funding that non-US banks were losing. Initially, the swap line with the ECB was doubled to $110 billion, and that to the SNB was quadrupled. The Fed agreed new lines for the Bank of Japan, Bank of England, and the Bank of Canada totaling $110 billion. On 29 September, central banks agreed to at least double all these swap lines.

On 13 October central banks announced fatefully that 'sizes of the reciprocal currency arrangements (swap lines) between the Federal Reserve and the BoE, the ECB, and the SNB [and the Bank of Japan on the following day] will be increased to accommodate whatever quantity of US dollar funding is demanded [at fixed rates].' As Jaime Caruana, General Manager of the BIS noted later, 'the extension of such swaps in unlimited amounts represents a turn in central bank cooperation that the founders of the BIS [in the 1920s] would have found unimaginable.'[18]

Non-US banks revealed a preference for the Fed's international lending of last resort through swaps over drawing on the domestic lending of last resort through the discount window. That is, as the swaps became unlimited, non-US banks responded by reducing their takings from the TAF even as they ramped up their takings from the swaps.[19] To continue with the metaphor, credit from the 13th Federal Reserve Bank displaced that from

the 2nd District Bank in New York. Non-US banks thereby retained scarce US collateral that would allow them to draw on the Fed's discount window late in the day. The credit risk of lending to non-US banks shifted from the Federal Reserve to the ECB and other central banks.

At the peak, the Fed had swapped almost $600 billion, mostly to the ECB, the SNB, the Bank of England, and a few other central banks. These in turn distributed the funds to banks that could offer collateral that these central banks found satisfactory.

The Fed's open-handedness worked to lower the short-term dollar rates that mattered most. After Lehman's collapse, expected overnight rates had trended unevenly down (lower line in the upper panel of Fig. 13.2), and the Fed lowered its target for the federal funds rate by 50 basis points at its October 8 meeting. But the Fed easing was not making itself felt in rates paid by US corporations on their bank loans or by US households on their adjustable-rate mortgages. Libor doubled from less than 3 percent before Lehman's failure. The spread between the Fed's expected overnight rates and Libor hit 4 percent (shaded area in the lower panel of Fig. 13.2). After 13 October, without ex ante limits on the swaps to the key central banks, this spread fell by half within weeks.[20] The compression of 3-month Libor might have happened even faster had the central banks offered unlimited dollar funding at this maturity in October, as they later did in November 2008.

Fig. 13.2 Central bank swaps lower dollar Libor, late 2008 (*Source* Refinitiv Datastream; Federal Reserve; author's calculations)

Likewise, the rate premium for borrowing dollars against foreign-exchange collateral narrowed in response to the expansion of the swap lines.[21] That is, the rate at which non-US banks could borrow dollars against the euro, yen, and other currencies fell back toward outright dollar borrowing rates like Libor or repurchase rates. Institutional investors outside the United States were able to roll over hedges of US securities holdings, instead of engaging in fire sales. Unlimited swaps effectively backstopped both the offshore deposit market and the forward foreign-exchange market.[22]

Often the motivation for the swaps is ascribed to the Fed's goal of financial stability,[23] and Daniel McDowell in his book, *Brother Can You Spare a Billion* stands out in recognizing their key role in fixing the Fed's monetary transmission to the US economy.[24] Libor priced not only trillions of dollars of derivative contracts but also, it bears repeating, US corporate loans and US adjustable-rate mortgages. While the October 2008 FOMC meeting dwelled on the difficulty of controlling the opening federal funds rate in New York given upward pressure offshore, the transmission of the Fed's policy rate to the domestic real economy required a lower 3-month Libor, not just hitting the overnight fed funds target.[25] Non-US banks dominated the panel of banks that reported Libor at 11 a.m., 6 a.m. New York time. So the New York Fed needed to ease term funding conditions by dawn for non-US banks offshore, and the swaps put dollars into the hands of central bankers in Frankfurt, London, and Zurich to do just that job.

Ultimately, the Fed reconciled its domestic Congressional mandate with its providing a backstop to offshore dollar banking. It extended hundreds of billions of dollars in central bank credit to stabilize trillions of offshore dollars for which non-US banks were liable. It did so not only to achieve the global public good of financial stability but also to assure the transmission of its monetary policy to US households and businesses.

The Fed Backstops Global Dollar Banking and Bonds, 2020

When a very different funding crisis next struck amid pandemia in March 2020, the Fed not only returned to its playbook but also extended it very significantly. Again, it sought to stop the run on MMFs. Again, it activated the swap lines with major central banks and extended them more broadly. But this time, severe disruption of the dollar bond market led the Fed to become a buyer of last resort in the bond market. Without targeting foreign involvement in the dollar bond market per se, domestic Fed bond

purchases accommodated sales of Treasury securities by foreign central banks and helped to stabilize prices of trillions of dollars of foreign-issued dollar bonds. Indirectly, the Fed backstopped the global dollar bond market.

When in March 2020 market participants began to understand the challenge of the Covid pandemic, they responded in a dash for cash. Firms worried that revenues would crash to zero, leaving cash flows deeply negative. The 'cash' resources of the corporate treasury, often invested more for yield than immediate availability, suddenly needed to be really liquid. And firms drew down credit lines with banks to bulk up on bank deposits. Banks did not suffer runs, as in 2008, but they prepared for large cash calls on committed lines of credit.

As in 2008, the riskier MMFs suffered runs. Investing in bank and corporate IOUs, 'prime' MMFs experienced redemptions of $125 billion in March 2020, 11 percent of their assets.[26] This was a smaller liquidation than in 2008, when this segment of MMFs was larger. This time none broke the buck or impeded liquidations. Still, as MMFs paid out to redeem shares, remaining shareholders worried that dwindling liquid assets would trigger 'gates'—constraints on redemptions mandated by regulators after 2008. A reform to deal with liquidity strains on MMFs turned out to accelerate runs.[27]

As in 2008, the run on MMFs had knock-on effects on other markets. It threatened to close the commercial paper market, a key source of short-term financing for firms. And, as in 2008, the run on MMFs left non-US banks scrambling for dollars. Onshore and offshore MMF funding of non-US banks dropped by $200 billion in February–March 2020.[28]

The dash for cash did not just disrupt money markets, however. It also led to the selling of US dollar bonds. This selling not only destabilized the global benchmark bond market—the US Treasury bond market—but also the main funding source for US corporations.

As background, US corporate bonds outstanding had grown very considerably since the GFC, in part as an *intended* consequence of the Fed's repeated rounds of bond buying. The Fed encouraged US corporations to issue bonds by buying Treasury and agency mortgage securities, reducing the so-called term premium demanded for locking in funding for years at a fixed rate. As an *unintended* consequence of the same Fed bond buying, firms, and governments outside the United States had also issued dollar bonds in size. As a result, the rest of the world's borrowing in the dollar had shifted over the previous decade away from bank loans to dollar bonds (Fig. 13.1, left panel).

In March 2020, heavy selling of bonds came from three sides. First, hedge funds dumped US Treasuries. Highly leveraged so-called relative value

funds held relatively cheap Treasury bonds (financed in the repo market) against short positions in Treasury bond futures. The normally modest spread between these two—certain cash bonds could be periodically delivered into maturing bond futures, linking their prices—widened amid rising volatility, increasing margins, and deteriorating liquidity. This wrong way move cost the highly leveraged funds dearly. Losses in turn forced them to deleverage by selling Treasuries in the hundreds of billions of dollars in March. Other hedge fund strategies magnified the moves.[29] Lots of leverage among holders could make even a safe asset risky. The data are partial, but something well over $200 billion in hedge fund selling is a reasonable estimate.[30]

Second, foreign central banks also dumped Treasuries. Recalling the pressure on their dollar borrowing banks and firms in 2008, and in many cases intervening in the foreign-exchange market to support their currencies by selling dollars, they sought to turn Treasury holdings into immediately useful bank deposits. Treasury data show $244 billion in US Treasury bond sales, or 3.3 percent of holdings, by foreign officials in March–May 2020.[31]

Third, responding to and magnifying these sales, households staged the largest and sharpest liquidation of bond mutual funds in memory, and the run forced fund managers to sell bonds in the market. Since the GFC, low interest rates had encouraged US households to reach for yield by buying bond mutual funds. US bond fund holdings as a share of the corporate bond market rose from less than a tenth to almost a fifth. Facing the uncertainties of pandemic and turmoil in the bond market, households liquidated an unprecedented 5.6 percent of bond fund assets in March.[32] One interpretation is that households originally viewed this investment as only slightly riskier than a bank deposit but in March 2020 suddenly viewed it as risky.[33] Another interpretation is that given the hedge fund and foreign selling of Treasury bonds and their resultant yield spike in early to mid-March 2020, bond fund holders redeemed about what one would expect in response to recently experienced price declines.[34] In any case, bond fund managers had little choice but to pass on the selling pressure to the bond market. The easiest bonds to sell were US Treasuries, and funds sold $260 billion in the first quarter of 2020.[35]

Stepping back, then, the Fed faced big runs on money and bond mutual funds and widespread dumping of US bonds. Holders of the riskier MMFs sought out, pulling dollars out of non-US banks. The Fed dealt with this as it had in 2008. But what to do in the face of large selling of US Treasury securities and an incipient run on bond mutual funds? This required a new playbook. At risk was the main source of funding for US corporations—and for nonbank dollar borrowers outside the United States as well.

The Fed responded with a combination of old and new policies. It dealt with the disruption of the money markets along the lines of its response in 2008 but innovated in its response to the disruption of the bond markets. To calm bond markets, the Fed became the buyer of last resort in a manner that had profound international implications. To underscore: the Fed did not target foreign holdings of US bonds or foreign-issued dollar bonds in particular. Nevertheless, the effect of the Fed bond buying on foreign holdings of US bonds and foreign-issued dollar bonds amounts to an extension of its international lender of last resort operations.

The Fed quickly consulted its playbook from 2008 to stabilize MMFs and thereby to stabilize their funding of non-US banks. The Fed rolled out facilities to inject its credit into the commercial paper market as a buyer of last resort.[36] In order to increase the confidence of MMF investors, on March 17 it revived a program to underwrite new issues of commercial paper, reassuring investors that maturing paper could be rolled over. On March 18, it revived a 2008 facility to allow the Federal Reserve Bank of Boston in effect to buy outstanding commercial paper (not just asset-backed commercial paper as in 2008) held by MMFs (technically lending on a non-recourse basis to banks to buy the paper).

To enable non-US banks to access dollars and thereby replace the loss of funding from MMFs, the Fed reactivated the swap lines. In 2007–2008, the Fed had taken a year to widen access to larger amounts for more central banks, for longer maturities, and in more frequent operations. Playbook in hand, the Fed took these steps in days in March 2020.

Once again, as non-US banks scrambled for dollars, Libor began lifting off from the Fed's policy interest rate. Even as the Fed lowered its federal fund policy rate, as reflected in the expected overnight rate (the overnight index swap or OIS, plotted as the lower line in the upper panel of Fig. 13.3), the key 3-month Libor rate began to rise on 12 March.

Swiftly, the Fed acted to keep the transmission of its interest rate policy to the real economy from breaking down by extending its credit offshore to bring down Libor. The very next day, the Fed eased its interest rate on central bank swaps from OIS+50 basis points to OIS+25 basis points for five core central banks with standing swaps; it also offered 84-day swaps. Libor fell but then began to rise again and the Fed extended the swaps to the other nine central banks on March 19 and started daily operations. The start of daily swap operations on March 23 marked the local maximum of Libor, which fell to within 25 basis points of OIS by early May. With these swift moves, Fed credit extended to central banks through swaps rose much more

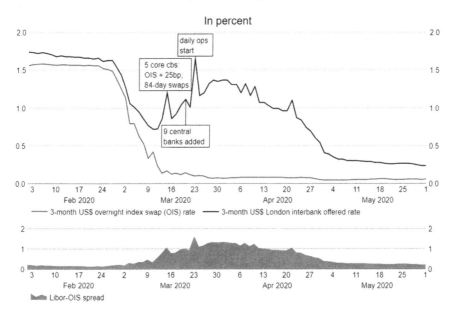

Fig. 13.3 Central bank swaps lower dollar Libor, early 2020 (*Source* Refinitiv Datastream; Federal Reserve; author's calculations)

sharply in 2020 than in 2008 but peaked at a lower level at less than $500 billion.

The political reaction to the use of swaps in 2020 confounded widespread fears that de facto the Fed faced a higher political hurdle to mobilize the swaps. In 2008 and after, the Fed fielded sharp questions from Congress regarding the central bank swaps.[37] In the end, the new banking legislation known as the Dodd-Frank Act did nothing to restrict the legal ability of the Fed to extend its credit to other central banks through swaps. This absence of constraint stood in contrast to new constraints on the Fed's use of its emergency lending powers, which proscribed deals for individual firms (as with Bear Stearns in March 2008 and AIG in September 2008) and required Treasury assent. Still, there was a practical political question about the use of swaps. In the event, central bank swaps caused little controversy in 2020.

The balance of the swaps shifted from Europe in 2008 to Asia, that is, Japan, in 2020. In 2008, the ECB borrowed about half of the dollars advance by the Fed; in 2020, the Bank of Japan did. This partly reflected the retrenchment of European banks after the traumas, near-death experiences, and nationalizations of 2008. It also reflected the fact that the international banking footprint of Japanese banks[38] had expanded since the GFC.[39] Strong growth in holdings of dollar bonds on a hedged basis by Asian insurance

companies also boosted demand to borrow dollars in the foreign-exchange market.[40]

In response to Treasury bond selling and the spike in Treasury rates, the Fed entered the market as a determined, rapid, and heavy buyer. The operating instruction to the open-market desk at the New York Fed charged it with buying Treasury and agency securities 'in the amounts needed' to restore the proper functioning of the market.[41] In the three weeks between 11 March and 2 April, the Fed bought no less than $900 billion of Treasury and agency securities.[42] Thus, Fed more than offset the domestic and foreign official selling of US Treasuries of as much as $800 billion over a longer period. From the standpoint of the foreign official holders of US Treasury securities, the Fed purchases allowed them to turn securities with wildly fluctuating prices set in suddenly and surprisingly illiquid markets into bank deposits or secured placements with the New York Fed (repos).

Watching central banks selling US Treasuries, only to see them sit on much of the cash at the New York Fed, led the Fed at the end of March to offer overnight advances to central banks using US Treasuries as collateral at a rate above private repo rates. This little-used facility, dubbed the Foreign and International Monetary Authorities (FIMA) Repo Facility, is discussed below.

Dislocations were evident in the corporate bond market as well and the Fed responded speedily. As mutual funds sold corporate bonds, these went to big discounts to levels implied by credit derivatives. Such market dynamics threatened to cut off US firms' major source of financing of investment and hiring, and even to cause defaults if maturing bonds could not be refinanced. On March 17, the Fed announced that it would use its emergency powers to lend to its primary dealers, i.e., its bond market counterparties, as it had in 2008. This gave them an assurance of funding that would allow them to make markets and arbitrage cash and derivatives markets. On March 20 the Fed extended the first loans to the primary dealers using these emergency powers. The primary dealers offered corporate bonds as collateral for the Fed advances, suggesting that the Fed credit was getting through the dealers to support the corporate bond market.

The Fed then took an unprecedented step as a corporate bond buyer of last resort. On March 23, it announced that it would buy investment grade US corporate bonds. The principle of the Fed buying corporate commercial paper at money market tenors had been set in 2008 and reinforced earlier in the month with the revival of the commercial paper buying program. What was unprecedented was the Fed going beyond the money market, the usual focus of its operations. The Fed was backstopping the longer-maturity private bonds on which US firms rely most for market funding.

The Fed's terms for the corporate bond purchases showed a sensitivity to the political hazard of being seen to help firms without a direct stake in the US economy. To be purchased, a bond issuer could be foreign-owned but had to be incorporated in the United States, have significant US operations and a majority of its employees based in the United States.[43] This targeted intention, however, did not preclude that the program would indirectly lift the prices of dollar bonds issued by foreign firms that did not meet these criteria.

More surprising was the announcement on April 9 that the Fed would buy junk bonds, the low-rated bonds of more leveraged and more risky firms. After all, the Fed as bank regulator had been flagging for years to banks the risks of lending to firms that private equity firms were loading up with debt, both bank loans and junk bonds. Indeed, ultimately the Fed bought mutual finds designed to hold the whole gamut of junk bonds, so the Fed bought some bonds that had been issued by firms that the Fed had cautioned banks not to lend to.[44]

In any case, one can imagine that the corporate bond purchases could affect non-Treasury dollar bond prices in one of two ways. The Fed buying could be a thumb on the scale of just those bonds purchased. There was certainly evidence for such: the Fed's announcement highlighted its intention to lower yields on short- to medium-term bonds, and their yields fell more markedly, for instance.

Alternatively, the effect of the Fed buying could diffuse from those bonds purchased across the spectrum of dollar bonds embodying credit risk. This diffusion could work through portfolio substitution by investors, as they sold into the prospective Fed bid for US corporate bonds and bought cheaper bonds not targeted by the Fed.

The prices of the biggest ETFs for investment grade US corporate bonds, junk US corporate bonds, and emerging market dollar bonds broadly support the second view. Prices of the ETFs for investment grade bonds (LQD) and emerging market bonds (EMB) had both bottomed between the Fed announcement of its lending to the primary dealers late on March 17 and its doing so on March 20 (Fig. 13.4). This timing points to funding liquidity rather than credit concerns, reinforcing the impression conveyed by the gap between US corporate cash bond prices and those of the corresponding credit derivatives. When the Fed announced that it would buy investment grade bonds, the price of their ETF rose for three days. With a one-day lag, both the junk bond and emerging market ETF prices rose for three days as well. When the Fed announced that it would buy junk bonds on April 9 and upped its overall maximum of corporate bond purchases, the prices of all three ETFs

jumped the same day. By mid-June 2020, the prices of all three ETFs had recovered substantially. Though the Fed bought corporate bonds and did not buy any of the emerging market dollar bonds, their price performance did not much differ. The effect of the Fed's purchase of US corporate bonds seemed to diffuse widely.

Flows into bond funds also point to the conclusion that the Fed's promise to purchase US corporate bonds turned around flows into global bond funds. Outflows from global bond funds seemed to respond more quickly to the Fed announcement than did outflows from US investment grade bonds (Fig. 13.5). But broadly flows into the bonds that the Fed never bought tracked those of the ones that it did buy. With the flows, as with the prices, the effect of the Fed announcement seemed to diffuse beyond US corporate bonds to dollar bonds from issuers in the rest of the world.

In sum, in March 2020, the combination of the Fed's lending of last resort to securities dealers and its buying of last resort of US corporate bonds had an unintended consequence. Not only US corporate bonds but also global dollar bonds bottomed in price between the announcement of the primary dealer lending and the first loans. One can interpret this observation as suggesting that Fed credit allowed the primary dealers to make markets in all sorts of dollar bonds embodying credit risk, both domestic and foreign. And the

Fig. 13.4 Emerging market dollar bonds rise as the Federal Reserve buys US corporate bonds (*Source* Refinitiv Datastream; Federal Reserve; author's calculations)

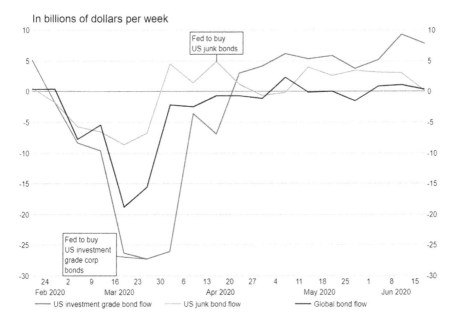

Fig. 13.5 Global bond flows recover as the Federal Reserve buys US corporate bonds (*Source* Refinitiv Datastream; Federal Reserve; Investment Company Institute; author's calculations)

subsequently similar price movements in the US corporate and global bonds point to investors' evident treatment of domestic and foreign dollar bonds as close substitutes in their credit portfolios. Lending to bond dealers and buying bonds domestically, the Fed halted an incipient run on funds holding dollar bonds issued by non-US obligors. Stopping the outflows from global bond funds in turn prevented fire sales of dollar bonds issued by borrowers outside the United States. In effect, if not in intention, the Fed backstopped the global dollar bond market.

The Who's Who of Swap Lines

In extending swap lines, the Fed has drawn three lines. The Fed has established standing swap lines with Canada, the Bank of England, the ECB, the Bank of Japan, and the SNB. These lines have no ex ante fixed limits in terms of the number of dollars extended. Drawing a second line, the Fed has established temporary lines with five advanced economies—the main Nordic countries (Denmark, Norway, and Sweden), Australia and New Zealand—and four emerging economies—Brazil, Mexico, Singapore, and South Korea.

The Fed has drawn a third line that includes any central bank that holds US Treasuries in custody at the New York Fed. Under the FIMA repo facility, any central bank with US Treasury securities held in custody at the New York Fed can raise overnight funding from the Fed using those securities as collateral.[45] Little used, the facility became a standing one in July 2021. It complements the New York Fed's reverse repo pool, which allows central banks to invest overnight cash.

As might be readily imagined, such line drawing has led to a great deal of discussion among all kinds of observers. One line of inquiry has been the reverse engineering of the Fed's choices: trade relations, banking exposure, politico-military relations, and UN voting alignment, among other factors, have attracted attention.[46]

An aspect of the who's who that has not received the attention that it deserves is the key currency aspect, that is, the coverage by the Fed's central bank swaps of private foreign-exchange market swaps against dollars. Recall from the description of non-US banks in dollar intermediation above that non-US banks borrow and lend dollars not only on balance sheet but also off-balance sheet against foreign currencies. In choosing its central bank counterparties, the Fed's focus on key currencies has resulted in quite high coverage of the largest segment, namely foreign-exchange swaps, of the huge global foreign-exchange market.

The central bank survey of foreign-exchange markets in April 2019 found daily total turnover of $6.5 trillion, of which swaps accounted for about half. More than 90 percent of the swaps had the dollar on one side of the transaction. Thus, every working day in April 2019, dollars were borrowed and lent against other currencies to the extent of almost $3 trillion. The currencies of the five central banks with standing swap lines with the Fed account for two-thirds of the daily dollar lending through swaps. The currencies of the other nine central banks chosen by the Fed account for another 16 percent of dollar swap transactions (Fig. 13.6). Overall, the coverage of the currencies of the Fed's 14 partner central banks in foreign-exchange swaps against dollars is five-sixths.

Thus, the standing swap lines draw what may seem to be a narrow circle around five central banks, but actually draw a broad circle in terms of the currencies against which dollars are borrowed in the foreign-exchange market.[47] Adding the temporary swap lines with another nine central banks makes for a very broad circle, judged by dollar borrowing against foreign exchange.

This perspective leads to a new interpretation of the finding of studies that the central bank swaps, especially in unlimited size, succeeded in lowering

- ■ EUR, JPY, GBP, CHF, CAD ■ AUD, DKK, NOK, NZD, SEK
- ▪ BRL, KRW, MXP, SGD Other

Fig. 13.6 The Federal Reserve's central bank swap lines cover most foreign exchange market swaps. Share of currencies by central bank swap line status in $2.9 trillion of daily dollar swaps, April 2019

dollar borrowing costs in the respective currencies compared to such costs in 'untreated' currencies.[48] If the problem is the global tightening of dollar rates, then the central bank swaps involving the key currencies can solve most of the problem. And the temporary swaps take the share of the problem solved up to five-sixths.

Even this way of looking at the swaps is liable to understate their effectiveness. In 2020, when the ECB obtained dollars from the Fed and lent them out to banks in the euro area, much of the proceeds were indeed lent in the foreign-exchange market in swaps against euros.[49] But by no means all were so lent.[50]

A particularly suggestive case was the Swedish kroner in March 2020. The premium on dollars lent against the Swedish kroner in the foreign-exchange market tracked that against the euro very closely.[51] In particular, the two narrowed in lockstep as the ECB drew on its Fed swap to make dollars available to banks in the euro area. This was days before the Riksbank had agreed a swap with the New York Fed and weeks before the Riksbank's first dollar-providing operation. A Riksbank study concluded: 'The foreign-exchange swap market in Europe, including Sweden, started to function better particularly once the ECB commenced its extensive dollar auctions.'[52]

How could this have happened? Among the dollar takers from the ECB could have been affiliates of Swedish banks in Frankfurt that used the dollars to lend against Swedish kroner in the swap market. Or a French bank might have seen more return in lending dollars obtained from the ECB against kroner than against the euro. In either case, a Swedish insurance company could have been the counterparty, rolling over its dollar borrowing through a swap against kroner in order to maintain a currency hedge on a US dollar

bond holding. As the Fed provided dollars to the ECB, the cost of the dollar hedge paid by the Swedish insurer normalized.

In general, what starts as an official swap of dollars against euros can ultimately fund a private swap of dollars against any currency. Dollar borrowing costs in the currency of the central bank providing the dollars might be the first to show the effect. But the effect of the Fed's swaps with the selected central banks can diffuse and lower dollar borrowing costs against other currencies. Such diffusion may have worked better in 2020 than it did in 2008, when big banks were not well capitalized, and possible credit losses inhibited transactions. One should not be surprised that the effect of the selected central bank swaps can spread widely across currencies in the foreign-exchange market.[53]

The upshot is that it may not make such a large difference as is generally supposed that the Fed offers most of its swaps to a handful of central banks, given the large share of their respective key currencies in the foreign-exchange market. Note the family resemblance between two suggestions in this chapter: that the seeming narrowness of the choice of central bank counterparties for swaps and the Fed's restriction of last resort bond buying to US bonds may not have mattered as much as one might suppose.

The Fed decides with which central banks to establish swap lines and which dollar bonds to buy, but market participants decide how broadly the effect of Fed credit spreads. Despite the lines that the Fed drew, it managed in 2020 to ameliorate offshore dollar borrowing costs broadly, in banking and bond markets alike.

In 2008 and 2020, the Fed proved willing and able to follow Kindleberger's rule for the international lender of last resort, swapping dollars without limit to central banks to onlend to non-US banks. In doing so, the Fed not only provided the global public good of financial stability but also ensured the effectiveness of its domestic monetary policy. In 2020, the Fed's unprecedented domestic bond market operations stabilized the global dollar bond market. Chapter 15 returns to these findings to pose two questions. How might central bank swaps support cooperative central bank operations in the global dollar bond market? And could politics constrain the Fed's provision of the public good of international last resort lending?

'Overfunding' by the Treasury: a complement to the lender of last resort?
A modern bank run is from bank deposits into Treasury bills as the ultimate safe asset, rather than into cash or gold. This was the case in 2008, but not in 2020, when the liquidity of bank deposits was more in demand than the

safety of Treasury bills. In the case of a bank run into Treasury bills, it makes sense to complement the lender of last resort with the borrower of last resort in precisely the instrument in demand. If Congressional constraints on the Treasury's debt permit, Treasury 'overfunding' in a crisis marked by a flight to quality can be stabilizing.

In 2008, two groups of investors ran from banks into Treasury paper. Foreign central banks, starting already in 2007, reduced their placements with commercial banks. In the third and fourth quarters of 2008, foreign central banks added almost $500 billion to their holdings of Treasury bills, while private foreign investors added half that sum.* After Lehman's failure, holders of 'prime' US money market funds, invested in the dollar debts of non-US banks, switched to government funds that invest in US Treasury bills.

An important but overlooked complement of the international lender of last resort operation by the US authorities in 2008 was the US Treasury supply of bills in excess of its borrowing needs, reaching an amount near $600 billion. The rationale of the Treasury's so-called supplementary financing account was to help the Fed to keep its target federal funds rate well above zero interest rates at a time when the Fed's credit operations were otherwise creating excess reserves for banks. (Technically, the Treasury sold bills and deposited the proceeds at the Fed; the Fed did not yet have Congressional authority to pay interest on excess reserves.) This cooperation between the Fed and Treasury ultimately proved short-lived as the Treasury approached a debt limit.

But whatever the intention and whatever the constraints, it was a useful tool of crisis management in late 2008 to supply the world's safest of safe assets in an elastic manner—not determined by the size of the fiscal deficit or normal debt management policy.

* Robert McCauley and Patrick McGuire, 'Dollar Appreciation in 2008: Safe Haven, Carry Trades, Dollar Shortage and Overhedging,' *BIS Quarterly Review*, December 2009, pp. 85–93.

Notes

1. Charles P. Kindleberger, *The Politics of International Money and World Language*, Princeton *Essays in international Finance*, no. 61 (Princeton, NJ: International Finance Section, August 1967), p. 6. See Emmanuel Carré and Laurent Le Maux, 'Kindleberger in Retrospect: the Federal Reserve's Dollar Swap Lines and International Lender of Last Resort Rules', *Industrial and Corporate Change*, vol. 31, no. 2 (April 2022), pp. 448–63. After the breakdown of Bretton Woods, Kindleberger made clear that he envisioned the need

for a lender of last resort in dollars to non-US banks outside the United States in the case of a run on their dollar books. See Charles Kindleberger, 'Why World Bankers Are Worried: Interview', *Challenge* (November–December 1974), p. 20. See Hawtrey in Chapter 12 for an earlier version of the Kindleberger rule.

2. Perry Mehrling, *The New Lombard Street* (Princeton: Princeton University Press, 2011).

3. Michael Bordo, Owen Humpage and Anna Schwartz, *Strained Relations: US Foreign-Exchange Operations and Monetary Policy in the Twentieth Century* (Chicago: University of Chicago Press, 2015).

4. Robert McCauley and Catherine Schenk, 'Central Bank Swaps Then and Now: Swaps and Dollar Liquidity in the 1960s', BIS *Working Papers* No. 851, April 2020, pp. 9–15.

5. Iñaki Aldasoro, Egemen Eren and Wenqian Huang, 'Dollar Funding of Non-US Banks Through Covid-19', BIS *Quarterly Review*, March 2021, Graph 1, p. 33.

6. Naohiko Baba, Robert McCauley and Srichander Ramaswamy, 'US Dollar Money Market Funds and Non-US Banks', BIS *Quarterly Review*, March 2009, p. 67.

7. Patrick McGuire and Goetz von Peter, 'The US Dollar Shortage in Global Banking and the International Policy Response', *International Finance*, vol. 15, no. 2 (2012), pp. 155–78.

8. McCauley and Schenk, 'Central Bank Swaps Then and Now: Swaps and Dollar Liquidity in the 1960s', pp. 19–40.

9. Saleem Bahaj and Ricardo Reis, 'The Economics of Liquidity Lines Between Central Banks'. *Annual Review of Financial Economics*, vol. 14 (2022).

10. The holdings in the United States are often overlooked in assessments of the role of foreign investors in the US housing bubble but including them takes the foreign (by nationality) holding of private mortgage-backed securities to 40 percent. See Robert McCauley, 'The 2008 Crisis: Transpacific or Transatlantic?', BIS *Quarterly Review*, December 2018, p. 58, footnote 8.

11. Robert McCauley and Jean-Francois Rigaudy, 'Managing Foreign Exchange Reserves in the Crisis and After', in *Portfolio and Risk Management for Central Banks and Sovereign Wealth Funds, BIS Papers* no. 58, October 2011, pp. 24, 27.

12. BNP, 'BNP Paribas Investment Partners Temporaly [stet] Suspends the Calculation of the Net Asset Value of the Following Funds: Parvest Dynamic ABS, BNP Paribas ABS EURIBOR and BNP Paribas ABS EONIA', press release, 9 August 2007.

13. Nathan Sheets, Ted Truman and C Lowery (2018): 'The Fed's Swap Lines during the Crisis: Lender of Last Resort on a Global Scale', Hutchins Center, Brookings Institution, and Program on Financial Stability, Yale School of Management, 11–12 September, pp. 9–10.

14. Francesco Papadia, 'Central Banking Cooperation in the Great Recession', *Bruegel Policy Contribution*, June 2013.
15. James Andrew Felkerson, '$29,000,000,000,000: A Detailed Look at the Fed's Bailout by Funding Facility and Recipient', Levy Institute, Bard College, *Working Paper* No. 698, December 2011; Efraim Benmelech, 'An Empirical Analysis of the Fed's Term Auction Facility', *CATO Papers on Public Policy*, 2, 2012, pp. 57–91.
16. See Linda Goldberg, C. Kennedy and J. Miu, 'Central Bank Dollar Swap Lines and Overseas Dollar Funding Costs', Federal Reserve Bank of New York *Staff Reports* No. 429, January 2010.
17. Baba, McCauley and Ramaswamy, 'US Dollar Money Market Funds and Non-US Banks', p. 77.
18. Jaime Caruana, 'Central Bank Cooperation: Reflections on the Experience of the Last Eight Decades', CEMLA's 60th Anniversary Commemorative Conference on Central Bank Cooperation at the Beginning of the 21st Century, 20 July 2012.
19. Linda Goldberg and David Skeie, 'Why Did U.S. Branches of Foreign Banks Borrow at the Discount Window During the Crisis?' *Liberty Street Economics*, 13 April 2011.
20. McCauley and Schenk, 'Central Bank Swaps Then and Now: Swaps and Dollar Liquidity in the 1960s', Graph 9, p. 19, citing Goldberg, Kennedy and Miu, 'Central Bank Dollar Swap Lines and Overseas Dollar Funding Costs'.
21. Naohiko Baba and Frank Packer, 'From Turmoil to Crisis: Dislocations in the FX Swap Market before and after the Failure of Lehman Brothers', *Journal of International Money and Finance*, vol. 28, no. 8 (December 2009), pp. 1350–74.
22. Perry Mehrling, "Elasticity and Discipline in the Global Swap Network", *International Journal of Political Economy*, vol. 44, no. 4 (October 2015), p. 317.
23. Bahaj and Reis, 'The Economics of Liquidity Lines Between Central Banks'. According to Adam Tooze, *Crashed: How a Decade of Financial Crises Changed the World* (London: Penguin, 2019), p. 206, 'If the Fed did not act, what threatened was a transatlantic balance sheet avalanche, with the Europeans running down their lending in the United States and selling off their dollar portfolios in a dangerous fire sale'. See also Ingrid Hjertaker and Bent Sofus Tranøy, "The Dollar as a Mutual Problem: New Transatlantic Inter-dependence in Finance", *Politics and Governance*, vol. 10, no. 2 (2022), pp. 198–207.
24. Daniel McDowell, *Brother Can You Spare a Billion?: The United States, the IMF, and the International Lender of Last Resort* (Oxford: Oxford University Press, 2017), Chapter 7, "The United States as an ILLR during the Great Panic of 2008–2009". See also Fabian Pape, "Governing Global Liquidity: Federal Reserve Swap Lines and the International Dimension

of US Monetary Policy", *New Political Economy*, vol. 27, no. 3 (2022), pp. 455–72.

25. According to the FOMC Transcript, 28–29 October 2008, only a minority of 7 FOMC members mentioned Libor 17 times. By contrast, FOMC members mentioned federal funds or its variants no less than 97 times. Many Libor-based US mortgages had been extended in 2006 with low, 2-year "teaser" rates and were due to reprice off of Libor in late 2008. So unless the Fed brought Libor down, holders of adjustable rate mortgages faced a 'Libor surprise'.

26. International Organization of Securities Commissions, *Money Market Funds during the March–April Episode: Thematic Note*, November 2020, p. 13. US MMFs that invest in public securities experienced larger inflows, of 30 percent of their net assets in March, and another 10 percent in April (ibid., p. 10), as investors switched from bond funds to safe money funds.

27. Financial Stability Board (FSB), *Policy Proposals to Enhance Money Market Fund Resilience: Final Report*, October 2021.

28. Aldosoro, Eren and Huang, 'Dollar Funding of Non-US banks through Covid-19', p. 33.

29. Andreas Schrimpf, Hyun Song Shin and Vladyslav Sushko, 'Leverage and Margin Spirals in Fixed Income Markets during the Covid-19 Crisis', *BIS Bulletin* No. 2, 2 April 2020.

30. Vissing-Jørgensen, op cit. Private foreign sales should be included to some extent, given the incorporation of US hedge funds in offshore banking centers.

31. Colin R. Weiss, 'Foreign Demand for U.S. Treasury Securities during the Pandemic', *FEDS Notes*, January 28, 2022.

32. Annette Vissing-Jørgensen, 'The Treasury Market in Spring 2020 and the Response of the Federal Reserve', BIS *Working Papers* No. 966, October 2021, Table 5.

33. Ibid.

34. Sean Collins, 'Bond Mutual Fund Outflows: A Measured Investor Response to a Massive Shock', Investment Company Institute *Viewpoint*, 4 March 2021.

35. Vissing-Jørgensen, op cit and Yiming Ma, Kairong Xiao and Yao Zeng, 'Mutual Fund Liquidity Transformation and Reverse Flight to Liquidity', Jacobs Levy Equity Management Center for Quantitative Financial Research Paper, 2020, revised 1 April 2021. Shelly Antoniewicz and Sean Collins, 'Setting the Record Straight on Bond Mutual Funds' Sales of Treasuries', *ICI Viewpoints*, 24 February 2022, argue that such estimates overstate the scale of selling. However, given shareholder redemptions, some bonds had to have been sold.

36. Robert McCauley applied the term 'buyer of last resort' to the Fed's 2008 and 2020 purchases of commercial paper and its 2020 purchase of corporate bonds in Izabella Kaminska, 'When Central Banks Take Over Bond

Markets', *Financial Times Alphaville*, 26 March 2020. https://ftalphaville. ft.com/2020/03/25/1585143723000/When-central-banks-take-over-securi ties-markets/, accessed April 6, 2022; Andrew Hauser, Bank of England Executive Director of Markets, applied the term to the Fed's and Bank of England's purchases of government bonds in March 2020 in 'Why Central Banks Need New Tools for Dealing with Market Dysfunction', speech given at Thomson Reuters Newsmaker, 7 January 2021. https://www.bankofeng land.co.uk/speech/2021/january/andrew-hauser-speech-at-thomson-reuters-newsmaker, accessed April 6, 2022.

37. J. Lawrence Broz, "The Politics of Rescuing the World's Financial System: The Federal Reserve as a Global Lender of Last Resort", *The Korean Journal of International Studies*, vol. 13, no. 2 (August 2015), pp. 323–51.

38. Along with Canadian banks, whose US retail presence is so extensive that their US dollar funding tends to be quite stable.

39. Robert N. McCauley, Patrick McGuire and Philip Wooldridge, 'Seven Decades of International Banking', BIS *Quarterly Review*, September 2021, Graph 6, p. 69; Committee on the Global financial System, *US Dollar Funding: an International Perspective*, CGFS Papers, no. 65 (2020), p. 21.

40. Ibid, pp. 24–5; Patrick McGuire, Ilhyock Shim, Hyun-Song Shin and Vladyslav Sushko, 'Outward Portfolio Investment and Dollar Funding in Emerging Asia', BIS *Quarterly Review*, December 2021, p. 57–8.

41. Lorie Logan, 'Treasury Market Liquidity and Early Lessons from the Pandemic Shock', Remarks at Brookings-Chicago Booth Task Force on Financial Stability (TFFS) meeting, panel on market liquidity, October 23, 2020.

42. Federal Reserve, 'H.4.1 Release—Factors Affecting Reserve Balances', 12 March and 2 April 2020.

43. Federal Reserve Bank of New York, 'Secondary Market Corporate Credit Facility: Program Terms and Conditions ', 28 July 2020. https://www. newyorkfed.org/markets/secondary-market-corporate-credit-facility/second ary-market-corporate-credit-facility-terms-and-conditions, accessed April 6, 2022.

44. Robert McCauley, 'How Should the Fed Buy Junk Bonds?' *Financial Times Alphaville*, May 1, 2020.

45. When the facility was announced, it was priced at the Fed's rate of interest on excess reserves plus 25 basis points, but when it was made a standing facility the rate was set at the top of the Fed's target range for the federal funds rate, then 25 basis points. See Mark Choi, Linda Goldberg, Robert Lerman and Fabiola Ravazzolo, 'The Fed's Central Bank Swap Lines and FIMA Repo Facility', Federal Reserve Bank of New York *Staff Paper* No 983, September 2021, p. 9, footnote 14.

46. Joshua Aizenman and Gurnain Pasricha, 'Selective Swap Arrangements and the Global Financial Crisis: Analysis and Interpretation', *International Review of Economics & Finance*, vol. 19, no. 3 (2010), pp. 353–65; Joshua Aizenman,

Hiroyuki Ito and Gurnain Pasricha, 'Central Bank Swap Arrangements in the COVID-19 Crisis', *Journal of International Money and Finance,* vol. 122 (2022), p. 102555 find US military alliances affect the Fed's choice of swap partners, while John Michael Cassetta, 'The Geopolitics of Swap Lines', Harvard Kennedy School of Government Mossavar-Rahmani Center for Business & Government *Associate Working Paper Series* No. 181, March 2022, finds that UN voting alignment makes a difference, though it is not clear how big a difference.

47. By turnover, one could argue that the Australian dollar is as important a counterpart currency as the Swiss franc or the Canadian dollar, but the force of this argument is lessened by the inclusion of the Reserve Bank of Australia among the partners of the temporary swaps.

48. Linda Goldberg and Fabiola Ravazzolo, 'Do the Fed's International Dollar Liquidity Facilities Affect Offshore Dollar Funding Markets and Credit?' *Liberty Street Economics,* December 20, 2021; Saleem Bahaj and Ricardo Reis, 'Central Bank Swap Lines: Evidence on the Effects of the Lender of Last Resort', *Review of Economic Studies,* 2021, pp. 16–21.

49. Gianluca Persi, 'US Dollar Funding Tensions and Central Bank Swap Lines during the COVID-19 Crisis', *ECB Economic Bulletin,* no. 5 (2020).

50. See discussion of the use of swap proceeds to replace dollar funding, lend dollars in the swap market or to buy US dollar assets in Saleem Bahaj and Ricardo Reis, 'The Workings of Liquidity Lines between Central Banks', in Refet Gurkaynak and Jonathan Wright, eds, *Research Handbook of Financial Markets* (2022).

51. Marushia Gislén, Ida Hansson and Ola Melander, 'Dollar Liquidity from the Federal Reserve to Other Central Banks', Sveriges Riksbank *Economic Review,* no. 1 (2021), pp. 37–8.

52. Ibid., p. 43.

53. Joshua Aizenman, Hiro Ito and Gurnain Pasricha, 'Central Bank Swap Arrangements in the COVID-19 Crisis'; McGuire, Shim, Shin and Sushko, 'Outward Portfolio Investment and Dollar Funding in Emerging Asia', p. 64: 'The expansion of Federal Reserve swap lines with major advanced economy central banks, including the Bank of Japan, mitigated stresses in global dollar funding markets. And the reopening of swap lines with the Bank of Korea and the Monetary Authority of Singapore on 19 March 2020 further narrowed the swap basis in Asian EME currencies'.

14

Bitcoin: Worse Than a Ponzi

The novel mania of the first decades of the twenty-first century was an investment in cryptocurrencies or cryptocoins. These are encoded units of value that are transferred over the internet from one holder to another on a decentralized ledger. In principle, if not in practice, no trusted institution oversees the transfers. And the electronic unit of value is not an IOU—it is a virtual asset but no one's liability.

Cryptocurrencies have proliferated as speculative assets, attracted many investors, and produced billionaires. Cryptocurrencies of various kinds have risen in number from one in 2009 to over 10,000 today. Despite the original promise of bilateral transfers, crypto holders can trade on hundreds of mostly unregulated exchanges. About 16 percent of Americans had invested in or traded cryptocurrencies by late 2021, including 43 percent of young men between 18 and 29 years of age.[1] The aggregate value of crypto reached about $3 trillion in November 2021, alongside the peak in US technology shares. In early 2018, Forbes listed 10 crypto billionaires, many of whom were founders of coins and exchanges. By March 2022, Forbes counted 19 crypto billionaires, including Changpeng Zhao, founder of the leading trading platform Binance.[2]

For the leading cryptocurrency, bitcoin, there are three main sources of supply and demand: so-called miners, early investors, and late investors. First, a miner wins new 6.25 bitcoins by using brute computational force to discover a code, using the code to bundle thousands of pending transfers into a block, and attaching the new block to the extant chain of blocks

R. Z. Aliber et al., *Manias, Panics, and Crashes*, https://doi.org/10.1007/978-3-031-16008-0_14

(hence 'blockchain').[3] Second are the early investors in bitcoin, including some miners who do not sell their bitcoin rewards. The miners and early investors traded the bitcoin higher among each other, alongside some criminals who prized the promise of anonymous transfers. Third are the late investors. Bitcoin throws off no cash flow and no one stands to redeem it. Ultimately, early investors realize a gain only with a sale to late investors.

Stepping back, one sees that investors became willing to pay a large sum for entries on no one's spreadsheet. This happened even as bitcoin's original rationale as anonymous means of value transfer gave way to a speculative and highly volatile store of value. As store of value, crypto turned out not to provide any hedge against inflation as crypto prices fell sharply in the first half of 2022 amid heightened inflation.

Many prominent economists have expressed skepticism regarding bitcoin and its ilk. Nevertheless, they have struggled to analyze it, often labeling it a Ponzi scheme. Given the remarkable trajectory of crypto, it merits a more careful characterization. The verdict here is that Ponzi scheme does not fit. Ponzi schemes like the original and Madoff's are subject to runs, but crypto is not. Investors cannot collectively call time on crypto. At heart crypto is less Ponzi than pump and dump, as described in the box below. Crypto ends not in a run, but in a price crash, a 'go to zero' as occurred in May 2022 to a sizeable coin. And unlike both a Ponzi scheme and a usual pump and dump scheme, the leading crypto is not just redistributive, taking from Peter and giving to Paul. Bitcoin is a deeply negative sum game, owing to the costs of mining. As a result, in a crash, aggregate losses would outweigh gains by the cumulated cost of mining.

Leonardo DiCaprio and *The Wolf of Wall Street*

A 2013 Hollywood thriller about pump and dump in a boiler shop is *The Wolf of Wall Street*. Leonardo DiCaprio plays the wolf; he makes his living—a high one, full of women, booze, drugs, private jets, and his own yacht—by selling penny stocks to the dentists of Newark and Jersey City and Peoria. Leonardo and his subordinates create or buy a shell of a company with an emotive name—Fusion Biometrics might be an example. Initially, they own all of the shares; then they sell a few shares to each other at slightly higher prices, and once they have a track record that shows that the prices increase day after day and week after week, they hustle the dentists and the undertakers and car-wash owners for their orders. Eventually, they sell all the shares to these investors. Their trick or skill is to sell a lot of shares to the public on the basis of the increases in prices that they have managed. And when they have no more shares to sell, they stop buying the shares, and the price falls through

the floor when one of the gullible dentists seeks to sell his shares and realize his profits so he can get the money to buy a Ferrari.

In a case of life imitating art, the movie was co-produced by the stepson of the Malaysian prime minister and funded with the proceeds of bond sales by a state-owned development agency in Malaysia that had been misappropriated by a combination of Goldman Sachs bankers, the prime minister and other officials, and a local fixer, still at large. Goldman Sachs ended up paying a 'criminal fine and disgorgement' of $2.9 billion for its role in paying $1.6 billion in bribes, the largest settlement to date under the Foreign Corrupt Practices Act.* Goldman bankers in the region have been convicted of a crime, but senior management had not enquired very energetically into why the firm received over $600 million to underwrite $6.5 billion of bonds, about ten times the going rate for an investment grade agency bond.

*U.S. Department of Justice, 'Goldman Sachs Charged in Foreign Bribery Case and Agrees to Pay Over $2.9 Billion', *Justice News*, 22 October 2020. https://www.justice.gov/opa/pr/goldman-sachs-charged-for eign-bribery-case-and-agrees-pay-over-29-billion, accessed June 1, 2022.

Minsky-Kindleberger Meets Bitcoin

Bitcoin had a nerdy start. It was first proposed as a 'peer-to-peer' means of encrypted payment in a white paper in 2008, complete with 8 references.[4] By making payments expensive, bitcoin could be transferred securely over the internet without the benefit of a financial intermediary and without the benefit of trust. A new technology promised 'every man a banker.'

This scheme resonated with those upset by the role of banks in the Great Financial Crisis in 2008 and the public support provided to them. Enthusiasts contrasted bitcoin's limited number to the rapid expansion of major central bank balance sheets at the time.

Bitcoin's price rose from less than a dollar at its launch in 2009 to $1000 in 2013. Bitcoin graduated from cryptographic esoterica and libertarian dream to financial mania. Investors diffused from the technically adept and ideologically committed to those with a fear of missing out (FOMO).

Referring to Minsky's phases of a financial mania, Joost van der Burgt, visiting the San Francisco Fed from the Dutch Central Bank, pinpoints the end of 2013, when bitcoin reached $1000, as the displacement—the moment when a new way of making money became apparent.[5] According to van der Burgt, bitcoin then entered its boom phase.

During the boom, bitcoin attracted an increasing number of imitators, and with the competition new opportunities for the application of leverage to crypto. Of course, free entry raised questions about the selling point of a strictly limited supply of 21 million bitcoin. The most important imitator, ether, started in 2015 on the Ethereum blockchain. Like Avis, this number 2 tries harder. The Ethereum blockchain supports not just transfers of ether but also supports automated contracts that execute transactions under certain conditions, so-called smart contracts. Ethereum enabled the development of so-called decentralized finance (DeFi) in 2021, bringing lending, borrowing, leverage, and automated trading to crypto[6] (as well as often silly non-fungible tokens—blockchained and transferable evidence of ownership of electronic objects). At its peak, much of the $250 billion of crypto assets 'locked'—perhaps parked would be the more accurate term—in smart contracts amounted to leverage.

Van der Burgt dates crypto's entry into its euphoria phase in late 2017, when bitcoin reached $20,000. He noted that classic signs of euphoria, namely taxi drivers talking about bitcoin investment and generous use of leverage by investors. A 'crypto winter' that saw bitcoin's price fall by two-thirds between early January 2018 and early February 2018 may question this timing of euphoria. However, its rise from $5000 to $60,000 between mid-March 2020 and March 2021, and its subsequent rise to $69,000 in November 2021, surely took bitcoin into euphoria.

Euphoria saw the development of crypto's own money, a development common to manias. The irony is that there was no general shortage: the US dollar money supply had risen hugely above trend owing to the combination of Treasury pandemic transfers to households and the Fed's buying of Treasury bonds in 2020–2021. Yet as crypto trading came to rely on centralized platforms (as described in the next section), it lacked a stable unit to settle trades and serve as collateral. Banks declined to convert crypto into dollars speedily and cheaply owing to constraints like know-your-customer and anti-money laundering rules. So crypto adopted its own dollar stand-ins, persuasively named stablecoins. These were also coded entries on blockchains, but their promoters promised to hold their dollar value stable. Liquidity in the crypto ecology, including the novel automated lending and borrowing programs that sprang up in 2021, came to depend on stablecoins, and their backing with real money, or lack of it, introduced vulnerabilities.

As described below, May 2022 saw the crash of the fourth largest stablecoin, terra, and the total loss of value of an associated coin, luna, that was intended to secure the stablecoin's value. These crashes shook the conviction that bitcoin would recover from its loss of half its value since November 2021.

Thus, the May 2022 crashes suggested that crypto euphoria was giving way to distress. Recall from Chapters 2 and 6 that distress denotes the period when some players realize that the door is closing on their ability to exit the object of speculation at a profit and to convert near-money to real money.

Bitcoin versus the South Sea Bubble

In 2013, Nout Wellink, former head of the Dutch Central Bank, judged bitcoin as 'worse than the tulip mania. At least then you got a tulip, now you get nothing.'*

Perhaps a different contrast better serves to highlight bitcoin's extreme nature. The South Sea bubble of 300 years ago was a mania with a government charter. As an anti-institutional project, bitcoin could hardly differ more from the South Sea Company.

- In 1720, Parliament legislated the consolidation of government debt into the South Sea; in 2009, an anonymous group of computer programmers launched bitcoin.
- A dominant schemer ran the South Sea Company, corrupting politicians, orchestrating its market operations, and self-dealing; to change bitcoin's code, some combination of core developers, numerous nodes, and numerous miners are the operators.
- In terms of the functions of money, the South Sea Company consolidated an existing store of value secured by state taxing power; bitcoin was intended as a means of payment and nothing but its supposed usefulness stands behind it.
- The South Sea Company should have been readily valued, holding government bonds bearing a known interest rate (5 percent then 4 percent) and callable in seven years; bitcoin is nigh-on impossible to value, as a zero coupon perpetual bond, an asset with no maturity and no promised cash flow (formerly a financial joke).
- The South Sea shares traded in 1720 in a range between 1000 and 100 in the months between hitting its lunatic note in April and collapsing in September; bitcoin between $100 and $70,000 in its long run since 2013.
- In 1721, after the crash, Parliament not only passed the Act to Restore Publick Credit to override contracts and to apportion gains and losses but also confiscated the estates of the Chancellor of the Exchequer and the Company's directors; it is hard to imagine any legal effort to reapportion gains and losses after a crypto collapse (see below).

The South Sea Bubble arguably advanced British public finances by trans-forming the bulk of public obligations into a more homogeneous and trade-able form. It remains to be seen whether and if the technological innovation spurred by crypto makes a similarly significant and lasting contribution.

*Alex Hern, 'Bitcoin Hype Worse Than "Tulip Mania", Says Dutch Central Banker', *The Guardian*, 4 December 2013.

The Institutionalization of Crypto

Bitcoin's boom and euphoria phases saw the development of institutions to make the trading of cryptocoins easier. Trading platforms developed to enable the trading of crypto against dollars and crypto against crypto. The conve-nience of trading crypto against crypto led to the development of stablecoins as proxies for the dollar. Contrary to the founding vision, these institutions centralized trading and required trust to operate. As if in a sped-up recapitu-lation of the history of financial abuses, these institutions operated in a way that seemed almost calculated to lose that trust.

A tellingly euphoric moment was the April 2021 initial public offering of crypto trading platform Coinbase, which mostly trades bitcoin and ether against the dollar. Its price settled on its first trading day at a valuation of $65 billion, within spitting distance of the valuation of the parent of the New York Stock Exchange.[7] This Delaware corporation claimed 6 million monthly transacting users in Q1 2021 (9 million by the first quarter of 2022) and $223 billion of 'assets on platform.'[8]

This centralization of trading brought conflicts of interest long prohibited in traditional finance. Although Coinbase was often described as an exchange, in fact, US states regulated it as a money transmission business.[9] As such, it dealt with its customers as a principal; such transactions represented 11 percent of its revenue in 2020.[10] A proper exchange is not simultaneously a principal. Coinbase is a founder of the consortium that established the stablecoin USDC, which it promotes on its trading platform.[11] Coinbase also comingled customer accounts and its own corporate holdings. Only in May 2022 did the SEC finally require Coinbase to disclose the implication that customers could end up as the firm's general creditors in the event of its bankruptcy—centralization with a vengeance.[12]

A second trading platform, Binance, epitomized overtrading. Here highly leveraged derivative bitcoin trades came to drive prices in spot trading of

bitcoin versus the dollar as conducted on Coinbase. In the first quarter of 2021, when bitcoin doubled in price from $30,000 to $60,000, a so-called perpetual swap contract for bitcoin averaged over $20 billion in turnover a day on Binance, about 20 times the spot trading on Coinbase.[13] Traders use this contract to take a leveraged position in bitcoin, putting down only a small fraction of their bet and settling gains or losses in crypto. After a flash crash in May 2021, when China prohibited financial institutions from dealing in crypto, the unregulated Binance announced the reduction of its maximum leverage from 100 or more to 20 times, still very high for an extremely volatile asset, but actual practice is not clear.[14] The upshot is an inverted triangle of highly leveraged bets that drive the prices on the relatively narrow foundation of bitcoin-dollar trades.

Thus, price discovery for crypto takes place on an unregulated platform that features high leverage. Moreover, Binance is said to have turned a blind eye to billions in illicit flows of funds well into 2021.[15] The institutionalization of crypto leaves its liquidity and price at the mercy of events in such a venue.

The largest crypto exchange depends on the largest stablecoin. Most of the bitcoin trades on Binance are perpetual swaps of bitcoin against the leading stablecoin, tether. It is easy to see why a dollar stand-in would be useful in this key derivatives market. If a trade of crypto against the dollar cannot use the dollar to post margin or to settle gains and losses, it is awkward to use the volatile bitcoin for these purposes. It is much more convenient to use the stable leg of the trade to post margin and to settle gains and losses than to use the highly volatile leg for these purposes. For an unregulated exchange that does not have good access to the dollar, an ersatz dollar is very useful.

More broadly, stablecoins became a useful vehicle currency in the crypto world and extended its reach. A trader selling bitcoin and looking to buy again or to switch into another crypto coin could avoid the delays and expense of acquiring and then selling dollars. In DeFi transactions, using smart contracts, i.e., coded instructions running on the Ethereum blockchain, rather than financial institutions, stablecoins can be lent out and borrowed at interest rates well above those on the corresponding dollars.

By October 2021, the aggregate value of stablecoins weighed in at $127 billion, with market leader tether amounting to over half of this sum.[16] This was just 3 percent of the value of outstanding cryptocoins. Despite the decline in the value of crypto overall in 2022, stablecoins reached an aggregate measured value of $180 billion at the end of February 2022[17] and held around that level into May.[18] Though still a small share of crypto market

value, they play a key role in the crypto universe: the turnover of tether in particular exceeds that of bitcoin and ether combined.

As the roles of Coinbase, Binance, and stablecoins have grown, the 'peer-to-peer' vision of the founders of bitcoin has dropped by the wayside. Partly this resulted from a design that sacrificed an efficient means of payment for a trustless, non-institutional system. Bitcoin proved by design pretty clunky when payment traffic turned heavy; transactions slowed and congestion led to higher transfer fees. A payments network should be 'the more the merrier,' but bitcoin proved to be 'the more the sorrier' at its local price peak in late 2017.[19]

Decentralization thus gave way to a centralization appropriate to a heavily traded speculative would-be store of value. By mid-2021, cryptocurrency exchanges and trading desks were estimated to be responsible for 80 percent of transactions on the bitcoin blockchain and about a third of holdings.[20]

Ideologically, the recruits to crypto investing did not share any libertarian vision. Rafael Auer and David Tercero-Lucas analyzed a survey by the Federal Reserve Bank of Atlanta and found that bitcoin holders did not stand out in their dissatisfaction with the standard financial system.[21]

But the institutionalization of crypto introduced vulnerabilities into its world. Problems at the two trading platforms, Coinbase and Binance, could lead investors to re-evaluate the value of crypto investing. Stablecoins made a very specific promise and under the best of management would still face the risk of runs. If the major stablecoins were to become unusable, crypto liquidity would be impaired, pushing down prices, and DeFi, which runs on stablecoins, could fall apart.

If tether were as well managed as a regulated money market fund it could still find itself losing money on an investment, 'breaking the buck' (i.e., reporting a share value below $1) and suffering a run, as did the Reserve Primary Fund in 2008. Then the Fed and US Treasury backstopped money market funds to limit the fallout. Even without any fund's breaking the buck in March 2020, regulated money market funds suffered runs and again the Fed rode to the rescue.

But there is ample reason to suppose that tether is not managed with the prudence of a standard money market fund. In early 2021, the New York State Attorney General fined the firm, accusing it of falsely claiming that its liabilities were fully backed by dollars, and required it to disclose its holdings.[22] Outrage greeted tether's first disclosure—a circle chart of its holdings in March 2021.[23] An SEC-regulated money market fund, by contrast, periodically discloses all of its holdings at the level of security.

Tether is a 'company that seemed to be practically quilted out of red flags',[24] concluded a *Business Week* cover story in October 2021. But the crypto world continued to rely on it. Remarkably, a leading business glossy shouted fire, but the crowded theatre's patrons just remained in their seats.

For over a year guesses as to the obligors and nature of tether's reported holdings of commercial paper ranged widely. Was it paper issued by distressed Chinese real estate developers? IOUs backed by cryptocurrencies? Or worse? In October 2022, Tether Holdings claimed that it had run its commercial paper holdings that back tether to zero. But as of 30 September 2022 it reported that 9% of the assets backing tether consisted of tether-denominated loans, that is, IOUs secured by undisclosed assets, likely cryptocurrencies. These could make the Lehman Brothers commercial paper that led to the run on the Reserve Primary Fund in September 2008 look solid. Since tether pays no interest and Treasury bills yielded 3% in September 2022, tether could make billions in annual profit without making such loans, leaving observers scratching their heads.

In May 2022, the unpegging of a minor stablecoin (terra) and the collapse of an associated $40 billion plus cryptocoin (luna) in weeks signaled the possibility of the onset of distress. At this stage, the inflow of new investors slows, and some current investors look to liquidate holdings and raise real dollar cash.

From Terra to Luna and Back

The unpegging of a minor stablecoin in May 2022 and the associated collapse of a widely held cryptocoin highlighted the risk posed by stablecoins to the crypto ecology and the potential of a widely held cryptocoin to 'go to zero.' Their creator, Do Kwon, promoted terra (UST) as a stablecoin maintained by an algorithm rather than backed, as with tether, by a more or less sufficient portfolio of more or less liquid assets. The algorithmic approach was sold as better, even more pure, in its lack of reliance on an institution. After all, if a backed stablecoin has a foot in traditional finance, the authorities could freeze its assets.

The idea was a fine piece of financial engineering to produce stability out of instability. If terra were to trade below $1 par value, a trader could buy it with a real dollar (or more likely tether) and exchange it for a dollar's worth of luna, whatever luna's price. At $100 per luna, one terra would fetch a hundredth of a luna; at $10 per luna, one terra would fetch a tenth of a luna.

Then the luna could be sold for dollars (or tether) and the trader could in principle pocket the gap between terra's price and par.

The short and the long of it was that the algorithm would enable arbitrage to support terra's stable value at $1—if there were always a market bid for the luna. Yet potential buyers would know that as much luna as necessary would be issued. The algorithmic stablecoin's parallel in traditional finance carried the telling Wall Street adjective, 'death-spiral'(box).[25]

'Death spiral' preferred shares and par reset junk bonds

Algorithmic stablecoins are cousins to two other clever pieces of financial engineering. A 'death spriral' convertible is a bond or preferred share sold as a fixed-income investment that, at maturity, converts into the common equity in the firm. However, the bond is converted not into a fixed number of shares, but into as many shares as are required to preserve the bond's par value. If the firm is in distress, the prospect of a massive dilution of the equity-holders' claim on the firm can lead the equity price to collapse—hence the name.

Another similar fine piece of financial engineering featured in the largest leveraged buyout in the 1980s. Par reset junk bonds formed part of KKR's 1989 buyout of RJR Nabisco. The coupon on these junk bonds was to be periodically reset to bring the securities to par. The worse the bonds were doing, the higher the coupon. Once RJR Nabisco's finances became distressed, an interest rate that would bring the bonds to par would bankrupt the company. Only KKR bringing new equity to the deal prevented the firm's finances from blowing up.*

* Robert N. McCauley, Judith S. Ruud and Frank Iacono, *Dodging Bullets* (Cambridge: MIT Press, 1999), chapter 4.

The stakes were not small. Terra had joined the top four of stablecoins and luna the top ten rank of cryptocoins. Demand for terra was turbocharged by a 19 percent interest rate paid by a smart contract called Anchor controlled by Do Kwon. (As with much 'decentralized finance,' in this case, decentralized governance was an illusion.) Terra's growth seemed to provide a (spurious) argument for holding the linked luna. On April 5, luna's price had risen to $116, up from 63 cents on 1 January 2021, and its market cap had reached $41 billion,[26] and outstanding terra had climbed to UST 17 billion (then trading near par and so worth $17 billion).[27] Thus the whole complex had reached a value of almost $60 billion, ostensibly on the promise of the uses for terra and luna under development, but mostly on the basis of the 19 percent promised on terra and a price trend for luna pointing to the moon.

Terra found little use as a means of payment, and by Friday 6 May UST14 billion of UST 18 billion was parked at the Anchor protocol earning 19 percent.[28] As the *Financial Times* quoted the author just before the run on terra, 'When you hear of a 9 or 19 percent short-term interest rate on an asset [stablecoin] that is supposed to have a stable value against the dollar, put your hand on your wallet.'[29]

The run started over the weekend, with holders of terra withdrawing UST 2 billion or more per day from Anchor on Sunday through Thursday. The conversion of UST at par to luna was limited ('gated') to a certain amount per day, and sales on exchanges saw terra slump to a discount.

The day-by-day number of outstanding luna provides summary statistics of the crash. In the week ending Friday 6 May, there were 343 million outstanding luna as the price fell from the $80s to the $60s. Outstanding luna rose 9 percent on 10 May, then almost quadrupled to 1.5 billion on 11 May. Outstanding luna gained two zeros to reach 169 billion on 12 May and the printing stopped at 6.5 trillion on the lucky 13th of May.[30] Four zeros had been added to the number of Luna outstanding in four days in a brief and spectacularly unsuccessful defence of terra's peg to the dollar. Luna fell to a rounding error away from zero and was delisted from exchanges. Terra hit 15 cents on Friday the 13th, and subsequently traded lower; UST 11 billion remained. Luna became worthless before half of the terra had been converted.[31]

In the weeks before the run, Do Kwon had sought to defend his creation by selling luna to buy $3.5 billion-worth of bitcoin. Practically, the downward trend of bitcoin prices undermined this would-be defence. Conceptually, the purchase undermined the argument for the algorithmic approach. In any case, the sale of the bitcoin did more to spread the selling to bitcoin than to rescue terra. Questions remain whether the sales of bitcoin against terra favored insiders.

The question can also be posed regarding how the promoters of terra-luna fared. As noted, at the peak in early April 2022, the value of terra and luna approached $60 billion. Almost all of those who had bought from the promoters were sitting on capital gains on their luna at that peak valuation, so this sum is too high as an estimate of the take of the promoters. One must also take into account that the promoters sold at widely varying prices. Binance was reported to have received 15 million luna for its $3 million investment in 2018, which were worth $1.6 billion at the peak.[32] In this case, the promoters only made $3 million. (Binance claims to have held the luna and to have taken the loss.) It is entirely possible that the promoters pocketed $1 billion

or more on a venture that a law professor in 2021 dubbed 'Built to Fail.'[33] Do Kwon's defence is that he thought it could succeed.

A widely held coin crashed from over $100 to 0 in five weeks and a stablecoin was implicated in the market dynamics. In the immediate wake of terra's unpegging, tether came under pressure and traded as low as 95 cents on 12 May 2022. It recovered to near par within days, but its reported outstanding amount declined from 83 to 67 billion at the end of June.[34]

The demonstration that what had been advertised by Binance as a safe asset could tumble in value took its toll on the willingness of investors to lend crypto through DeFi protocols. The total value of coins 'locked' on such smart contracts had reached $250 billion—including considerable leverage[35]—around the turn of the year 2021–2022 and had already declined by a fifth by March.[36] From around $200 billion in early May, it reached $75 billion by mid-July and $43 billion in December.[37]

The institutional toll from terra/luna contagion spread fast. On 12 June, a crypto borrowing and lending platform, Celsius, which claimed a million customers who earned 17 percent on over $20 billion in assets in August 2021, froze withdrawals.[38] It has since filed for bankruptcy, along with crypto lending platform Voyager and crypto hedge fund Three Arrows. At issue in the Voyager bankruptcy is the issue that we have highlighted for Coinbase, namely whether the crypto assets on deposit are held for the customers, or are Voyager's property.[39]

Many of those who had bought luna felt like victims, but had a hard time putting their finger on what had befallen them. Even critics of cryptocurrencies have had a hard time characterizing them.

FTX: Pump and Dump with a Twist

In November 2022, the second largest crypto exchange, FTX, declared bankruptcy after suffering a run. A million customers and creditors were left with about $8 billion of losses. Founder Sam Bankman-Fried (SBF) saw a peak fortune of $26 billion evaporate, and his lieutenants rapidly pled guilty to federal criminal charges of defrauding customers and misleading investors on SBF's orders. FTX's new CEO, who liquidated Enron, was shocked to find lemonade stand accounting and emoji controls. Discussion of this crash has ranged from SBF's dressing and sleeping habits to his political contributions and 'effective altruism.' Here the focus is on how a worthless token became cash.

SBF pumped and dumped with a twist. He founded crypto trading firm Alameda Research in 2017, and FTX in 2019. That July, FTX created out of nothing its own token called FTT, which offered holders discounts on FTX fees. FTX minted 350 million FTT, kept half and 'pre-sold' a fifth before its exchange listing at an average price of 14 cents, raising $10 million. Major holders FTX and Alameda dominated a thin and illiquid market in which FTT traded up from its advertised listing price of $1 to peak price of $80 and a market cap of $10 billion (based on Coinmarketcap's implied float of 125 million FTT) in September 2021. Alameda seems to have borrowed billions of dollars against FTT collateral from various sources. *Securities and Exchange Commission v. Caroline Ellison and Zixiau "Gary" Wang* of December 21, 2022 (22-cv-10794, SDNY, paragraph 4) accused the head of Alameda: 'Ellison, acting at the direction of Bankman-Fried, engaged in automated purchases of FTT tokens on various platforms in order to increase the price of those tokens and inflate the value of Alameda's collateral, which allowed Alameda to borrow even more money from external lenders at increased risk to the lenders...' Then, after the May 2022 collapse of Terra/Luna, Alameda lost access to external loans and repaid them by apparently pledging FTT for loans by FTX of its client assets—dollars, bitcoin, tether, ether. Where, beyond a $1 billion loan to SBF and other loans to FTX executives, the funds went is not clear at writing.

The twist is ingenious. After FTT's price was pumped up by the FTX 'bots', it was not dumped in a myriad of investor phone calls, the usual retail approach. Instead, 'secured' borrowing 'monetized' FTT: a novel wholesale dump. Ultimately, customers' misplaced trust in FTX was turned into cash. But along the way was discovered a new (automated) pump and wholesale dump through 'secured' borrowing.

Worse Than a Ponzi[40]

What is bitcoin from an economic perspective? Probably the most frequent answer by skeptics among economists and others is that it is a Ponzi scheme. In early 2021, Brazilian computer scientist Jorge Stolfi made the following argument that Bitcoin is a Ponzi scheme[41]:

1. Investors buy in the expectation of profits.
2. That expectation is sustained by the profits of those that cash out.
3. But there is no external source for those profits; they come entirely from new investments.

4. And the operators take away a large portion of the money.

All of this rings true. Yet in calling it a Ponzi scheme, skeptics are too kind to bitcoin on two counts. First, bitcoin makes no promises and cannot have the same endgame as a Ponzi scheme. Second, it is a deeply negative sum game from a broad social perspective.

It is unfair to Charles Ponzi to call bitcoin a Ponzi. In 1920, Ponzi promised 50 percent on a 45-day investment and actually paid out to some investors. He suffered and even survived runs before the authorities caught up with him. The scheme did not last a year because of the extravagant return, but Ponzi made a promise, paid some initial returns, and suffered runs.

In the largest and probably the longest running Ponzi scheme in history, Bernie Madoff paid returns of around 1 percent a month. He offered to cash out his scheme's participants, both the original sum 'invested' and the 'return' thereon. As a result, the scheme could and did suffer a run; the Great Financial Crisis of 2008 led to a cascade of redemptions by participants and the scheme's collapse.

But the resolution has extended beyond its collapse on account of remarkable and ongoing legal proceedings. These have outlived Madoff himself, who died in early 2021.

Many are unaware that a bankruptcy trustee, Irving H. Picard, has doggedly and successfully pursued those who took more money out of the scheme than they put in. He even managed to follow the money into offshore dollar accounts, litigating a controversial extraterritorial reach of US law all the way to the US Supreme Court.[42] Of the $20 billion in recognized original investments in the scheme (which the victims had been told had reached a value more than three times that sum), some $14 billion, a striking 70 percent, has been recovered and distributed.[43] Claims of up to $1.6 million are being fully repaid.

By contrast to investments with Madoff, bitcoin is bought not as an income-earning asset but rather as a zero coupon perpetual. In other words, it promises nothing as a running yield and never matures with a required terminal payment. It follows that it cannot suffer a run. The only way a holder of bitcoin can cash out is by a sale to someone else.

Bitcoin's collapse would look very different from that of Ponzi's or Madoff's scheme. As noted above, one possible trigger could be the collapse of a big stablecoin; other possible triggers lurk in the trading platforms. Given their record, the lack of regulation and scant disclosure, it is not hard to imagine a big stablecoin persistently breaking the buck. This could so disrupt

the whole ecology of crypto that there could be no bids for bitcoin. The market might close indefinitely.

In this event, there would be no long-running legal effort to chase down those who cashed in their bitcoin early in order to redistribute their profits to those left holding bitcoins. Holders of bitcoin would have no claim on those who bought early and sold.

In its cash flow, bitcoin resembles a penny stock pump and dump scheme[44] more than a Ponzi scheme. In a pump and dump scheme, traders acquire basically worthless stock, talk it up and perhaps trade it among themselves at rising prices before unloading it on those drawn in by the chatter and the price action. Like the pump and dump scheme, bitcoin taps into the pure desire for capital gains. Buyers cannot stand the sight of friends getting rich overnight: they suffer an acute fear of missing out (FOMO). In any case, bitcoin makes no promises and cannot end as a Ponzi scheme ends in a run.

This is not to say that Ponzi schemes of varying sophistication do not abound in crypto and DeFi. In the terra-luna scheme, inflows into terra chasing the 19 percent interest pushed up the price of luna, sales of which funded the 19 percent return, according to Binance's founder and head Changpeng Zhao.[45] His after-the-fact description is ironic in view of Binance's having advertised the terra investment as a 'safe and happy' opportunity.[46] In any case, here was a return promise, more generous than Madoff's in a lower interest rate environment, and a story for a stable principal as well. One can think of this scheme as a Ponzi scheme grafted onto the standard crypto pump and dump.

The other big difference between bitcoin and a Ponzi scheme is that the former is, from an aggregate or social standpoint, a negative sum game. To the extent that real resources are used up to make bitcoin run, it is costly in a way that Madoff's two- or three-man operation was not. (This was also true of ether up until September 2022, when it converted from its energy-intensive mining ['proof of work'] to a more environmentally friendly means ['proof of stake'] of keeping its participants honest.) From the social standpoint, what Madoff took out of his scheme and finally consumed is a redistribution in a zero-sum game (the trustee sold his penthouse). Stolfi's fourth observation above, 'the operators take away a large portion of the money' lumps together Madoff's take and bitcoin's miners' revenues, but these are very different in economic terms.

With bitcoin, the game is to name the country whose electricity consumption equals that of all the puzzle-solvers (miners) who get to effect transactions and receive bitcoin in reward. Even if the electricity were priced to

include its contribution to global warming (its 'environmental externality')—which presumably it mostly is not—this represents a real cost.

How big a cost? At the beginning of 2021, Stolfi put the cumulative payments to bitcoin's miners since 2009 at $15 billion.[47] At the then price of bitcoin, he put the increase in cost at about $10 million per day, which mostly pays for electricity.

At higher bitcoin prices in the 'teens of thousand dollars, the hole is growing faster. About 900 new bitcoin a day require most of $20 million a day in electricity and computer wear and tear. Thus, the negative sum in the bitcoin game is in tens of billions of dollars and rising at most of a billion dollars per month. If the price of bitcoin collapses to zero, the gains of those who sold would fall short of the losses of holders by this growing sum. To liken bitcoin to a Ponzi scheme or even to a pump and dump scheme, both basically redistributive, is to flatter bitcoin.

Bitcoin is a long-running, decentralized pump and dump scheme with a negative sum. True, there are many early investors with an interest in new investors (although recent research points to much more concentration among early miners than previously thought[48]), rather than a single 'Wolf of Wall Street,' the real-life pumper and dumper played by Leonardo DiCaprio. True, they are more likely to sport beards than slicked-back hair. True, many are sincere in their belief that trustless transfers or stateless money will somehow contribute to human happiness. But it must be said that, since bitcoin, promoters of coins commonly allocate coins at the outset to insiders, ranging from 15 percent for Ethereum to about 50 percent for Binance.[49] Since bitcoin, crypto promoters are openly 'talking their own books.'

And true, it is a pump and dump of a remarkably shambolic character. An industry source has estimated on the basis of inactivity that some one-fifth of bitcoin is held, if that is the right word, by those who have lost their codes.[50] One regretful holder sought to have a public dump in South Wales dug up to find his discarded laptop with his codes for 3000 bitcoin.[51]

To conclude, an economic analysis of bitcoin finds it unique in the history of manias. As an object of speculation, bitcoin is unprecedented in the degree to which there is no there there. This post-modern mania features big prices for entries on nobody's spreadsheet. A zero coupon perpetual has arrived not as a joke but as a trillion-dollar asset. Unlike a Ponzi scheme, bitcoin cannot end in a run. However, the centralized institutions that have grown up to accommodate mass investment in bitcoin and others could fail investors and precipitate a crash.

In a crash, the holders of bitcoin will have no one to pursue to recover what they invested. Unlike a Madoff-style Ponzi scheme, early investors who

get out before the crash need not fear that a court will demand their winnings. Collectively, the losses will exceed gains by what investors cumulatively paid the miners for bitcoin. This sum has gone up in smoke, a social loss. The holders of bitcoin and other crypto might in the end only wish it had been a Ponzi scheme.

Play to Earn

Developers of cryptocoins are on the lookout for 'use cases,' and gaming is a natural use. The pitch to those who play normal games on their cell phones is, 'Why not earn while you play?'.

For a time, Axie Infinity was the biggest online crypto video game. Its promise was to make work and play become one. Its achievement was millions of low-income players working on gaming as a cottage industry and paying away much of their earnings to the owners of the gaming tools.

Its rise had much in common with that of terra-luna: it offered unsustainable rewards to players that propelled growth. In both cases, one can think of the rewards as marketing spending, within a business model of bringing money in, thereby building demand for the venture's main coin, and then selling it at fancy prices. The climax of this game story is not a run, as with terra-luna, but instead the largest hack in DeFi's short history. By then, the promoters had had plenty of opportunity to unload the venture's coin on 'investors' drawn in by the coin's price rise.

The game really took off in April 2021 when its developers moved the game off of the Ethereum blockchain network to avoid its delays and fees owing to the same decentralized, slow, expensive, and energy-intensive validation process as the Bitcoin network uses.* The game's developers opted for nine trusted validators to authorize deposits and withdrawals into and out of the game of number two coin ether (ETH) or Coinbase's stablecoin (USDC).

In the game, players use at least three digital pets called Axies to compete in battles. 'The monsters are cartoonish blobs distinguished by their unique mixture of interchangeable parts, not unlike Mr. Potato Head.'** So far, this is like the 1990s video game Pokémon, but there are two twists. The first twist is that players must buy these Axies, non-fungible tokens (NFTs) with varying battle strengths. At the peak of the game's growth in mid-2021, three Axies cost the equivalent of hundreds of dollars, or even a thousand dollars for more potent ones. First, pay to play, then play to earn. In Fig. 14.1, in the left three columns, dollars are converted to ether, then bridged onto the Axie Infinity blockchain ('Ronin') and are used to purchase Axies.

Fig. 14.1 Axie Infinity flow of funds (*Note* Axie = non-fungible token (NFT), digital pet used to play game; ETH = ether; AXS = Axie Shards, main 'governance' coin; SLP = Smooth Love Potion, in-game reward coin; USDT = tether stablecoin. *Source* Authors' elaboration)

The second twist is that successful players earn an in-game coin, known—why not?—as smooth love potions (SLPs) as well as Axie Shards (AXS). AXS is the game's main coin, shown in Fig. 14.1 in the column 'Play Game.' These can be 'cashed' out of the game in the last column in Fig. 14.1 by moving them to the Binance exchange, exchanging them for tether (USDT) and selling the tether for US dollars. Or, remaining in the column 'Play Game,' the coins can be used to 'breed' new Axies, starting with two extant Axies. A newly bred Axie can be taken to the Axie market and sold to new players or old players looking to step up their game, with a 4.25 percent transaction fee paid to the game's treasury, controlled by AXS holders. Given this need for SLPs and AXS to breed Axies, new players created a demand for the winnings of the current players.

In sum, take dollars, buy Axies, play with them to earn SLPs and AXS, and then cash them out or use them to breed Axies for sale. With no promises of X percent return or stable Axie values, this is not quite a Ponzi scheme packaged as a video game. Still, players brought real money to the game and hoped to make a return. When new players were bringing in more money than was being cashed out, the prices of Axies, SLP, and AXS rose. The game's developers and their venture capital backers were playing a game of setting player rewards to recruit new players and their money, generating activity in the game that would draw buyers to AXS. The developers then sold their AXS at elevated prices to 'investors' who had no interest in playing the game.

Generous player rewards did generate a rapid growth of players. From April 2021, daily active players grew rapidly and reached 2.7 million by November 2021.*** At the peak in growth of new players in July–August

2021, when new players almost tripled, SLPs fetched as much as 35–40 cents, with lots of demand for breeding. Skilled players were quitting their jobs.**** Though the developers resided in Vietnam, perhaps half the players were in the Philippines, with Venezuelans a distant second.

Many, perhaps most, players did not have the required upfront money to buy Axies, and virtual sharecropping developed. Impecunious players obtained 'scholarships,' under which they would use sponsors' Axies and pay them a third or a half of their earnings. By September, one sponsor group (a 'guild' organized as a 'decentralized autonomous organization,' almost a blockchain corporation) in the Philippines had most of its $850 million in assets in Axie, and had raised money from US private equity.*****

Axie Infinity's coin AXS, ostensibly entitling holders to govern the game, rose from $6 in early April 2021 to $160 in November 2021, reaching a market value of almost $10 billion.****** The game's developers raised $7.5 million from venture capitalists in May 2021, and $152 million in October 2021, the latter valuing the startup at $3 billion.

But as growth slowed and the rewards stayed generous, inflation set in. By September, players were earning SLPs at twice the rate that they were using them to breed new Axies; their cashing out pushed the SLP price down into the 5- to 10-cent range. The developers severely tightening the terms on which SLPs are earned and spent in February 2022, but their price still fell to a cent or two.******* At this rate, players could not earn the minimum wage in the Philippines and the number of daily players fell by about half.

Thieves broke into this already very troubled game on March 23, 2022. Hackers lifted over $600 million dollars worth of ETH and USDC held in the game's stash on the Ethereum network. The game designers had cut corners and depended on only nine trusted validators for withdrawals rather than the thousands for Ethereum or Bitcoin blockchains and the hackers were able to compromise five of them. On May 6, the US Treasury identified the hackers as a group linked to North Korea as it sanctioned a crypto-mixing service that obfuscated the origin and destination of crypto transfers for the hackers.********

Amazingly, despite an evident lack of attention to security, private equity backers, led by crypto exchange Binance, stumped up $150 million in May 2022 to pay back gamers, who owned two-thirds of the $600 million stolen.********* The market capitalization of the AXS coin fell to $1 billion, embodying the hope that players could be compensated fully and the developers could figure out how to make play-to-earn work.

Stepping back, a high price of AXS depended on the game's success in drawing players, activity, and money. Somewhat like the developers of terra-luna, unsustainably high rewards drove very rapid growth. Thanks to the digital sharecropping, the game excited potential buyers of AXS with the idea

of introducing millions of people of modest means to the world of crypto wallets, exchanges and so on. The game only flourished for some months. But perhaps it lasted long enough for the developers and the more astute venture capitalists to cash out plenty of AXS. If so, a pump and dump scheme with lots of bells and whistles succeeded.

* Molly White, 'The Axie Infinity Hack, What Happened, and Why People Keep Talking about Bridges', March 30, 2022, www.blog.mollywhite.net, accessed May 9, 2022.

** Joshua Brustein, 'A Billion-Dollar Crypto Gaming Startup Promised Riches and Delivered Disaster', *Bloomberg* June 10, 2022.

*** Sidhartha Shukla, 'Axie Infinity Was Losing Gamers Even Before Record Crypto Hack', *Bloomberg*, April 4, 2022.

**** Naavik, 'Axie Infinity: Infinite Opportunity or Infinite Peril?' November 12, 2021, www.naavik.co, accessed May 9, 2022.

***** Miles Krupp and Tim Bradshaw, 'Crypto's Hottest Game Is Facing an Economic Maelstrom', *Financial Times*, November 26, 2021.

****** https://coinmarketcap.com/currencies/axie-infinity/, accessed May 29, 2022.

******* https://coinmarketcap.com/currencies/smooth-love-potion/, accessed May 29, 2022.

******** U.S. Treasury, 'U.S. Treasury Issues First-Ever Sanction on a Virtual Currency Mixer, Targets DPRK Cyber Threats', *Press Release*, May 6, 2022.

********* Tim Bradshaw, 'Makers of Axie Infinity Game Raise $150 mn After Massive Crypto Hack', *Financial Times*, April 6, 2022.

Notes

1. Andrew Perrin, '16% of Americans Say They Have Ever Invested in, Traded or Used Cryptocurrency', *Pew Research Center*, November 11, 2021. https://www.pewresearch.org/fact-tank/2021/11/11/16-of-americans-say-they-have-ever-invested-in-traded-or-used-cryptocurrency/, accessed June 6, 2022.

2. Pamela Ambler, Angel Au-Yeung, Grace Chung, Jeff Kauflin, Alex Konrad, Laura Shin and Nathan Vardi, 'The Richest People in Cryptocurrency'. *Forbes*, February 6, 2018; John Hyatt, 'The Richest Crypto and Blockchain Billionairees in the World 2022', *Forbes*, April 5, 2022.

3. Bitcoin is a big production. The ledger contains the whole history of anonymous transactions. By mid-2021, blocks on the bitcoin chain numbered

689,000. Igor Makarov and Antoinette Schoar, 'Blockchain Analysis of the Bitcoin Market', *NBER Working Paper* 29,396, October 2021, p. 7.

4. Satoshi Nakamoto, 'Bitcoin: A Peer-to-Peer Electronic Cash System', https://bitcoin.org/en/bitcoin-paper, accessed May 23, 2022.

5. Joost van der Burgt, 'Making Sense of Bitcoin Price Levels', Federal Reserve Bank of San Francisco *Fintech Edge*, April 2018.

6. Serio Aramonte, Weqian Huang and Andreas Schrimpf, 'DeFi Risks and the Decentralization Illusion', BIS *Quarterly Review*, December 2021, pp. 21–36.

7. Miles Kruppa and Aziza Kasumov, 'Coinbase Valued at $76bn in Coming-of-Age Moment for Cryptocurrency', *Financial Times*, April 14, 2021.

8. Securities and Exchange Commission, 'Coinbase Global, Inc., Form 10-Q, for the quarter ended March 31, 2022', p. 42. https://www.sec.gov/ix?doc=/Archives/edgar/data/1679788/000167978822000048/coin-20220331.htm#i6ff81ac294904d009a3ab35125a1d5f6_178, accessed May 23, 2022.

9. Securities and Exchange Commission, 'Coinbase Global, Inc., Form S-1', February 25, 2021, p. 50, https://www.sec.gov/Archives/edgar/data/1679788/000162828021003168/coinbaseglobalincs-1.htm, accessed May 23, 2022.

10. Ibid., p. 103.

11. Ibid., p. 146.

12. SEC, 'Coinbase Global, Inc., Form 10-Q, for the quarter ended March 31, 2022', p. 83.

13. Carol Alexander, Daniel F. Heck and Andreas Kaeck, 'The Role of Binance in Bitcoin Volatility Transmission', *Working Paper*, August 2021. https://ideas.repec.org/p/arx/papers/2107.00298.html, accessed May 29, 2022.

14. Adam Samson and Joshua Oliver, '"I Was Panicking": The High-Risk Bets Sparking a Backlash at Binance', *Financial Times*, July 21, 2021.

15. Angus Berwick and Tom Wilson, 'How Crypto Giant Binance Became a Hub for Hackers, Fraudsters and Drug Traffickers', *Reuters*, June 6, 2022.

16. President's Working Groupon on Financial Markets, the Federal Deposit Insurance Corporation, and the Office of the Comptroller of the Currency, *Report on Stablecoins*, November 2021, p. 7.

17. https://cointelegraph.com/news/total-stablecoin-supply-hits-180-billion-report.

18. https://www.theblockcrypto.com/data/decentralized-finance/stablecoins/total-stablecoin-supply-daily.

19. Hyun-Song Shin, 'Cryptocurrencies and the Economics of Money', speech to the Bank for International Settlements Annual General Meeting June 24, 2018, https://www.bis.org/speeches/sp180624b.pdf, accessed June 2, 2022.

20. Makarov and Schoar, 'Blockchain Analysis of the Bitcoin Market', pp. 12, 28.

21. Raphael Auer and David Tercero-Lucas, 'Distrust or Speculation? The Socioeconomic Drivers of US Cryptocurrency Investments', BIS *Working Papers* No. 951, July 2021.

22. https://ag.ny.gov/press-release/2021/attorney-general-james-ends-virtual-currency-trading-platform-bitfinexs-illegal.

23. For tether's risible disclosure, see Jemima Kelly, 'Tether says its reserves are backed by cash to the tune of... 2.9%', *FTAlphaville,* May 14, 2021. https://www.ft.com/content/529eb4e6-796a-4e81-8064-5967bbe3b4d9, accessed June 2, 2022.

24. Zeke Faux, "Anyone Seen Tether's Billions?", *Business Week*, October 7, 2021. https://www.bloomberg.com/news/features/2021-10-07/crypto-mystery-where-s-the-69-billion-backing-the-stablecoin-tether.

25. See Nasdaq glossary entry, 'Death Spiral Convertible' https://www.nasdaq.com/glossary/d/death-spiral-covertible, accessed May 27, 2022.

26. See https://coinmarketcap.com/currencies/terra-luna/historical-data/, accessed May 27, 2022.

27. See https://coinmarketcap.com/currencies/terrausd/historical-data/, accessed May 27, 2022.

28. See https://app.anchorprotocol.com/earn, accessed May 27, 2022.

29. Eva Szaley, 'Crypto's Evolution Adds New Risks to Potential Rewards', *Financial Times*, May 6, 2022.

30. See https://coinmarketcap.com/currencies/terra-luna/historical-data/, accessed May 13 and 27, 2022.

31. See https://coinmarketcap.com/currencies/terrausd/historical-data/, accessed May 27, 2022.

32. Marco Quirez-Gutierrez, 'Binance Chief Jokingly Tweets "Poor Again" After Disclosing Loss on Luna Investment from $1.6 billion to Under $3,000', *Fortune,* May 17, 2022 https://fortune.com/2022/05/17/binance-ceo-changpeng-zhao-poor-again-luna-twitter/, accessed June 6, 2022.

33. 'Built To Fail: The Inherent Fragility of Algorithmic Stablecoins', *Wake Forest Law Review,* vol. 11, October 25, 2021, online http://www.wakeforestlawreview.com/2021/10/built-to-fail-the-inherent-fragility-of-algorithmic-stablecoins/, accessed June 6, 2022.

34. https://coinmarketcap.com/currencies/tether/historical-data/, accessed June 28, 2022.

35. Aramonte, Huang and Schrimpf, 'DeFi Risks and the Decentralization Illusion', pp. 29–30.

36. International Organization of Securities Commissions, *IOSCO Decentralized Finance Report,* OR01/2022, March 2022, p. 29.

37. https://defillama.com/, accessed July 15, 2022 and December 11, 2022.

38. Celsius Network, 'Celsius Network Assets Are Officially over $20 Billion', *PRNewswire,* August 24, 2021. https://www.prnewswire.com/news-releases/celsius-network-assets-are-officially-over-20-billion-301361803.html, accessed June 18, 2022.

39. Debevoise and Plimpton, 'Recent Crypto Bankruptcy Filings May Provide Clarity to Critical Unresolved Questions', *Debevoise Update,* July 14,

2022. https://www.debevoise.com/-/media/files/insights/publications/2022/07/20220714-crypto-bankruptcy-filings-may-provide-cla.pdf, accessed July 15, 2022.

40. See Robert McCauley, 'Why Bitcoin Is Worse Than a Madoff-style Ponzi,' *Financial Times Alphaville*, December 22, 2021 and 'Here's Why Bitcoin Looks Worse than a Madoff-Style Ponzi Scheme, Says Robert McCauley', *CNBC*, December 22, 2021. https://www.cnbc.com/video/2021/12/27/heres-why-bitcoin-looks-worse-than-a-madoff-style-ponzi-scheme-says-rob ert-mccauley.html, accessed July 13, 2022.

41. Jorge Stolfi, 'Bitcoin Is a Ponzi', blogpost, January 2, 2021. https://ic. unicamp.br/~stolfi/bitcoin/2020-12-31-bitcoin-ponzi.html, accessed June 2, 2022 consolidating Stolfi's number 3 and 4.

42. https://www.supremecourt.gov/DocketPDF/19/19-277/114023/201908291 15406902_Appendix.pdf, accessed June 2, 2022.

43. 'Thirteenth Pro Rata Interim Distribution of Recovered Funds to Madoff Claims Holders Commences; Totals More Than $112 Million', The Madoff Recovery Initiative press release, February 25, 2022. https://www.madofftru stee.com/statements-19.html, accessed June 2, 2022.

44. Jorge Stolfi letter to Securities and Exchange Commission, July 28, 2018, https://www.sec.gov/comments/sr-cboebzx-2018-040/srcboebzx2018040-4064523-169183.pdf, accessed June 2, 2022.

45. 'CZ's [Changpeng Zhao's] FAQ 8—On LUNA/UST and Taking the Right Risks', *Binance Blog*, May 20, 2022. https://www.binance.com/en/blog/from-cz/czs-faq-8--on-lunaust-and-taking-the-right-risks-421499824684903883, accessed May 28, 2022.

46. Adam Samson and Joshua Oliver, 'Binance Promoted Terra as "Safe" Investment before $40bn Collapse', *Financial Times*, May 25, 2022.

47. Jorge Stolfi, 'Yes, Bitcoin Is a Ponzi', January 16, 2021. https://www.ic.uni camp.br/~stolfi/bitcoin/2021-01-16-yes-ponzi.html, accessed June 2, 2022.

48. Jaron Lanier and Glen Weyl, The Decentralized Mystique', *CoinDesk*, June 7, 2022. https://www.coindesk.com/layer2/2022/06/07/the-decentral ized-mystique/, accessed June 28, 2022.

49. Aramonte, Huang and Schrimpf, 'DeFi Risks and the Decentralization Illusion', Graph 3, right-hand panel, p. 28.

50. 'Bitcoin's $30 billion sell-off', *Chainanalysis*, June 8, 2018. https://blog.cha inalysis.com/reports/money-supply/, accessed May 29, 2022.

51. D. T. Max, 'Half a Billion of Bitcoin, Lost in a Dump,' *New Yorker*, December 13, 2021.

15

The Lessons of History

It is time to pull the threads of the argument together. But before we do, there remains one difficult, unanswered question: Does it make a difference if there is no lender of last resort? For one thing, for most of the financial crises covered from 1720 to 2020, both national and international, a lender of last resort did swing into action in response to the pressures of the market—though often protesting all the way. The role was not always dispatched with efficiency, so that a refined analysis would categorize the aftermath of crises not only by the presence or absence of a lender of last resort but also by how well the role was discharged. Second, the aftermath of an economic downturn depends not just on how the crisis was handled but on a host of other variables, especially the factors affecting long-term investment: population growth, the existence of a frontier, demands arising from war, exports, the presence or absence of innovations that are not fully exploited, and the like. A speculative crisis like that of 1847 in England was likely in any event to be pulled quickly back into prosperity by renewed investment in railroads, regardless of whether the Bank of England suspended the Bank Act of 1844 and stood ready to provide liquidity to all borrowers with sound collateral.

Despite these difficulties, we are prepared to make the case, tentatively, that a lender of last resort does shorten the business depression that follows financial crisis. The evidence turns mainly on 1720, 1873, 1882 in France, 1890, 1921, and 1929. In none of these was a lender of last resort effectively present. The depressions that followed them were much longer and

© The Author(s), under exclusive license to Springer Nature
Switzerland AG 2023
R. Z. Aliber et al., *Manias, Panics, and Crashes*,
https://doi.org/10.1007/978-3-031-16008-0_15

deeper than others. Those of the 1870s and 1930s were both known as Great Depressions.

When a lender of last resort comes to the rescue, even maladroitly, downturn after the panic is seen to be momentary, transient, ephemeral, episodic, slowing the economy down only briefly. Panic marks in many instances the peak of a normal cycle with a recovery period of about two years, but without deeper significance. Not so, it is claimed, with 1720, 1873, 1882 in France, 1890, 1921, and 1929.

The South Sea bubble and its collapse in 1720 proved not so economically damaging, perhaps because the Bank of England's stabilizing role. Carswell contends that the South Sea bubble's collapse marked an epochal turning point, but he does not address the narrow claim that a lender of last resort shortens the recovery time.[1] In contrast to this view, Schumpeter characterizes the South Sea bubble as nothing more than an excess and breakdown of speculation.[2] Judged by the bankruptcies—220 in 1720, 288 in 1721, and 240 in 1722—the depression ran the normal two-year course.[3] Ashton puts 1722 as the bottom and 1724–1725 as the peak of the next cycle, with a new, milder crisis from October to December 1726.[4] Hoppit argues that the South Sea bubble did not much disrupt industrial output and overseas trade, although the joint effect of the Mississippi and South Sea bubbles disrupted the foreign-exchange market.[5] One might argue that the Bank of England did in fact act as a lender of last resort in taking over the stock of the South Sea Company. It originally contracted to do so at 400, later reneged when the Bank itself came close to collapsing, and finally converted the stock only a little above the market when South Sea stock had sunk to 135.[6] Hoppit broadens this view: the 'Bubble's effect was not generally felt across Britain and Ireland partly because of the symbolic support for the Bank of England from the king and Prince of Wales…, partly because in turn the Bank of England made strenuous efforts to support credit.'[7]

The eighteenth century in France may be more relevant to our claim. There the trauma of the Mississippi bubble and the collapse of John Law's system slowed down the development of banking and the expansion of industry. Together with the collapse of the assignats during the Directorate in the 1790s, it made the French neurotic, or even paranoid, about banking for years-just as the Germans were rendered paranoid about inflation by the inflation of 1923 and the British about unemployment after their experiences during the 1920s. We are left then with 1873, 1882 in France, 1890, 1921, and 1929.

There was no lender of last resort in 1873 in Vienna, Berlin, and New York, the storm centers of the crash. In London there was no panic, hence

no need for a lender of last resort. The French let the Union Générale go to the wall in 1882 with minimal intervention. In 1929, the lender of last resort function was inadequately performed in New York (as suggested earlier, though the verdict does not command general agreement), and in 1931, international operations to halt the spread of collapse and the decline of prices and to restore business confidence were notoriously feeble.

On every other occasion from 1763 to 1914, more or less effective steps were taken. It would be helpful if one could discriminate carefully between the rescue operations, to determine which were more and which less adroit and to compare them separately with the length, depth, and width of the depressions that followed. Unhappily, we discriminate only crudely, if at all, limiting the analysis to whether recovery was fast or slow.

There can be little doubt that the depression of the 1870s was severe. After 1857 and 1866 (1864 in France), prices declined for two years and then picked up. After 1873, however, they declined for six years to 1879.[8] In the United States there was a severe recession through 1874 and then five long years of severe depression.[9] This would appear to support the hypothesis. But one is given pause by an explicit statement in McCartney that this was the result primarily of a breakdown in basic industries, rather than the disruption of financial machinery.[10] There is no need to identify the entire 'Great Depression' from 1873 to 1896 with the absence of lenders of last resort in Berlin, Vienna, and New York—at least one writer doubts whether it was a depression at all rather than merely profitless prosperity.[11] Our inclination, however, is to associate the extended depression of the 1870s in Central Europe, in the United States, and by propagation in Britain with the sharpness of the collapse of prices and the absence of a lender of last resort. This is far from an irrefutable case.

In 1882, in France, the speculative banks of Lyons were allowed to fail, with only limited assistance to mitigate some of the disastrous consequences for the brokers who had supported the speculators. Recovery in France was long drawn out, conditioned partly by the slowness of recovery in Britain, the United States, and most of the Continent.[12]

The 1890 Baring crisis can be classified either way, either as having or as lacking a lender of last resort. For Britain, there was the equivalent of a domestic lender, that is, the guarantee of the Baring Brothers liabilities, and an international rescue committee, organized by William Lidderdale, the loans from the Bank of France and the State Bank of Russia, plus the latter's commitment not to withdraw its deposit. But for the world outside Europe, there was no such therapy, and the depression was deep and long, lasting until 1896. The troubles of 1890 in Argentina, Brazil, and Chile were echoed in

1893 in Australia and the United States,[13] with little or no intentional help from abroad.

There was, however, a *deus ex machina*. The product of serendipity rather than design, the rapid rise of gold production in South Africa followed the discoveries of 1886 in the Rand. The contrast in the response of the world economy to gold discoveries in 1849 and 1851 on one hand and 1886 on the other is striking. In the middle of the century, the Californian and Australian gold strikes were quickly translated into a boom in Europe; in the 1890s, there was no such rapid response. The difference lay in external circumstances: buoyant in the early 1850s, depressed from 1890. The surge of gold production finally produced an effect after 1896, however, serving as a lender of last resort by pouring high-powered money into the system. In the United States, for example, gold coin in circulation rose from $374 million in 1890 to $495 million in 1894 and $679 million in 1899, over a period when US production rose only from $33 million to $79 million, a large increase in terms of percentage, but a modest one in absolute terms and as compared with the rise in circulation.[14]

In 1920 and 1921, there was no lender of last resort because the recession was deliberately engineered—by Britain, as a step on the route back to the gold standard, and by the Federal Reserve System in the United States, in order to halt inflation. The United States recovered 'fairly quickly,' but the abrupt fall in prices and output in Britain 'hastily spread to a number of other highly industrial countries and developed into a depression of extreme severity and duration.'[15] Pedersen speaks of 'the quasi-permanent depression inaugurated in 1920,' although he does not associate the extent of the decline with the absence of a lender of last resort, and he allows, as he should, for the importance attached by the British authorities to a return to gold. He blames the American authorities, however, for deflationary policies that prevented European countries from returning to gold:

> The authorities seem to have been guided by a somewhat vague idea that conditions were unsound, that prices were too high, that the budget should be balanced, that things would not correct themselves, and that some action 'cleaning up' the aftermath of the unsound wartime policy was necessary.
>
> Now it is my thesis that this state of mind and the action which it engendered was fateful, because so much depended on the policy carried out in the U.S.A
>
> ... For these reasons I think it safe to conclude that the U.S.A. monetary authorities by stimulating demand in the spring of 1920 instead of contracting it could have prevented the permanent depression of the countries struggling

to return to gold, mitigated inflation in a number of countries, and made the attempt of monetary reconstruction of the countries easier, and diminished the structural fall in the prices of primary and agricultural products.[16]

The argument that the depression of the 1930s was exacerbated by the lack of effective lenders of last resort-domestically in 1929 in the United States, worldwide in 1931—has been dealt with at length above, in a number of places.

This evidence through the 1930s by no means constitutes a conclusive demonstration that intervention of a lender of last resort in a panic softens the depression that follows. Too many other factors are at work, both long and short term, and the occasions when a panic has been allowed to run its course are so few that the material is not abundant enough for strong conclusions. At most there remains a presumption, but perhaps not a strong one, that halting a cumulative deflation helps shorten the depression that follows.

The major crises in the forty-plus years since this book was originally published have featured some version of the lender of last resort, generally criticized for doing too much and too little. Warts and all, it is a reasonable judgment that the subsequent recovery would generally have been slower in its absence.

The aftermath of the Mexican crisis of 1982 echoes in some ways that of the 1890 Baring crisis. Big creditor country banks avoided insolvency and creditor countries enjoyed an economic recovery in the early 1980s, but the borrowing countries recovered slowly. The analogy breaks down in the innovative international lender of last resort operations for Latin American and other debtor countries, which had no parallel in 1890. Going beyond IMF lending with conditions attached, creditor country officials managed commercial bank lending, leaning on commercial banks to stump up 'new money.'[17] Latin American debtors used the new money, along with IMF and other official funding and trade surpluses, to service their (rescheduled) bank debt. This management supported borrowers' growth by maintaining international trade credit, although Mexico still endured a prolonged growth setback.[18] Creditor banks avoided depositor runs and government takeover and worked their way back to solvency, but a more balanced conditionality might have precluded their paying dividends along the way.

In the Asian financial crisis, the much-criticized international lender of last resort operations set up a generally solid export-led recovery in the debtor countries. On the creditor side, the Asian financial crisis only slowed the upswing that continued until the bursting of the Dot.com bubble in 2000. The IMF drew criticism for treating the problem in Asia initially as more one of overspending than an international run on fragile structures of debt.[19]

After announcements of large public loan packages failed to keep banks from exiting, in Korea, creditor officials led by the Federal Reserve Bank of New York eventually leaned on the banks to roll over short-term credits.[20] On the creditor side, the stakes were generally lower in the Asian financial crisis, with major banks more modestly exposed than they had been in the 1980s in Latin America. That said, Japanese banks' struggle with their post-crisis bad loans was coming to a slow climax as the Asian financial crisis hit, so there was potential for vicious circles that the last resort lending forestalled.

With hindsight, the 4th edition of this book argued prematurely that Japan's weak recovery after the bursting of the bubble in 1990 might count against the efficacy of the lender of last resort there. The 4th edition suggested that the poor recovery might reflect 'how well the role was discharged': Japan's 'efforts at salvage were slow, widely spaced, and caught up in political maneuvering'[21]—all points well-taken. The authorities finally stepped up to the plate in 1997–1998 to support a troubled bank and a securities firm and to nationalize two banks. In 1999, the government injected preferred shares across the major banks.[22] To be sure, the Japanese lender of last resort had none of the speed, decisiveness, and democratic buy-in of the Nordic lenders of last resort in 1990–1992.[23] But given the immense scale of the Japanese bubble, in retrospect, the economy performed respectably when account is taken of the evolution of its working-age population. Economist Paul Krugman, once a sharp critic of Japanese policy-making after the burst of the bubble, quipped after the 2008 Great Financial Crisis that he owed the Japanese emperor an apology for his criticism.[24]

The major argument regarding 2008 is whether the lender of last resort should have been more inclusive by saving Lehman Brothers, thereby making the subsequent global decline in economic activity less severe and the recovery more robust. The 7th edition of this book devoted a chapter to Lehman that argued that the decline in employment and GDP and the increase in the fiscal deficit owing to its failure well exceeded the plausible cost of rescuing it.[25] Lawrence Ball argues at length that the Fed could have rescued Lehman, but did not do so because of political considerations and because of a failure to understand the cost of the failure.[26] Ball claims that without the Lehman collapse 'the whole Great Recession wouldn't have been so great.'[27]

However one interprets Lehman, the domestic lender of last resort—restarting within days of the Lehman collapse—and the international lender of last resort arguably prevented a far worse outcome in 2008. 'The counterfactual of how the system would have adjusted without the swap lines is too grim to contemplate,' write three ex-officials who were directly involved.[28] As argued by policymakers Ben Bernanke, Timothy Geithner, and Hank

Paulson in *Firefighting: The Financial Crisis and Its Lessons*, which includes cameo appearances by Kindleberger and Minsky, the whole Great Recession could have been the Great Depression.[29]

The tentative judgment is that domestic and international lender of last resort operations promoted a stronger recovery from the Covid recession of 2020. The argument is whether the scale of the fiscal response, particularly in the United States under two presidents, and the two-year persistence of ultra-easy monetary policy, overdid stimulus and stoked global inflation.

Does the Lender of Last Resort Forestall Crises?

A wider claim is made for lenders of last resort that they make it possible to avoid financial crises altogether. The record shows that financial crises were less frequent in Britain after 1866: 141 years separated the retail run on Northern Rock in 2007 from that on Overend Gurney in 1866.[30] And in the United States, a half of a century separated 1929–1931 from the Mexican default of 1982. In addition, the record can be interpreted to reveal that crises were less terrifying. History is full of hyperbolic statements about the various crises:

1772 Britain: 'One of the fiercest financial storms of the century.'[31]

1825 Britain: 'A panic seized upon the public such had never been witnessed before.'[32]

1837 United States: 'One of the most disastrous [panics] this nation ever experienced.'[33]

1847 Britain: 'In the last nine months more reckless and hazardous speculation than any other known in modern times.'[34]

1847 Britain: 'It may safely be affirmed, that since the fall of Napoleon, the City has never been in a state of greater excitement.'[35]

1857 Britain: 'Crisis of 1857 the most severe that England or any other nation has ever encountered.'[36]

1857 Hamburg: 'So complete and classic a panic has never been seen before as now in Hamburg.'[37]

1857 Hamburg: Panic 'of a violence hitherto unknown.'[38]

1866 Britain: 'Crisis of 1866 most serious in modern times.'[39]

1866 Britain: 'Wilder than any since 1825.'[40]

1873 Germany: 'In 56 years, no such protracted crisis.'[41]

1882 France: 'Never have I seen an equal catastrophe.'[42]

1929 United States: 'The greatest cycle of speculative boom and collapse in modern times—since, in fact, the South Sea Bubble.'[43]
2008 United States: 'The worst financial crisis since the Great Depression.'[44]

This rhetoric mostly moderated after 1866 in Britain.

Consistent with the decline in hyperbole, the view was put forward by a group of distinguished economists in the 1930s that the existence of a lender of last resort, while it may exacerbate overtrading, calms anxieties when overtrading occurs. In July 1932, the Committee on Economic Information, a high-powered group consisting of Sir Josiah Stamp (as chairman), G. D. H. Cole, J.M. Keynes, Sir Alfred Lewis, Sir Arthur Salter, Sir Frederick Leith-Ross, with H. D. Henderson and A. F. Hemming as joint secretaries, wrote the following:

> As the [19th] century wore on, the knowledge that the Bank Act would be suspended in case of need, and that, as a consequence, harassed debtors with good security to offer would be able to obtain advances from the Bank, sufficed to prevent panics from arising.[45]

This group of economists, advising the British cabinet, was advocating an international lender of last resort and may have exaggerated the effectiveness of suspending the Bank Act. The committee further seemed to overlook the fact that suspension of the Bank Act had not been a certainty, as Lidderdale went to great length to demonstrate in 1890, concerned as he was about the subversive effects of continuous suspensions.

This view that manias were moderating was fairly persuasive in the decades after World War II up to the 1970s. Putting aside 1970s speculation in real estate, farmland, and oil production, the mania for syndicated bank loans to developing countries that figured prominently in the first edition of this book in 1978 suggested that manias had not become historical curiosities. The Japanese mega-bubble marked the 1980s and the Asian financial crisis marked the 1990s. Talk among macroeconomists of the 'great moderation' at the beginning of the present century exploded in 2007–2008. It is hard to avoid the conclusion that the succession of last resort operations in the 1980s, 1990s, and 2000s does not calm anxieties when the Minsky moment hits, though many worry that it exacerbates overtrading.

A particular version of the question whether the lender of last resort forestalls crises is why the successful use of central bank swaps in 2007–2009 did not make their use unnecessary in 2020. The first answer is the botched nature of 'reform' of money market funds after the runs on them in 2008.

But the second answer is that the Fed's extension of credit through central bank swaps stirred political controversy at home that undermined the force of the precedent.

The 'reform' of money market funds left them still exposed to shareholder runs without a standing lender of last resort. In March 2020, firms seeking to raise cash in the face of a possible collapse of revenues took little comfort from the reform's tweaking of money funds' liquidity requirements. Worse, the reform mandated that, in the face of extreme demand from shareholders for cash, limits, or 'gates,' be applied to redemptions. Limits excite, and the prospect of such limits accelerated the run. When $150 billion took flight from the funds in days in March 2020, a run on the dollar funding of non-US bans was the mechanical result.

In responding to this run, a non-US bank borrowing, hoarding, or lending dollars had to reckon the likelihood of the swap lines being fully reactivated in size and frequency. Here the question was not a legal one. The Congress had in its post-crisis Dodd-Frank Act limited the Fed's use of its emergency lending powers at home, requiring that the US Treasurer approve and that the Fed target the credit to a class of borrowers and not a single firm.[46] However, Dodd-Frank had not touched the Fed's ability to offer swap lines. And indeed, in early 2020 the Fed had permanent swap lines with five major central banks.

But Congressional hearings featured questioning of the swap lines after the 2008 crisis and their use again during the European sovereign strains of 2011–2012 generated controversy. Consequently, despite the swaps among the major central banks having become permanent, their role in the next crisis was ambiguous. On one reading, market participants anticipated swaps: non-US banks from the five swap jurisdictions could bargain for cheaper funding from money market funds in calm times.[47] Still, questions remained regarding the effective availability of swaps.

In the event, when the Fed reactivated the swap lines in March 2020, there was no political reaction. Perhaps in the next crisis, the anticipation of the swap lines may calm market participants. Indeed, some observers worry that non-US banks may overdo dollar intermediation on this anticipation.

Looking forward, two challenges confront the international lender of last resort as the Fed is currently playing the role. The first follows from the shift of global dollar credit from bank lending to bond markets. The second is the political dimension.

Bond Market Buyer of Last Resort?

While the Fed was set up as a lender of last resort to banks, it has had to innovate to play a parallel role in securities markets. It has used its emergency powers to become a lender of last resort to securities firms, including ones not affiliated with major banks. Using the same emergency powers, in 2008 and again in 2020, the Fed bought outstanding commercial paper and underwrote new issues, assuring issuers, including nonfinancial corporations, of their access to credit. In 2020, the Fed used its emergency powers to buy US corporate bonds.

We have argued in Chapter 13 that the Fed's promise to purchase US corporate bonds ramified widely, lifting prices of dollar bonds issued by non-US firms and sovereigns. In this case, the extension of the domestic lender of last resort to the bond market proved to serve as the international lender of last resort at one remove, or by proxy.

But what if this did not work, and, as funds dumped dollar bonds issued by non-US borrowers, the market threatened to spiral downward? Such a collapse could not only inflict illiquidity and wealth losses on holders but also lead to unnecessary defaults as issuers found themselves unable to roll over maturing bonds. The US credit markets would not be immune to such developments in the global dollar bond market.

One could imagine new uses for central bank swaps under these circumstances. For instance, the Fed could extend dollar credit to major central banks that in turn could directly buy or underwrite dollar bonds. Such an approach would follow the principle of the central bank swaps: the Fed extends dollar credit to central banks and the latter take on the credit risk of operations with the private sector.

The Fed directly buying up dollar bonds of non-US issuers would depart from this principle but could benefit from speed and relative simplicity. An intermediate approach might be to have major central banks agree to indemnify the Fed for losses on bonds of 'their' issuers.[48]

This discussion may strike the reader as far-fetched. The point is that as the US financial markets have evolved from banking to bond markets, the Fed has come to intervene in domestic securities markets as lender, buyer, and underwriter of last resort. The evolution of US financial markets has its counterpart in the dollar market outside the United States: nonbanks there have more debt in the form of bonds than bank loans these days.[49] So the question may arise of how the Fed's intervention in the bond market might work in the international context. The practical issue of whose paper to buy

is the new version of the old question of the lender of last resort: who can borrow? This brings us to the political dimension.

The Political Dimension

Domestic lender of last resort operations can have a crucial political dimension. Events during 2008 crisis and the 2020 crisis highlight this dimension.

Ball contends that a big reason for letting Lehman fail in 2008 was the political decision by the Republican Treasury Secretary (who legally had no veto over a Fed decision) not to be seen as 'Mr Bailout.'[50] Ball rejects the darker interpretation that the Treasury Secretary as the former head of Goldman Sachs was happy to see off an aggressive competitor of his alma mater.[51]

In 2020, the US Republican Administration supported the extension of the US domestic lender of last resort to ensure that it not be seen, as in 2008, as overly or even exclusively concerned with the fate of big banks. The CARES Act passed in late March 2020 put US Treasury loss-absorbing funding behind emergency Fed lending to small and medium-sized businesses and smaller non-profits under the Main Street Lending program. Fed purchases of municipal paper as well as bonds of the New York City transit system and the State of Illinois had similar backing. 'Although Fed officials may have been reluctant to wade too far into private credit markets, they also sought to dispel notions that their emergency support was reserved for Wall Street.'[52] A broader domestic lender of last resort operation set risky precedents but provided political cover in Congress.

The international lender of last resort as practiced by the Fed drew two lines that have an inevitable political dimension.[53] In the inside circle are the major central banks that were eventually offered dollar credit to distribute to their banks with no ex ante limits. In the next circle are central banks to which the Fed offered dollar credit up to a certain amount *at times of acute funding strains*. This circle comes and goes with crises, but remained the same in 2008 and 2020. In the outer circle is any central bank that holds US Treasury securities at the Federal Reserve Bank of New York, which can be borrowed against.

The drawing of lines leaves countries out. On 28–29 October 2008, the Fed's Open Market Committee discussed a denial of a swap line to Iceland and approaches by Chile, India and South Africa.[54] Other applicants were evidently Indonesia, Peru, and the Dominican Republic.[55]

Those inclined to lay emphasis on the political basis of the choice face the question of why the Swiss National Bank but not the Monetary Authority of Singapore is among the five permanent swap partners. For the politically minded, a glance at US State Department fact sheets shows extensive US military cooperation with Singapore, while security cooperation with Switzerland seems limited to antiterrorism.[56]

Looking forward, could for instance the response to the Russian invasion of Ukraine in 2022 bear on the choice of dollar swap partners? While Brazil voted in the United Nations to condemn the invasion, it declined, like Mexico, to join the United States, its allies, and others in putting sanctions on Russia.

The more general point is that the dollar is widely used by banks from countries like China where the central bank has not had a swap line with the Fed. Such banks have dollar liabilities amounting to trillions of dollars, the overwhelming majority of which are booked outside the United States.[57] Even the Fed's provision of US banknotes could involve political considerations, as with shipment of US cash to Buenos Aires during the Falklands/Malvinas war in 1982.[58] So far, the crucial political dimension has not kept the international lender of last resort in dollars from working. Can central banks continue to reconcile the politically possible and the economically stabilizing in a fracturing world?

Notes

1. John Carswell, *The South Sea Bubble* (London: Cresset Press, 1960), pp. 271–2.
2. Joseph A. Schumpeter, *Business Cycles: A Theoretical, Historical and Statistical Analysis of the Capitalist Process* (New York: McGraw-Hill, 1939), vol. 1, pp. 250–1; John Carswell, *The South Sea Bubble* (London: Cresset Press, 1960), pp. 271–2.
3. T. S. Ashton, *Economic Fluctuations in England, 1700–1800* (Oxford: Oxford University Press, Clarendon Press, 1959), p. 121.
4. Ibid., p. 172.
5. Julian Hoppit, 'The Myths of the South Sea Bubble', *Transactions of the Royal Historical Society*, vol. 12 (2002), pp. 152–8.
6. Carswell, *South Sea Bubble*, pp. 184, 205, 213.
7. Hoppit, 'The Myths of the South Sea Bubble', p. 158.
8. Clement Juglar, *Les crises commerciales et leur retour periodique en France, en Angleterre et aux Etats-Unis*, 2nd edn (1889; reprint ed., New York: Augustus M. Kelley, 1967), p. 99.

9. E. Ray McCartney, *Crisis of 1873* (Minneapolis: Burgess, 1935), pp. 113, 117.

10. Ibid., p. 117.

11. S. B. Saul, *The Myth of the Great Depression* (New York: St. Martin's Press, 1969).

12. W. Jett Lauck, *The Causes of the Panic of 1893* (Boston: Houghton Mifflin, 1907), p. 55.

13. C. P. Kindleberger, 'International Propagation of Financial Crises: The Experience of 1888–1893', in idem, *Keynesianism vs. Monetarism and Other Essays in Financial History* (London: Allen & Unwin, 1985), pp. 226–39. See Carmen Reinhart and Kenneth Rogoff, 'Recovery from Financial Crises: Evidence from 100 Episodes', *American Economic Review*, vol. 104, no. 5, pp. 51–3, on the US in 1893, and among the top 35 most severe crises on their measure, Argentina, Brazil and Uruguay in 1890 and Australia in 1893.

14. Bureau of the Census, U.S. Department of Commerce, *Historical Statistics of the United States, 1789–1945* (Washington, DC: U.S. Government Printing Office, 1949), pp. 151, 275.

15. Jørgen Pedersen, 'Some Notes on the Economic Policy of the United States During the Period 1919–1932', in Hugo Hegelund, ed., *Money, Growth and Methodology* (Lund: Lund Social Science Studies, 1961); reprinted in J. Pedersen, *Essays in Monetary Theory and Related Subjects* (Copenhagen: Samfundsvidenskabeligt Forlag, 1975), p. 188.

16. Ibid., pp. 193–4.

17. See Robert McCauley, 'IMF: Managed Lending', in Michael Claudon, ed., *World Debt Crisis* (Cambridge, MA: Ballinger, 1986), pp. 123–45. The Federal Reserve stymied US banks' attempt to crank up the spread on the 'new money' syndicated loans.

18. Reinhart and Rogoff, ibid., p. 53.

19. IMF, Independent Evaluation Office, *The IMF and Recent Capital Account Crises: Indonesia, Korea, Brazil* (Washington: IMF, 2003), pp. 3, 37.

20. Woonchan Kim and Yangho Byeon, 'Restructuring Korean Banks' Short-term Debts', in David Coe and Se-Jik Kim, eds, *Korea Crisis and Recovery* (Washington: IMF and Korea Institute for International Economic Policy, 2002), pp. 405–48.

21. 4th edition, pp. 207, 213.

22. Hiroshi Nakaso, 'The Financial Crisis in Japan During the 1990s: How the Bank of Japan Responded and the Lessons Learnt', BIS *Papers* No. 6, October 2001.

23. Claudio Borio, Bent Vale and Goetz von Peter, 'Resolving the Financial Crisis: Are We Heeding the Lessons from the Nordics?', BIS *Working Papers* No. 311, June 2010.

24. Paul Krugman, 'Apologizing to Japan', *New York Times*, 10 October 2014. See also Gauti Eggertsson and Paul Krugman, 'Debt, Deleveraging, and

the Liquidity Trap: A Fisher-Minsky-Koo Approach', *Quarterly Journal of Economics*, vol. 127 (2012), pp. 1469–513.

25. See Chapter 14, 7th edition of this book, 2015.

26. Laurence Ball, *The Fed and Lehman Brothers: Setting the Record Straight on a Financial Disaster, Studies in Macroeconomic History* (Cambridge: Cambridge University Press, 2018).

27. Isaac Chotiner, '"That Is What These Days Is Called an Alternative Fact"', *Slate*, September 12, 2018.

28. Nathan Sheets, Edwin Truman, and Clay Lowery, 'The Federal Reserve's Swap Lines: Lender of Last Resort on a Global Scale', Brookings Hutchins Center and Program on Financial Stability at the Yale School of Management, September 11–12, 2018, p. 17. https://ypfsresourcelibrary.blob.core. windows.net/fcic/YPFS/14%20B%20International%20Swaps%20Prelim% 20Disc%20Draft%202018.09.11.pdf, accessed June 27, 2022.

29. Ben S. Bernanke, Timothy F. Geithner and Henry S Paulson, Jr., *Firefighting: The Financial Crisis and Its Lessons* (New York: Penguin Books, 2019), pp. 11–3. The book argues that the Federal Reserve lacked the legal authority to rescue Lehman Brothers.

30. Hyun Song Shin, 'Reflections on Northern Rock: the Bank Run that Heralded the Global Financial Crisis', *Journal of Economic Perspectives*, vol. 23, no. 1 (Winter 2009), pp. 101–19, argues that the invisible electronic run on Northern Rock was the essence, and the retail run relatively unimportant. In this case, the interesting interval would be the 107 years that separated Overend Gurney from the Secondary Banking Crisis of 1973.

31. Ashton, *Economic Fluctuations*, p. 127.

32. Thomas Joplin, *Case for Parliamentary Inquiry into the Circumstances of the Panic, in a letter to Thomas Gisborne, Esq., M.P* (London: F. Ridgeway and Sons, n.d. [after 1832]), p. 14.

33. Reginald Charles McGrane, *The Panic of 1837: Some Financial Problems of the Jacksonian Era* (1924; reprint ed., New York: Russell and Russell, 1965), p. 1.

34. James Wilson, *Capital, Currency and Banking* (London: Economist, 1847), p. 1101.

35. D. Morier Evans, *The Commercial Crisis, 1847–1848*, 2nd edn (1849; reprint ed., New York: Augustus M. Kelley, 1969), p. 111.

36. D. Morier Evans, *The History of the Commercial Crisis, 1857–1858, and the Stock Exchange Panic of 1859* (1859; reprint ed., New York: Augustus M. Kelley, 1969), p. v.

37. Fred Oelssner, *Die Wirtschaftskrisen, vol. 1, Die Krisen in vormonopolistischen Kapitalismus* (Berlin: Dietz Verlag, 1953), p. 237, quoting Friedrich Engels.

38. Albert E. Fr. Schaffle, 'Die Handelskrise von 1857 in Hamburg, mit besondered Rucksicht auf das Bankwesen', quoted in Wladimir d'Ormesson, *La grande crise mondiale de 1857: L'histoire recommence, les causes, les remedes* (Paris-Suresnes: Maurice d'Hartoy, 1933), p. 119.

39. A. Andreades, *History of the Bank of England* (London: P. S. King, 1909), p. 357.

40. E. Victor Morgan, *The Theory and Practice of Central Banking, 1797–1913* (Cambridge: Cambridge University Press, 1943), p. 177.

41. Fritz Stern, *Gold and Iron: Bismarck, Bleichroder, and the Building of the German Empire* (London: Allen & Unwin, 1977), p. 189, quoting a letter of October 1875 from Baron Abraham von Oppenheim to Bleichroder.

42. Jean Bouvier, *Le krach de l'Union Générale* (Paris: Presses Universitaires de France, 1960), p. 145, quoting a director of the Crédit Lyonnais.

43. John Kenneth Galbraith, *The Great Crash, 1929*, 3rd edn (Boston: Houghton Mifflin, 1972), p. vii.

44. Andrew Lo, 'Reading About the Financial Crisis: A Twenty-One-Book Review', *Journal of Economic Perspectives,* vol. 50, no. 1 (2012), p. 151.

45. Fourth Report of the Committee on Economic Information, 'Survey of the Economic Situation, July, 1932', in Susan Howson and Donald Winch, *The Economic Advisory Council, 1930–1939: A Study in Economic Advice During Depression and Recovery* (Cambridge: Cambridge University Press, 1977), pp. 277–8.

46. Philip A. Wallach, *To the Edge* (Washington: Brookings Institution, 2015), Chapter 7.

47. Egemen Eren, Andreas Schrimpf and Vladyslav Sushko, 'US Dollar Funding Markets During the Covid-19 Crisis—The International Dimension', BIS *Bulletin* No. 15, May 12, 2020, Graph 3, p. 5.

48. This phrase introduces a host of practical issues: would a central bank buy bonds according to the residence or the nationality of the issuer? The Fed was generally more careful on this front in 2020 that it was in 2008, purchasing a bond only if its issuer had a substantial presence in the US economy. This meant that the Fed could buy the debt issues of a firm headquartered abroad, so long as it had sufficient US employees. However, in buying US corporate bond ETFs, it outsourced such distinctions to the compiler of the index on which the ETF was based.

49. See BIS Global Liquidity Indicators, https://stats.bis.org/statx/srs/table/e2?m=USD&f=pdf, accessed June 15, 2022.

50. Ball, *The Fed and Lehman Brothers*, chapter 12, 'Explaining the Lehman Decision'.

51. Guy Rolnick and Asher Schecter, 'Could the Fed Have Rescued Lehman Brothers? Q&A with Laurence Ball', *Promarket*, Stigler Center, University of Chicago Booth School of Business, January 30, 2017.

52. Lev Menand, 'The Logic and Limits of the Federal Reserve Act', May 6, 2022, p. 68. https://papers.ssrn.com/sol3/papers.cfm?abstract_id=4031875, accessed June 28, 2022.

53. Perry Mehrling, 'Where's My Swap Line? A Money View of the International Lender of Last Resort', Boston University Global Development Policy Center CEGI *Working Paper* No. 52, October 2021, concentrates on the

permanent swap lines and FIMA, and so has two tiers interacting with the Fed to backstop dollar intermediation.

54. Sheets, Truman and Lowery, 'The Federal Reserve's Swap Lines: Lender of Last Resort on a Global Scale', p. 15.

55. Eswar Prasad, *The Dollar Trap* (Princeton: Princeton University Press, 2014), pp. 203–13.

56. US Department of State, Bureau of European and Eurasian Affairs, 'Relations with Switzerland', January 4, 2022. https://www.state.gov/u-s-relations-with-switzerland-2/; Bureau of Politico-Military Affairs, 'U.S. Security Coopera-tion With Singapore', April 20, 2021. https://www.state.gov/u-s-security-coo peration-with-singapore/, both accessed July 13, 2022.

57. Iñaki Aldasoro, Torsten Ehlers, Patrick McGuire and Goetz von Peter, 'Global Banks' Dollar Funding Needs and Central Bank Swap Lines', BIS *Bulletin* No. 27, July 16, 2020. Only some of the central banks without Fed swap lines hold enough US Treasury securities at the New York Fed for its overnight repurchase facility to provide much of a backstop.

58. Under the Extended Custodial Inventory program, the Federal Reserve Bank of New York vault in effect extends to commercial bank vaults in London, Frankfurt and Zurich in Europe and Hong Kong and Singapore in Asia (and formerly Buenos Aires in the Americas). See Joseph Botta, 'The Federal Reserve Bank of New York's Experience of Managing Cross-border Migration of US Dollar Banknotes', *China's Capital Account Liberalisation: International Perspectives*, BIS *Papers* No. 15, April 2003, pp. 157–8.

Epilogue: A Property Mania with Chinese Characteristics

In September 2021, the headlines of the financial press carried warnings that China's second largest property developer, Evergrande, could default on a dollar bond sold offshore. Its bonds traded hands at 20 cents on the dollar, suggesting little hope that default would be avoided. After months of drama, Evergrande along with competitor Kaisa defaulted on dollar bonds in December 2021.

Evergrande had grown like topsy. It was reported to have 778 projects in 233 cities. In common with other developers, it financed itself by preselling apartments. It pre-sold 1.4 million apartments, generally for full value. The $200 billion (interest-free) obligation bulks large in its total liabilities, said to be $300 billion, including debt to banks, bondholders, and nonbanks. The firm also owes suppliers and construction firms.

Along the way, Evergrande had diversified into electronic vehicles, health, and drones. Its chief economist had predicted in 2015 a doubling of house prices in a decade and signed on for the equivalent of $2.3 million per year in 2017. The firm pledged $115 million to a Harvard University-led consortium to research COVID-19 in early 2020.[1]

Financial distress among developers led to a deterioration in cash flows across the big Chinese property companies. New home sales and starts have fallen by 30–40% year over year from the latter months of 2021 into 2022. By mid-2022, about a score of Chinese property companies had gone into default on most of the $100 billion of dollar bonds.

The global financial press featured the question of whether China's property market was approaching its Minsky moment, that is, the moment of transition from mania to panic and crash. This phrase, the Minsky moment,

© The Editor(s) (if applicable) and The Author(s) 2023
R. Z. Aliber et al., *Manias, Panics, and Crashes*,
https://doi.org/10.1007/978-3-031-16008-0

dates back to the Asian Financial Crisis, and was coined by Paul McCulley, an economist at the money manager Pacific Income Management Company (PIMCO).[2] The term received a lot of play after the Lehman collapse in September 2008. Extraordinarily, in 2017, Zhou Xiaochuan, Governor of the People's Bank of China, used the term to warn of over-optimism that had led to very high corporate debt and rapidly rising household debt in China.[3] (One looks hard in the memoirs of US Federal Reserve leaders and US Treasury secretaries for similar evidence of a familiarity with Minsky.) A question that divides informed observers is whether China's leaders' awareness of the risks of financial stability, along with the multitude of policy measures at their command, could allow them to avoid a Minsky moment.

The challenge that confronts the Chinese authorities is formidable, pressing, and threefold. First, China must adjust to the depletion of the pool of labor in the countryside that allowed millions to move to factories and cities every year. The urban share of the Chinese population rose from about 20% in 1980 to 65% in 2021. Recall that in the 1960s Germany drew in over 100,000 Turks and Southern Europeans per year as guest workers in order to postpone, or at least to stretch out, its 'Lewis turning point' when the excess supply of labor ran out.[4] At this turning point, an economic model based on an elastic supply of labor at the going wage requires wrenching change to slower growth.

Second, China must adjust to the decline in housing investment as a source of demand. Given an already elevated share of GDP devoted to investment, an increase in the wage and consumption shares of GDP is required.

And finally, and most controversially, China must adjust to lower house prices. Lower apartment prices can sap consumption by making households feel less wealthy and could threaten the solvency of some banks that have provided mortgages.

Displacement: Urbanization and Privatization

To start the exposition with the first stage of Minsky, the displacement that led to the Chinese property boom was the combination of rural–urban migration, a political decision, and a new means for the accumulation of household wealth. From the 1980s, hundreds of millions of Chinese would leave the countryside for the city. Never before in human history had so many left the countryside for the city.

The government made a key decision to leave the giant job of housing mostly to the private sector. In the late 1990s, the government decided to sell off the stock of worker housing at state-owned enterprises at low prices

to the occupants and mostly to leave the construction of new apartments to private real estate firms. By then, Hong Kong property companies operating on the Mainland had been building high-end, often expatriate housing, but home-grown developers came to dominate the market.

From early on, it became clear that shifting from holding bank deposits paying interest rates at best modestly above the rate of inflation to buying an apartment could do wonders for one's wealth. Seeing one's friends becoming richer in this manner could change one's mind about taking the risk of borrowing to the hilt, as became necessary as housing boomed.

Euphoria: Rising Prices and Debt, Buy-to-Wed and Buy-to-Hold

In the years between displacement and distress, the Chinese property market sent out many signs of euphoria. Apartment prices multiplied. Of course, so did incomes, but the ratio of median apartment price to median income reached world-beating levels by 2018 in Beijing and Shanghai, with Shenzhen in fourth place just after neighbor Hong Kong. In these cities, it took 40–50 years of median income to pay the price of the median apartment.[5] It took 'only' 20+ years in London and around 15 in Tokyo and New York.

Rental yields tell a similar story. These are 1–2% in the top Chinese cities, but 3% in London and 4% in New York.

Property borrowing by households rose rapidly. The state-owned banks made floating-rate mortgages a major line of business from the late 1990s. Mortgage debt has grown rapidly, pacing a more than tripling of the ratio of household credit to GDP between 2008 and end-2019. That said, household debt in China at 62% of GDP at the end of 2021 had not reached the burdens carried by households in the United States at 78% of GDP or Hong Kong and Great Britain, at around 90% of GDP.[6] Still, Haibin Zhu and colleagues describe the increase in household debt as 'alarming,' since it brings it to the burden of Japan in 1989 and suggests the absence of a 'cushion against a housing bust and potential spillover to the macroeconomy.'[7]

A Chinese characteristic of the property market has boosted mortgage debt. Chinese property developers presell apartments when they start construction. And Chinese banks extend mortgages to households at the point of purchase, before the collateral for the mortgage exists. Thus households have taken on debt through bank mortgages of purchased but uncompleted apartments. Preselling occurs in the United States in, say, Miami when its property market is hot, but it is very common in China.

Property developers in China came to rely on pre-sales as their most important source of funding and faced perverse incentives. The rapid growth of projects and slow construction boosted developers' cash flows: 'starting construction in order to receive approval to presell projects' while 'stretching delivery deadlines beyond contracted deadlines.'[8] Pressed by the authorities to reduce debt in 2021, the most leveraged property developers slowed construction. In the summer of 2022, Chinese households began to chat online about not paying on mortgages on uncompleted apartments where construction had slowed to a crawl or stopped.

It is not clear whether the Chinese data on private business debt includes all of the real estate developers' debt from pre-sold apartments. This debt is in effect construction loans by households to developers. (In recent years, developers also borrowed from households through the means of so-called wealth management products, in effect high-coupon medium-term commercial paper marketed by banks and near-banks.)

In any case, real estate debt in the household and the business sector contributed materially to the rise in the debt of the non-government sector in China. Such debt in China has reached and surpassed the peak readings during the Japanese stock and real estate bubble of the late 1980s (Fig. E1). What is more, such debt in China is well above the ratio reached by US private debt before the Great Financial Crisis of 2007–2008. If the debt owed directly by property developers to households is not well accounted for in the Chinese data, the Chinese private debt ratio may be higher than that shown by 2.5 or 5% of GDP.[9]

In addition to high prices and high debt, the sheer contribution of property to the growth of the Chinese economy is very high. In the US housing bubble of the 2000s, the share of GDP devoted to home construction rose sharply but never exceeded a single-digit share of GDP. In China, the property market accounts for an estimated 15–20% of GDP.[10]

Another important Chinese characteristic distinguished the Chinese property mania. Given the disproportion of marriageable men and women, families competed for scarce women with an apartment for the newlyweds. The more that other families offered, the more one's own family had to offer: the essence of a rat-race.[11] Real estate acquired a social meaning absent from other asset classes. But the number of marriages in China has been declining since 2013.

A related but distinct salient characteristic is the demand for empty apartments as a portfolio asset. Bank deposit and bond yields have tended to be low in relation to nominal GDP growth, albeit generally positive in real terms.

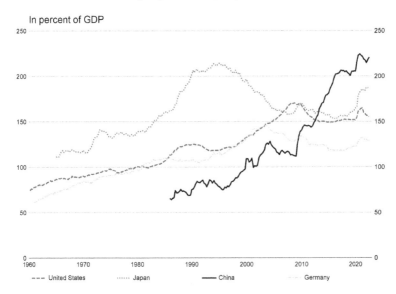

In percent of GDP

--- United States Japan —— China Germany

Fig. E1 Credit to the private nonfinancial sector (*Source* Refinitiv Datastream; Bank for International Settlements)

Capital controls have generally bound, despite leaks. And wealth management products offering juicy returns are relatively recent innovations and fraught with credit risk.

In most markets, a speculative demand for housing shows up as 'buy to let.' But in China, the social value attached to newness in apartments (and cars) is high. Moreover, as prices have risen relative to incomes, they have also risen in relation to rents, so the reward for renting at 1–2% in the top Chinese cities is low. So rather than buying to let, Chinese investors 'buy to hold' empty. This produces not so much the infamous ghost cities, but rather a Swiss cheese of empty apartments in generally occupied buildings. An estimated 22% of Chinese households own more than one home.[12]

The fraction of the urban housing stock that is owned but vacant is naturally a matter of some dispute. An analysis at Capital Economics, an economic consultancy, agrees with Chinese analysts on a vacancy rate of about 20% but highlights that half of the empty apartments are old privatized stock awaiting sale to a developer and demolition.[13] On this reckoning there could be 30–50 million owned but empty recently constructed apartments in China's cities, storing value more than housing people.

A consequence of high prices, high rates of home ownership, and the portfolio demand for housing is that housing wealth represents a very high fraction of household wealth. One estimate puts housing wealth at 60% of urban households' portfolios.[14]

From Distress to Panic and Crash?

Clearly, Chinese residential real estate has entered distress. Developers' business models depended on growth to generate cash and did not take into account the prospective decline in rural-urban migration. Developers are defaulting or scrambling not to. Housing activity is declining rapidly, although prices are declining only marginally in the official data. Government policies are shifting gears from restraining to promoting housing investment.

Residential investment as a share of GDP is bound to fall in China. US residential investment fell by almost two-thirds between the end of 2005 and the end of 2010. Even with stepped-up government investment in housing, residential investment could fall by 10% of GDP in China.

Normally real estate prices grind down overextended periods, but the Chinese characteristic of a large portfolio demand for housing could speed things up. As developers slash prices to move inventory, they undermine the store of value motive. Those who bought to hold most recently among the holders of the 30–50 million empty apartments, might put their apartments on the market. And as prices declined further, less recently acquired empty apartments could be offered for sale, and so on.

A substantial fall in housing prices in China would tend to lower consumption, given the high share of housing wealth in household assets. This would only increase the challenge of adapting to the change in labor supply and only make it more difficult to adjust to the decline of residential investment spending as a share of output.

A sustained decline in Chinese property would ramify globally. Chinese residential blocks stand tall thanks to steel milled from tons and tons of Australian iron ore and metallurgical coal. The wealth represented by residential property sends millions of Chinese tourists and students abroad. Lower Chinese demand for commodities and lower Chinese interest rates to offset economic weakness would put downward pressure on the renminbi and other emerging market and commodity currencies.

Another Chinese characteristic, heavy government involvement in the housing sector, is often cited as a reason not to anticipate a crash. The consolidated government sector depends on land sales for 25% of its revenue, with local governments particularly dependent on them.[15] And local governments have borrowed substantially, in effect using land sales as a fall-back means to service debt should project revenues prove disappointing. Government finances are vulnerable to a property downturn, but this gives the Chinese authorities even more reason to manage the real estate market.

Not least, the Chinese government at various levels has used macropru-dential policy to manage the property market. Controls on borrowing and other measures have been turned on and they can be turned off. Indeed, the strains in the finances of the Chinese property developers in the fall of 2021 were in part owing to the 'three red lines' drawn by the Chinese authorities that set limits on their leverage. Now, to support the property market, the government can provide guarantees on the bonds of selected developers and guide banks to lend to them. In addition, as noted, the authorities have the scope to reduce interest rates in general and the mortgage rate benchmark in particular.

Those who argue that the government can prevent a property crash empha-size its capacity to use administrative means to prevent a major home price decline.[16] They also cite the need for public housing to enable those who have lived in the cities without proper household registration to settle down. They also cite China's capital controls that limit the diversification of household assets.

It is an open question how the authorities will manage the challenges of the decline in housing demand and the decline in house prices in China. The stakes are high.

Notes

1. Rebecca Ostriker and Dierdre Fernandes, 'Evergrande Reneges on Multimillion-Dollar Pledge to Harvard-Led COVID Project, Another Stumble in Its Ties to School', *Boston Globe*, January 16, 2022.
2. Akhileshi Ganti, 'The Minsky Moment Defined', *Investopedia*, https://www.investopedia.com/terms/m/minskymoment.asp, accessed June 9, 2022.
3. 'China Central Bank Warns Against "Minsky Moment" Due to Excessive Optimism', *Reuters*, October 19, 2017.
4. Charles P. Kindleberger, *Europe's Postwar Growth* (Cambridge: Harvard University Press, 1967), Table II-3, p. 31.
5. Kenneth Rogoff and Yuanchen Yang, 'Has China's Housing Production Peaked?', *China & World Economy*, vol. 29, no. 1 (2021), Fig. 4, p. 7, citing www.numbeo.com. The following data on rental yields are December 2021 data from the latter source.
6. Bank for International Settlements, Credit to the household sector, https://stats.bis.org/statx/srs/table/f3.1, accessed July 13, 2022.
7. Haibin Zhu, Grace Ng, Tingting Ge and Ji Yan, 'China's Attempt to Avoid a Japan-Like Housing Bust', J. P. Morgan, *Global Data Watch*, August 11, 2022.
8. Jonathan Kemp, Anirudh Suthakar and Tom Williams, 'China's Residential Property Sector', *Reserve Bank of Australia Bulletin*, June 18, 2020, p. 72.

9. Ibid., Graph 9, p. 73.
10. Ibid., Graph 1, p. 68; 'Measuring the Universe's Most Important Sector', *Economist*, November 27, 2021.
11. Shang-jin Wei, X. Zhang and Y. Liu, 'Home Ownership as Status Competition: Some Theory and Evidence', *Journal of Development Economics*, vol. 127 (2017), pp. 169–86.
12. Kemp, Suthakar and Williams, 'China's Residential Property Sector', p. 67.
13. Julian Evans-Pritchard, 'China Property Handbook (2020)', *Capital Economics China Economics* (no date), p. 15; Kemp, Suthakar and Williams, 'China's Residential Property Sector', citing Gan on the China Household Finance Survey, p. 68.
14. Zhu, et al., 'China's Attempt to Avoid a Japan-Like Housing Bust', Kemp, Suthakar and Williams, 'China's Residential Property Sector', p. 67.
15. Ibid., p. 68.
16. Zhu, et al., 'China's Attempt to Avoid a Japan-Like Housing Bust'.

Index

© The Editor(s) (if applicable) and The Author(s) 2023
R. Z. Aliber et al., *Manias, Panics, and Crashes*,
https://doi.org/10.1007/978-3-031-16008-0

www.ingramcontent.com/pod-product-compliance
Lightning Source LLC
Chambersburg PA
CBHW070330090125
20112CB00005B/281